T0365216

Gravity

My

Enemy

WHEELCHAIR ADVENTURES IN THE WILDS OF
TROPICAL COLOMBIA

Edmund Elsner

Order this book online at www.trafford.com
or email orders@trafford.com

Most Trafford titles are also available at major online book retailers.

Cover: Gold Tairona anthropomorphic figure: courtesy of Colección
Museo del Oro Banco de la República, Colombia

Author with blacktip shark, photo by Raymond E. Belding

Cover design by Ryan Harker, Mesa, Arizona

Printed in the United States of America.

ISBN: 978-1-4120-0658-3 (sc)

Trafford rev. 01/03/2013

 www.trafford.com

North America & international
toll-free: 1 888 232 4444 (USA & Canada)
phone: 250 383 6864 ◆ fax: 812 355 4082

Dedicated to the Colombian people — courageous, humorous, hospitable, generous, well mannered and highly intelligent. They have suffered more than any I know, yet are the proprietors of an astonishingly beautiful country. They speak the finest Spanish on Earth. After decades they remain among my best friends. Equally, I would like to dedicate this book to George A. Hubbard of Tamworth, New Hampshire, and Ray Belding of Torrington, Connecticut, without whom these remarkable experiences would not have been possible. And to my sons Ed (Chiqui), Piet and Marco, who provided the encouragement to carry this through to completion.

Piet, Ed (Chiqui) & Marco

Foreword

This collection of stories is all true. Most of the names mentioned are real. Any change in events is merely to condense them into a single story, but they otherwise remain as they happened. It portrays a period of time spanning from mid-1964, to late 1975 when I lived in the colonial, university city of Popayán, Colombia. I was a teacher with many holidays, strikes and long vacation periods that gave me the freedom to wander.

I prefer to downplay the fact that I am a quadriplegic in a wheelchair. This came as a result of polio contracted in my first year of college in Whitewater, Wisconsin. To satisfy some people's wishes, I added a prologue and re-wrote small parts of the book as reminders of my condition, and apologize for doing so because it is not my nature to sing this tune.

I have made an attempt to stay out of politics, yet Colombian política is a fascinating stage of events and characters, so in part I was unsuccessful but I trust the reader will not only appreciate the importance of these events and their protagonists but become a student of Colombia's past as I did. Where much U.S. history is distant and out of our personal effective reach, Colombia's history is still in the air. During my tenure there I had the good fortune, and indeed the great honor, to have Colombian friends who are now firmly imprinted in history books.

What I have avoided is what deserves avoiding in such a book: political controversy and the drug trade. Colombians are some of the finest people on the planet. They are well-read, involved in their destiny more than we Americans tend to be; they suffer, cry, laugh, feel more than most and are cursed with the ancient (and present) coca leaf, a commodity as common as the Inca potato, used throughout time innocuously but now a major player in the world of crime, thanks in great part to an insatiable appetite for cocaine within United States and a rather arbitrary policy of prohibition. Colombians themselves are not significant consumers of illicit drugs. The average Colombian has no connection with them. Despite our characterizations of them, all Colombians are no more drug traffickers than all Americans are drug addicts. The recent marriage between Colombian guerrilla forces (FARC and ELN — Armed Revolutionary Forces of Colombia and National Liberation Army) and the drug cartel has resulted in a lethal and wealthy partnership. Unlike Al-Qaeda, they are located at the very doorstep of the United States, dedicated to terrorism and the destruction of everything we and the Colombians stand for.

But this book is about pre-drug Colombia, its breathtaking natural riches, beauty and adventure. Calling it a collection of stories is just that: They can be read independently despite some chronology.

Edmund Elsner
Mesa, Arizona
July 2005

Contents

Illustrations

Photographs without credits by the author

Prologue

As I gradually awoke and my eyes focused, all I could see was a grid of tiny holes in a ceiling of white over my head.

I wondered where I was. I tried to move my head to look around but my head would not move and felt as though strapped to the bed. Slowly coming to reality, I felt the shock of my situation and experienced once again the feeling of utter devastation and gloom, sensing the full impact of what was happening. I was totally paralyzed. As I surveyed my body, I noticed I could slightly move my right big toe and my fingers, though weakly. I opened my mouth. My jaw moved, and I could move my eyes from side to side but could not rotate my head. I realized the holes I saw were the tiny holes in a ceiling of acoustic tiles. With no one near, I tried to distract myself from the present tragedy and shock by counting the holes in an acoustic tile.

"Multiply," I told myself, and counted the holes on one side but could not. It was then I realized that the muscles controlling my eyes were also affected. I could not keep my sight focused on any single point. My eyes jumped involuntarily from their center of focus.

How I had arrived to this state of affairs involved a sequence of events that took me like a whirlwind in the preceding four or five days. I was too fragile emotionally and shocked to know what to make of it.

Just four days earlier on October 15, 1959, I was a student majoring in music at what was then called Whitewater State College in southern Wisconsin, later to become a branch of the University of Wisconsin. Ironically, my yearnings just days

Gravity My Enemy

ago were to play football at the University of Wisconsin in Madison.

I was as fit as a gladiator at 210 pounds. I had a 34-inch waist and could do over a hundred push-ups. I ran the 100-yard dash in under ten seconds.

Just four days earlier I could have out-fought and out-run almost anybody I knew, but I woke up that first morning with a painfully sore, stiff neck. It was Thursday. My first class that day started at eight a.m. I found it was almost impossible to turn my head that morning as I prepared for class. When I tried to put my chin on my chest, I could not. Somewhere, in the recesses of my memory I had heard that was a symptom of polio. But I had had stiffness before, so I took a hot shower and had a light breakfast, feeling confident I could shake this off and it would loosen up as the day progressed.

But as the hours passed that morning, the stiffness got worse. It was now very painful. By suppertime, I was miserable. My neck was really hurting terribly but I didn't want to miss practice with a small choral group in which I sang. The other members were all fellows with unusual talent and interest. We sang traditional college songs in those days, like Gaudeamus Igatur. That particular night we worked on a favorite, The Bells of Saint Mary's.

One of the guys in the group broke the news that his fraternity brother had been diagnosed with polio that day and was in the hospital. We were taken aback by the news. How could polio come to southern Wisconsin? This was found only in the septic confines of the Big City, where people didn't engage in many summer sports or spend time in the sun. How bad was he?

II

Prologue

When would he be back? No one knew. Our knowledge of polio was zero. (Months later, I was to find out that this fellow and I were the only ones on campus that had gotten polio, and the extent of his paralysis was a slight weakening in the lower part of one leg. He eventually recovered completely.)

That Thursday night became a nightmare. I suffered through practice but was relieved to get back to my apartment. The soreness in my neck was now almost intolerable, and my symptoms worsened by adding a reeling headache. I put on hot compresses to clear what seemed like sinuses, but they brought no relief. I felt a slight fever and a dull pain started in the back of my pelvis, which got worse as the night progressed. Having had no sleep all night the first night, I was almost happy to see the day dawn on Friday. Daylight brings optimism. Daytime meant I could do something besides suffer. I resolved to take some action to find relief.

As soon as I could get moving, I went to the college infirmary. The doctor, bored, performed a cursory examination and pronounced me sick with the flu and sent me home with advice to rest, drink fluids and take an aspirin. I felt some relief learning that it was nothing serious.

Yet this did not feel like ordinary flu. The pain in the back of my pelvis was worse than ever, making me almost disregard the stiff soreness in my neck and the headache.

I decided to return home, thirty miles away, and called a girlfriend to see if she could pick me up. After arrival to my hometown, I headed to her house and we ran to a nearby doctor her mother recommended. He gave me some pain pills. I still had not told my parents that I was back home in Williams Bay. The pain pills helped somewhat and

Gravity My Enemy

I sat down for dinner at my girlfriend's house. Her mother served chicken noodle soup.

I was embarrassed to discover I was having difficulty bringing a spoonful of soup to my mouth. My hand trembled terribly. I spilled repeatedly as I leaned over the bowl in an effort to eat. I finally had to give up, as it couldn't be done. I lamely said I wasn't hungry and pushed the soup away, deciding it would be wise to head home to my family. I was feeling worse then ever and it was time to let my parents in on this strange malady, as I was now sure it was something serious. As happens in small towns, my folks had heard through the grapevine I was back home and feeling pretty sick. They were irritated I hadn't gone home first, which was just a few blocks away.

To get there, I walked past the school and a residential area and went via a shortcut through thick woods behind our house. There was a well-worn path from all the years my sisters and I went to school over the same route. Here and there was a fallen tree crossing the path. These required nothing but simply stepping over them. As I routinely tried to do so, I found it impossible to lift my foot over to the other side, and had to actually lift my leg behind the knee with both hands each time to place my foot on the other side.

At home, I went straight to bed. My parents' ushered me to their bed, which was a signal that they felt I was unusually ill. I spent a fitful night.

The next day, Saturday, I was still in severe pain but now feeling in a state of shock, detached, as one feels when he knows something is very bad. They called our family doctor, Clifford Wiswell, who made a home visit, as was the custom in those days. He and I had done some duck

Prologue

hunting together, but he was characteristically stone-faced and non-committal. Though he had been a friend of the family from the time I was a kid, I disliked the smell of his office. It smelled of alcohol, pain, and fear. He checked me out and, if he said anything, it wasn't to me. I recall saying to him, "Gosh, I hope it's not polio."

This was ironic. I had no idea at the time what the symptoms of polio were. Only skinny, pale kids from the city got polio, not a sun-tanned athlete from a small town in Wisconsin.

Doc Wiswell left.

Sunday, I changed beds. The pain wasn't quite as bad, but I was very weak. When I tried going to the bathroom, I bent my knees to sit on the toilet, but as soon as I flexed my knees to sit, they gave way and I fell hard and painfully on the toilet. When it came time to get up, I couldn't stand. I struggled as hard as I could but could not get up. In my effort, I fell to the floor with my pants down around my knees, and was embarrassed to call my parents for help — a hard thing to do after years of physical independence. My parents hadn't seen me like this, of course. After a lot of grunting and groaning, my parents got me to a standing position and, by locking my knees, I was able to walk back to bed.

That was the last time I ever walked. It was October 18. In four days, I had gone from a powerful athlete to this.

When I awoke on Monday morning, October 19th, I could not get up at all. I tried to sit up and could not. I tried to raise my arms and that was impossible as well. I couldn't even bring my fists to my shoulders or turn my head from side to side. My parents called an ambulance and in a short while, a couple of fellows hauled me out the back door on an aluminum stretcher to the

Gravity My Enemy

ambulance parked in back. I was in the local Elkhorn hospital a half-hour later.

The only thing of note that happened that Monday, other than entering the hospital paralyzed, was that Doc Wiswell came in to give me what I later learned was called a "spinal tap."

I also learned in retrospect that it was probably the first time since medical school he had ever done a spinal tap. He laid me on one side and brought my knees to my chest, in a fetal position. Behind me on the bed out of my sight, he clattered little metallic surgical things and finally poked me rather painfully in the spinal column with what felt like a big needle. He seemed to be probing around with it. He grunted in frustration, withdrew it, and tried again, and then again, and again. I counted twelve attempts. My legs twitched and jerked with each attempt. My lower back was getting very sore from the repeated punctures. On the thirteenth try, he struck pay dirt. He called it spinal fluid. He showed it to me triumphantly. It looked like champagne without the bubbles. This curiosity about medical things was to become a habit I would acquire in coming months as a defense against all the unpleasant and painful surprises hospitals have to offer.

That first night in the hospital, I was, for some reason perhaps, left alone in my room. The nurse clipped a signal light button to the pillowcase next to my head and asked if I was all right — a rather silly question, I thought, for someone who just arrived in an ambulance.

"If you need anything, just push the button," she said cheerily, and walked out, clicking the door shut.

It never occurred to me to try the button, or at least try to reach for it. This whole business

Prologue

was very new to me and my mental state was as though
I were on a very distant and dangerous planet.

I had no roommate or the customary television
set. Fortunately, the room light had been left on
so I could see. I soon started feeling somewhat
short of breath. Or was it my imagination? Perhaps
it was the uncertainty of the moment. In time,
however, almost in answer to my own question, my
breathing definitely worsened and became labored,
requiring a conscious effort. I soon was alarmed.
Gasping for air became more difficult and I
panicked. After some time pondering this new
crisis, I finally gathered the nerve to reach for
the signal button and found to my horror I could
not move my arm enough to reach it. I was unable
to reach it when the nurse left it but it never
occurred to me to try. My whole concentrated effort
was now spent on breathing and, in time, by some
Divine mercy, I found oblivion — or exhaustion —
and entered a great void.

In the morning, as I gazed straight upward
at the acoustic ceiling, I gradually came to my
senses and began recalling what had happened
the night before, and felt jubilation upon the
realization I had survived. I took a conscious
breath. It was difficult but was actually no worse
than the night previous. Something also told me
it would get no worse.

I knew I had made it.

It must have been very early, because no one
came to my room. If anyone had entered to check
me during the night, I was unaware of it. For some
reason, it became important to me to know how many
holes were in the acoustic tiles above my head. I
tried to visually count the number in each rank
and file. After much effort and recounting, I felt
I finally had the two numbers committed to memory.
Now the challenge was to do a big multiplication

in my head, without benefit of paper and pencil. The mental exercise was totally absorbing. I had to go back to the mental beginning several times, as though to erase my work and start over, but I learned more about my mathematical abilities that morning than I would ever believe, and finally reached what I was convinced was the answer. Then, to augment the challenge, I calculated the number for the entire ceiling — not counting the partial tiles — that was asking too much. The biggest challenge was getting the correct number of zeros.

This kind of complex mental exercise became my way in later years of grappling with life's major problems, and providing a distraction from some of the more vulgar horrors of illness and mortality. I realized years later that it was unusual for a boy of seventeen to get involved in such philosophical issues, but these were extraordinary times.

It was now Tuesday, October 20th. The night before, after the nurse left, I probably came closer to death than at any other time in my life, or at least I thought so. When the nurses came in that morning and noticed my shallow breathing, they began scurrying around and raising their voices in alarm. I was actually amused. My breathing problem had become an outright emergency to them, but I was not allowed to participate in the discussion, something many handicapped people learn in time.

I tried to explain to the nurses rushing in and out of my room that my breathing was no worse than the night before, but could not get their attention. Also, I found I could only whisper, as I did not have enough air to produce a voice.

Two orderlies soon had me on another collapsible aluminum stretcher and were running

Prologue

with me down the hallway. They banged open swinging doors and we were out in the cold air and into an ambulance. This time, as we sped out of the hospital confines and careened onto the highway, the red lights were flashing and the siren wailing. We were off to what I later found was Madison General Hospital an hour away.

The two men in the front of the ambulance made no attempt to talk to me, or show any interest in my fate, as though I were dead. This should have come as no surprise, since they came from a mortuary. Their entire topic of conversation up front dealt with mortuary issues, in a very matter-of-fact way.

We arrived to Madison shortly, for which I was glad, as I was getting depressed with the topic of conversation in the front of the ambulance. After delivering me to the open twin doors of Madison General, I never saw them again, and hoped I never would.

***

The following year was to be a virtual odyssey. The experience at Madison General was a nightmare in itself.

Upon arrival, I was treated with haste, rushed down old, dark hallways, people running and uttering in urgent voices. They were getting me to an iron lung. We soon arrived next to one of these medieval-looking tanks, like something out of a story by Edgar Allen Poe or Jules Verne. It looked like a huge boiler with rivets and it scared me to death. There about a submarine hatch at one end, openly awaiting my arrival like the hungry jaws of a giant, steel monster. Inside lay a thin mattress. There were smaller portholes on the sides with tight rubber gaskets through which

Gravity My Enemy

attendants could reach in, supposedly to give injections, pills and whatnot. Underneath this tank near the floor was a massive bellows. This was sighing rhythmically up and down, powered by an electric motor to create a slow sequence of internal pressure and vacuum, to force my lungs to take in air and expel it. The only thing lacking, I soon learned, was to perform a tracheotomy on my throat, a small incision for a tube to provide me a clear air passage. I felt in shock. Somewhere in the past, I had learned that polio victims placed into iron lungs became dependent upon them. The dependence made it difficult to develop the diaphragm sufficiently to breathe independently. This little tidbit of information created in me an increased desperation to tell someone that my breathing had not worsened since the night before. But no one would listen to my urgent whispers.

Just as a small surgical tray was brought for the incision, a stately, barrel-chested man in an expensive gray suit approached. Everyone treated him with deference. He came to me with a kindly twinkle in his eye and introduced himself as Dr. George Berglund, my new doctor in Madison General. He was a neurologist and brain surgeon. And he was the first person to listen to what I had to say, stooping down with his ear close to my mouth. I spoke.

With a friendly pat of reassurance on my chest, he told me not to worry, ordering that the surgical tray to be taken away.

"What we'll do, Eddie, is put a nurse with you round the clock to monitor your breathing.

We'll park the iron lung just outside the door." I knew I had a friend.

The first night I developed a strange hypersensitivity between my toes. It was so

X

Prologue

intense and agonizing, I could bear it no longer and the nurse rolled up wads of gauze and placed them between all my toes. My father told me weeks later that I had called home that night insisting they come up to Madison immediately.

How I called is anyone's guess. Perhaps the night nurse assisted me. During the first couple of weeks everyone entered my room wearing a mask. Outside, I learned, there was a quarantine sign. The recent epidemics had taught these people well.

Soon, to everyone's collective relief, the breathing emergency passed and I was moved into a room with another roommate. The quarantine sign was removed and I was allowed visitors without need of a mask. Among the first were two fellow women patients from the ward. They had bubbling personalities. They giggled. They had brought me an apple.

"Thanks," I said, as they held the apple out to me.

"I can't use my hand to take it," I explained, so they placed it in my hand.

"Aren't you going to eat it?" one asked after some moments.

Sheepishly, I admitted I could not lift it to my mouth. One took it from my hand and put it in my mouth, but I found I did not have the strength in my jaws to pierce the skin of the apple with my teeth. I was learning how badly I was afflicted.

On another occasion, a small boy who was among those visiting my roommate came to talk to me. My voice was coming back somewhat. In friendliness, I smiled at the boy. He said, "Your face is all crooked." This, I learned, was facial paralysis.

During the first nine days in the hospital, I had had no bowel movement but had eaten all three meals every day, so I had at least twenty-seven meals compacted in my lower intestine. Copious quantities of laxatives did nothing to alleviate the state of advanced constipation. Enemas had no effect.

Finally, the nursing staff decided to "dynamite," as they called it. Dynamite, I soon learned to my horror, required a rubber glove, Vaseline and a long, stiff finger.

They rolled me onto a cold, metallic bedpan. Snapping the cuff of her rubber glove, the nurse announced cryptically,

"This won't take long."

I never had a baby but could now imagine what it was like. I held my breath and sweated.

When the job was done, I lay back on my pillow exhausted. I expect the nurse did not feel much better.

I was still unable to sit up. Each time they transported me it was done on an OR (operating room) cart. My fever had passed and I was no longer "sick" but still in considerable pain, for which I was given a morphine shot every few hours. In time, this was reduced to a capsule. My roommate was also on morphine from surgery. While talking on the phone with a friend I overheard him mention, "Beats martinis all to hell."

Dr. Berglund came to visit me daily and I always looked forward to seeing him. He usually arrived well into the night after 10 p.m. because he had spent the entire day in surgery. He was a prominent neurosurgeon, known throughout the country and was often called upon to travel long distances to perform the most difficult and challenging operations. Despite his importance, he was always cheerful and personable, and soon became a good friend. My curiosity in his trade prompted him to bring me instruments he used in surgery as "show and tell." I was fascinated.

Prologue

He brought the little flexible saw used to open a hole in the cranium, and explained that he often spent the entire day doing an operation through an opening in the head no bigger than a silver dollar.

One day I received a visit from several of my school buddies.

I was beside myself with joy and excitement. They brought a big television set that had been donated by the townspeople of my hometown of Williams Bay. It changed my life. The days and nights were no longer endless and terrifying.

In those early days in the hospital, I had to go to physical therapy every day. The therapist, with her white uniform and traditional triangular yellow patch on her shoulder proclaiming her to be certified, was a skinny redhead with the features of a hawk. She scared me. My muscles and tendons were severely inflamed and painful. She wretched my arms and legs in impossible positions, stretching joints to the extent I almost passed out. I gritted my teeth. I had known pain before but this polio episode was an experience where I felt trapped, victimized by this horrible scarecrow woman.

"It's gotta hurt if you want to get better," she scolded sternly. I thought to myself, "Lions, tigers and bears. Oh, my!" The statement was both a warning and a justification for her daily atrocities. I was always made to feel that I was responsible for all of this.

Worst of all was stretching my back. She sat me up on the table and got behind me on her knees, pushing me forward with a strong hand on the back of my neck. It was excruciating. She explained that the back was the most important. Until it was properly stretched, this process could not end, she said. I was a strapping 210-pound seventeen-year

Gravity My Enemy

old, afraid of nothing in my entire life. Yet I was so terrorized by her I found myself laughing at her stupid jokes, feigning entertainment and interest in her silly musings.

Finally, I resolved to put an end to the agony. One day I made a decision. I was rolled upstairs through the ancient hallways of the hospital, looking at dusty pipes overhead as I neared the dreaded PT department. I hated and feared this young woman more than anyone in my entire lifetime. She was a bully; she was insensitive and overly rough. And she was ugly.

I hated myself for kowtowing to her out of fear. It was a manifestation of the "Patty Hearst Stockholm Syndrome," developing an alliance and false friendship with your enemy out of fear and the instinct for self-preservation. When she finally began stretching the back, I announced that the back was now stretched enough, and invited her to see for herself. With admirable discipline, I forced myself to relax all my muscles as she pushed me forward onto my knees.

She very slowly counted, "One, two, three, four, five, six, seven, eight, nine," and then after a long hesitation and one final push, "ten." She was convinced.

It was finally over. Physical therapy was to be no longer like The Rack in The Inquisition.

During my time in Madison, three hospital roommates died before my eyes, all of heart attacks. One man was forty-two years old. Having just celebrated my eighteenth birthday in the hospital, he was "old" by my standards.

By Christmas I was transferred to Sherman Hospital in Elgin, Illinois, the city in which my father worked. I was glad to get out of Madison. Some months later, my parents received a letter

Prologue

from Dr. Berglund confirming my paralysis to be caused by poliomyelitis Type 3[1].

GEORGE A. BERGLUND, M.D.
110 EAST MAIN STREET
MADISON 3, WISCONSIN

NEUROLOGICAL SURGERY

TELEPHONE ALpine 5.0881

January 6, 1960

Mr. E.G. Elsner, Jr.
92 Upper Loch Vista Road
Williams Bay, Wisconsin

Dear Mr. Elsner:

Thank you for your letter of December 15, 1959. Indeed I am pleased to hear that Eddie is happy at Elgin and that the therapy is good. Please remember me to him and tell him that I would appreciate a progress note from him inasmuch as I consider him a personal friend as well as being his physician in Madison.

I just had a report from the State Laboratory of Hygiene informing me that "poliomyelitis virus type III has been isolated and specifically identified". This definitely establishes the diagnosis as poliomyelitis.

I am enclosing a statement relative to the bill rendered by the practical nurse.

My best wishes to you and Mrs. Elsner, as well as to Eddie.

Yours very truly,

George A. Berglund, M D

GAB:nz
Enc.

I had entertained hopes I had a more temporary affliction called Guillain-Barré. Most people with this strange disease recovered completely within eighteen months. But deep down, I knew I was handicapped for the long haul.

On March 21, 1960 I was flown in a Lockheed Electra to Warm Springs, Georgia, a rehabilitation facility made famous by President Franklin Delano Roosevelt.

---

[1] n. Polio. The picornavirus that causes poliomyelitis. Serologic types 1, 2, and 3 are recognized, type 1 being responsible for most cases of paralytic poliomyelitis and most epidemics. Also called poliovirus, poliovirus hominis.

XV

Gravity My Enemy

The Georgia Warm Springs Foundation was an Idyllic setting. And so began a new, and very different, life for me. It was located at the foot of the cool, Pine Mountains outside the little town of Warm Springs south of Atlanta. It smelled of pines. The complex itself was in the shape of a large quadrangle on a gradual slope, with open grounds in the center bisected with walkways running between tall pine trees. The entrance opened into Georgia Hall, a sprawling vestibule of buffed floors, leather lounge furniture and expensive framed watercolors on the walls. The windows sparkled. The right side of the quadrangle housed the patients, forming three floors. Since the advent of the Salk vaccine for polio, the lower floor was closed off and abandoned for lack of patients, and the foundation, originally dedicated to treating only polio victims, had to take in other types of paralysis in order to survive.

Staff referred to patients by the name of their affliction. A person who had had polio was "a polio." A person injured with a broken neck or back was called "a traumatic lesion," one with multiple sclerosis was "an MS," and so on. Unlike my previous hospital experience, we all wore street clothes and spent the day up and around, in recognition of the fact that we were no longer "sick" but in rehabilitation. Instead of the dinner tray in bed, we all ate in a large dining hall served by waiters.

When I first arrived, the medical people rolled me on a stretcher, as it was called, to a

---

Prologue

room that resembled a classroom. Doctors, nurses and physical therapists of several nationalities surrounded me, as the Georgia Warm Springs Foundation (GWSF) was also a training facility of international renown. I had to appear wearing my full regalia of leg braces and any other orthopedic equipment I had been issued in Illinois.

"Beautiful but useless," Dr. Bennett said, as he paced around me, indicating my expensive leg braces to the surrounding staff. "Beautiful but useless." He was dressed in an expensive suit. Those gathered around wore the uniforms of their trade, mostly white. The visiting doctors all wore a white smock, with the usual stethoscope folded in a front pocket.

"We have here," he went on, as though I were less human than a medical specimen, "a young man of eighteen years of age, obviously well-developed physically, most likely an athlete." He continued strutting around me as he talked.

"We don't know why," he continued parenthetically, "but we find that often those in the best physical condition become the worst affected by polio. This young man had Type III poliomyelitis with some degree of meningitis." He went on, "He obviously didn't get his shots, probably thinking his athletic abilities made him immune," came the final indictment.

"Am I correct?" He directed his attention to me as a person for the first time. The hushed group awaited my answer in silence.

"Yes, sir," I replied in a weak voice.

Guilty as charged. Were I sitting up, I probably would have hung my head in shame.

"He is a quadriplegic," Dr. B went on in a clinical tone, and with rather severe involvement. The virus reached the bulbar region but he was fortunate enough to avoid a respirator. His

Gravity My Enemy

involvement is somewhat lateral, the left side being slightly less affected than the right, which is virtually without any muscular movement at all. He lost some sensory in his hands and feet initially. These two symptoms led medical staff in the north to believe at the outset he might have Guillain-Barré syndrome but spinal fluid later revealed Type III poliomyelitis.

"The task ahead with this man is a long one," he went on. "Here at this foundation, we firmly believe that muscles in a relaxed, but flexed position have a better chance of some recovery." He went on as I reviewed in my mind all that had happened in the past months and felt rather excited as I viewed my new surroundings. I felt greatly encouraged by seeing other patients cruising back and forth in the hallways in shiny wheelchairs, dressed in slacks and sport shirts.

"... so the first order of business," Dr. Bennett interrupted my musings, "is to get him to our brace shop and get him fitted with hand splints and leg braces. Overhead suspension rods with springs will raise his arms at shoulder level to help the deltoids — no chance of you pushing around your own chair, m'boy," he said to me.

And so, after the medical staffing, I was the next day sent to the brace shop, where they had a myriad of power tools, grinders, and cutters for work on aluminum, steel and leather. This was also a training facility for brace makers from afar. As I lay on the stretcher (the OR cart) men bent and fitted sheet aluminum to fit my hands while others, as though I were in Santa's workshop, fitted pieces to my legs, adding, riveting, and polishing. All the tailoring took several hours. They raised the seat of my wheelchair, since I was tall. They also raised the armrests, attached a bracket in back to carry crutches, and provided

Prologue

me a portable tray in front and a number of other
adaptations. A day or so later, I received all
this equipment. Wearing it, I must have been
quite a sight.

The most encouraging to me was being the
owner of a new, tailor-made pair of crutches,
fastened behind my chair, to proclaim my intention
of walking again.

Each day was as busy as going to college.
Everyone was rousted out early for breakfast
and baths. The orderlies rushed everyone to a
bathroom at the end of the hall, bodily lifting
each patient into a tub, rapidly scrubbing him,
toweled him off and raced back down the hall to
our individual rooms, two at a time. Then, we
all went our separate ways — some to regular
physical therapy involving stretching and gauging
muscle strength throughout the body. Others went
to Occupational Therapy to learn to do everyday
functions like making transfers from wheelchair
to car, to bed, to the toilet, kitchen work, or
handicrafts for manual dexterity. The foundation
had a yellow '58 Chevy with a hand control and
we used this to learn how to drive. Since each
person's handicap was different, each one had to
learn everyday tasks in a different way.

One of our favorites was the pool, supplied
with natural, warm spring water, for which the
foundation was named. The pool was only about
three feet deep and had a number of underwater
wooden platforms on which the patients lay to
receive more therapy, based on the fact that water
buoyancy rules out gravity and allows greater
freedom of movement, which is otherwise not
experienced by the very weak. Using adjustable
aluminum leg braces and "walking" in water to one's
waist, without much risk of falling, accomplished
the beginning stages of walking as well.

Gravity My Enemy

My therapist was a solid, female Army captain named Fran Parks, originally from Pennsylvania, on a training mission at Warm Springs. She was a friendly but tough gal; about five feet two inches tall but handled my six-foot frame with ease. We became close friends over time, as we did with most of the visiting staff, with the exception of a six-foot-three-inch German redhead gal named Ursula, who had to be a relation of Himmler's. Drawing her for physical therapy was like getting Attila the Hun. She stretched joints like she was taking apart a cooked chicken. The therapists I came to like the most were three cute girls from Lisbon, Portugal. I had a bad crush on a dark-haired gal named María Teresa Figuereido who took it upon herself to push me all over the campus on weekends and introduce me to their favorite music called Fado.

The orderlies at Warm Springs, mostly black, made life worth living also. This was a menagerie of characters named O.C., a skinny fellow about seven feet tall that should have been making millions in the NBA. Another named Ben, was bucktoothed and stupid as a chicken. Henry was the smart guy, always with a joke, like O.C. Tommy was a tough white guy with a nasty scar down his cheek and splitting his chin, the work of a knife attack he received at the hands of a Japanese soldier in the Second World War. Then, there was Phillip, an effeminate blond orderly who's song of every day was, "Put your sweet lips a little closer to the phone, and let's pretend that we're together all alone..." sung in a high-pitched southern twang.

My roommate, Cecil Corson, came from the edge of the Okeefenokie Swamp in Waycroft, Georgia. He spoke so unintelligibly that even fellow Crackers couldn't understand him. Cecil

Prologue

used to enjoy picking on Phillip because he was evidently gay. Cecil would fill a small syringe with urine and hide it under the bed sheet and turn on his signal light. When Phillip arrived at the door, Cecil would shoot him in the face with a fine stream of urine. Phillip, not knowing what it was, wiped his cheek and said, "Qui-it!" as Cecil and I burst out laughing.

The truth is, we all wanted out of Warm Springs, despite the good food and camaraderie. We were all there for the wrong reasons. Most of us were young, far from home and family, and spending months in the routine of rehabilitation became tiresome. So we resorted to pranks for amusement.

There were big laundry chutes in the hallways at floor level, with doors opened by push bars similar to those in high schools. Each patient's wheelchair was readily recognizable by its special features. One day, we snuck off with Lewis's wheelchair. Lewis was our accomplice in this. We then opened a laundry chute and hung Lewis's chair by the handles inside the chute, leaving the doors partially open, and ran to the nurse, Mrs. Roberts, exclaiming, "Mrs. Roberts! Mrs. Roberts! Lewis fell down the laundry chute!"

She tore out of the nurse's station and ran to the site of the "accident."

"Oh, my God!" she screamed as she spotted Lewis's chair hanging in the mouth of the chute. She ran to the nurse's station and sent orderlies down to the lower, abandoned floor to recover Lewis. Needless to say, he wasn't there and we all had a good laugh. Mrs. Roberts was characteristically a very angry woman and she gave us all a good dose of her character that day, but she was a good sport.

Despite her tough demeanor, Mrs. Roberts fortunately had a sense of humor, and we got along

Gravity My Enemy

fine with her for the most part. The nurse we disliked heartily was a robust brutish woman named Miss Bullock. She was too thick skulled to have a sense of humor. She was mean and unforgiving, and treated us all like children. One day, she paid the price.

On a quiet evening, she was in charge of the second shift, which ran from three p.m. till eleven at night. It was her duty to collect everyone on the ward and get them to bed, with lights out, before turning the shift over to the Third Shift. After supper, we played cards, watched some TV and visited together but by around nine at night she sent nursing staff and orderlies to begin collecting everyone and getting them to their rooms.

At around seven on this particular night, we started organizing everyone to gradually disappear. In one's and two's, patients got on the elevator at the far end of the hall and headed downstairs to the abandoned floor, where they took up their card games and whatnot. By about nine, all but the most incapacitated were nowhere to be found. Miss Bullock sent people looking down in Georgia Hall first, as was routine. Finding no one, they began looking outside in the courtyard and on the different porches and balconies that were areas of common congregation, but found no one. They checked the movie theater. Perhaps there was a movie going on she was not aware of. But it was dark and closed. By ten, Miss Bullock could be heard even by us as she roared for her staff to search different areas, even the parking lot out in front of Georgia Hall and the dining hall. Was there some activity about which she hadn't been informed? She made calls to no avail. She was now desperate. It was her responsibility to turn over the floor to the next shift in good order, but she could not account for most of her patients!

Prologue

Downstairs, we played cards, told stories and giggled with uncontrolled mirth.

Close to eleven-thirty, it dawned on someone — most probably by process of elimination — that the only place so many people could hide was on the lower abandoned floor, and someone burst on the scene to find us laughing hysterically. I think Miss Bullock's "foul-up" that night even reached the ears of the foundation director, Dr. Bennett.

Inside the courtyard from the elegant Georgia Hall was a fountain that shot water up in the air from the center of a circular pool that was about twenty feet in diameter. It was a shallow pool, perhaps only a foot deep. We discovered it circulated the same water.

Cecil and I were the ringleaders of many pranks, but this we were about to embark on one of the worst. We had gotten scolded soundly for what we pulled on Miss Bullock but, as Cecil said, "What are they gonna do? Kick us out?"

On this particular day, Cecil and I had someone buy us seven large cans of Lux Liquid Detergent. As an afterthought, Cecil ordered some small bottles of red dye.

In the beginning, we had no intention of flooding Georgia Hall, but seven cans of dishwashing detergent is quite a lot. Only a capful is required to make a sinkful of soapy water. Cecil pushed his chair over to poolside and I joined him as he was opening the paper bag and withdrawing the first blue can. He then looked around furtively to make sure nobody was watching, and then up-ended it, letting its contents gurgle out into the water. Then, he dumped in a second, and a third, then a fourth, until all seven empties were hidden back in the bag. He quickly added the bottles of dye.

At first, nothing happened.

Gravity My Enemy

We sat and watched. But after some moments, the constant falling of the column of water from the central fountain splashed and began to make a few suds in the center and around the edges of the pool. After a few minutes, they were becoming quite visible, and we sat back to enjoy our handiwork. Before long, the soap was beginning to billow up in small piles around the pool. They were pink. It didn't take long for the suds to begin overflowing the pool. Then they ran out onto the grass. In alarm, Cecil and I backed off from the pool, deciding it was safer to watch this Vesuvius from a greater distance. By now, the suds were three feet high, and flowing liberally downhill towards Georgia Hall thirty feet away. A gust of wind picked up a huge billowing mass of foam half the size of a refrigerator and swept it towards the building, pasting it wetly on the windows. Eventually, quite a lot of the slop flowed right into the hall itself and I guess the mopping job took some time. We knew we would have to face the music but, as Cecil said, "Best thing that could happen is they send us home."

In August, at long last, I was sent home. Whether it had anything to do with the suds in Georgia Hall, I never learned, but it was good to be out of the hospital for the first time in almost a year. As I said, close to a year is a long time to keep an eighteen year old in the hospital, especially when he's not sick.

When I returned to Wisconsin, my real life began. At first, it was no fun living in a wheelchair. It never was, but I figure it beats many other afflictions.

People at times have asked: What is it really like to be handicapped in a wheelchair?

The answer depends, of course, on the person. But more importantly, it depends on the stage in

Prologue

which one is at a given time. For my part, in the first days and weeks I was in a state of shock and dismay, much as I have been told animal prey feel upon being caught by a predator. There is little rational thought. Soon, the shock is replaced by a blind hope that everything will in time return to normal. Otherwise well-intentioned people foster some of this. They tell stories, true or made up, about a "cousin" or someone who "had the same thing but fully recovered." Though well meaning, I think much of this is intended to alleviate their own discomfort in the presence of an uncomfortable situation. But all it does is increase the disappointment and desperation on the part of the handicapped person. The miracles told are just that — rare exceptions, often exaggerations of reality or later explained to be something other than how they have been represented.

The sooner the handicapped person accepts this condition and devises ways to live with it, the sooner he'll begin to lead a productive life and feel contentment with his accomplishments. The fact is, in life, we all must live with our individual setbacks. Some of us are overweight, some slower of foot, some ugly and others dull-witted. Some fail to learn to express themselves well and others have dismal luck with the opposite sex. Some of us do miserably with numbers while others have mechanical genius. We all must learn over time to capitalize on those assets that come easily to us, and even develop them more for survival, while we also do some "muscle-building" in areas of dysfunction where we perform least. If we get better, that is so much gravy, but we cannot waste valuable time wishing things were different. We all must play the hand we are dealt, and get on with it. Life is a gift. Having a physical handicap is not easy, partially because

Gravity My Enemy

it is visible. Social stigmas hinder achievement because of other people's pre-conceived notions of what one can or cannot do. This must be overcome — not with heroism or a Hollywood version of "courage" but with proof in the form of everyday hard work and achievement of common goals.

Also, it is axiomatic that those who give compassion more than seek it find true solace. As a people in a wheelchair or otherwise handicapped, it behooves us to focus outwardly and see other people's needs and suffering, and address those rather than living a life of grievance and dependency on handouts.

To a person handicapped in mobility, as I was, gravity is the enemy. The most severely handicapped person could get along just fine if he lived on the moon's surface, weighing one-sixth his Earth weight. Gravity is the great enemy.

With severe paralysis or weakness, mobility is the biggest challenge. Today's technology has come up with truly great marvels. Wheelchairs and hand controls are a far cry from FDR's day. Funding sources put virtually all of it within reach of everyone. The pull of gravity is what makes life difficult or impossible to the handicapped person to get around, but if one has intellect, curiosity and imagination, coupled with empathy and compassion toward others, the mind and genuine friendships will bring greater freedom. Adventures of the imagination are far more exciting than those of reality.

In the years to come, as following chapters will illustrate, I was to prove that even the wildest dreams can become reality and the most severely handicapped person can even escape the bonds of gravity and a "handicapped" body.

1 Early Adventures

I had a great time as a kid. We had little material wealth but made up for it with a vivid imagination. From an early age I used the imagination as a vehicle to distant lands and distant times.

History as it was taught in school had no effect on my delight with history. In fact, some teaching was so uninspiring that I confess my fascination with the past came about despite the history courses.

I loved the museum. It was there I saw my first Java Man, the man-killer lions of Tsavo, my first dinosaur and a real Egyptian mummy. I roamed the halls of the Chicago Field Museum of Natural History in utter rapture, going from one display to the next.

Imagery is a wonderful thing. It costs nothing and the person using it effectively can make it as good or elaborate as he wants, based on either real happenings or conjectures. Books and movies sketch in details of the salient issues but the reader or viewer is the one who ultimately converts it to his own reality.

Imagery is also responsible for great achievements: The basketball player can actually raise freshot percentages by systematically imagining he is sinking more freshots. Einstein was unable to formulate the final details of his famous Theory of Relativity until he actually used imagery to ride on a light beam.

Nobody ever had to tell me to read books as a class assignment. Most kids cheat anyway. We had a wonderful, one-room library in our little southern Wisconsin school. I will probably never know who put this collection together but I would

Gravity My Enemy

like to pay tribute to that person's unrewarded genius. I am certain I read more than my teachers did. The theory of sea travel from South America to the South Pacific on a balsa raft by Thor Heyerdahl's "Kon-Tiki" was common knowledge to me before reaching high school. I liked some of Stephen Crane's poetry more than his "Red Badge of Courage" and I knew from an early age that "Swiss Family Robinson" was pure lies and fabrication in contrast to "Robinson Crusoe," which actually happened, opening for me the door to the careful thinking, innovation and the strong heart needed to survive alone on a desert island. But "Swiss Family Robinson's" treehouse inspired me to build several far less elaborate versions at dizzying heights in the red oaks behind the house in my boyhood years.

I knew the true location of Timbuktu because I traveled in my imagination with the Tuaregs on the salt caravans in books taken from the shelves of that humble library. Josh Slokum's incredible solo voyage around the world in his thirty-six-foot wooden sloop Spray took place late at night under my reading lamp. The Horatio Hornblower series, I learned, was really based on C.S. Forester's admiration for the real Admiral Horatio Nelson who brazenly confronted the entire Spanish and French fleets together off Trafalgar, Spain in the heavily armed, five-decked, massive ship o'-the-line HMS Victory and defeated them, but gave his life in his triumph. Thus began a legacy of British superiority of the high seas that would last over a century. James Fennimore Cooper's Hawkeye, with his trusty muzzleloader Killdeer in hand, resided in the woods just outside my bedroom and

Early Adventures

in my mind as a kid, and I met the true Benedict Arnold of our Revolutionary War though Kenneth Roberts' "Rabble In Arms."

I considered myself lucky to get a passing "C" grade in high school history but I did not care because I knew that real history was far more exciting and important than textbooks.

Today's film industry has an edge over the movies of the past as concerns special effects but those films of my youth in the 1950's had an irresistible allure and they fueled a fertile imagination: I sailed with pirates on a creaking wooden deck in the Caribbean after witnessing the heart-breaking, puzzling duplicity of Long John Silver in "Treasure Island," I helped hoist their sails and fire their cannons, and I smelled the acrid odor of the smoke from black powder. Robert Taylor of Sir Walter Scott's "Ivanhoe" made me into a black knight in my dreams, jousting against the Normans to the approving roar of a medieval crowd. I made my own shield of Masonite with a cross painted on the front. My helmet was fashioned from a large Jay's potato chip can. An old broom was my lance. I needed no tedious history course to learn about William The Conqueror and Harold of the Saxons because Sir Walter Scott taught me before I ever entered a history class.

As young boys, we used to buy quarter-inch dowels at Hollister's lumberyard in town, for ten cents apiece. These we used in sword fights inspired by the movie "Scaramouch," featuring some of the best sword fighting ever between Mel Ferrer and Stewart Granger. We began learning what it was like to fight with foils by simulating the fights in the movie with these quarter-inch wooden

Gravity My Enemy

dowels. The red welts on our arms attested to the sincerity of effort we put into each combat.

We crawled on our bellies through the brush on commando spy missions to save our country and rid the world of tyrants.

From early boyhood I imagined chugging down some far-off jungle river with dangerous hippos snorting near the boat and crocs plunging into the swirling river current as my little, one-lunged steamer chugged tirelessly through the dark forest. This was inspired by Humphrey Bogart in "African Queen."

I yearned to sit in a narrow dugout canoe with Indians as we silently paddled through the mysterious depths of the Amazonian jungle, revealing new and exciting panoramas as we came around each bend of the river.

(Little did I know that I would actually do this very thing in later years.)

I dreamt many times of being on safari on the African veldt after seeing Stewart Granger in "King Solomon's Mines." Once again, I had no way of knowing I would one day conduct my own safaris across uncharted plains in Colombia.

I loved the old Tarzan movies. We swung from wild grape vines while, in our imagination we swung from vines with Johnny Weissmuller. Years later, I would visit a tiny corner of a surprisingly small Mexican jungle called Mismaloya, and actually see the setting for those Tarzan movies, among others.

There always was and always will be uncertainty about the future. The past, however, is largely known and brings with it authenticity. And the more archeological discoveries we make, the more exciting and defined the past becomes and the more relevance it brings to the present,

Early Adventures

because the past is what shaped and gives meaning to the present.

Our time machine is imagination based largely on fact. With more discoveries to be found in the ground and in old archives we develop an informed imagery and can more easily "travel" to any time and place we choose in history to different, intriguing cultures and places with their strange belief systems and values. The panorama suddenly differs from anything in our "real" experience. Forests appear where today there are none. The dress, language, daily pursuits and activities, the sounds and smells — and dangers — become those of another time and place.

I lived most of my youth in Williams Bay, Wisconsin, population 700 at the time. To me that small town was the whole world.

My father, as a young man, was lean, with a dark complexion. And, aside from work around the house, he was always involved in projects, most very clever, innovative ones that ended up really working. He grew up in Forest Glen in northern Chicago, the second generation of German and Spanish immigrants. His dreams were engendered by aviation heroes like Charles Lindbergh who crossed the Atlantic non-stop in 1927. My dad was only ten at the time. He earned money as a boy selling meticulously hand-made airplane models at air shows. They were as light as a feather. When older, he earned money by parachute jumping at air shows — a real death-defying stunt in those days.

My father was never drawn by organized sports, so I never got a baseball mitt for Christmas, or a basketball hoop on the front of the garage.

Gravity My Enemy

At age 5, with my old man and my 1st .22 rifle

He was a commercial artist by trade and a visionary by choice. He was instrumental in getting me into the business of using my imagery. He took me on trips. Once, we traveled to an area called Lac du Flambeau where there was an Indian reservation. There he bought me a hand carved bow with arrows that really worked. The most exciting was the pair of brain-tanned beaded moccasins he got me. Made by an elderly Chippewa woman, they smelled wonderfully of smoke, as I imagined the old Indian villages must have smelled. I put them on immediately and refused to take them off for the remainder of the trip. With those moccasins on my feet, I walked as silently as Hawkeye and ran faster than the wind.

For all the wonders of books and movies, radio then was a wonderful thing. A bit similar to books but unlike movies, radio left it all up to the listener to visualize. "Straight Arrow" was my favorite. These programs aired every Tuesday and Thursday afternoon after school. They led me to cut off cereal box tops ("N-A-B-I-S-C-O, Nabisco is the name to know . . .") to send in for a "golden" arrowhead and Indian ring with a gold nugget from his gold cave, where he kept his palomino horse, Fury. I used to paint my face with the different schemes he painted as he emerged from the cave on Fury in the comics. This sparked a life-long fascination with the Native American, leading to seven years of intermittent study

Early Adventures

of Plains Lakota religion with a holy man named Frank Fools Crow of Kyle, South Dakota on the Pine Ridge reservation. To this day, their view of God (*Tunkasila* in Lakota) and their spiritualism make the most sense to me.

"Sky King" inspired an interest in aviation, and "Sergeant Preston of the Yukon" taught me that a snowy wilderness could really be home. As a teen, I enjoyed being alone in the woods, and I never was afraid of the outdoors or the dark, as most kids were. I learned early that there is nothing to fear in nature: It was the city where bad things happen. My relationship with nature became personal and very spiritual. At around fourteen, I slept out in the snow with no tent for over a week, living off game I got with my .22 Remington Targetmaster Dad bought me. I fried rabbits and squirrels in goose grease in a heavy iron skillet and slept remarkably comfortably in a snowdrift next to the fire.

Aside from my books, radio and movies, for fun and adventure I had to go no further than my own family. My dad was a big dreamer in his own right. He, as an adult wage earner, had the means to make many dreams come true. He took me trout fishing on a dark, swift stream where I caught my first brook trout and saw my first water moccasin. I mentally had gone trout fishing with Ernest Hemingway after repeatedly reading his "Big Two-Hearted River."

One June, Dad and I paddled into the Canadian wilderness with my uncle Buddy, in the beautiful Boundary Waters, and a year or two later, as an extra-special thrill, we flew in to a remote lake in Ontario from Ft. Francis. The floatplane was a massive Norseman with a 650-hp Pratt and Whitney radial engine that raised a 100-yard rooster tail behind it on takeoff. We strapped a canoe onto the

Gravity My Enemy

struts of the Edo pontoons and pumped gasoline from their built-in tanks for a week's supply for the outboard motor, and we camped totally alone for a week on a rocky point where we could watch beaver and listen to the thump-thump-thumping of ruffed grouse in the nearby woods. We saw moose browsing at the water's edge and once spotted a black bear among the brambles.

Dad got drafted late in the war and was sent off to Camp Fannin, near Tyler, Texas.

Despite his later claims of hating the military, he seemed to really get caught up in everything related to it. He and his two brothers inspired me. His younger brother, Buddy, had joined the Army Air Corps and ended up flying a P-38 fighter in the Aleutian Islands when the Japanese invaded the islands near Kiska. His plane was even painted like a Flying Tiger. Their kid brother, Ralph, was rather sickly as a boy. He went in to take tests at age seventeen to join the Air Corps as well and got high scores but being under-age, needed his father's signature to join. His father refused, so my Uncle Ralph had to wait another year. He was finally accepted and after flight training was shipped to France where he flew missions deep into Germany in his P-47 fighter. Being farther away, my father was less in touch with Ralph than with Buddy. Uncle Buddy once called my father in Texas from Alaska and offered to fly down in his fighter and pick him up for a trip home to Chicago for Christmas. Even before jets, the little time this took was astonishing. The two crammed themselves into a cockpit designed for only a single pilot. My dad sat on Buddy's shoulders, bent uncomfortably over his head with the canopy pressing down on his back. When they reached Chicago, Buddy made a hard bank as he

Early Adventures

announced "Turning down Foster Avenue!" where we lived at the time. My dad, not accustomed to violent flight maneuvers as his brother was, blacked out from the turn.

Uncles Buddy (above) and his P-38 Lightning in the Aleution Islands, and Ralph with his P-47 Thunderbolt in Etain, France

Gravity My Enemy

He took me to air shows to see and hear the "heavy iron" of high-performance warplanes as they roared past excited crowds at ground level, trailing smoke as they did slow rolls.

I built model fighter planes and imagined racing though billowing clouds in search of a very dangerous and skilful enemy in the skies of Europe. This was not difficult to imagine: My uncles, Buddy and Ralph told me their tales (much too modestly, I later realized). Both got hit with enemy fire but luckily made it back to base. When the war was over, they brought home their leather helmets, goggles and leather jackets, along with thick, fleece-lined boots. My uncle Ralph even showed us reels of 16 mm combat film taken right from his P-47. I later read several old mission reports he kept. One was about his little fighter group receiving a commendation from General George Patton for shooting up a Panzer division that had Patton's people briefly surrounded.

These uncles were never condescending to a young boy like me. They treated me with affection and told stories as though to an adult.

My dreams were perhaps only dreams but they were all firmly rooted in the authenticity of history. Did I ever hear of Genghis Kahn? I dreamed I rode on horseback with his huge Mongolian army as they set up hundred-mile encirclements on wild game hunts across Asia. Almost two thousand years earlier, I rode with Alexander the Great in the battle at Gaugamela and later as he crossed the Hindu Kush.

Too many need prodding to study history, because the way it is taught is totally wrong. Too few history teachers really feel the emotion and impact of history, beyond simple dates, names and places. Too few history teachers are true dreamers. They have no comprehension of what it

Early Adventures

was like to ride with the Arapaho in search of buffalo, or travel with Marco Polo to the Orient. It never occurs to them what it would have been like to sail around "the Horn" with Captain Cook or see Tahiti before the European took disease and corruption to the South Pacific paradise. No history teacher I ever knew understood or knew about the architectural genius of Hadrian, or ever read the teachings in Stoicism of Marcus Aurelius and become interested is his wars on the Danube against the Barbarians. None felt in their hearts what it must be like to hunt whales from an Umiak in the Arctic ice floes, or fight the Persian army of a million highly-trained, disciplined soldiers as did the far better-trained, much better disciplined Spartans at Thermopylae in 480 B.C. How could a mere college degree prepare a teacher to feel the awe of viewing Machu Pichu for the first time, or the Pyramid of the Inscriptions in Chiapas? Or the temples of Copán and Tikal? Did our high school history teacher (we called him "Thomps") ever hear the hoof beats and choke in the dust in the chaotic battles of Trajan, when the Roman Empire was at its greatest expanse? I felt I did all these things through the reading of books. There are many worlds waiting in books. I read and dreamt about Hannibal from Carthage and learned of his genius. How did he take African elephants through the snowy Alps? I felt I was there. I could see in my mind's eye Julius Caesar as he courageously rode to the front to inspire his already-loyal troops in his last battle at Munda against Sextus Pompey in what now is Spain. The infantry was rank-and-file in the center, the standard phalanx of the day, with the light, mobile cavalry to the right. Highly skilled, professional slingers and archers formed on both sides as javelin-throwers in the front hobbled the

11

Gravity My Enemy

big shields of the enemy as opponents approached each other with just a few yards of separation, seconds prior to the actual flow of Roman blood.

Unlike many, I lived out some of my fantasies. After seeing "20,000 Leagues Under the Sea" my father took me to the Chicago Sports Show. There was a booth on scuba diving, a sport almost unknown in those days. This booth had a mannequin dressed in a rubber suit with mask, and a tank strapped on its back. The device was called an Aqua Lung, invented by Jacques Ives Cousteau. I stood there and stared at it in awe. We made the rounds, saw Labrador retrievers fetch live-trussed ducks under impossible conditions in front of thousands of yelling people. We saw a daredevil skier jump off a ski jump lined with straw and do a forward flip before landing at high speed on the slanted floor below.

But I kept returning to the booth on Aqua Lungs. The promoters gave me a blue pamphlet illustrating the different models of Aqua Lungs, from three tanks to a single, small tank. In months to follow at home this pamphlet joined my other books, and it became worn and fell apart after I went through it hundreds of times, wistfully dreaming of the day I might have the means to buy one for myself.

Around then, in the dead of winter, the movie theater in Delavan, seven miles from home, was featuring a movie about deep sea diving called "Underwater" with Jane Russell. I begged my parents to drive me to the movie, but to no avail, so when the night of its first showing arrived, I set out on foot and hiked through the snow to see it.

The day I was to get my own diving outfit came when I was about thirteen. I was out on the front porch flipping through the pages of a Field & Stream magazine.

Early Adventures

One ad caught my eye.

This advertised a Navy surplus Diving Outfit with everything included: a mask, a high-pressure hose, harness and a brass pump made by the Miller-Dunn company of Florida.

The price was $32.95 — a lofty sum — but I was now working on the weekends as a stock boy for 75 cents an hour.

In those days, we sent cash in the mail and never lost a cent. I had often taped quarters onto cereal box tops and stuffed them in an envelope for decoder rings and a tiny "gold" arrowhead flashlight from Straight Arrow. Once I got a small submarine that alternately floated and sank in the sink with a charge of Arm and Hammer baking soda. Most of these orders went to Battle Creek, Michigan. I guess that was where they made breakfast cereals.

For this diving outfit, I folded dollar bills onto a piece of cardboard, securely taped the proper change to it, and sent it off.

Every day in following weeks I stopped by the post office downtown and asked Mr. Iverson if anything had come for me. Finally one day, he said he had a box for me, and invited me to come around the back of the mailroom to get it.

I was about to burst with excitement. The huge box was misshapen from its journey. I hefted it. It was perhaps thirty pounds. I hauled it all the way home on my shoulder, a mile over steep hills. When I arrived, I set it down carefully next to the front porch outside the house and caught my breath, then opened the box with trembling hands.

Inside, there was a heavy solid brass pump with two cylinders, bolted onto a wooden base. Lying lengthwise in the box was a three-foot flat galvanized steel bar to be used as a handle for the pump. This inserted into the top of a rocker arm to operate the pistons. There was a coil of black high-pressure hose with brass couplings at each end. Tucked in a corner of the box was a heavy-duty canvas harness with buckles and a ring in the back through which I was to pass the hose, according to the crumpled illustration sheet. Then there was a black mask that looked like a World War II gas mask, but with big letters USN embossed at the top. It had flex hoses like those of the Aqua Lungs I so admired, and they were clamped under the eye lenses and joined together in a Y at the back.

I rounded up a couple of neighborhood buddies and we excitedly headed to the pier down at the lake a couple of blocks away, each hauling a part of the equipment. It was decided my friend Gordy Roth would man the pump while Eddie Maher fed the hose over the side of the pier to avoid tangles. As the owner, I got to try it first. I nervously strapped on the harness and Eddie screwed the hose to the Y through the big ring on the back of the harness. I readied the flex hoses over my shoulders and adjusted the straps of the mask on my face so it fit tightly. Gordy gave the pump a few tentative strokes and I smelled the rubbery odor of new hose as the air hit me in the face. I gave him thumbs up, meaning, "Pump like hell!" With excitement, I jumped off the edge of the pier feet first and plunged into the cold water. The air on the lenses kept them from fogging but being curved, everything was distorted. Gordy hesitated pumping once and I found myself desperately sucking for air — there was no reserve in the system. Eventually, though with regret, we decided we had to discard the mask in favor of a regular French diving mask, and simply sucked from the hose grasped in our fists

Early Adventures

like an ice cream cone. And a warning to Gordy of dire consequences kept him pumping furiously. Although the dives were limited by his endurance to only a couple of minutes, it opened up a new world of fantasy for all of us.

In time, we got a heavy, lead-weighted helmet made from a hot water heater at Johnny Ladd's welding shop, and thus we joined the ranks of the Nautilus crew in "20,000 Leagues Under the Sea." The helmet had an abundant air reserve with all of the pump noises and bubbling straight out of the movie.

Another fantasy I entertained as a boy was flying. Having uncles who were pilot heroes undoubtedly had an influence, though they had little good to say about their war experiences. I spent as much time as I could at the airport in the nearby town of Elkhorn, helping out, polishing windshields, pumping gas to earn change and tips to take flying lessons, which were ten bucks an hour. Often I only had two or three dollars but the instructor cheerfully

Diving helmet & pump

Gravity My Enemy

indulged me for a mere fifteen minutes, "enough for three take-offs and landings." I never got my license because the law required an age of sixteen to solo but I finally beat the law.

The airport manager, a burly guy named Jim Price, told me to practice taxiing the J-3 Piper Cub, as I was having difficulties mastering this on the ground, being a "tail-dragger" rather than the more modern tricycle gear. Jim advised me to start slow and work up in speed.

The J-3 has no electric start, so we had to have one person in the cockpit while the other out front cranked the propeller. There is a strict procedure for this, as it was a dangerous operation. The guy at the prop was to never grab the edge of the prop with crooked fingers, but crank it with hands flat. Then, he yelled "Off" to make sure the magnetos were off and it would not start as he cranked the prop several turns to suck gas. The guy in the cockpit had to confirm "Off!" When the 65-hp Continental could be heard to suck gas, the guy at the prop then yelled, "Left Mag!" & was answered by "Left Mag!" confirmation from inside the cockpit. Kicking his right leg forward first to gain momentum, the guy at the prop cranked hard downward with a backwards kick, to flip the wooden Sensinich prop. The engine was finely tuned and usually started on the first or second try. The guy at the prop jumped clear as the person in the cockpit put the switch on "Both" magnetos and lightly accelerated by "cracking the throttle."

Since this was a lonely small-town airport, I was taught an "illegal" way to start the Cub without a second person. After turning the prop a couple of times to prime the engine, I stayed behind the prop with the right foot in front of the right wheel and left behind it, then reached

Early Adventures

inside the cockpit with my left hand, "cracked" the throttle slightly to give it a little gas, and set the switch on Left Mag. Reaching forward with my right arm, I grabbed the prop, flipping it downwards as hard as possible. When it started, the trick was to quickly jump inside and take over the throttle, and then buckle up. Jim knew I had mastered this technique, so didn't bother coming outside to help me to start it. In a few moments, I smelled the wonderful smell of burnt aviation fuel and was slowly going down the grass strip all alone, my hair blowing in the prop blast, as it was customary to leave the doors open on the J-3 in the summer, even when flying.

Following his advice, I taxied slowly down the strip, trying to keep the plane in a straight line, a task much easier said than done, as it tends to zigzag back and forth as the rudder pedals are over-controlled. I then in time picked up a little more speed and found the job easier as more propeller blast hit the rudder surface. This was getting to be a snap, I thought. I pushed on more throttle after turning around at the end of the runway. The tail wheel was beginning to come clear of the ground as I was virtually racing along next to the tall, waving grass. I was controlling it perfectly! The feeling of almost flying was exhilarating.

Suddenly, the sensation of rumbling along the sod surface became smooth as I realized to my horror that I was completely airborne!

I quickly chopped the throttle. The plane suddenly lost its lift and dropped, bouncing awkwardly on the ground, then nose-up high in the air. I had been told of this danger, which could lead to a stall and an accident, so I frantically pushed the throttle forward for more gas to gain control, only to find myself

Gravity My Enemy

flying again. As the plane leveled out, I could see the fence at the end of the runway approaching fast. Out of the corner of my eye,

The J-3 Cub

I also saw Jim Price running out onto the field, waving his arms. While still blessed with some remaining runway, I desperately cut the throttle and accelerated in a series of embarrassing uncontrolled bounces down the entire length of the strip but quickly saw my demise, and the plane's, immediately ahead. I was faced with a decision: a possible crash at the fence or pour on the coal to go all the way around in the air, which I had never done alone. Of the two alternatives, the worst was facing Jim with a wrecked plane. I hit the throttle lever and took off in a gradual ascent and made a slow turn over the road to go "around the patch" to approach from the other end. I was almost giddy with relief as I made a smooth landing and finally, in sweaty triumph, got the plane stopped and cut the throttle. The

Early Adventures

engine made a couple last turns and came to a halt. All was silent except for the metallic pops and clicks the engine made from the heat. I sat there in the cockpit, my heart pounding. My tee shirt was soaked with the sweat of fear. Jim ran breathlessly up alongside my door, puffing heavily from the sprint out of the building, and with a violent arm gesture, ordered, "Get out of the damn plane!"

That ended my flying career in Elkhorn. I went home in shame that afternoon, wondering how I could ever face him again. But at night while musing in bed over the experience, I thought, "At least you soloed." And I was not yet sixteen.

I never had the nerve to ask Jim to write that solo flight in my logbook.

***

Besides flying planes, I loved flying hawks. I read books as an addiction from the earliest age. (I somehow learned to read before kindergarten.) The library was my treasure trove. Books of falconry accumulated in my room and became dog-eared. My cousin Dave and younger brother Tim discovered a redtail hawk's nest near home and I cajoled my cousin into climbing to the top of the dead oak fifty feet up. Dangling from his lofty dead limb, he fastened a rope onto it and took to it with a carpenter's saw. The limb suddenly snapped, the rope broke and the limb with the large nest crashed to the ground.

Gravity My Enemy

My first redtail hawk

One of the two white-fluffed chicks survived. I began training it as soon as feathers started coming in. After a time, I had a lovely male (called a *tiercel*) redtail hawk flying and hunting rabbits.

All of these dreams took place in the span of only a few short years, though they seemed a lifetime. I later went to college, got polio and entered into a new and quite different life. During this time I met foreign friends and became interested in languages and different cultures.

My first introduction to organized sports was on the high school football team — the only team sport that attracted me. I don't believe my father attended a single game except the last in which I played, when I ran for three or four touchdowns — I cannot remember which. He took a picture of me as I left the field at the end of the game, and

Early Adventures

I suspect his presence was at the insistence of my mother. The University of Wisconsin could have saved us a heap of money, as they had offered me a football scholarship for the next fall season. But I was dissuaded from playing football by a player on the University of Wisconsin team[1] who explained that the physical demands coupled with academics made this the "toughest way to work your way through college." So I went to school closer to home and got polio mid-semester. Once out of the hospital almost a year later, I headed for a wheelchair-accessible campus, the University of Illinois in Champaign-Urbana.

While at the university, I met a number of students from Colombia, who were there under a program called ICETEX. An American friend from Portland, Oregon, was a teacher in the Spanish department and had spent a year in Colombia, teaching English at a bi-national center called Centro Colombo-Americano. Under their influence and tutelage, I gained some proficiency in Spanish and went through a learning process on Colombia.

After graduation, I worked for a publishing company in Elgin, Illinois. Being in a wheelchair, I was unable to work at the company itself. My father found me a small office in Elgin near the company, which allowed me to accomplish an unusual amount of work undistracted, and provided me a phone and unlimited freedom. Between jobs one day, I picked up the phone and dialed my friend Jack in Portland.

"What's this Colombo thing you were always talking about in Champaign?" He gave me a brief rundown, explaining that both the U.S. and Colombian governments sponsored the program. There were a number of centers throughout different cities in

---

[1]   Center George Crist

Gravity My Enemy

Colombia. Teaching positions paid modestly, much
like the Peace Corps, to which I had also recently
applied. He gave me the address and I got busy
writing a letter to the Centro Colombo-Americano
in Bogotá.

I was a bit apprehensive about traveling
alone to a Third World country. One day, I
received a letter offering me a one-hundred-
dollar-a-month salary to teach English at the
Centro Colombo-Americano in the small city of
Popayán, in southern Colombia for a year. The
contract offered round-trip transportation from
Miami and one hundred pounds of unaccompanied
baggage. There was no hesitation on my part. I
signed and sent the contract in the mail the
same day. In a whirlwind of activity in the days
immediately following, I got my passport and many
shots. I packed two army duffels with books, as
my unaccompanied baggage.

In less than a month, on September 16, 1964,
I found myself aboard a Lockheed Constellation
flying over the Caribbean to South America.

The Avianca "Connie" (courtesy Avianca)

2 El Dorado

My arm felt sore from the yellow fever shot, as I bid farewell to my family, boss and friends. My needs, mostly books, were packed in two army duffels. Thus began my journey to South America.

I was headed to the small colonial city of Popayán in southern Colombia. The United States Information Service, known then as "USIS," had several bi-national cultural centers, BNC's, throughout the country. In Colombia each was called "Centro Colombo-Americano," or more commonly "Colombo." These were essentially schools dedicated to teaching English as a second language and vocational courses such as accounting, sewing and bilingual secretary studies. They were also libraries and centers for cultural events, as well as outlets for scholarships to study in the United States. As such, most were important social hubs in their respective towns with large numbers of people coming and going at all hours.

The Colombo in Popayán was in trouble for lack of teachers from the U.S. When the Centro

23

Gravity My Enemy

Colombo-Americano of Bogotá, which headed the operations throughout the country, received my letter of inquiry, they decided to chance sending me a contract to see if I would bite. At the time, they already had in Bogotá a married couple from North Carolina, Jerry and Caroline Whitmire, who had arrived originally to teach in Bogotá's center. In the event I accepted, the Whitmire's had agreed to transfer to Popayán where Jerry would serve as director, while his wife Caroline and I would teach.

And so it happened. I signed the contract.

Just days later, I found myself on a flight from Chicago to Miami in a Lockheed Electra, which was modern for its day but was falling out of the sky at an alarming rate due to a design problem.

In Miami I boarded a Lockheed Constellation, the sleek triple-tailed airliner lauded as the best intercontinental airliner in the pre-jet era. It was one of the first truly high-altitude aircraft, with a pressurized cabin and a speed in excess of 300 mph. Movie stars and politicians were often seen in slick magazines, waving from the ramp of the fashionable "Connie."

It was late at night in Miami when I looked out the big observation window of the Avianca waiting area prior to boarding the huge plane. The floodlights illuminated a shiny, silver aircraft with "Avianca Colombia" proudly painted in dark blue letters on the sides. Stunning, dark-haired stewardesses in bright red ponchos, called "*ruanas*" in Colombia, scurried about readying for the flight.

I was twenty-two. I needed a wheelchair to ambulate, and was about to leave my country for the first time, and live in a faraway land on my own.

Once helped aboard, I buckled in. One by one, the reciprocal engines coughed to life,

24

El Dorado

belching a cloud of white smoke and the vibration
of the engines could be felt through the airframe.
They smoothed out to a roar as we crept away from
the terminal. In minutes, we were in the night
sky over a carpet of lights comprising Miami.
They twinkled below in neat rows, and then ended
in pitch-blackness as we left the coastline and
thundered southward over the Caribbean. On what
was I embarking? Could I handle the challenge of
the language, a totally different culture, with a
wheelchair in a country probably inaccessible to
wheelchairs? These questions nagged my tired mind
as we droned over Cuba in the wee hours of the
night. I noticed only one set of headlights below
as we passed over Cuba. Not much life down there
anymore since Castro, I thought to myself.

Dinner was served. It was terrific. Many
years later, when I learned it was a common
joke to deride airline meals, I had always been
well-disposed toward them, no doubt owing to that
first dinner on Avianca that prejudiced me in
their favor. We passed the island of Jamaica, also
barely lit.

An American woman sat next to me. She was a
resident of the Colombian city of Medellin.

The only subject she wished to talk about
was the size of the cockroaches there. Bored with
her limited repertoire, I finally dozed off as the
Connie's four engines throbbed rhythmically in
the night as we flew on to our destination high in
the Andes. I intermittently dozed and mused over
what little I had read of Colombia's tumultuous
history.

Colombia was the birthplace of South American
independence marshaled by Simón Bolívar. Called
Nueva Granada, it comprised today's republics of
Colombia, Ecuador, Panama and Venezuela, its capital
city being our destination of Santa Fe de Bogotá.

Gravity My Enemy

All but Panama have almost identical flags, the top yellow and blue, with the bottom half of the flag red, evidently in graphic representation of the blood spilled throughout its unusually bloody history. The Battle of Boyacá on August 7, 1819 was the turning point in their struggle, finally winning independence from Spain, but culturally, the original Spanish hidalgo nature of the people is still very prevalent.

Panama seceded from Colombia in 1903, at Teddy Roosevelt's urging, to build the canal.

Previous to that, Ecuador and Venezuela had become independent republics.

As Colombia developed, two major political parties emerged: the Liberals, which used the color red, controlled the ports, and the Conservatives, using the color blue, held power in the interior with the banks. Decades of animosity and strife between them followed the country's independence during the 19th, and first half of the 20th, centuries, giving Colombia the distinction as one of the most violent countries in Latin America, despite and in contrast to its renown as a seat of learning and high culture. The size of Texas and several adjoining states combined, Colombia claimed a population of over twenty million at the time of my arrival.

Colombia is a land of sharp physical contrasts. It has, in a sense, three coasts. The Atlantic or Caribbean lies on the northern extreme, the rocky and densely forested Pacific to the west, and the Amazon River to the south, which accommodates ocean-going vessels six hundred miles beyond the point where Colombia extends south to touch it for 72 miles. Ports at all three fronts feed the country from abroad. Running north to south along the western side of the country is a jagged spine of three *cordilleras*, or mighty Andes mountain

El Dorado

ranges, mostly volcanic, reaching dizzying, snow-capped heights of almost 20,000 feet. To the east of the mountains lie vast, hot, undulating, grassy plains, called the *Llanos Orientales*. This region is largely unpopulated cattle country where one finds independent, tough-minded cowboys in their own distinct culture, spreading into Venezuela. Their alluring music, called the *joropo*, is played with a harp. East and south of this vast savanna stretch the seemingly endless rainforests of Colombia, Venezuela, Brazil, Ecuador, Peru and Bolivia. To the east lies the Orinoco Basin, while to the south spreads the huge Amazon Basin, the largest forest on the planet, much still unexplored. Blanketed with triple-canopy rainforest, which is home to numerous little known native tribes.[1]

Colombia shares its southern border with Ecuador and Peru in a region little known and often disputed. The northern Pacific Coast is a combination of impassable fever jungle and rugged mountains, also home to Indian tribes such as the *Cholos*, thus far unknown and unaffected by modern cultures. This is the area of the Darien, where the construction of the Pan American highway has been thwarted to this day, due to its inhospitable terrain, forest growth and swamp, also mostly unexplored.[2] The Darien region borders Panama.

---

[1] There has been much discussion among anthropologists regarding the origin of the Amazon tribes. Originally, the predominant theory was based on the migration across the Bering Sea from Asia but recent theories lend credence to African origins as well.

[2] An estimated 25,000 died of mosquito-born disease and accidents during the construction of the Panama Canal, an estimate by Chief Sanitary Officer Dr. William Crawford Gorgas. Precise number is unknown because the French, failing in the construction, also failed to keep good records.

Gravity My Enemy

As one would expect, the fragmented nature of the country has contributed to distinct cultural and dialectic separations of its people. Even a novice can distinguish Colombian people's origins from their accent, manner of speech and dress, as well as their unique musical rhythms. These evolved into exciting and exotic beats such as the *Cumbia* and the *Bambuco*. Colombia is a leader with some of the richest musical and artistic talent in the Americas.

These same geographical and cultural differences have led to violent conflict and jealous regionalism as well, and the Colombian political system is designed to overcome these regional differences by bonding loyalty and political affiliation to a strong centralized system of government. The resulting dynamic is an ever-changing political scenario that is fascinating and often entertaining, with a menagerie of key actors playing such interesting roles that most of Colombia's populace is much more involved and well-informed in politics than the average American.

The sudden change in the engines' revolutions interrupted my train of thought, as the plane began its long descent to Bogotá's El Dorado airport.

El Dorado of myth and legend, The Gilded One, was a *Muisca* Indian prince coated in oil and gold dust while celebrating the crater lake's creation. From a balsa raft he plunged into the lake and washed off the gold dust, while the Indians on the shores tossed gold trinket offerings, called *Tunjos*, into the dark waters. Thus, the bottom of the lake has been the object of massive efforts even to present day, largely unsuccessful, to retrieve the gold.

When early Spanish *conquistadores* reached this land in the early sixteenth century, they

28

El Dorado

found a country populated by several different cultures of Native Americans, from the *Sinú* and *Tairona* cultures on the Caribbean coast, to the best goldsmiths of the New World, the *Quimbayas*.

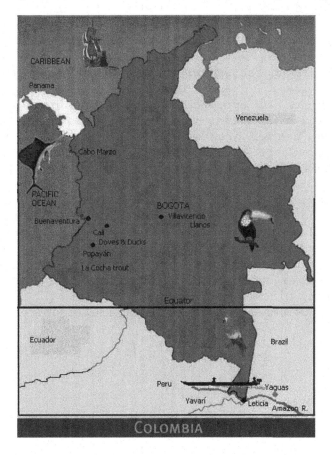

I gazed out the porthole in an effort to catch my first glimpse of my new homeland for the coming year. It was getting light. Below the wing I could make out the verdant rolling hills, devoid of roads and only an occasional twinkling cluster of lights revealing a tiny settlement.

Gravity My Enemy

Much, as I could make out, was a patch-quilt work of varying greens, as small farmsteads emerged into view and passed under the wing.

The plane came perilously close to jagged forested peaks as it banked steeply to make its final approach to El Dorado airport. To one side, I spotted the precipitous mountain of Monserrate, its pristine white chapel perched on the top, overlooking the sprawling city of Bogotá below.

Lower green hilltops passed rapidly below as we approached. The thundering plane crossed over a long row of eucalyptus trees just as we neared ground level and within seconds the pavement of the runway streaked under the plane's wings, it hesitated momentarily and then its tires screeched to herald our landing. I was amazed to note black and white dairy cattle grazing alongside the pavement, virtually under our wingtips, and was curious to see concrete, rather than the familiar wood, light poles in a line along the runway fence. The air was fresh and quite chilly. Large, black vultures wheeled in lazy circles overhead.

Colombia was such a beautiful country.

3 Popayán

Air accidents were common in Colombia. There were few navigational aids such as VOR. Many local aviators relied on ADF (automatic direction finder) that could be used with regular AM radio, which pointed in the direction of the transmitter. All that was required was to identify which transmitter it was and where it was located. It was still unknown how far the aircraft was from the transmitter, and was hard to use in a crosswind, but at least one knew approximately where he was.

Weather is a big problem for flying in Colombia. Poor visibility due to fog and clouds were the rule throughout the country. Colombia has three, very lofty Andes mountain chains, and the clouds, as pilots there tend to say, have "rocks in them."

During the first five days in the country, I met up with old university friends who lived in Bogotá and were delighted to show me around their city and its environs. We had been together at the University of Illinois in Champaign-Urbana for several years and had become very close. They proudly took me everywhere of interest. I had my first experience watching a professional soccer game, which to me seemed too long and tedious for so few points scored. We went to the famous underground Salt Cathedral, carved entirely from a salt mountain in Zipaquirá. We climbed in a Swiss-built cable car to the dizzying heights of Monserrate overlooking the city. Since there were so many gracious people who wanted to see me, I had the embarrassing experience of going to dinner to three different homes in a single night, and became ill from over-eating.

Gravity My Enemy

When it was over, I finally had to head to my destination in the southern part of the country, Popayán, for which I had signed my teaching contract. I returned to El Dorado and took another Constellation flight to what was then the diminutive, old tropical Calipuerto of Cali. The flight took us over what is commonly called *La Línea*. This is the razorback of the central *cordillera* of the Colombian Andes. Strong prevailing winds roaring over this chain cause violent updrafts. Low-flying aircraft usually experience some degree of buffeting as they cross to the west. I was sitting back in my seat enjoying the spectacular view of the snowcapped volcano Nevado de Ruiz when this phenomenon took me by complete surprise.

The first impact was like a giant hammer blow in the solar plexus of the Connie. It was so violent, it made a cracking noise, making me suspect there was structural damage. The huge plane rocked and the engine pitch increased momentarily. Just as it settled once again into normal flight, another powerful shock convulsed the plane.

Whenever scared or alarmed on a commercial flight, it is wise to check the reactions of the flight crew to gauge the severity of the situation. One stewardess had been distributing cold sandwiches and drinks to the passengers from a wheeled stainless steel cart in the aisle. She was now on her knees on the carpeting, her mouth agape and her eyes wide in stark terror. I knew we were in trouble. She had completely lost her air of self-assured calm she had been taught to display in the presence of passengers during turbulence. The cart had tipped on its side against a seat and Dixie cups of drinks were spilling onto the floor. I noticed droplets hanging from the ceiling, evidence of the jolt.

Popayán

Passengers who had unbuckled their seatbelts were thrown in all directions, some in the aisle, and others on top of fellow passengers. I noticed one elderly lady with her feet in the air, lying across the knees of what seemed to be a stodgy businessman wearing glasses, which were comically askew on his face.

Several hard blows followed in quick succession and I felt seriously concerned that the plane was damaged, as these were not the common smooth bumps usually encountered even in violent turbulence, but jarring impacts that made the cracking, breaking noise of metal giving way. For the first time in my life, I considered the possibility of dying in an airplane crash.

But then the air smoothed out and the triple-tailed airliner resumed its steady roar as though nothing had happened. The stewardess regained her feet, smiled in embarrassment and quickly pushed her cart down the aisle in our direction to return to the nook behind a curtain where it had originated. People who had been tossed about quickly got untangled, straightened their ties, ran fingers through their hair and returned to their seats in embarrassment, apologizing to those they had inadvertently visited during the tumultuous moment in flight. All showed visible relief in their gestures. Even the businessman resumed his feigned, bored perusal of the stock market section of the newspaper, as a show that flying was to him a very routine experience.

The young fellow next to me took up a nervous conversation and when he learned my destination was some hours south of Cali to the city of Popayán, he suggested we share a taxi, which we eventually did upon our arrival. Cali was hot compared to Bogotá and we were sweating when we taxied up to the small terminal, but I doubt it

Gravity My Enemy

was due only to the heat. We soon set out for the south, as I saw three crosses high atop a hill beyond the city.

The trip was beautiful, reminding me of films I had seen of the African plains, with animals grazing in vast, green pastures, accompanied by snow-white cattle egrets. Flocks of tree ducks flew in the distance.

By the time the red sun began to set over the low mountains to the west, we reached the tropical town of Sandander de Quilichao. We stopped for a brief snack. I had no experience with roadside fare. My new friend suggested I try *chicharrón* and a meat *chuso*, essentially a shish kabob of extremely tough meat with a tasteless flour *arepa sin sal* stuck on the end of the stick for an appetizer. The *chicharrón* was deep-fried sowbelly, and rather tasty. I drank an orange pop to wash it down, and we continued our journey from the flat plains and began to enter the mountains, as I saw a large bat flutter in the darkening sunset. The road had been gravel since Cali, and our driver avoided billows of choking dust by keeping his distance behind preceding vehicles, most of which were canvas-covered trucks. Lightening cracked ominously ahead as we toiled up the steep grade. It was starting to rain. The light drizzle turned into a downpour.

In a half hour, we were bogged down behind a line of buses and trucks, churning their wheels in deep mud as the line advanced slowly. For periods of up to an hour, our progress stopped altogether. After several hours, we reached the point that was holding everything up. Two bulldozers were busily clearing a landslide by pushing mounds of mud off into the abyss below. As soon as we passed this area of deep mud, glistening wetly in the headlights of oncoming trucks, we broke free

Popayán

and got up to about thirty miles per hour. It was refreshing to be moving again. The mountain air became cold, and I rolled up my window.

Late into the night we finally reached Popayán, which looked very nondescript in the late darkness. We were exhausted, and asked the taxi driver to drop us off at the first hotel.

It was called Hotel Victoria. The big, double doors were closed. My friend Ovidio got out and hammered on the door with his key ring. In a moment, a smaller, inset door opened tentatively and a small Indian boy with a shock of straight, black hair hanging in his face sleepily gazed at us.

"Can we stay?" Ovidio asked.

The Indian boy nodded wordlessly.

The taxi driver opened the trunk of the car and he and Ovidio got out my wheelchair and bags, along with others Ovidio had brought. We paid the driver and he sped off into the night. The streets were dead quiet. As we asked the Indian to open the bigger doors so I could enter, he informed us there were no rooms.

"Why didn't you tell us, you idiot?!" Ovidio shouted at him indignantly.

"Let's get the owner," I said. The boy was apparently very uneasy about waking his boss, but we were insistent.

After a few moments waiting nervously, the owner came down the stairs. She had a smile and greeted us warmly. She was middle-aged and rather attractive, introducing herself as Josefina. She was Swiss. Josefina assured us that we could stay if we could convince another American to share his room with us. She knocked on a door. "Robin," she called twice.

Finally, a tall, thin American with acne stuck his head out the door and we explained our predicament. He readily accepted us, and Josefina scurried off to bring another folding cot and mattress.

Robin Sandefur was a Peace Corps volunteer who had just arrived to Colombia to engage in what was called *Acción Comunal,* whatever that was. It seemed Robin was in some doubt himself. He was from some suburb of Cincinnati.

In a few moments, Josefina again appeared with a large platter of sandwiches.

Dios le bendiga, I said enthusiastically. God bless you. She served us coffee with a thick skin of milk on the surface. Ovidio dumped in about ten spoonfuls of dark, semi-refined sugar as Robin and I watched in alarm. The sandwiches were made from a thick loaf of bread with ham and boiled egg slices. We ate hungrily and quickly fell asleep.

I was in my new home.

Popayán

4 The Payaneses

When I signed a teaching contract with the Centro Colombo-Americano, it was to work in the city of Popayán, one of the oldest cities in Colombia, founded in 1536 by Sebastian de Belalcazar, one of Francisco Pizarro's lieutenants, who also founded Quito in Ecuador to the south and the lovely city of Cali to the north. Popayán was small in area for its population of 90,000, a grid of narrow streets tucked between clusters of whitewashed adobe houses with Spanish tile roofs. A big university complex formed its center. The city is perched high at 5,700 feet in the central *cordillera* and enjoys a perpetual spring-like climate at about 68 degree F. daily, but is often quite rainy. It is famous as an educational center. Many families throughout the country send their sons and daughters to study in local secondary schools and the famous Universidad del Cauca, which produced no less than fifteen of Colombia's presidents.

More than any other place I have seen, Colombia is replete with a menagerie of interesting characters and unbelievable contrasts and social contradictions. To the average American, the disdain for life and the level of violence is shocking; even more so when we who have lived there recognize the contrast with their Old World culture and lofty educational accomplishment that permeates the upper classes of Colombian society. Visible poverty right at one's feet on the sidewalks is astounding, while obvious opulence and incredible wealth display a stark contrast. These contradictions are exhilarating and inspiring as well as horrifying. It may come as a surprise that I saw very little corruption in Colombia. Many of its leaders participate in the political process

Gravity My Enemy

out of fervent patriotism often at great personal and economic sacrifice. Judges are virtually impeccable in carrying out their duties in one of the cleanest judicial systems in the world, which may explain why so many were assassinated years later for convicting members of the Medellín and Cali drug cartels. Certainly, these contrasts also exist in other parts of the world but are shrouded by the activities and complexities of society. Or they are institutionalized. Colombia is socially much more transparent. Its press is painfully honest and people openly discuss national problems and issues in the numerous cafes, without fear of reprisal. Interesting characters come to the fore, are appreciated for what they are, talked about with fondness and amusement, or disgust, in open forum. With this, it would not come as a surprise that the use of descriptive and ingenious nicknames, or *apodos*, as they are called in Spanish, is rampant and highly entertaining in and of itself. A friend in town who had the nervous habit of blinking was called *semáforo*, "stoplight." Another rotund, five-foot-four-inch, bald fellow named Luis Hernando López was commonly called *"Balín"* López — "Ball Bearing." A rather skinny fellow who had trouble spotting birds as they flew right past him on a dove shoot was called *Ojo de Aguila* — "Eagle Eye," of course.

"Bullfrog" Bruno Mantilla was a very nice fellow, affable with everyone and a very good English teacher, but as irresponsible with money as a small child. He was constantly forgetting important things, like paying his rent. In fact, he was in serious hock most of his life. When a bill collector approached him, he dug deep into his pockets as a sign of destitution and, with a warm, wide smile that wrapped across his entire face, (from which he earned his nickname) told the

The Payaneses

collector, "I'll have it for sure, without fail, next Tuesday when I get paid." Colombians are a patient, tolerant people. And "next Tuesday" he was nowhere to be found, or had not been paid yet, he said, or had been sick or whatever other excuse he could establish.

Bruno played the lottery, as do all desperate people in Colombia. There is an official lottery in each Colombian province. Popayán's province is Cauca. Its lottery was not big compared to other, more wealthy provinces, but still represented a windfall that could change a person's life. Lottery tickets are sold as "fractions," or the entire sheet of ten fractions. The fractions are torn off the whole perforated sheet and cost what the name implies — a fraction, and pay off a fraction of the grand prize as well.

Habitual lottery players often buy their tickets from the same vendor each week and they become acquaintances over time. A winning ticket will usually bring a hefty tip to the vendor.

I suppose due to the Catholic religion and a people who have been subjugated by higher political powers throughout history, Colombians have a blind faith in fate or destiny. Call it luck if you wish. They are not in control of their fate (which explains many of their social attitudes and behavior). The Virgin Mary or God handles that, and in Their devine benevolence will someday change a person's fortune. Thus, Colombia is very ripe ground for lotteries. Bruno bought a whole ticket every Friday, the day the Cauca lottery played. In the late afternoon every Friday, on the steps of the *Gobernación* in the main park, those entrusted with the lottery brought out the big wheels and spun them in the eyes of the public and the winning number was announced, to be followed by some jubilant winners and a large number of

39

Gravity My Enemy

losers, who tore up their tickets in disgust and tossed them in the gutter. "Next time."

This particular Friday, Bruno as usual ran across his lottery vendor, who had his favorite number all ready. Bruno dug deep into his pockets and for once was skunked. He only had enough for a fraction of the ticket.

That afternoon, when they publicly spun the wheels in the large doorway to the *Gobernación*, his number won. Even in terms of good luck, Bruno's luck was bad. He had not bought a mere fraction in longer than he could remember. Even so, the payoff was a whopping 22,000 pesos, a fortune in those days almost two years' salary for him.

With Bullfrog Bruno, pleasure comes before obligation. Oh, sure, he was going to pay his four months of rent arrears, and his phone bill, and his light bill (his phone was disconnected). But first, he had his eye on some fishing equipment. And an inflatable boat. He went out and bought a new rod and reel, a spool of line and a nice collection of lures as well as all the paraphernalia anglers so much love. Of course, a tackle box was necessary, a rather big one, in fact. Then boots, a rain poncho, a little stove and cooking utensils, stringer, filet knife, designer sunglasses and, as an afterthought, a foot pump for the boat. By the time he had completed his purchases, only a small handful of cash remained and not enough to pay a single bill.

Saturday, the very next morning, found Bruno riding an express taxicab in the pre-dawn hours heading for a cold mountain stream in Paletará, where rainbow trout had been planted years ago by the conservation department, Inderena. The stream ran into a high-altitude lake of ice-cold water.

As the sun peeked over the horizon, Bruno was excitedly unloading his gear from the trunk

The Payaneses

of the taxi, including his packed lunch. The taxi driver slouched into his seat to await Bruno at the end of the day, closed his eyes and readied himself for a day of boredom and easy money.

Once the inflatable raft was pumped up and loaded, Bruno carefully pushed off and inserted his collapsible plastic oars into the holes provided for the purpose. He was wearing his tall rubber boots as he awkwardly rowed out toward the middle of the lake.

At first all was calm, the surface of the lake like a mirror, but as soon as the sun came up, small gusts of breeze made small cats paws on the surface. As happens in the high cloud forest, clouds intermittently scud across the low sky and then the sun comes out again, only to be obscured once again in cloud. It often drizzles as well. The surrounding area is spongy and covered with lichen and moss, the dwarf trees festooned with moss and dripping.

Bruno was an enthusiastic angler but, in truth, largely unsuccessful and not possessing knowledge or much experience. Yet he was happy and eager to describe himself as a close follower of the sport. He was even less of a boatman, tending to be clumsy and with little coordination or understanding of which oar to pull to achieve a given direction. He was out from the shore perhaps a hundred yards when he stood up in the small craft to ready his fishing pole. A sudden gust caught him unawares and he lost his balance and fell overboard, losing his pole overboard in the process, as well as every loose item in the boat. Desperate, he grabbed a line attached to the side of the raft but in so doing, unknowingly popped the plug loose on the air chamber on one side and the boat started to deflate. His boots were full of water and he feared being pulled to the bottom, so

Gravity My Enemy

he kicked them off and shed his rain poncho as well. The designer, wrap-around sunglasses were gone in the initial plunge into the frigid waters.

Bruno

The breeze was taking him to the opposite, uninhabited side of the lake and, as deflated as the boat now was, he could not control it to get back, so he opted to push off from the boat and swim for it. Being a poor swimmer and given the frigid temperature of the water, he was lucky to make it back. He arrived exhausted and lay on the shore for a time before gathering the strength to get to his bare feet and hobble to the taxi, where the driver was still sound asleep.

Bruno threw himself, dripping, onto the car seat and returned to Popayán. All his fishing equipment was either on the bottom of the lake or washed up on the other inaccessible side of the lake.

Upon reaching his apartment, he was greeted by his landlord, who had learned of Bullfrog Bruno's good fortune in the lottery. (Word gets around quickly in a small town.) The landlord smiled warmly in anticipation of good news. Bruno smiled back with his big, wraparound bullfrog smile and, out of habit, dug deep in his sodden pants, hunched his shoulders, showing the empty palms as a sign of "no money," as he had done a thousand times previously. He was back where he started. With the possible exception of the time he burst his waterbed on his second-story

The Payaneses

apartment, this event took the prize for someone plagued by bad luck.

Popayán is one of only two, truly colonial cities in Colombia. All the houses adjoin and have red tile roofs, blackened by the acid from nearby volcanoes. The walls are three to four feet thick adobe. Streets are narrow, some cobble stoned. Everything is whitewashed, and the eaves of all houses and stores overhang the sidewalks, allowing pedestrians to walk around without getting wet in a town where it rains more often than not. The elevation is 5,700 feet and chilly as a rule. The narrow streets are crowned to allow quick draining of the rainwater. Some old houses from colonial times have huge double wooden doors with elegant iron hinges and lion-headed doorknockers.

I was on my way to class one day early in the morning when I detected a strange thundering sound. A young fellow named Luis was pushing me in my wheelchair.

"*Escuche!*" I said. Listen! "What's that?" I thought it might be an earthquake, which was a frequent phenomenon in this part of Colombia. We felt no tremor. Suddenly, from one block away, a large herd of cattle with long horns came around the corner at a dead run and headed straight for us. Luis deftly got me up on the narrow sidewalk but we could see the cattle were also on the sidewalks. Urgently, he rushed me over to the big doors of the Santo Domingo church, and pushed me inside. The herd of cattle thundered by, shaking the ground. My heart was pounding. This was every bit like Pamplona, but without the warning. We had missed tragedy by a hair's breadth. Why someone had decided to herd long-horned cattle through the middle of a city of 90,000 people always remained a mystery. But there was always impunity. In Colombia, there are more pressing issues.

43

Gravity My Enemy

I worked as director of a bi-national center and found myself usually either attending the public or doing the paperwork one has to contend with when using government grants. On one Monday morning, deeply mired in financial reports, my secretary, Silvia, stuck her head in the door. With raised eyebrows, which signified "you'll just love this" she said a gentleman was there to see me. I asked who and she replied, "You'll see." It turned out to be a very tall, elderly Black man, as skinny as a beanpole and somewhat bent over from his height, which had to be no less than six feet five inches, and osteoporosis. He had a very friendly countenance and I bid him in.

"*En qué le puedo servir?*" I asked, hoping it would be brief. How can I help you?

"*En nada, maestro . . .*" Nothing much, calling me "maestro" which is a form of deference the extremely poor show those they regard as higher status. He was hesitant, but finally pulled out of the pocket of his wrinkled and soup-stained suit a long, browned reed flute. He was a minstrel. His flute was hand-made, stained dark brown and shiny from much use. "Oh boy," I thought to myself. "Now, I've gotta put aside urgent work to indulge a flute minstrel.

"How much do you wish?" I asked. Money is always involved in these cases.

"O... *lo que su merced disponga,*" Whatever you wish, he said in eloquent Spanish. He seemed so kindly and gentle, I couldn't help but feeling an immediate fondness toward him. Gesturing him in, he came to the center of my office and poised his flute in position on his chin and began the first hesitant, quiet notes. The tune was folkloric in flavor, melancholy and unknown to me. As it gained in rhythm and he opened up in volume, I became amazed at the mellow sweetness of the

The Payaneses

sound exuding from this crude instrument. The notes came as though from a celestial source, not of this earth. They wavered in a lovely vibrato and filled the area with an enchanting melody. I felt a rush of emotion at the sounds he produced, and felt my hair standing on end. I was in the presence of something heavenly, an angel in a pauper's clothing. The old man then broke off from playing the flute and began to sing in a beautiful, rich voice that can only come with age. The quality of the concert was incredible. I felt tears welling up in my eyes.

My secretary and the librarian, Gladys, by now had entered, and several teachers and students crowded in to hear this fantastic, genius musician. As the office was getting crowded, even from people off the street who had heard this as they passed on the sidewalk outside, I asked him to move out into the library where there was more space. He graciously moved out and resumed the concert. In a matter of minutes the library was full, with people using all the chairs, sitting on desktops and on the floor. There were people from the street outside, now easily numbering perhaps fifty or sixty. I signaled to Eva, our office helper, to please get some coffee ready and in a short while she was serving all around, as we asked the old man to take a break and join us. The applause was instant and sincere. He graciously bowed but remained very modest. We all took up a collection and gave him a considerable amount of money, much more, I am sure from the look in his eyes, than he ever expected. And much less, I thought to myself, than he deserves. Why couldn't the Chicago Symphony Orchestra recruit such an unusual talent? This old man with his old, stained flute was every bit as good as any flute soloist I had seen in the best concert halls in the United States.

45

Gravity My Enemy

The gaunt, old man gave us a long encore, the richest, most vibrant tones I had heard in my life. People watching were literally moved to tears. The old man's voice was a perfect mate to his flute, much like Louis Armstrong's trumpet replicated the sound of his voice, but less flamboyant and more humble as is good folk music of a humble people. His sounds filled the entire school and library. When it was over, he came over and embraced me.

"When can you return?" I asked eagerly, and was joined by many others. "We'll schedule a full concert," I encouraged him, "with advertising and tickets."

The elderly man smiled but brushed off my inquiry with a wave of the hand. His cheekbones protruded and shined like rubbed mahogany, and his eyes danced in joy. "Someday, perhaps."

And the next thing I knew, just like that, he was gone.

"What was his name? Did anybody get his name? Where's he from?" I asked in dismay.

"I think from the coast," someone volunteered, but it was no doubt a guess based on the coast having the greatest Black population. "The Coast" in Colombia meant the Caribbean. Perhaps someday.

We always remembered this old musician fondly and wished he would return, but it took three years to see him again, and he wandered in just as unceremoniously as he did the first time. Taking us unawares, we were unable this time, too, to make the preparations his talent deserved, yet a small crowd still gathered to hear him.

Over the years, the old flutist blessed us with his music three more times. We never learned his name, or where he came from. I learned a year later that, being homeless, this street gamines

The Payaneses

stole his beloved flute from his fiber bag as he slept. With an admirable philosophic acceptance that we could all do well to emulate, he cheerfully said, "They stole my flute, but not my music."

There were other less-welcome visitors.

One who occasionally showed up at my office was a religious freak that looked like a twin of Charles Manson. He dressed like a monk and had a tiny picture of Christ encapsulated in clear plastic stitched to the skin of his forehead.

Another was the owner of a family-run two-bit radio station in Popayán. His name was Luis Dario Valencia (no relation to the president). Usually, he came in to discuss any political or news item that had some relationship to the United States, and demonstrated a friendly demeanor. But occasionally, he was openly hostile and argumentative, lambasting the U.S. and its entire people with some of the most preposterous claims. He became physically threatening on these occasions and I had the good fortune of having a perceptive secretary that knew, just from the look on his face, when I was going to have trouble with him, and she sent for help. On those occasions he had to be removed bodily from my office.

These "lunacy attacks" seemed common, at least in Popayán. A diminutive fellow the people called "*guineo*" (the name for a tiny banana) went on a periodic rampage in town, beating on people and breaking windows, until he was hauled off. A local dentist, a well-educated, informed, pleasant man in general, would, perhaps once a year, wearing rags, go berserk and stand out on a busy street corner and shout outrageous epithets and obscenities to the passing public. After a short while the police would take him away.

Other than being mildly amusing, there were dangers. In those days the influence from Peking

Gravity My Enemy

and Cuba had reached a high pitch, and bombings and street riots were frequent. The public schools and the Universidad Del Cauca law school were hotbeds of ideological dissent. Ernesto "Che" Guevara was in the process of exporting violence to other Latin American countries, under the auspices of Cuba. Ironically, they all claimed an ideology of solidarity with labor groups, students and *campesinos* (peasants or mountain people) but these same groups suffered most under attacks. Student strikes deprived the majority from attending classes, workers could not venture onto the streets to practice their trades and support their families, and the people of the countryside (or *campo*) often lost their lives at the hands of guerrillas and army alike.

Being a representative of the U.S., I was under constant threat of bombing and assassination and from the first it became my custom to go everywhere armed. In the beginning, this was simple adventurism but as time passed and I gained experience, this measure was adopted in earnest, and had the support of the local authorities. I was given a permit and even encouraged to defend myself and my home. Naturally, we had bomb threats in my office but a bomb incident was never actually carried out. On the advice of experts, I kept a fifty-five gallon drum hidden in a back corner, with sand in the bottom, for a "bomb deposit," to divert the blast upwards to avoid property damage and bodily injury. CARE offices, known for donating food to country schools, were not so lucky, and had quite a bit of damage done. I personally had to vary my routes to and from work, as well as my schedule, and live well out of town.

I practiced shooting frequently with friends from the local gun club "Junín" and from the

The Payaneses

secret police D.A.S. and regular police. D.A.S. used a 9mm Danish Madsen submachine gun with which we practiced. Over time I became fond of a pistol I had - a double-action Mauser HSc of World War II vintage, which was as small as a Walther PPK but more solid and heftier. I had the original grips changed to smooth grips made of a rosewood called *granadillo,* and carried the gun in a Hunter shoulder holster, the side of which I cut down to gain a better grasp on the gun. It had a spring device that was adjustable and I spent many hours doing fast-draw exercises at a man-sized target seven meters' distant and, in time, could put two shots in the middle in about two seconds.

One night about ten I was returning home with a girlfriend along deserted streets. We had picked up carryout dinner of a wonderful, thin, hammered and breaded pork chop from Restaurante La Parma and anticipated a quiet evening dinner. Suddenly, out of a recessed doorway, a young man with light, curly hair jumped out at us, brandishing a chromed pistol with mother-of-pearl grips. I was too startled to attempt reaching for my gun, and found myself resorting to diplomacy instead. He put the gun to my forehead and showed every intention of killing me on the spot. I pretended I did not take his threat seriously and instead feigned interest in his shiny gun.

"No, wait," I said, "that's a neat gun — let's see it." I was flabbergasted to hear myself say this. I was about to die. He pressed his attack, pushing the muzzle against my head. My girlfriend got excited and started to scream and I told her to shut up, that this guy really was not going to hurt us.

He snicked off the safety. I cringed in anticipation of having a bullet scramble my brains.

49

Gravity My Enemy

"Hombre, Dios mio!" I said. *"Cálmese!"* Take
it easy. "Just let me see your gun for a second —
I won't touch it!" I got a glimpse of his face in
the streetlight and he looked like a certifiable
nut. This was no rebel with a political agenda,
or even a robber. I was scared to the bottoms
of my feet. There was no reasoning with someone
like this, but my feigning interest in seeing his
gun was my only option. To my utter astonishment,
pride in his piece seemed to momentarily halt
his murderous intent, and he took it away from
my forehead for just a second to admire it from
a side angle. Amazingly, the attack on my life
degenerated into admiration for his shiny pistol.
I was nervously fingering the butt of my Mauser
under my jacket, ready for a fast draw. But, with
a motion to my girlfriend, we turned cautiously
away and slowly left. As we made the turn at the
next corner, I surreptitiously peered back and
saw our would-be assailant standing by himself
in the middle of the lonely street under the
streetlight, examining his gun.

As good as they may have been, I don't even
remember how tasty the breaded pork chops were
that night.

That was the first of two almost identical
situations that took place in Popayán over the
years. The second occurred when a huge guy jumped
out of a recessed, dark doorway, this time with
no gun that I could detect but he had a face
straight out of a horror movie. His teeth were
yellowed and widely separated, he was slobbering
from his mouth and one eye was askew in a totally
expressionless face. He was hunched forward with
rounded shoulders and his arms dangled like a
monster grave robber, and the end of which his
hands curled like meat hooks. He came at us
surprisingly fast but stopped short, much to our

The Payaneses

relief, groaning guttural nonsense. Somewhere, I had seen him before. I frantically searched my memory. Where had I seen him? Then, it came to me. Once, I had gone to the *riña de gallos,* cockfights, with friend and Colombo director, Jerry Whitmire, who referred to them as "chicken fights." I had seen this Frankenstein monster there. If allowed among the public, I presumed he posed no real threat, at least in daylight. As best we could, we casually kept our pace, though my heart almost jumped out of my chest, and we distanced ourselves, leaving this monstrosity standing there, confused.

The Ayerbe family is well known in Popayán. Its patriarch, El Coronel Ayerbe was an ex-military man who fathered several sons and only one daughter. Much of my hunting was done with the Ayerbe brothers, among them a very close friend named Santiago. He was a medical student at the local Universidad del Cauca (and later became a prominent pediatrician). A classmate of Santiago's named Alfredo pestered him continually about taking him out to shoot. Finally, Santiago agreed to take him to shoot a .22 pistol in a small gravel pit located about a long block behind the San José hospital, where both he and his classmate received much of their hands-on medical training. Much like me, Santiago was reluctant to take a novice out shooting because their lack of expertise always constituted a degree of danger.

When they reached the gravel pit on foot, Santiago upholstered his pistol and began showing Alfredo first how to handle it. He loaded the clip and slid it into the grip first, explaining as he did so, that he always had to keep the muzzle of the gun pointed away from people, "down range" as it is called. With the loaded clip pushed up into the grip, Santiago explained that the gun

Gravity My Enemy

was still not ready to fire until he pulled the slide back and let it fall, thus picking up one round and chambering it. Santiago did a careful demonstration, pointed the pistol in the general direction of the target area. He then showed where the safety was, snicked it off and, adopting a perfect sideways stance, extended his arm and fired all ten shots from the clip at some cans he had set up as targets. The cans bounced with the impacts. Alfredo was very impressed, anxious to try it himself, reaching for the gun. Santiago withheld it, as he wanted to make sure his classmate understood the basic rules of safety first.

"Okay," he said, "the gun is now unloaded, but even unloaded you always keep it pointed either straight up or down range while you're loading."

"*Sí, sí, hombre,*" he answered impatiently. "*Dame la pistola!*" "Give me the gun."

"Okay, take it easy, *cálmese.* First, you load the clip, but with only three rounds to start." Alfredo loaded the clip with the rounds Santiago gave him and then jammed the clip into the grip.

"Now, I'm going to get behind you and you pull back the slide and chamber the round, take off the safety and aim at those cans."

Santiago then turned away to get behind Alfredo. As he did so, Alfredo turned facing Santiago and shot him in the back of the neck. In total shock, Santiago fell down. Standing over him, Alfredo carefully aimed the gun at his head and pulled the trigger.

Click! There was no shot.

Santiago struggled to get up and finally got to his feet as his classmate pulled back the slide of the pistol in another attempt to chamber a round, again pulling the trigger. But again, it just clicked. By this time, Santiago feebly took

The Payaneses

off running toward the hospital with Alfredo close behind, feverishly working the action of the pistol and clicking it without a shot behind fired.

Apparently, Alfredo had inadvertently pushed the button that releases the clip so one can pull it out and reload the pistol, and the clip fell out just enough so that the slide could not pick up another round. Had it loaded a second shot, Santiago would have been dead.

Running in desperation, losing blood and going in and out of consciousness, almost falling each time, Santiago finally made it to the emergency entrance, with Alfredo close at his heels. By this time, Alfredo realized the wisest thing was to conceal the pistol and pose as a concerned friend, so he stuck it in his waistband and covered it with his shirt.

The emergency staff took immediate action to care for Santiago, whom they knew well. He was going in and out of consciousness from shock and blood loss, but he tried in vain to tell the emergency people to keep Alfredo away from him, as he wanted to kill him. The bullet had entered from the back of his neck and traveled forward into his jaw, making it almost impossible for his to speak. In desperation, he kept trying to warn the staff but they told him to stay calm and try not to talk, busying themselves with an IV and administering other medical help. Santiago knew he could not stay conscious much longer and if he didn't warn the hospital staff, they would think that Alfredo was there hovering over Santiago out of concern and friendship.

After some minutes, the staff ushered Alfredo out and only then was Santiago able to blurt out, "He shot me! He still has the gun! Don't leave me alone!"

Gravity My Enemy

By then Alfredo had guessed that the game was up and he not only fled the hospital but fled the city as well. In coming days, a police search in his hometown ended with his capture and he was tried and put in a mental facility.

Thus ended the horror story. Santiago, happily, fully recovered. He never learned why his friend had turned on him as he did other than mental illness, nor did he or anyone else ever see any sign that Alfredo was abnormal in any way, or felt any animosity toward Santiago, who was always well liked among all of his friends.

***

Some years later, we made a late-afternoon trip to Cali. We went in a taxi. As we approached the city near the bullring, people began shouting at us. The taxi driver finally caught what they were shouting and said to me, "Riots ahead." My heart jumped. Despite having faced many dangers, there was something about mob rule that truly scared me.

"We may have to turn back," I told him, but he, as many Latinos, saw this as an opportunity to show his mettle, and insisted on penetrating deeper into the area of disturbance. I was getting very concerned, as were my two American friends who were down on a visit for hunting.

We headed down a narrow street, having been diverted, and got halfway down the block when a sea of angry people boiled around the corner ahead and filled the street, running in our direction and yelling. The cab driver yanked the steering wheel abruptly to the left and slammed the front wheels into the left curb, bumping up onto the sidewalk. He threw the car into reverse in the same motion, and slammed the car into the

The Payaneses

opposite curb, hitting a storefront with his back bumper, and screeched into a sharp turn to the left as we bounced back onto the street. The mob was only ten feet from us. He clipped the back bumper of a parked car on the opposite side as he got into the center of the street, accelerating for all he was worth. Two rioters had gotten onto the trunk of the car and were angrily hammering the back window of the car with their fists. The window buckled under the pounding but stayed in one piece. My head craned around in terror, I saw they were losing their grip on the slippery trunk. The cab driver jerked around the corner and both rioters slid off onto the street. We raced several blocks to a quieter area. When we saw the sign of a police substation, I told him to stop, that we could seek refuge here.

Happily, he got out and popped the trunk and my friends opened up the folded wheelchair and brought it to the side. I hopped in quickly; we paid the taxi driver, admonished him to be very careful where he went, wished him luck, and ducked inside the police station. The police inside all held batons, and asked us what we wanted.

"*Refugio!*" I said. The rioting was all around us and we obviously had to get inside somewhere to avoid a lynching.

"*Es peor!*" one said, "This is worse! This is where they come!" he said. It made perfect sense. The mob wanted to target the establishment, meaning not only gringos but cops. But a crescendo of noise outside told us we were too late to change and we buried ourselves inside behind a couple of handguns. To our great relief, the noise passed after a time and seemed to move on. We ventured out to the main doorway cautiously and peered out. It was like a war zone. Cars were burning and smoldering, trees were down across the road.

Gravity My Enemy

At the end of the block, a pile of tires was furiously burning, belching black, acrid smoke.

After about two hours holed up with the police, a gray and white police truck pulled up to the front of the building and the police asked us if we needed a ride somewhere.

"How is it out there?" I asked.

The uniformed police from the truck said, "It's bad, but we know a safe route into the center of town — I think," he smiled. "It's likely to get worse here as the night passes," he warned. "They're targeting police!"

We took the hint, and gathered our belongings quickly and jumped into the police vehicle. It was a panel truck, and we could only see out the front as we sat hunched over in back. The driver knew his way around, turning constantly as we wove our way through the extensive Cali neighborhoods. People were all out in the streets, excited and curious about the riots. Many made nasty remarks to the police and once, a heavy projectile thumped into the side of the truck. Incredibly, we reached Parque Caicedo in the very center of town. Tall royal palms were toppled and crisscrossed the streets. Windows were broken everywhere. Whatever the reason behind the riots, it seemed everyone was the target. Stores, vehicles, houses, roadside vending kiosks were all severely damaged, many burning.

The police dumped us out, urging us to hurry. We expressed our gratitude and headed for the hotel just off the corner, and registered. We were probably the only clientele they had. The center of town was totally deserted. George made a quick foray out to find something to eat and came back a half-hour later with some large, oblong cans of sardines in tomato sauce and several sticks of French bread. In a bag, he carried several

The Payaneses

bottles of Pilsen beer. We were in business, at least for the duration.

During the night we heard gunshots periodically, sirens and the ebb and flow of shouting in the distance. As we gazed out the hotel window, fires could be seen in several areas.

The next day, after intermittent sleep, we went out into the street. All was quiet. I was immediately challenged by soldiers. I confidently flashed my passport and said, *"Oficial."* I was "official" something or other and they let me pass. The streets in all directions showed incredible destruction. Down near the travel agencies and airlines offices, the crowd had captured a Coke truck. It was probably symbolic of Yanqui Imperialism and they had overturned it and used the bottled Cokes as missiles for smashing every plate glass window in sight. Not a store or office was spared. Several empty bottles of Coke were mute testimony to the fact that the rioters had drunk a lot of Coke as well. So much for symbolic imperialism.

***

Colombians are avid chess players. The good ones are practically unbeatable. A close friend named Alfonso Hernández was one of these, and he took it upon himself to train me into a respectable chess player. Alfonso was the University Chess Champion of Colombia. He was a little fellow, extremely affable and intelligent. Professionally, he taught ecology in the Universidad del Valle in Cali, but was doing a stint with the Universidad del Cauca in Popayán, so we got to see a lot of each other. Daily, in fact. He stopped by my office and got me into the irresponsible habit of playing a game each afternoon. This series taught me a lot. Alfonso was not only good — he was a fanatic. When a major confrontation took place between two Russian chess masters in Montevideo, Uruguay, Alfonso bought a plane ticket from his impoverished salary and flew there to see it personally. Uruguay is halfway around the world from Colombia, despite both being part of Latin America.

He brought in hefty volumes of famous chess games. Mildly interested, I glanced through them and was dismayed to see only blocks of letters and numbers, depicting the moves. He would excitedly come into my office, book and chessboard under his arm, and set up. Then, with a great flourish, he would open the book and start making moves as he read from it, jumping on the edge of his chair in excitement.

"The genius of that move!" he would exclaim.

"I don't see it," I said, dully.

"Just look! He moved his queen's bishop here," he then would dramatically place the piece on a square. "Don't you see? Just look at it! Take your time."

I would look at the array for perhaps five minutes, and impatiently wave it off.

"Alfonso, please!"

"Don't you see? He precludes his opponent from moving his pawn over here (pointing to the square) and thus sets it up so he can advance his knight . . ." and so on. He was six moves ahead. I had trouble playing from a crisis one move ahead.

In time, he made a fair player of me. I was no champion but managed to beat over half my opponents. This developed into a routine chess game every Friday afternoon with the local police commandant, el Coronel Cárdenas. In Colombia, people anxiously anticipate the weekend by calling Friday, *Viernes Cultural,* or "Cultural Friday" for all the drinking

The Payaneses

and whore mongering that took place starting on Fridays. It was an accepted part of life.

In our case, however, it really was cultural. We both knocked off work early, I headed to his dispatch and two or three police who knew me carried me up to the second floor, where the colonel's office was located. We would set up the chessboard and coffee was served, and we locked horns in a serious contest. I never won a game. In fact, I couldn't even get near El Coronel, as he was the Colombian Military Chess Champion. He was also a dramatic, flamboyant player, moving his pieces with great theatrics and hand movements. The colonel was a picture in uniform, the essence of spit and polish. His black hair was slicked back and shiny. His shoes were black mirrors and his brass sparkled.

One day, I decided to introduce my two friends to each other — the University champion and the Military champion — and watch the sparks fly. Alfonso was well dressed and formal, as Colombians tend to be, with a coat and tie, but there was something a little humbler about him. He looked for the entire world like Dustin Hoffman. They were both very gracious to each other. Colonel Cárdenas raised his eyebrows when I told him about Alfonso having been university chess champion.

"Indeed?" he said. "Perhaps you'd enjoy a game," *una partidita* he called it, "a tiny, little game." Alfonso happily accepted.

They sat facing each other as I watched, amused. After several moves, I could sense that two titans were grappling, there was tension and the air was thick. I could also sense that Alfonso was mildly irritated with the colonel's flamboyance and theatrics, but he remained quiet and withdrawn, moving his pieces with a degree

Gravity My Enemy

of humility in sharp contrast to the colonel's style. Halfway through the game, Colonel Cárdenas casually picked up an El Tiempo newspaper from the chair alongside him and opened it, perusing the pages. This was an affront. I sensed Alfonso stiffen, but he remained intent on the game before him. The colonel interrupted his reading only to glance at the board and finally make another move, with a quick, dramatic movement of his hand, and went back to the newspaper.

Alfonso lost soundly.

I mentioned to the colonel that we had gotten caught up in the Cali riots the previous week.

"*Fue muy malo, eso,*" he said. "What these groups are looking for is a martyr."

"So," I remarked, "the authorities must be very careful how they handle these things."

"*Tienen que tener mucho cuidado,*" he agreed, "because one dead student provides their martyr. It's a big problem, with nation-wide ramifications." Then, he looked at me very meaningfully and said, "However, thirty dead is no problem." We immediately understood. Thirty was more an issue of serious intimidation and no longer simple martyrdom.

The conversation quickly shifted. They agreed on another game. *Un desquite,* the colonel called it, a second-chance, get-even game. The colonel set up the pieces.

They were well into the mid-game when I noticed the colonel had lost interest in the newspaper, and was leaning forward intently examining the board. He began taking a little longer with each move, and his once-exuberant moves took on a slight hesitancy. They were now into the end game, and about even in pieces, but from my limited knowledge, I felt that Alfonso had a slight edge in position. It was a real battle of the minds.

The Payaneses

Finally, Alfonso meekly slid one piece over and, in so doing, placed the colonel in a double check. He looked at the array for a long moment, and finally let out a heavy breath, making a hand gesture to say, "What can I do?" He gazed at the board for a few more moments and then reached his hand across to Alfonso in a handshake of concession.

"*Felicitaciones.*" Congratulations, he said. "You play a very skillful game," he admitted. "You're a dangerous chess player!"

Alfonso smiled. "And so are you! I've rarely had such an adversary."

As we left the police headquarters, Alfonso remarked to me, "A very fine fellow. In that second game, I swore he would not read that newspaper!

The law school of the Universidad del Cauca in Popayán was a hotbed for revolutionary ideologies. There were issues that cropped up with surprising frequency, both domestic and foreign. At the drop of a hat, the law school students cancelled classes and organized some sort of protest. This usually started with placing outdoor speakers in the law school balconies facing out toward the stone patio adjoining the Santo Domingo church. This gave every discontent an ample opportunity to provide a public harangue to whoever wished to stop in the corner of the street outside and listen. Common participants were the students from the public high schools, known as *colegios de bachillerato,* which were so crowded and ill equipped that they were delighted to call a strike for any reason, and head for the law school to listen to inflammatory rhetoric exported from Cuba and Peking.

Following the lengthy speeches, when the gang outside was deemed to be sufficiently large, a mob would form and they would head like a

Gravity My Enemy

tide of lemmings down the street, usually toward the park a block away. The park was bordered by the *Alcaldía* or mayor's office which included the elegant municipal council chambers decorated with old paintings of national leaders, the Colombian flag, wood paneling and the long, hand-carved and polished council table with ornate, carved, high-backed chairs. On the one side of the municipal building was the Governor's palace, or *Gobernación,* which housed the departmental offices as well as the governor's office. To the other side, as tradition had it, was the *Curia,* the seat of ecclesiastical government, a large, white church with old, domed roofs.

Thus, the park was a good and obvious first target for student revolt. They arrived inspired and armed with rocks and Molotov cocktails.

On this particular day, there were rumors of impending riots but I had errands to run and decided to get on with my day. My errands included a trip to the mayor's office for some paperwork, but no sooner did I get inside the building than people came running down the streets announcing a student uprising. The doormen clanked the wrought iron gates shut, and I was stuck inside. I sent a message up to the second floor to the mayor to see if he was in, and he in response sent down an invitation to go up and join him. Spanish colonial buildings had no elevators, so I asked help from the doormen. Throughout Colombia, I found people always eager to hoist my wheelchair up steep staircases, often for many floors. This was usually done between three of four men, so the task seemed effortless and went swiftly. I was soon in the mayor's office.

César Negret was a tall, rather handsome fellow in a rustic way, a hank of dark hair hung in his face like Li'l Abner. His handshake was

The Payaneses

firm and genuine. Negret was an ex-colonel from
the army, and very pro-United States.

Schooling in the U.S. Jungle Warfare School
in Panama explained his fitness and confidence.
"Edmundo, qué gusto! Sigue," he beckoned.

Popayán is known for its old churches and colonial
architecture. La Ermita (above) is the oldest. Note
roofs overhanging sidewalks, allowing people to walk
under shelter in the rain.

Gravity My Enemy

Santo Domingo church (top) at the entrance of the
Universidad del Cauca. The Valencia house (bottom).
Foreground shows colonial Spanish arched bridges made
of brick, concrete and ox blood.

The Payaneses

I wheeled in and looked around the elegant surroundings, always enjoying the ornate luster of Old Spanish governmental trappings. We both acknowledged I was trapped — I was with him for the duration, and he sent downstairs to the Lonchería Belalcázar restaurant for grilled ham and cheese sandwiches, and gestured me to a ringside seat, as it were, on the park side front balcony. I was a little hesitant, but with a warm smile he insisted we sit there to watch developments. I did notice we had to sit inside somewhat, so we could not be readily seen from the street. Like popcorn at a movie, the sandwiches arrived and he and I sat back to watch just as a seething mob of students entered the park, chanting in unison the slogans common to Communist demonstrations of the time: "Ho-Ho Ho-Chi Minh!" Etcetera. In profile, César Negret had a receding jaw to go with an obvious overbite, and it gave him a characteristic charm as he laughed.

"Notice the students!" he shouted above the din. I looked carefully, but could not determine what he was referring to, and said so.

"See? Look closely!"

I still shook my head in puzzlement.

"They're not all students! Look at those over there!" He pointed and, sure enough, there was a large contingent of rabble that had no resemblance to students at all, but more to overgrown street urchins and common thieves.

Just then, three army trucks with canvas covers pulled up and parked on the opposite side of the park and camouflage-clad soldiers jumped off the back, some carrying transparent riot shields and others with German G-3 assault rifles with bayonets fixed. All had clear Plexiglas face shields. Amid shouted orders from several sergeants, they formed up into a phalanx and with

Gravity My Enemy

a loud order, "Ar-rr-re!" they stomped heavily and began advancing toward the rioters.

The mayor and I sat riveted. I felt very nervous at the impending confrontation but he exuded a show of calm, even amusement.

Several rioters ventured out from the group to hurl rocks into the group of soldiers, and quickly retreated back into the masses. One rock caught a soldier in the foot and he interrupted his cadence to hop painfully off to one side. Another shouted order from a sergeant brought their weapons to a horizontal position at waist level, and they continued their advance toward the mob.

When there was only about thirty feet separating them, one rioter lobbed a Molotov cocktail amid the soldiers. It broke and spread a knee-high flame with a lot of black smoke. At the same time, I noticed three soldiers setting up a larger machinegun in the park, mounted on a tripod, and were opening a metal container of ammunition on a belt to feed into the breech.

The flames from the firebomb were somewhat ineffective, as it evidently was not made of pure gasoline for some reason, but it scattered the troops in the immediate area of impact momentarily.

Suddenly, the block of soldiers fired a volley in the air over the heads of the mob and the thunderous roar jolted us. The students visibly recoiled as well, some running in the opposite direction. But others stayed their ground in defiance. Two of them hurled fire bombs into the troop formation, which had their shields up against a hail of rocks. Both burst into flames, scattering several soldiers. One of them had his pants in flames and was rolling on the street while others tried to beat out the fire. The next volley went into the mob itself, and pandemonium broke loose.

The Payaneses

People were running in all directions. We noticed several lying on the street. One was writhing from his wounds and two others were still, looking like discarded laundry. I was amazed that there were not more, as the row of rifles had to be at least twenty. Another roar from a third volley sent the rest of the people in the street bolting like sheep. Within minutes, only shouting could be heard but it appeared that the organizational aspect of the student revolt had disintegrated, and the rioters were nowhere in sight. The soldiers were regrouping into their original formation, while a small knot of them helped their ailing comrade back to one of the trucks.

We learned later that there had been sporadic "unrest," as the press calls it, in different parts of the city, but news reached the mayor that the area was secure and I soon felt safe enough to return to my office.

When I arrived, several soldiers were occupying the block to protect the Colombo against any further insurrection, but we nervously went back to our duties and the remainder of the day was calm.

The next day I ordered a big steel door installed in the entrance, against the advent of future riots. In the years to come, I was gratified for having made the adaptation, as we several times had to withstand the onslaught of angry mobs. Never once did they penetrate, but there were many tense moments. In all my years with dangers, to my mind, nothing is quite as worrisome as an angry mob whose collective daring and conviction is more than the sum of its individual parts.

Popayán for the most part was a quiet city and very picturesque with its white buildings and aging tile roofs, and the traditional three crosses high atop an adjacent hill, overlooking the city.

Gravity My Enemy

One of the most memorable characters in Popayán's menagerie, indeed in my entire life, was Roberto "El Loco" Lehmann. On the hoof,

Callas Park (top) & Hotel Monasterio

The Payaneses

he looked like a bandit straight out of a Pancho
Villa movie set. He was swarthy, had a huge, black
moustache, hairy black eyebrows and was one of
those few men who had a five o'clock shadow at
eleven in the morning. Though well liked among all
of us with a great sense of humor and story-telling
ability, he was a true scoundrel, a man not to be
trifled with. His worst enemy was his wife, Sonia,
a diminutive, feisty shrew of a woman with a shrill
voice who stood up to her husband fearlessly and
was really the only person in El Loco's life that
he truly feared. Like most of us, El Loco was a
faithful friend of President Guillermo León Valencia
and the Conservative party. Sonia was a staunch
Liberal and had no trepidation about getting in
his face in defiance. Despite this, he was a
noted woman's man, and cheated on her constantly.
His frequent hunting trips lent themselves to
this infidelity and also, coincidentally, gave him
an opportunity to collect different wild animals
such as deer and birds, which were brought in by
acquaintances he met in the field. His house at
times was a veritable zoo. During one period he
had a girlfriend, a very attractive young street
girl we all referred to as the *cusumbu*, the term
used for the raccoon-like Coati Mundi so common
in the tropics. Roberto was director of the local
branch of an insurance company. When he was in
town, he made token stops to the office to make
sure all his girls (all attractive, of course) had
their nose to the grindstone. One morning while
in his office, his personal phone rang. He picked
it up. It was his wife, Sonia, at the other end,
livid and shouting at him.

"Roberto, I'm coming down there and I'm
gonna kill you!" she shrieked. Shaken but trying
to show calm in the presence of his office staff,
he asked what the problem was.

Gravity My Enemy

"You come and get this goddamned *cusumbu* out of this house! She's tearing the place apart!"

El Loco's heart went to his throat. His girlfriend had often threatened a confrontation with his wife, but he felt reasonably assured it was all bluff. Now it had finally happened and he was sure the end result was going to be someone getting hurt — physically. With his tail figuratively between his legs, he dashed home, trying to muster enough courage and bravado for the occasion.

When he arrived, he discovered the melee was being caused by a real *cusumbu,* an animal brought in by a campesino he knew from his hunting trips. It had escaped from its makeshift cage and trashed his house. His wife was genuinely puzzled when he simply laughed and showed such relief at the devastation.

During our early trips to the Santander area of the Valle del Cauca for doves and ducks, the highway department, *Obras Públicas,* (known as OO.PP.) was working on completing the Pan American Highway between Cali and Popayán, a stretch of about eighty miles. The project was taking an inordinate amount of time and we were all thoroughly disgusted. Each trip coated us with a fine, white dust after riding behind choking clouds raised by vehicles preceding us. Newspapers carried complaints daily about the time and money the highway was consuming. If we wanted to go to Cali for whatever reason, we were forced to get a hotel upon arrival and take a shower and change clothes after the four-hour trip, or go by narrow-gauge railroad called the Autoferro, a small, two-car train that wobbled side to side so much that we arrived at our destination almost sick to our stomachs. Bullet holes in the train's windows were testimony to the dangers of going this route. We

The Payaneses

all wanted the Pan American highway finished, and soon, but the work dragged on for years.

When we went on our weekend hunting trips, Roberto Ayerbe often drove his Willys pick-up. "El Loco" detested the confinement up front in the cab, preferring to stand up behind us outside. This also gave him ample opportunity to shout obscenities and threats at the highway workers that he saw goldbricking along the way. Many were often insolently lying down taking a nap, using a pile of dirt as a backrest. El Loco lived up to his name on those occasions by pulling out a .22 caliber Star pistol he had and firing shots around them, screaming, "Get up, you lazy bastards, and finish this damned highway, or I'm gonna kill every one of you!" He was fortunately an excellent shot, or we would have felt he was shooting much too close to their feet, but of course, they didn't know that and literally ran for the hills in fear for their lives. By the time we had made several trips, we noticed that the workers were strangely occupied, casting wary glances when cars passed. We don't know if it had much effect, but we like to think to this day that El Loco had some influence in finishing the Pan American Highway sooner than they otherwise would have.

The choking dust on the roads was always a problem. Once, while traveling south of Popayán to hunt deer in a hot, flat area called Patía, El Loco was driving around miles and miles of tedious switchbacks in the mountains. Unfortunately, we got stuck behind a *chiva,* which actually means "goat," the word used for the open-sided buses used to haul campesinos with their chickens and pigs, as well as firewood. The heat did not allow closed windows. The *chiva* was kicking up billowing plumes of fine dust and our hair and eyebrows became coated. Glancing to the side, I noticed that Roberto's bandit moustache was almost white. The road was too narrow to pass till the road widened. At these points, it is customary to allow a vehicle to pass if needed, but the driver of this *chiva* was obstinate despite frantic horn honking by El Loco, and would not let us pass. We were obligated to plod tediously behind the bus, swallowing choking dust. After a couple of missed opportunities to pass, I could see that El Loco (wild man) was about to give more meaning to his name. In a fit of anger, he said for someone in back to hand him his Remington 1100 shotgun and a shell. Without interrupting his determined driving, he pulled the gun out of its case and dropped the shell in the open breech, hit the button and the action slammed shut. El Loco was a southpaw, so it made it relatively easy for him to hold the shotgun one-handed out the driver's side of the window and skillfully blast the rearview mirror off the side of the *chiva,* shattering it to pieces three feet from the driver. The bus came to a halt and the driver got out at the same time El Loco did, shotgun in hand. The driver, when he saw this wild man approaching angrily with a shotgun in his hand, felt he was a dead man and got to his knees pleading. El Loco ran up to him and put the muzzle of the shotgun between the driver's chattering teeth and said, "Don't you ever block my way again." We held our collective breath but he hopped back in the car and calmly passed the bus.

Someone told me that when Roberto was younger he rode his horse to the municipal swimming pool near the statue of Popayán's founder, Sebastian de Belalcázar. For some reason, the bathhouse had three stories. El Loco was probably just beginning to acquire his nickname when he rode the horse up the staircase to the third floor. After arriving,

The Payaneses

amid the laughs and amazement of people present, he could not persuade the horse to descend the stairs. He was stuck. Finally, they had to bring the local vet, Virgilio Pinzón, to sedate the unfortunate horse. Nearby construction workers knocked out part of a wall and they had to lower the horse down on the outside with ropes.

Far to the south of Popayán lies a jungle area surrounding the Amazon tributary, the Putumayo River, a wild area that extends for hundreds of miles. It was the closest area where jaguars could be found. Called El Tigre, it was the one game animal Roberto wanted above all others. With several friends, he organized a hunt to the Putumayo area beyond the town of Mocoa, and for this he was determined not to fail. When he got to the area, he purchased a small goat to use as bait. He had a local Indian take him off some miles where jaguar tracks had been seen, and left instructions he was not to be bothered for several days. The Indian left. Tethering the goat, El Loco climbed into an overhanging tree with his gun, a small wooden box of food and some jugs of water. He wore a head net against mosquitoes, and resigned himself to sit it out until he got his tigre. El Loco was probably the most determined hunter I ever knew. Days later, on instructions, we all went back to his tree to pick him up, wondering if he was even alive. We were relieved to see him climb down the tree, his joints creaking and looking like an angry pirate, with a three-day growth of black beard. He was disappointed that he neither saw nor heard a jaguar in his time there, his eyes were red bloodshot, but he seemed surprisingly content.

"*No ví ningún tigre,*" I saw no jaguar, he said, "but it was wonderful being in the jungle!"

Gravity My Enemy

We had shot a few jungle turkeys we called *pavas* and a jaguar in his time there, his but saw no large animals, as I learned was often the case in the rain forest.

"El Loco" (left) & "Eagle Eye" with doves

The Payaneses

After a week of heat and mosquitoes, we were all ready to head back on our three-day journey to a much cooler Popayán.

On the way, we had to go through the lofty, cold city of Pasto, which was home to Colombia's only insane asylum, called *El Manicomio,* in the days when the criminally insane were simply locked up. Once through Pasto and heading north toward Patía, someone had the wild idea of representing "el Loco" Lehmann as a literal *loco.* His bloodshot eyes, swarthy pirate appearance had the look of someone rather unstable. When we stopped to eat at a little roadside restaurant, one of the guys got a length of chain out of the back of one of the trucks, and wrapped it around El Loco's wrists and his ankles. As he shuffled in, all of us trying to hold back our laughter, we all sat down at a large table.

"Don't mind him," one said to the waitress, "but be sure to keep your distance." He went on to tell her that we were from the D.A.S., the plain-clothed secret security police of Colombia. He said that El Loco was an escaped serial killer and we were bringing him back to El Manicomio (insane asylum) in Pasto.

The small restaurant was filled with people and it didn't take but a minute for the word to get around. We were light-hearted, though tired from the trip, but were enjoying our first real meal in civilization in over a week. Finally satiated, we sat back and were having something to drink when, all of a sudden, El Loco got up, still in chains, and jumped up on the table and let out a blood-curdling yell. The stampede that ensued cleared out the restaurant in less than thirty seconds. He let out another yell as we could still hear hurried footfalls outside.

Gravity My Enemy

We all burst out laughing. The restaurant was empty. Minutes passed. It was time to clap our hands, as is customary in Colombia to call the waitress, but no one appeared. One member of our group got up and looked back in the kitchen but came back with a gesture indicating that no one was to be found. They looked everywhere but could find no one to whom we could pay the check. After some time, we got in our cars and left, feeling a combination of shame and silly laughter over what El Loco had done.

Being a bit nuts ourselves, I guess, we went through the same Crazy Man routine twice more, with the same results. "Hell, we could travel across the country for free with this guy!" one remarked. Looking back, we were awfully lucky that he didn't get shot for his acting ability.

Roberto had several brothers, each a bit nuts in his own right. His brother Federico was shot and killed some years later by a jealous husband. Another brother, Fabricio, a noted angler, was accused of tossing his wife off a bridge. Another, the oldest, Carlos, was a self-styled expert in almost everything connected with hunting and shooting. One day, he obtained a new gun from Europe somewhere, a 9.3x62mm, similar ballistically to an old caliber called the .35 Whelen. He was very excited and wanted badly to try it out. Carlos was a very tiresome, fastidious fellow. He invited several of us to witness the marvels of this new rifle. Unfortunately for him, he invited his brother, Roberto, El Loco.

We all headed out to the nearby countryside in two cars. Carlos brought along a small table and chair to shoot, as well as the rifle, the ammunition and a sandbag to rest it on for a firm shot. It may run in the family, but he also this time brought along a live goat for a target and

The Payaneses

tethered it off about two hundred yards distant. Then, he set up the table and chair, carefully aligning them just so for the proper angle. When the table wobbled slightly, he jammed small stones under the legs until he was satisfied it was firm. Then he sat in the chair, rocking back and forth, placed pebbles under a leg to stabilize it, and got up to fetch the rifle with its cigar-sized ammo. This he placed meticulously on the table, after removing it from its case and lovingly wiping it off with an oily rag. He lay the rifle on its side on the table with the bolt open, and set the box of ammo alongside. He then, looking downfield at the unsuspecting goat, put on his shooting glasses and adjusted them carefully. Somehow, all the preparations and fastidiousness reminded me of Ed Norton in The Honeymooners.

"My earplugs," he said. He then got up to get his earplugs out of the car. We let out a collective sigh of impatience. We were all standing around poking jokes and ridiculing this display of fussiness when, suddenly, we heard a loud bang!

Carlos jumped out of the car and hit his head on the doorjamb in his haste to see the cause.

Standing next to the table with his brother's new rifle in his hands, a thin wisp of smoke exiting the muzzle of the rifle and a big smirk on his face was El Loco. The goat was down without a movement.

Carlos, totally disgusted, silently packed up all his stuff without saying a word. I don't know who ended up with the goat.

El Loco was not exempt from having gags pulled on him, either. His first love was a vintage '55 Chevy, which he cared for daily. We put a gag whistle in the exhaust pipe once, which caused

Gravity My Enemy

him days of anxiety over his car's strange noise until one of us mercifully popped it out.

One day I went by his office and saw him inside sitting at his desk. He looked like hell. His beard was overgrown, much like the Putumayo trip, his eyes bloodshot and he was bedraggled. Expecting to hear an interesting story about a hunting trip, I went in and said,

"*A Dónde en diablos fuiste?*" Where in hell did you go this time?

He motioned me over to his desk, rather conspiratorially, and put his finger to his lips in a gesture of hush-hush.

"*Estuve de cacería,*" he said. I've been hunting. I thought I noticed a strange emphasis on the word "hunting."

"That's obvious," I replied. "Hunting what?"

"I don't want you to breathe a word of this!" he said.

"Well, what?" I asked.

"*Lo más peligroso **en el mundo**,*" The most dangerous game in the world! he said under his breath.

"My goodness! Here in Colombia?" Could it be jaguar or what? I thought, hardly 'the most dangerous in the world.'

"Now I repeat: You keep quiet!"

Intrigued, I continued listening. "Man."

"Man?"

"Yes, man. The most dangerous game in the world."

Somewhere, I had read a short story like this called, I believe, 'The Most Dangerous Game.' It was about some nut who had hunted everything imaginable. He devised the hunt of all hunts by releasing a clever human captive and hunting him down.

"You really are 'loco'," I said.

The Payaneses

It turns out that they had just formed a new civil defense unit in town, in response to a crime wave that was out of control. Roberto was elected chairman. They were issued walkie-talkies, a police scanner and other odds and ends like badges, handcuffs and Billie clubs. We had a new Barney Fife club. They ran scruffy hippies out of town and chased down thieves. In the evenings, they sat around listening to their police scanner to intercept phone calls from citizens who heard their houses being broken into, and beat the police to the address, search the bushes around the house to apprehend the criminals. Occasionally, there was armed resistance and this resulted in the hunt of "the most dangerous game" to which he referred. The Colombian people had been victimized for years, and now the pendulum had swung the other way.

Guillermo León Valencia had been Colombia's president during the early part of the National Front, a four-term coalition government he co-authored to put an end to the worst epoch of violence in the country's history. When I first met him, he was on a visit to Popayán. Someone close to him ushered me into the Hotel Monasterio where he was staying during the visit. In my wheelchair, I was brusquely pushed through a multitude of people, chafing shins and ankles with the footrests of my wheelchair on the way, and finally up to his table in a rush. Whoever was "driving me" bumped into the table so hard it spilled drinks. So, his first impression of me was an embarrassment. My first impression of him was that of an incredibly angry, scary old man. (He was highly amused years later when, as friends, I told him this. He explained to me that the press had gotten into his face a lot in those

Gravity My Enemy

days and, in fact, a famous picture in a major newspaper showed him furiously reaching for the photographer's camera, which he smashed to pieces on the pavement. He confessed to me then that the happiest day of his life was the day he got out of the presidency. Yet, when he died years later, and to this day, he was heralded as The President of Peace, a eulogy well-deserved, and evidence of the great love his people had for him.)

After the sunset of his active political career, he settled down in his hometown of Popayán, a city that produced no less than fifteen presidents. It was during this time that we became fast friends. The first time we met socially he actually made a visit to my house. A dear friend, Aurelio Velasco (father of present-day air force general, commander of the Colombian Air Force and close friend Héctor Fabio Velasco) brought him over to the house because the president wanted to watch me reload ammunition, a pursuit of mine for which I became known among friends, despite its illegality. A knock came at the door and my wife answered. In seconds, she came running in to me with a look of great excitement and anguish, *"Es El Presidente!!!"* she said, snapping her fingers in nervousness, as Colombians do when greatly embarrassed.

"El Presidente who?" I asked calmly.

"EL Presidente!! Apure!!" Hurry up! This was THE President.

I invited him in and he spent a good hour with me watching reload ammunition, taking careful measurements, lubricating empty shell casings and seating bullets. He seemed genuinely interested and asked many questions. As he was finally leaving, I asked him what he thought about reloading.

"Fascinante. Si quiere joderse." Fascinating — if you want to go nuts. This was my first

The Payaneses

sampling of his sense of humor. I guess he found reloading interesting but too tedious for his tastes.

In the months ahead, I visited him in the evenings at his house several nights each week, where he always enjoyed a small political and social group of friends. We engaged in story-telling for the most part, some politics and history, but mostly about hunting, his favorite topic. He had been "banished" politically for some time, as happens in Latin America when they want to remove a key person's influence from the local political scene. This was after his presidential term, to serve as Colombian ambassador to Spain. It was during this time of El Generalíssimo Franco, with whom he frequently went on boar hunts. President Valencia, in his stories, often referred to Franco as "*ese viejo pendejo*" — "that old asshole." Guillermo León was the son of a famous Colombian poet named Guillermo Valencia. Judging from old photographs, they looked very much alike. With this upbringing and cultural background, the president's verbal expression was extremely eloquent; his choice of words skillful, and it was a joy to listen to his tales told in pure classical Spanish. Thus it was not only his fame and notoriety that attracted the small gatherings each evening but the allure of his words. Above all, he was incredibly humorous. His choice of words itself was enough to keep us all in stitches. When we occasionally went on dove shoots together, I quickly learned that it was advisable to pick a spot distant from the president, since his quips kept us laughing so hard we could not concentrate on our shooting.

Around his table at night it was customary to eat black bread and honey right from the honeycomb, his favorite, and tell hunting stories and jokes. I got to know him well enough to tell

Gravity My Enemy

him translations of dirty jokes I had heard in English, and he became quite a fan.

His primary addiction, however, was hunting hounds. I spent many nights translating stories to him out of outdoor magazines like Outdoor Life and Field and Stream, articles of hunting with hounds and, in fact, often spent long periods discussing the content of ads for blue tick and black-and-tan hounds from the Ozarks. We even placed some orders and I later had to go to the airport to pick up his howling, slobbering acquisitions.

Some few years prior to this period, I had occasion to become acquainted with a renegade defrocked priest named Padre Camilo Torres. This Communist advocated the forming of a coalition between labor groups, students and peasants much as did Ernesto "Che" Guevara, to finally overthrow the government and remove the yoke of "Yanqui Imperialism." Despite his anti-American views, we had a cordial, intellectual exchange for some time and expressed a mutual respect for one another.

Headline news one day announced that Padre Camilo Torres had been gun running and was hunted down and killed by the Colombian army.

One evening years later while eating honeycomb and black bread with strong coffee, I asked the president about the incident, which occurred during his presidency. He said, in essence, that *el padre* was a thorn in their side for a long time but the government was never in a position to curtail visits to universities and labor groups because of his constitutional right to free speech. Guillermo León Valencia was, more than anything else, a staunch supporter of the constitution, even if it protected the enemies of his country. The Colombian constitution was virtually copied from the Constitution of the

The Payaneses

United States, and those leaders engaged in the fight for freedom from Spain consulted the likes of Thomas Jefferson and Benjamin Franklin.

"Then army intelligence reached me that El Padre Camilo Torres was engaged in receiving and distributing arms sent from Cuba," he told me soberly.

"Now, that was different from considerations of free speech! I had the reports verified. When there was no doubt of his activities, I ordered him to be killed." And so he was.

I thought it an interesting and a unique experience to have met and known both the rebel insurrectionist and the president who ended his career.

Above all, it was an honor to have a deep trust relationship with a man who is now prominent in Colombian and Latin American history books.

Valencia

I used to enjoy going out to the airport "Machángara" in the early morning to hunt shorebirds, quail and ducks. The strip was paved and long enough to accommodate small business jets, so I had the unique circumstance of being able to hunt a large tract of grassland in the wheelchair. I had memorized the location of several coveys of bobwhite quail and shot only one or two from each, as though they were my personal property. I had a pointer bitch called Reina that was extremely good, though very high strung and tended to cast out beyond shotgun range. Watching her work the coveys was a joy rarely experienced by hunters. Two small ponds had blue wing teal during the season of migration, and I had the

Gravity My Enemy

pleasure of taking one home on occasion. Over the years, I got three that had been banded. I sent in the numbers and requested information. All had come from Saskatchewan, a pretty long trip. Shorebird hunting was a thing of the past in the United States, but no Colombian regulations prohibited hunting them, so in the early fall when we heard the unmistakable nighttime cry of the greater yellowlegs, called *chorlos,* we quickly phoned friends and went out for these tasty birds. Wilson's snipe also migrated down and several friends shot them out of sloughs and bottomlands.

Early mornings at the airport were wonderful. There was almost no air traffic. Only three scheduled planes landed per week, so I felt reasonably safe as I hunted along the runway. The view of Popayán was lovely, with the white cupolas and spires, and the mountains in the background. When there was no cloud cover very early in the morning, I could see the Puracé volcano towering over the city in the distance, small fumaroles of smoke

Reina and quail

rising from its crater. To the right lay another cone-shaped volcano called Sotará, which had never been active in recorded history. In recent years, however, cattle had moved down from its slopes,

The Payaneses

supposedly because it was heating up, but when Japanese seismologists came to measure and study it, their equipment was stolen from the hotel and the project ended. To this day, I have often wondered what thieves would do with seismology equipment but, as is commonly said in Colombia, "They'll even steal a hole."

5 Volcano Puracé

Alberto was a stocky fellow built with a low center of gravity, an indication of original Chibcha Indian stock with the barrel chest, large heart and lungs, and short extremities that comes from millennia of human development in the lofty oxygen-starved Andes.

He had long, black hair, which he slicked straight back Rudolph Valentino style. His affable smile was broad, cheek-to-cheek, showing an even line of teeth that looked like Chiclets. Alberto was an architect. He lived in the apartment above mine with his small family. Through the customary open windows of the tropics, I often heard him fighting with his wife, like a Colombian Jackie Gleason in The Honeymooners.

One Friday afternoon, he caught me outside the entrance to our apartments as I came in from teaching classes, and asked me if I liked fishing. I said I did, but hadn't gone out in several years, what with college studies and all. He explained he belonged to a local fishing club that often went as a group to favorite angling spots, and would I be interested in going with them on Sunday? Enthusiastically, I said yes, and we agreed on a pre-dawn departure in his car.

The next Sunday morning the stars were still shining brightly as they do in the clear Andean air of 5,700 feet altitude, and it was surprisingly cold when we got in his square-boxed Nissan Patrol jeep, with fishing poles, brown bags of lunch and Thermoses of hot coffee. As we wound our way through the streets to leave town, we went by a large, sprawling public school of Popayán, called simply El Liceo. With a gesture, he smiled, and said "My old Alma Mater."

Gravity My Enemy

In the pre-dawn hours, the school, with its graffiti on white stucco and stone-base walls, was dark and showed no activity, but I knew it well, having had to substitute teach there on occasion. Being a public school, it was inexpensive to study there and students of common upbringing were often unruly. They were also the first ones in the streets when a strike or unrest was in the making, throwing rocks and Molotov cocktails.

"When I was in my last year of school there," Alberto said somewhat gravely, "we went on a field trip that was to later become famous nation-wide." "How so?" I asked, half-interested. "Well, I'll tell you a story like you've never heard before, I'll bet you," was his challenge.

"We had planned to go on a field trip with the senior class. This was my compañero, Ruben, and I. We hung out together a lot in those days. That was back in 1957. There were forty-three of us in the whole class," he explained.

They were to take a large school bus on the trip up into the mountains of the central range, or *cordillera,* of the Colombian Andes. There are three Andes ranges in Colombia and the colonial city of Popayán rested in a lofty valley between the central and western ranges. The destination of the class trip was the huge volcano known as Puracé that loomed over Popayán. It still had active fumaroles that could be seen spewing smoke, usually in the early morning before the clouds gathered and covered it over.

Puracé was one of a chain of volcanic peaks within sight of the city. They seemed very close due to their monstrous size but actually it took over two hours by car to reach Puracé.

The Colombian conservation department, INDERENA, was in the process of building tourist facilities to make the Puracé area a national

Volcano Puracé

park. It had a network of picture postcard trout streams tumbling through black rocks among the mountains, little ice-cold lakes, the home of the elusive Andean teal and black-and-white torrent duck.

In the wet, dripping forest surrounding the base of the mountain was a rich inventory of intriguing bird life and thermal pools and baths. The volcano itself, other than the small amount of gases escaping from its jagged mouth at the top, was docile and no one regarded it as a threat, as they did Sotará, a huge, cone-shaped volcano farther east. Geological rumor had it that the entire Popayán plateau was once a giant lake, and Sotará filled it level in prehistoric times. Increasing heat in recent years on the slopes of Sotará, people said, was causing grazing cattle to move farther down the slopes. Obviously, both Sotará and Puracé, names given them by the Paez Indians of the region, their meanings now long forgotten, were volcanically fed by the same hot caldron far below the Earth's surface.

Puracé was a popular climbing volcano to those bent on adventure. Most could reach the summit and return in a single morning, being able to say they had looked down into the maw of the sleeping giant and seen the fumaroles first-hand. This was the plan for the class trip.

The night before, however, as often happens on weekends to those in Colombian high schools, Alberto and his pal Ruben went out drinking the famous Colombian aguardiente, a licorice-flavored anisette that, despite its innocent, clear-water appearance, has a rude kick to it and a long-lasting effect.

Aguardiente in Spanish actually means "firewater." And, as also happens, they lost control. "We completely forgot we had to get up early the

89

Gravity My Enemy

next morning for the class trip," Alberto smiled. "We barely made it home in time to get any sleep at all." "The next morning, when it came time to be at the school to be on the bus, we were sound asleep." Alberto's younger sister, realizing he had planned to go on the field trip, rushed into his room the next morning and shook him awake. When he was coherent enough to see his watch, he jumped from his bed in a panic and quickly got dressed. "I didn't even have time to get clean clothes," he said. "I just jumped into last night's pants and put on a jacket as I went out the door to run to Ruben's house. There was no answer. So I just went in and he was lying on the floor in his room. I went in my father's truck, and by the time we were on the road to the school, it didn't dawn on me that I didn't have permission to use it."

He had had to drag Ruben out in a stupor and push him into the vehicle. By the time they were awake enough to realize the time, it was already too late to make the bus departure, and they continued in Alberto's father's car up into the mountains to Puracé, risking his dad's wrath, but not wanting to miss the outing.

The class had a good hour's head start.

Having a faster car did not provide much of an advantage, since the gravel road was steep, and was known for its constant tightly-curved switchbacks, making it impossible to gain any speed. They raced the engine, ground the gears and raised clouds of road dust behind them in their haste but were unable to catch sight of the bus during the entire journey.

Undaunted, they continued and finally reached the foot of the volcano two hours later.

"We found the bus parked there when we finally arrived, its engine already almost cool. Our classmates were nowhere to be seen. Quickly,

Volcano Puracé

we put on jackets, locked the car, and started following their tracks in the deep ash, heading toward the summit," he related.

"The ash was deep — really ugly and gray," he went on.

"It got in our shoes, in our clothes and up inside our pants. The right thing would have been to wear boots for this, but we were in too much of a hurry when we left Popayán," he said.

"Just at that moment," Alberto said, "I got a strange feeling. At first I thought it was just dizziness from the *guayabo* of all the drinking but Ruben grabbed my arm, too, and we almost fell over together. The ground was shaking! We felt, or rather heard, a deep rumble and it changed to a low roar." His face was dimly illuminated by the dash lights as he spoke, in the dull green glow of the dashboard lights. As I gazed outside, the horizon was beginning to show a slight pink.

"We stopped and listened but then heard nothing," he continued, "and thought it was just our imagination. The *aguardiente*. The ash was almost to our knees, and it was hard to walk, especially on a steep grade like that, where we often had to go on all fours. We went up two steps and slid back one!"

He chuckled, "And we were still awfully drunk, which didn't help matters much! Being kids, it never even occurred to us what our teacher would say if we arrived drunk. And worse, my Dad was going to kill me when we got back but, with him, it was easier getting forgiveness than permission. In those days, the most important thing was to impress or amuse our buddies, go where they went and that was all we cared about."

"Were you interested in the volcano too?" I asked, cautiously. It was now getting light enough to discern our surroundings without headlights.

Gravity My Enemy

"Not really," he replied. "I don't think we ever really gave it a thought. I had been up the mountain before with friends, and had seen it. It was impressive, and rather scary to look down into the crater, but we didn't really think much about it other than being a trip out of town."

I looked at him and awaited the rest of the story, feeling a little drowsy and wondering if I was going to be able to get through a long day's fishing.

"We were just starting out — Still at the very bottom of the mountain. Looking up, we could see what a trek we had in store for us, and neither of us was feeling all that great. We were feeling sort of silly, giggling and falling down, getting ash inside our shirts, smeared on our faces and acting like a couple of clowns. Ruben went ahead of me several meters, and I remember stopping to take a drink of water from the canteen, and that's the last thing I remember!"

I waited for him to continue, but he was silent for a time, and I was forced to ask, "What do you mean?"

"Taking that drink was the last thing I remember. I had no memory of anything. When I woke up, I was laying on the ground all covered in ash. I was all confused, didn't even remember why I was there. Everything around me was smoke and ash. I was lying next to a huge boulder as tall as I was and as fat as a car," he said. "I was all covered with this nasty gray ash, and was coughing. The ash was in my throat. The air smelled really foul and the ground was shaking violently, like an earthquake. In fact, it was an earthquake." As I looked over at him, he seemed tired, with a rather woeful expression coupled with a grim smile.

"After some minutes, I finally got to my feet and felt a terrible headache, like I had been

Volcano Puracé

hit over the head with something hard. I looked all around and couldn't see Ruben anywhere. I was really confused. Ruben had been right near me just a minute ago . . . or what I thought was a minute ago. I started to think that maybe I had just passed out and he had gone on without me, so I just started walking up the slope again when, suddenly, I stumbled over something. I looked down and it was a foot sticking up through the ash," he explained, still as though in shock.

"It was Ruben."

Ruben's body was buried in ash. From what Alberto was best able to figure, Ruben had stepped out into the open at the same time Alberto was shielded by a boulder when the blast from the volcano occurred. The explosion was so violent that the shock wave knocked Alberto unconscious. A rock or some other ultrasonic debris had decapitated Ruben, for his body had no head.

"He never knew what hit him," Alberto said. "They never later found his head," he said solemnly.

When the volcano erupted, as far as they were later able to determine, Alberto's entire senior class minus the two of them was probably up standing at the rim of the crater, and they were literally vaporized, for no one ever found even the body parts.

"Today, if you ever go up there," Alberto said softly, "look for a little bronze plaque with the names of my classmates. I'm the only survivor of that graduating class."

We were quiet as we got out of the car and assembled our fishing poles. We were going to fish for a small, salmon-like fish called *sabaleta*, a miniature tarpon, as the name implies.

"Want some avocado?" Alberto asked.

Gravity My Enemy

"No, thanks, I already had some breakfast," I replied.

"Not for breakfast!" he laughed. "For bait!"

I accepted half an avocado from him, carved off a small piece and put it on the hook. I felt foolish. I had never imagined using avocado for fish bait, but in Colombia, everything was always different. The river was fast and rough, the water slightly milky, roaring through rocks as it created flecks of white foam.

"Fish from the bridge there and just let your bait be swept downstream a little."

It was fifteen feet down to the water level. I looked down with some hesitation.

"And don't fall off!" he shouted. "I've already lost too many friends!"

I cannot honestly recall if I caught any fish that day.

The Puracé volcano erupted 12 times in 20th Century

Indian of the high Andes

6 Tiro Fijo

In my first years in Colombia, I renewed my love for hunting. I had always enjoyed it very much but the sport was interrupted by my college years. Hunting from a wheelchair at first seemed impossible.

Though I had done some plinking around with a .22 in the states after becoming handicapped, I never really got into hunting and shooting

Gravity My Enemy

seriously until I lived in Colombia and met the fellows from the *Club de Tiro Junín*, a shooting club in Popayán in the southern part of the country. These guys had a fancy club next to the country club just outside of town, with several shooting ranges and elaborate facilities. They hunted and competed with total passion. Most had very fancy guns of European manufacture. Makes such as Bernadelli, Perazzi, Victor Sarasqueta, Darne, Browning and Aguirre y Aranzabal were common among them, usually double barrel. Much of this influence came from President Guillermo León Valencia, who was a native of Popayán and made hunting more than just his casual pastime. He hunted with Generalíssimo Francisco Franco of Spain while serving as Colombian ambassador there, (In Latin America they give ambassadorships to people they want to remove from the political scene) and he had literally hundreds of rifles and shotguns that had been awarded to him by friends and foreign governments.

There's camaraderie among Colombian hunters and shooters that I have seen nowhere else. A hunt is a veritable party, with lots of story-telling, laughs and good fellowship, often combined with an eloquent banquet at someone's *finca* — or hacienda, as it is called elsewhere.

I tend to be a loner myself, as a preference when hunting, but the Colombian style has much to say for it, and makes for many fond memories.

Being from the U.S., there was a tendency for me to be arrogant in many things, among them issues of guns and hunting, since our history was formed by this expertise and activity. I, in the beginning, felt myself to be quite an expert, but humiliation was not long in coming, however, as some Colombians are incredible shots, primarily wing shots with a shotgun. But that's another story.

96

Tiro Fijo

Group of Colombian deer hunters.
President Valencia 3rd from left
in pith helmet

Some friends of mine, the Ayerbe family, had potato farms high up in the mountains of the central Andes, in the *páramo*, a cold, drizzly cloud forest, near a little mountain village called Malvasá, beyond the towns of Totoró and Gabriel López. It took two full hours to get there from Popayán over tortuous, winding mountain roads of mud and gravel that kept going up, virtually into the clouds.

Colombia has several species of deer. As a general rule, the larger species are found at the lower altitudes. The biggest is similar to the U.S. whitetail deer but has bifurcated antlers like the mule deer, and is found in the *llanos*. Naturally, it is called the *venado llanero*. Slightly higher altitudes have the *vallo* deer, a bit smaller. Up high in the majestic Andes forests are found the *soche* or *colorado* (red) deer, known as the brocket, and the smallest, with only spike horns is the *venado conejo*, literally meaning Rabbit Deer, the Pudu.

Gravity My Enemy

A cloud forest is a gnarled mass of stunted trees, mossy and perpetually dripping wet, enshrouded in mist and it is cold. Being right up in the Olympus of Andean weather, clouds whisked by rapidly, soaking everything in sudden, cold drizzles one minute and opening up with glaring, pallid high-altitude sunshine the next, with that quickly disappearing in turn to be replaced by sleet. The ground was often covered white, which remained for hours or a day or so. Such was the cold.

In this hostile environment, we often hunted out of a campsite. We piled leaves from the cactus-like *frailejón* plant (*espeletía*) under our bedding as insulation from the cold ground. The leaves were thick and very furry, the size of small doormats. The plants themselves grew all over the open grassy portions of the cloud forest, and looked like miniature saguaro cacti of a strange, alien world.

Everywhere in this region were little, icy rivulets that formed with other rivulets into fast streams, which were home to little rainbow trout. These were also home to the lovely Andean teal and an occasional black-and-white torrent duck.

The forest on the surrounding mountainsides was thick and impenetrable, hanging with moss and dripping. The twisted, black branches of the dwarfed trees looked like something out of an Edgar Allan Poe novel or a medieval fantasy, and the dense undergrowth was habitat for the ponderous mountain tapir and the smallest deer in the world — the Colombian pudu.

This miniature deer lives higher than any other in the world, has black bristly hair and simple, straight spikes for horns instead of the bifurcated antlers of other deer around the world. And it measures only about sixteen inches at the

Tiro Fijo

shoulder — about the size of a small lap dog. The pudu is virtually impossible to hunt without the use of dogs in this tangled mass of vegetation of the *páramo*. And the hunting dogs had to be special. Not just any dog went running around in such a tangle of black, grasping, clinging vegetation.

Nor did we. In fact, we never went in the brush ourselves. It would have been impossible, almost suicidal. These were a very special people, just like their dogs, who hunted the pudu deer, actually went in after them neck-and-neck with the dogs, and we all marveled at how they managed to do it. Among these rare mountain hunters were two of renown, who happened to be friends of many years. They were tall, strapping, rosy-cheeked brothers named Roberto and Sixto Manquillo. Their ruddy complexion came from the oxygen-starved altitude and perpetual cold. They always had about four days' growth of black beard, and both were as tough as thick leather and friendlier than anybody in the city. They grew up in the *páramo* and lived contentedly with their dogs, a simple life in the frigid climate. They were always ready to go hunting without notice, any day we might arrive. They had a pack of hounds that lived for hunting just as they did, and were equally as independent. Looking at the Manquillo brothers, they even resembled their dogs.

We showed up in Malvasá the afternoon before the hunt, this time to the modest Ayerbe ranch. The night before, we sat around an open fireplace in the mountain hut, rubbing our hands together to get warmth and drinking strong, heavily-sweetened coffee and hefty homemade bread with white peasant cheese that was wrapped in banana leaves. And we talked with the Manquillos well into the night about the next day's hunt, as we stared into the flickering cooking fire.

99

Gravity My Enemy

They told us where they had seen deer last and all the other gossip and details connected with hunting the strange pudu, and we listened attentively. We ate, drank coffee and smoked, till we all nodded off to sleep. The thin mountain air was very nippy; we were cocooned in wool blankets to stay warm, so sleep came quickly.

The next morning came in what seemed only a few moments and it was pure torture crawling out of warm blankets into the sub-freezing morning, still as dark as midnight. We loaded dogs and guns in the trucks, rain gear and all our hopes for a good day. With trucks coughing, belching smoke and rattling up the road, we headed even further up among the peaks to what seemed to be the top of the world.

We let the Manquillos out ahead of time with their dogs, about a dozen or so of them, all scruffy, brown and black in color as hounds tend to be, with the long ears and the lack of discipline for which hounds are known. There is nothing endearing or lovable about a deerhound. And they have no love of humans, the most greeting one can expect from a hound is for him to jam his muzzle into one's crotch, but know their business to a point of arrogance, they thrive on lousy weather, terrible food and rough terrain, and they slobber all over everything with long, wet tongues. They're lean, ceaselessly moving around, their testicles dangle 'way down and they're constantly scratching at fleas. Hounds have a "voice." Hound hunters refer to their howling in Spanish as *canto* or "singing" which requires some stretching of the imagination to coin such a term.

After dropping the Manquillos off with the pack of hounds, we proceeded to the other end of a long curve and got out with creaking bones,

Tiro Fijo

pulling guns from cases and loading them, the smell of gun oil in the air, muttering quietly amongst ourselves in the pre-dawn gloom.

Carefully picking a way to a good stand for each, we dispersed ourselves to cover a wide area between the rushing mountain stream and the woods. The pudu always headed downhill to the stream to evade the hounds.

As the pudu deer head to the stream to shake their pursuers, more often than not they're successful. But we tried to position ourselves so as to intervene.

At first, we could barely discern the Manquillos' presence several hundred yards up the ridge in the thick forest and off to the left, as it started getting light. Only an occasional yip or yap told us where they were, and, as all mountain people tend to do the world over, they had their own language of human yells and yodels too, that only they could understand, their voices echoing off the ridge and canyon walls almost melodically.

It was not long before we started hearing the wailing and howling of the dogs as they struck a scent and it makes a chill run down one's spine that is totally unrelated to the cold — sort of a primeval reaction to the sounds of the ancient hunt, something we unknowingly carry deep within our genes, born from millennia. If we think we are products of the "Industrial Age" we must first realize that it represents but the blink of an eye when it comes to the time involved in human evolution.

I quickly learned that the deer is not where you hear the dogs, but far, far ahead, much like the distance between the sound of a jet and the jet itself in the sky. Though it is tempting to search the brush at the wood's edge where the

Gravity My Enemy

dogs can be heard, it's wiser to look in all the other areas, far ahead.

After what seemed too short a time for all that went into the hunt, a dull thud of a large-caliber rifle echoed across the river basin and we saw the Manquillo brothers emerge from the woods. Some excitement and yelling could be heard from that direction, but I could see very little. After a moment, a small grouping of friends formed in the distance, and they began heading toward me, closer to the road, one of them with a small, black deer slung over his shoulder.

And just like that, the hunt was over. Friend Santiago had been the lucky one that morning. He pulled the deer off his shoulder and stretched it out on the ground in front of me. It was about the size of a giant rabbit, with black bristles for hair and a little, wet, black nose. Its eyes were brownish-black and shiny, like those of a stuffed toy. It was a little buck and on top of his head, angling backwards, were two, cute six-inch spikes. I was fascinated. The smallest deer in the world! Still quite an interesting prize.

We later attempted another drive with the dogs in a different sector of the ridges that stretched along the valley and, although the dogs gave evidence of hitting a scent at one time, no deer was seen. Many of the dogs had run off after Santiago shot the first deer, and we were working with a much smaller pack, less effective. Where the other dogs had gone, only a mountain hound-man knows, but the burly brothers seemed unconcerned, undoubtedly trusting the dogs would eventually show up at the house miles away sooner or later. After gathering everything and everybody, and all willing dogs, we headed back to the farmhouse, had a rough but hearty lunch of beef soup with yellow, mushy Indian potatoes called *papa guata*,

Tiro Fijo

its origin from the Incas. This, combined with
more white mountain cheese, which I realized was
really nothing other than compressed cottage
cheese with lots of salt, and the ubiquitous
syrupy-sweet black coffee, sweetened with chunks
of unrefined sugar cut from a brown block called
canela. It had a very distinctive flavor.

Bellies full from lunch, and warmed by the
mid-day sun, most of us fell off to sleep and
didn't come to till late afternoon, when we began
another round of hunting stories and plans for
the following day, which dawned very much the
same as the first.

The next morning the stars shown like
bright diamonds in the black sky as I was sitting
in the same spot as the morning before, and was
somewhat uncomfortable from the drizzle and frigid
wind, daydreaming to myself, my head momentarily
nodding occasionally in a compelling doze, I
began to believe I was in a bad spot and should
perhaps consider moving elsewhere, when the dogs
let out a howl up on the ridge in front of me, and
I could see Roberto Manquillo literally running
through the maze. I was reminded of Batman.
He was actually running on top of the trees.
I thought I was seeing things. He wore a white
plastic hat the style of a fedora, rainproof, and
a giant black rain poncho called a *ruana*, and
black rubber boots almost to the knee. With the
poncho flared out, he looked for all the world
like a huge, black bat chasing through the trees,
letting loose with an inhuman howling just like
his dogs, punctuated with high-pitched whoops and
shrieks, evidently intended to stir the dogs on.
As I stared, fascinated in open-mouthed disbelief
at this scene and super-human endeavor of running
through the brush by running on top of it eight
feet above the ground, I happened to glimpse a

Gravity My Enemy

small, black object like a bouncing ball, coming toward me, and with a jolt realized a deer was coming my way! This whole surrealistic exercise was taking place in my behalf alone.

Quickly gathering my wits, I shouldered the shotgun and let loose a load of No. 4 buckshot at the approaching deer.

It fell immediately, struggled back up, and was quickly downed by a second shot.

When friends came running, they said "It sounds like a war going on!" and several other comments about needing two shots for such a small deer. But everyone was genuinely happy, mostly me, and I was anxious to see my first pudu up close.

It was also a little buck. I say "little" because they are little compared to any other deer, but far bigger in importance to me because of its rarity. Who can tell if this buck wasn't a veritable giant among pudu's?

As is customary among hunters, we were all gathered around talking, recreating the hunt, eating and opening Thermoses, when several fellows, wild and woolly in appearance, came galloping on horseback down the road toward us. They jumped off the lathered horses and one seemed to be urging us to come with them, while the other was evidently saying the opposite — that we should get out of there as fast as possible. The excited chatter went back and forth, and the overlay of voices was hard to understand specifically, but there was a sense of urgency and fear about it. From what I could understand, a shooting had just taken place in a small village just down the road on the other side of the mountain, practically within earshot. Some freak of wind direction at that moment had denied us the sound of the event, but at the same time had possibly even saved our lives, as the sound of our shots had not reached them, either.

Tiro Fijo

The village in which this event took place
was Inzá. It seemed that early that morning, just
as dawn was breaking (and we were getting started
with our hunt), about 120 bandits had come out of
the mountains on foot and on horseback and raided
the village.

They first wanted the mayor, our messenger
said. The mayor of a small settlement like Inzá
was nothing more than the *ad hoc* spokesman for its
people. The mayor had appeared with his pregnant
young wife and they were both immediately seized
by the bandits and tied high off the ground on
posts, in a public display of barbarism. The
mayor was inflicted with what was in those days
of violence was commonly called "*corte franela,*"
referring to a "necktie cut" where they cut his
throat and pulled his tongue out the wound like a
tie, and let him bleed to death. They gutted his
wife like a hog, pulling out her entrails with the

Gravity My Enemy

fetus, and left her to die. The townspeople stood by in horror.

In an obvious effort to get money, the gang on horseback surrounded a mountain bus that had just arrived. This was the type called a *chiva*, with open sides and covered with canvas flaps to protect passengers from the rain, and with a big rack on the top to carry firewood, crates of chickens and the usual peasant luggage. These bandits (we called them *"bandoleros"* then, but now "guerrillas." More recently Freedom Fighters — probably the 'politically correct' term among the New Liberals) had various types of weapons, pistols, shotguns and some had submachine guns, a courtesy sent by Fidel Castro in the twisted hope of creating a continental revolution.

As they were extorting money from the passengers at gunpoint (I never understood how they hoped to gain the support of the *campesino*, which was part of their operational doctrine, by robbing them and cutting their throats), some fool on the bus pulled out a little, rusty .32 caliber short revolver and fired an errant shot, provoking a fusillade from the bandits with their automatic weapons, blowing out glass, and killing seventeen people, including two nuns. The steering wheel was blown right out of the hands of the driver, but he survived without a scratch.

After so much gunfire, the bandits quickly departed, possibly in fear of some Army reprisal.

We got there, very apprehensively and with guns ready, just minutes later, and everything was stunned chaos. People were weeping, coming to us with a hysterical recounting of events, and general shock of the aftermath. Across the little town square we could see the limp bodies of the luckless mayor and his wife, strung up on posts. With some reluctance and morbid fascination, we

Tiro Fijo

slowly approached the scene and stared silently up at the two victims. Strangely, their faces seemed still lifelike and with expressions of calm. It seemed the mayor gazed at me under drooped eyelids. Below, all was a grisly reminder of the atrocity. The ground under them was splattered with large pools of blood and viscera, still bright red in its freshness.

The "Chiva"

Luckily for us, the bandits were long gone by the time we arrived. Short-wave radio messages soon reached the police and army back in the closest city, Popayán, and army patrols were quickly dispatched to the area, but would take hours to arrive.

As often happens in such places in times of stress, it is very dangerous to be in the vicinity, especially with firearms — even if one is merely on a deer hunt. The reactions of over-zealous

Gravity My Enemy

army commanders, soldiers with low I.Q., and their desire to make the news with a killing of some of the "culprits" made it advisable for us to get out of the area, and back to Popayán as soon as humanly possible. So we raced back to our hunting area to pick up the Manquillo brothers and returned to Malvasá, packed our gear, bid a fond farewell and thanks, and returned to Popayán.

I lived at the time two blocks down the street from the police headquarters. Later that night, despite my weariness from a day's hunt and all the excitement, I was too keyed up from the experience and had to go out. I ventured onto the street and learned the news had shocked the entire public. Word had gotten out that the leader of the bandit group was none other than Manuel Marulanda, otherwise known as *Tijo Fijo*, (Sure Shot) the most bloodthirsty of all the bandits in South America at that time, on a par with Che Guevara, but for a time at least, to achieve less notoriety. He did not care much in those days about *La Revolución*: He just enjoyed killing people and extracting revenge for some unknown atrocities he himself perhaps had suffered in the aftermath of *La Violencia* that arose from the assassination of Jorge Eliécer Gaitán in April of 1949. Had Marulanda's gang heard our shots that morning, there is little doubt they would have come and killed us to get our guns, and any money we might have had. But, by sheer luck and a quirk of fate, and the swirling winds of the cloud forest, our lives were spared.

It was dark, the streets lit only by dim streetlights, and the air seemed sultry in comparison to the rarified air of the *páramo* we had just visited. I went up Calle 4 by the police headquarters. In front of the big, palatial white building, the red, yellow and blue Colombian flag

Tiro Fijo

hung limply from a mast jutting out diagonally from the front of the building. Outside in the street in front were parked two army trucks and one yellow public works dump truck, stenciled "OO.PP." on the door. They had just returned from Inzá. The *Obras Públicas* dump truck and was piled high in back with loaded caskets.

After note

Manuel Marulanda was until recently the leader and political representative of Colombia's *FARC (Fuerzas Armadas Revolucionarias Colombianas,* or Colombian Revolutionary Armed Forces), with which the Colombian government, under President Andrés Pastrana, was negotiating a peace settlement to include political legitimacy and participation in the constitutional government. When this failed, today's president Uribe has engaged in an all-out war against the *FARC* and their cohorts in the drug cartel.

A leering assassin,
Pedro Antonio Marín,
alias Manuel Marulanda
or more commonly,
"Tiro Fijo."
At 75, he was the
most dangerous
terrorist in our
hemisphere, having
murdered more
civilians than
Osama Bin Laden. He died
of a heart attack.

Author fording a stream

7 Wandering

No place I have seen equals Colombia for unspoiled adventure, camping, hunting and fishing. The country has unlimited environments and climates, over half the world's bird species, and scenery out of a fantasyland. Few people in Colombia, possibly due to past decades of violence and banditry, enjoy going out in the countryside to camp or engage in sports, so the natural surroundings are virtually untouched.

Another side to this is the fact that few Colombians have the outdoor experience to give accurate advice on where to go or what to do, so I was a novice in the truest sense in my earliest years. Many, eager to help, gave me advice that sent me on the proverbial wild goose chase, almost literally. I put together a rudimentary

Gravity My Enemy

set of equipment for a campsite and hitched rides, hopped buses and sat out in the rain for many long hours in an attempt to find some good hunting. More often than not, I ended up hunting nothing or very little, or shooting species not ordinarily the best for the pot. When I finally discovered the Valle del Cauca region from Santander de Quilichao up through Obando, this was idyllic country, though I was still unversed in the hunting and fishing skills needed to bring much to bag. In desperation I found myself downing shrilling, slow-flying lapwings, which are a type of plover with spurs on the leading edge of their wings, as though from the age of the dinosaurs. Another was the white cattle egret, also slow and easy to down for a novice, but surprisingly tasty. I found diminutive doves called *abuelitas* (literally "little grandmothers"), the little ruddy ground doves, and another equally small species that was powder blue in color. I shot mud hens and jacanas. Luckily, they were quite palatable, although local hunters I came to know later were very amused that I had shot and eaten such things.

One April, we were camped in a lovely spot under a giant shade tree on a friends' farm, called *Machín*. This was a dreamland.

I had a yellow Labrador retriever named Mike who was a retriever like no other I had seen. One late afternoon it was getting dark and I happened to be in a small grove of trees where doves were coming to roost. They were going by like rockets, in the dozens, and I was swinging my Charles Daly shotgun frantically, picking up incoming birds and shooting until the barrels became hot to the touch. In the beginning, I disciplined Mike and made him sit still, and then sending him to fetch each time a bird was down. I then waited for him to retrieve it and bring it to my hand.

Wandering

Ray & Peacock Bass

So many birds were flying by in the meantime I was losing many opportunities by being a dog trainer, so I quickly dispensed with the discipline and just let Mike run. He was so busy fetching one dove after another that I soon had to stop him to clear all the loose feathers from

Gravity My Enemy

his throat. I think he was enjoying himself as much as I.

It was getting darker and the doves were thinning out. A big bat flew by and I took a poke at it, in violation of my own rules of never shooting what I do not intend to eat, and the bat crumpled and fell on the other side of the trees. Mike took off after it. I tried to stop him, as I was afraid he would get bit if it was still alive, but he paid me no heed and raced toward the downed bat. In a few moments, he returned. With nothing. I swear, if this is possible for a dog, he gave me a dirty look, as though to say, "That wasn't funny, boss."

"Mike"

Gold was common in the area south of Cali. To the west of Santander de Quilichao was a small, Godforsaken village named Suárez on the Cauca River. We had to cross a couple of rickety wooden plank bridges to get there. Nearby, along the riverbanks were endless piles of gravel. An American company left these from extensive dredging for gold in the river many years earlier. They had taken the bulk of the alluvial gold but

Wandering

left sufficient quantities for the local Black women to eke out a living by panning the riverbeds on a daily basis, bending over in the hot sun and working heavy, wooden pans in the gravel. By week's end of backbreaking work, the women were able to accumulate a few pinches of gold dust in the bottom of a glass pill vial.

On Saturday mornings market day was held in Suárez. People brought their fruits and vegetables for sale, chickens and pigs, women deep-fried sowbelly in hot grease to sell with beer and bread to the hungry visitors. Most of the small market area was protected from the hot sun by awnings stretched tightly over thick bamboo frames. People wandered about, buying what they needed, talking, laughing and sitting for a cold drink or to eat some *pan de yuca* made from the cassava plant.

Arriving also early each Saturday were several gold buyers. These were a seedy, dangerous lot, barrel-chested and beer-bellied for the most part, wearing small fedoras and contemptuously had a toothpick sticking out of the corner of their mouths and a pistol in their waistbands. They were friends of no one. They all set up their scales in open windows of a row of motels near the market place, the shutters thrown back to announce they were open for business. The international market price for gold was $35.00 per ounce but these buyers paid less than half that. Gaunt, Black women with small children in tow timidly approached the windows and, without a word, offered their pill bottles of gold. Without ceremony, the angry buyer dumped the yellow dust on a sheet of paper and ran a magnet over it to remove ferrous material, then curved the paper and dumped the rest into the pan of the scale for a reading. Then he peeled off some pesos from a wad in his back pocket, thrust them out the

Gravity My Enemy

window to the expectant woman, and she was gone without question. More often than not, the gold buyer stole part of the pannings with slight of hand, and the woman wasn't the wiser. She went to buy meager food and cloth to make clothes for her children and, by morning's end the gold buyers packed up their scales and gold, got on a bus and headed back to Cali.

My friend George became fascinated with the idea of panning some gold. He bought a carved wooden batea from the Suárez market place when we stopped in for some lunch to take a break from shooting ducks. It was perhaps eighteen inches in diameter and about three inches deep. Anxious to try for gold, he asked the advice of one of the women we had seen selling gold. He offered to pay her a small fee to take him down to the river and give him a lesson in panning gold, while I sat back watching girls and drank a refreshing *fresco de guanábana*, a delightful white fruit done in a blender with milk and ice. After a time, George returned and proclaimed that he now knew the secrets of panning gold.

"It's back-breaking work," he said, "but it should be fun. When that batea is full of sand and water, it must weigh twenty pounds!"

In following weeks, George tried panning for gold each time we went on weekend hunting trips to the Santander area. Our friend Gabriel Paris from the local office of *Ingeominas*, the geological surveyors, gave George pointers on the best locations based on their studies. I think George got a few flakes of gold but not enough to call the effort an economic success. Yet he enjoyed trying and continued panning each week.

With us many times went an old friend, Alfonso Hernández, who had played some rounds of chess with the local police commander at my urging, since both

Wandering

were national champions. Alphonse, as we called him affectionately, did not hunt but was always eager to accompany us on hunting trips, being an ecology professor at the Universidad del Cauca. While we were shooting, he was often off on his own bird watching or whatever. He was such pleasant company, with such a terrific sense of humor, that we always enjoyed having him along. He was also a good-natured victim of our dirty tricks.

Before a dove-hunting trip one weekend, I turned on the grinding wheel in my little shop at home and ground a small amount of filings from

The batea

Gravity My Enemy

a brass curtain rod. These were as golden color as gold itself. I dumped them into a glass pill vial and took them on that weekend's hunting trip with George and Alphonse.

We had a lovely little campsite at the top of a knob hill and under the shade of a big, tropical tree. The scenery of the surrounding mountains of the central *cordillera* was breathtaking and, in the early mornings, we could usually make out the glistening snow from the Nevado del Huila to the east. At the base of the hill ran a little stream of clear water. George took Alphonse in tow down to the stream to try to pan some gold. Alphonse was very excited as we described exaggerated results. George briefly showed him the procedure and then left him to work at it for a while. We went back to the camp to have a coffee and gaze at the scenery.

After about an hour, a bedraggled Alphonse came moping up the hill to the camp, the *batea* hanging from one hand.

"*Es muy difícil!*" he said with a smile. He had predictably gotten nothing. We were relieved he was still good-natured about it.

"C'mon, Alphonse, you're not doing it right, is all!" George needled him. "Let me show you how it's done." And they walked off. I followed in the wheelchair, as I wanted to witness this.

From the top of the small hill, I watched George wade into the stream with the wooden pan while Alphonse followed close behind. George was six foot two while Alphonse was a diminutive five foot five. George scooped out what looked like a shovel-full of sand and gravel from deep behind some rocks and started washing out the rough gravel, gradually getting it down to a fine silt at the bottom of the pan. In a moment of distraction when I pointed out the snow-capped mountain in

Wandering

the distance to Alphonse, George quickly tossed in a small pinch of brass filings. Giving it a few more swirls in the water, George held the pan up triumphantly.

"Look at this! Y'see, there's nothing to it!"

Alphonse gasped at the result. George quickly thumbed out the filings into another pill bottle, put it in his pocket and handed the wooden pan to him, saying somewhat impatiently,

"Just do it the way I told you!" and walked away.

We went to have another coffee. A half-hour later, Alphonse came trudging up the hill, his head hanging in exasperation. He raised his eyebrows, still good-naturedly, and said, "I just don't know what I'm doing wrong!"

George took him down to the stream again and went through the whole routine of showing how it's done, and then at the end, palming in some brass filings. Alphonse again returned after a time, totally discouraged, and George played the same trick on him again.

The next time, however, Alphonse came up the hill exuberantly. He proudly showed two or three gold flakes in the bottom of the pan.

George and I almost fell over in surprise and burst out laughing.

"*Qué es tan chistoso?*" he asked, puzzled.

"What's so funny?"

We couldn't stop laughing. George almost fell on the ground, he was in such a state of mirth. Finally, we told Alphonse about the nasty joke we had pulled on him, and he began laughing hysterically as well. Soon, he showed more than his usual sense of humor, laughing even harder.

George became serious and asked him now, "What's so funny?"

Gravity My Enemy

Alphonse turned to us, still with a big smile, "I guess the joke's on you! I got some gold!"

***

In the southern part of the country close to Ecuador there is the city of Pasto, cold and rainy. Nearby is the valley of Sibundoy, above which, perched high in the mountains, is a large Andean lake called La Cocha. A very pleasant Swiss couple had built an attractive lodge on its shores, called Hotel Guamuéz. It had a large fireplace at one extreme of the glassed dining room, which overlooked the lake. Its fire added a measure of comfort in the chilly confines of the lodge, where they served a wonderful "blue trout," a name from the color acquired after first dipping in boiling water prior to cooking.

We went out daily in large, wooden, flat-bottomed boats piloted by sullen, non-communicative mountain Indians. We criss-crossed the lake slowly, passed by shores of large seas of cane, trolling with mostly a lure called a flatfish, which was the most successful. The trout were rainbows, not particularly feisty but gorgeous and very tasty on the dinner table.

Before discovering the Hotel Guamuéz we tent-camped near a frigid stream that emptied out into the broad lake near a picturesque island. Shivering in our sleeping bags, we enveloped our trout in tightly sealed aluminum foil. Inside, we added a small amount of water and a measure of powdered onion soup, and then cooked them on a small gas stove. They were extraordinary.

La Cocha was a good illustration of the vast variety of climates and scenery that Colombia offered. From lofty peaks, we could

Wandering

La Cocha (top) & author with rainbow

see miles of valley low in a multi-colored patchwork quilt of green fields. It was certainly a beautiful area if one could keep warm. The locals, mostly Indians, and a somber people, had

Gravity My Enemy

the typical, rosy-cheeked appearance that comes from a scarcity of oxygen at these high elevations, and their physique was short in stature with short limbs, developed from the need to conserve heat and energy. Almost all of them chewed coca leaves all day long, as they had done for millennia, to provide energy and stave off hunger. They often added a touch of lime to activate the effect of the drug, much as their ancestors had done hundreds of years previous. Both men and women wore the traditional fedora hats of the Andes Indians, draped a blue or gray poncho called a *ruana* over their torsos, and walked in rubber boots. The region was extremely rainy. The chilly climate and steep mountain scenery was for us a welcome respite from the fetid tropics.

Colombia-Ecuador border

South of Pasto lays the border between Colombia and Ecuador. On the Colombian side is the small city of Ipiales. On a quest for more adventure, I flew from Popayán to Ipiales one Friday with plans of crossing over to the Ecuadorian town of Tulcán to spend the weekend.

Wandering

An elegant bridge spans a deep gorge, which constitutes the natural border between the two countries. I took a taxi from the airport and crossed at this point, where I had to show my passport to some scruffy, monosyllabic border guards. They waved me though without ceremony. When I reached Tulcán a few short miles on the other side, I was taken by its forlornness. I had had two friends from here at the University of Illinois when I was a student there. They were brothers from this town and I had vague hopes of finding them to say hello and learn what had become of their lives. I had no guess where they would apply a university education — much more so one from the U.S. — in this unimpressive town. I asked the *taxista* to take me to the best hotel. At least I was going to find some comfort in this frigid berg. He took me to the Hotel Atahualpa, which turned out to be not only the best but the only hotel in town. Atahualpa was named after the Inca king who was held ransom by Francisco Pizarro for a room full of gold. Though the Incas delivered on the bargain, Pizarro, true to Spanish treachery, lopped off Atahualpa's head and took the gold anyway. The justice has only come over the centuries. The Inca's meek and subdued nature has survived in the end, and their religion and Quechua language are the most prevalent in Ecuador today.

I was given a barren, cold room in the hotel and after dropping off my bag, ventured out into the dining room to find some lunch. I was delighted to spot a big fireplace at the end of the room but, as I took a table, noticed no fire was lit in it. A quiet waiter with mostly Indian blood came to the table and handed me a mimeographed sheet for a menu. The first lunch I requested was not available, he said. Nor was my second choice. I asked about two more and he said,

Gravity My Enemy

finally, that the only thing they had was a kind of potato soup with bread. They did have coffee, I was happy to discover.

"*Entonces, qué le provoca*?" he asked. What would I like?

"I'll have the potato soup with bread," I answered. He nodded, wrote it down on a little pad for the purpose, and began to walk away. He then turned back and added, "*Con café?*"

"*Si, por favor, con café,*" adding, "*bien caliente.*" Real hot. It was probably in the forties in the dining room.

When he came back to serve me the soup, which was surprisingly good, I asked why they didn't have a fire going in the fireplace. He explained that they only did this when it was very cold. I asked how many guests they had staying at the hotel and he said I was the only one that day.

"Well, then," I said, "let's start a fire in the fireplace." He said they could not do this. I offered him a healthy tip if he would not only get a fire going but also move me to a table next to it. My feet were already as cold as if I were in a duck blind in Wisconsin.

He repeated that they could not start a fire in the fireplace. I asked if they lacked firewood, and offered to send for some, but he still refused. Pressing the matter far beyond his indulgence, I finally pinned him down and asked why they could not start a fire in the fireplace.

"*Es solo adorno,*" he finally said, "*no sirve.*" End of the mystery. It was not a real, working fireplace, only for show.

Duck hunting was a special treat throughout the country. Locally, there were three varieties of tree duck that provided excellent shooting — the fulvous, the black-bellied tree duck and the white-faced tree duck found in the northern part

Wandering

of the country closer to the Caribbean coast. These actually roost on trees and fence posts, and nest in holes in tree trunks like wood ducks. They're very vocal, each with its own version of a high-pitched whistle that often announces its arrival, and they tended to be nocturnal in their movements, so they were popular for night-time shooting on moon-lit nights. We often sat near one another talking quietly, waiting for the telltale whistle of approaching tree ducks. When we spotted their dark shapes overhead, we shot much like in the daytime, but with the added challenge of finding them in the reeds and swamp with a flashlight, guided only by the splash we heard if there resulted a downed duck.

Black-bellied tree ducks

One especially dark night, the tree ducks were moving a lot but it was too dark to spot them. A friend with us that we called *"Pecoso"* (freckle face) Peña was an excellent wing shot. He claimed he could see the ducks this dark night when no one else could, and invited us to watch him in action. As we sat to witness this ability he claimed, in some time, whistles told us ducks were coming our way.

Gravity My Enemy

Near Santander de Quilichao in our homemade duck boat we strained our eyes in the night to see them but could not. *Pecoso* suddenly brought his shotgun to his shoulder and fired a shot. Orange flame jetted from the muzzle of his gun and an instant later we heard the splash of a duck falling into the nearby marsh. We were astonished. The night was pitch-black.

A short while later, he fired another shot at tree ducks passing overhead. As usual, we heard rather than saw them. Once again, the sound of a downed duck impacting the water told us he had scored. Amazed, we commented at how *Pecoso* Peña must be one of those few people who could see in the dark.

Moments later, he fired a double at the sound of passing ducks and, to our surprise and delight, two splashes followed. This was incredible! Four shots, and he had four ducks down, while we could not ever see each other's faces a few feet away.

One of the fellows in our group, Roberto Ayerbe, became suspicious and walked off into the night as we awaited more of this display. A few minutes later, we heard a ruckus in the marsh nearby and some yelling and laughing. Roberto had discovered the secret. *Pecoso* Peña had previously planted his oldest son a distance away in the marsh. Roberto discovered him lying down on a dry hummock and, when a shot was fired, the son whacked the water with his hat to make the sound of a downed duck!

Other than these foibles, duck hunting was pretty serious business where we lived. Blue-wing teal came down from Canada and the northern states by the many thousands. Nothing is quite as startling as sitting in a small duck boat in a hot marsh, sleepily watching a set of decoys, than to have the sudden rush of a large bunch of teal

Wandering

swing over, sounding like the lightening attack from a fighter jet. Usually, by the time one has almost had a heart attack from the suddenness of the surprise, they're long gone.

Most ducks came from the United States and Canada, as the occasional leg band testified. We got shovelers (otherwise known as spoonbills) near the coast. At times we experienced a wave of ruddy ducks that provided wonderful shooting, as well as the rare pintail or cinnamon teal.

After a morning of shooting in hot country, we often went to a friend's *finca* for lunch. The *finca*, or farm, is as much a place of luxury as it is a working enterprise, with cattle and crops. The houses were often equally as opulent as those they had in the city, but with added amenities like a swimming pool or tennis courts. There is no host like a Colombian host. Lunches were served almost on a moment's notice and included salads, fruits, cold meats and dessert in extravagance, accompanied by a well-stocked bar and cold drinks fashioned from exotic fruits. The host even provided swimming suits on loan. The only equivalents to the beautiful Colombian *fincas* I can think of are the posh, millionaire safari clubs of Kenya, overlooking vast, lovely stretches of wild landscape.

Colombians were not, as a rule, enamored with camping as we Americans were, so hunts with them were entertaining, involved lots of people, but were generally limited to one morning. As we went on extended dove and duck hunts, George, Ray or other Americans and I set up beautiful, comfortable tent camps in nicely-shaded little spots that provided good scenery and often a little, nearby stream for bathing and washing dishes. Prior permission from landowners years previous was always sufficient to go onto the

Gravity My Enemy

land repeatedly and treat it as our own, the ground rules always being to close gates and clean up afterwards. It was also expected that we keep other people off, a duty we carried out with pleasure since it guaranteed quality hunting and solitude. We never were worried about our personal safety. Much like the laws of the Old West, people in these outlying regions had a way of enforcing their own justice with the gun, and this commanded respect and kept the possibility of cattle rustling and other crimes to an almost unheard-of minimum.

The Valle del Cauca is a huge plains area nestled between the central and western *cordilleras*, at an altitude of 3,400 feet, making the area warm and pleasant, as well as very beautiful. Evidently, this was also a favorite area of the pre-Columbian cultures as well, as we often found remnants of their civilization near our campsites. Among these were potsherds and stone grinders. After a rainy period, we searched along washed-out stream banks and found hundreds of incised and painted potsherds encrusted on the mud banks. Some were especially attractive, but we never found entire ceramic pieces.

Local peasant people told us of seeing a "blue flame" shooting up from the ground at certain places in the night. Like much folklore, we paid little attention to it, but later reading and research revealed that, indeed, this phenomenon had been explained to be the result of a flammable gas produced from ancient, decaying organic matter in old gravesites. Our helper, Oscar Mosquera, said they once found a deep, vertical pit in which there were "*muñecos.*" Dolls? We probed further. He explained that some fellows were using a device they called a *mediacaña* or a tube cut in half lengthwise, to take out core samples from the earth.

Wandering

By studying these carefully, they could surmise where the soil had been disturbed even centuries before. In these locations, they dug down and on occasion found intact pottery, bones and small gold artifacts. These *huaqueros*, or treasure hunters, were after only the gold. They took nose rings from ceramic pieces and discarded the ceramics, often destroying them in the process. Ironically, pre-Columbian artifacts have a high value despite the material, whether gold, ceramic or stone, so in their ignorance, they were destroying valuable treasures. The *"muñecos"* Oscar referred to were small, gold anthropomorphic figures.

As one would expect, we became fascinated with Colombian archeology and pre-Columbian cultures at least as much as we were with hunting and fishing adventures. Over time, we managed to collect a small number of pieces, which are now part of the collection at the Milwaukee Public Museum. Most of the gold pieces were made by the Quimbaya culture, who were the masters of goldsmithing, often using an alloy with copper which is called *tumbago* and is detectable by a greenish tinge. They used the lost wax process to create many of these lovely figures. Since pure gold does not corrode, they are today in the same condition they were many hundreds of years ago. The ancient pre-Columbian cultures in Colombia, such as the Tairona, Sinú and Quimbaya were especially fond of making frog effigies, to symbolize fertility, since small frogs come out in profusion after the rains begin. This in itself has a connection to their artwork, since agriculture and the resultant ability to store foods was what permitted them to have the sedentary time to develop such skills. As accomplished goldsmiths, few in history can equal the Quimbayas, who were the basis for all the legends that gave the

Gravity My Enemy

Spaniards their fever that ultimately conquered a continent. Entire flotillas of ships hauled unspeakable treasures first to Cartagena where they were stored in the castle of San Felipe, and then on to the Old World. One of history's great tragedies is that most of the gold art of Hispano-America was melted down into ingots for transportation to Spanish royalty, thus reducing its value to a small fraction of what it would be if in its original form. Today relatively few original pieces exist. The best collection in the world now is found in the Gold Museum in Bogotá, which will take anyone's breath away.

Quimbaya (r.) & Tumaco
(l.) cultures
Author's collection

8 Doves

The Eared Dove flies at 70 miles per hour without effort. If you compared him to the stateside mourning dove, you'd swear there is no difference in appearance in the hand, except for the long center tail feathers of the mourning dove, which the eared dove does not have or need. In size, color and shape, they're identical. They share the same genus, *zenaida,* but the mourning dove is of the species *macroura* while the eared dove is *auriculata.* But the similarity ends there.

On the wing the Colombian variety is so fast it practically leaves a vapor trail.

In the hot, sunny Valley of Cauca in western Colombia there live virtually millions of eared doves, roosting in scrub trees on the slopes of two *cordilleras,* or mountain ranges, of the Andes that form the eastern and western boundaries of the 120-mile long valley. And, a scourge to

131

Gravity My Enemy

farmers, they fly down into the valley to feed on sorghum and rice crops, diving from their roosts into the valley and getting up a good head of steam as they make a straight shot to the dinner table, making them one of the fastest game birds in the world.

The valley is a flat, green table of hot, lush farm country, shimmering in the heat of perpetual sunlight. The Valley of Cauca is the breadbasket of Colombia. Cali, its capital city, is a cosmopolitan commercial center of over a million people, boasting modern hotels, restaurants and shopping centers, and the most gorgeous girls in the world (although the Brazilians may dispute this). Its modern, large international airport hails the arrival of wingshooting fanatics from all over the world, but mostly shotgun enthusiasts from the southern United States, where bird shooting is nothing less than a religion.

Cali is the world's Mecca of dove shooting, and anyone lucky enough to make the pilgrimage once in a lifetime will treasure the experience as much as a Muslim does in his own.

Cali is beautiful, with a combination of modern and Spanish colonial houses. It has a lovely climate and at an altitude of 3,400 feet, it is not uncomfortably hot.

For many miles around the city in all directions, grain crops attract countless millions of doves. And no other country will argue that these game birds are the fastest in the world. The eared dove even humbles the world's finest, most adept wingshots. Many "top guns" of notoriety in their home towns have arrogantly arrived to Colombia with fancy Perazzi's, Charles Daly's, custom-made Churchill's, Bernadelli's, Holland and Holland's, competition model side-by-sides and over-and-unders from the world's most renowned

Doves

and expensive gunmakers. And most commonly, one sees guns from American companies that produce fine guns untouched by human hands during their entire manufacture, but each represents a fortune and a pride to their owners. They arrive eagerly with an air of supreme confidence, their mouths agape as they gaze out into the fields for the first time in utter amazement as they watch uncountable birds flying by. They uncase their treasures ceremoniously, with trembling hands, from leather trunk cases lined with red felt, fine leather leg-o'-mutton cases. And they leave three or four days later with shoulders deeply bruised after a daily fifteen to twenty boxes of ammo fired per day with no more protection than a thin tee-shirt against recoil, totally humiliated and frustrated. For no bird flies in the United States as fast or with such agility as the Colombian eared dove. No bird in the world but this dove has earned the right to thumb its nose, as it were, at the world's top wingshots.

In singles and in small groups or often dozens in a veritable cloud of birds, the gray rockets whiz by at such speeds that only the best shotgunners can achieve respectable scores.

They are such a menace to crops that local Colombian ranchers, financed with government subsidies, commonly poisoned them, until American sportsmen learned of the four-ounce Colombian treasure and began coming to shoot thousands in a single day, with no visible difference in numbers after months of shooting.

To better understand the difficulty of hitting these birds, the average "good wingshot" will down maybe one bird for every five shots — about 20 percent. A top wingshot from, say, Fort Walton Beach in the Florida panhandle, or places like Shreveport, Louisiana, Georgia or countless

Gravity My Enemy

towns with a reputation, even revered in his home town for downing birds with surprisingly little expenditure of effort or ammunition, might achieve a percentage of perhaps thirty birds for four boxes of shooting — 30 percent. The best we ever saw from the states was a remarkably funny character from Shreveport, Louisiana, who had shot "buhds" all over the world, from Argentina geese and ducks, to driven grouse in Europe, to frigid James Bay waterfowl. His scores averaged around sixty percent, shooting a fine OU Merkel at times, but preferring his old standby, a Remington 1100 semi-auto in 12-gauge with a full choke.

It had to be totally taken apart and cleaned two or three times in a morning's shoot in Colombia. When we once asked him if this tropical shooting was the best he had ever seen, he answered in typical Southern fashion: "Does a pig have a pork ass?" And so we nicknamed him 'Pork-ass' Killgore.

(Incidentally, the best shot we ever saw on doves, of all time and all nationalities, to shoot the Valle del Cauca dove fields, was Roberto "Loco" Lehmann, a swarthy Colombian insurance agent from Popayán. He was the Pelé of soccer, the Walter Payton of running backs, a miracle in his own right. He had the features of a Mexican bandit and wore a broad, black mustache and his characteristic wide-brimmed hat typical of that worn by peasants throughout the Colombian mountain country. To watch him shoot was an inspiring, breathtaking experience.

His favorite angle was directly overhead at distances most shooters would pass up as out of range. He twirled athletically on the balls of his feet as he took aim at birds far overhead. Each shot spat out a hot, empty hull on his bare right arm, as he was a southpaw.

Doves

While some local shooters had the luxury of an imported Labrador retriever, a dog which never likes doves due to the loose feathers that tend to clog its throat, most hired very experienced and efficient pick-up boys from local villages. "El Loco's" retrievers were his own young sons who not only retrieved dead birds on the run but relentlessly chased cripples under his iron-fisted and ruthless discipline, with dread fear of losing a single bird.

(In local competitions where one could see some of the finest wingshots in the country, many of whom, incidentally, won medals in the Pan American Games, the local shooting club held shooting competitions in the field whenever an unusually large flight of birds was present. Officers went out to the location ahead of time and staked out numbered shooting sites, and on the day of the shoot club participants drew numbered chits from a hat, and each shooter entered the field to his designated site after being scrupulously searched to assure he carried only one hundred shells. Each had to exit the shoot for the bag count by eleven a.m. or be disqualified.

("El Loco," on this particular shoot, took in his hundred shells, wearing his big hat, with three totally scared boys in tow. He carried two worn-out Remington 1100's, with no bluing or varnish remaining, and the grips wired and taped, as he needed both to cannibalize parts. They were choked "full." Wearing the big hat, twisting as an acrobat in a pirouette to follow a bird passing like a bullet far overhead he shot down birds with astonishing regularity. It was a sight to see.

(Another competitor who on this particular day had finished his supply of ammo went over to ask one of "El Loco's" sons how he was doing. "Ninety-eight birds on the ground and four shells

135

Gravity My Enemy

left." El Loco had skillfully picked crossing shots and downed two at a time twice, a virtual miracle of shotgunning, especially if done deliberately. Unfortunately, he missed two of his remaining shots, as he was hurried by the clock, and came out bitterly disappointed, with a perfect score of one hundred birds.

(The loser? A fellow everyone called El Mocho [a person missing a body part or otherwise handicapped] Iragorri, who came back with a single, big, green parrot.)

The majority of well-known people in Popayán had nicknames, "El Mocho" coming from the fact he was deaf. Another, who always had great difficulty spotting incoming birds was, of course, called *Ojo de Aguila* or Eagle Eye, and another with a nervous blinking habit as he talked was called *Semáforo* for "semaphore" or "stoplight." *Balín* López, or "ball bearing," was the name given a five-foot, four-inch, extremely rotund, totally bald shooter.

At the time, partner George and I were running an outfitting and guiding service throughout Colombia for foreign hunters and anglers. Most came from the U.S., so we saw many shooters of all kinds. Few wingshooters came from northern states and those who did were twenty-percent guys on average. The very best shots were the Colombians, who enjoyed a hunting season that lasted all year long, with no bag limits other than those imposed by a constant scarcity or high price of American-brand shells. Colombia made a local brand shotshell ammo called Bochica, which we never used except in an emergency of prolonged scarcity of good ammunition. Bochica's were of vintage design with antiquated fiber wads and corrosive primers. They kicked like a mule and rusted out the most carefully oiled shotgun barrel in two days of neglect, unless the

Doves

shooter immediately poured boiling water through the barrel upon arriving home, as though it were a muzzle-loader flintlock.

To the northern ear, listening to good southern wingshots, our most common clients, was always amusing, just as it was to the Spanish-speaker to hear the banter going on between the Colombians. Like the Colombians, the comments that went on in the field between them was a comedy show of the highest caliber. They had us laughing hysterically much of the time.

As a hunt was customarily set up for tourists, we had a very attractive base camp in a lovely shaded area adjacent to the shooting fields. It consisted of open-walled tents and lounge chairs, in sight of the shooting so those resting could observe their friends in the field. Shooters (and I make the distinction from "hunters," as no stalking was involved) usually spread out along a natural barrier such as a fence line to form a firing line, with a separation of about seventy yards between them. Most shots were twenty-five to thirty yards in range. Young, black pick-up boys from tiny, nearby villas, all known to us for years as old friends and real pros in their own right, came to help and made a good buck in doing so, not only from the pay we provided but well-earned tips from the shooters. They also received camouflage shirts, hats, sunglasses, insect repellent and whatnot that visiting shooters invariably left behind out of quickly-acquired fondness for their helpers and companions, and to reduce baggage. A single tip often exceeded what their entire family made in several months. There usually one boy assigned to each shooter, and the boy led the shooter to his respective post, as a mother leading a small child. The pick-up boys would then hunker down with a ten- or twelve-foot,

Gravity My Enemy

bamboo pole, to which was tied the white or brightly-colored shirt he had been wearing. And the boys watched attentively for birds, calling shots in a low voice to their respective shooters, who soon came to understand the short Spanish commands. Any bird approaching midway between shooters caused the boy to suddenly stand up with his flag, making the bird swerve into one shooter or the other. From the tent camp, where I usually was with other field helpers making lunch, if the group of shooters was eight or so, it often sounded like a veritable war of gunshots. As the morning progressed and got hotter, the shooting often intensified. Gun barrels after the first hour were too hot to touch.

Two kitchen boys from the camp were sent out about midmorning to wend their way among the shooters, carrying a big ice chest with complimentary sodas and beer, and catered to individual needs, de-capping an ice-cold drink and giving the shooter a welcome respite from the hot, frantic shooting.

By about eleven, most shooters were physically played out and completely exhausted of ammo. Many who came for three or four days of shooting were physically unable to continue after the first day due to serious bruising, which often extended from the middle of the chest down the inner arm to the elbow, colored black, blue, green and even yellow. To some, we had to administer prescription painkillers. As they came back to the shaded camp area one by one, their pick-up boys brought their bags of doves, attached together in a cluster by their legs to leather *pateras,* and hung them up on a nearby fence. The shooters often threw themselves on the cool grass in the shade in utter exhaustion, marveling among themselves at how incredible the shooting had been. Pictures were taken. Cold meat

Doves

sandwiches, salads and drinks were served while the shooters engaged in animated conversation about the shoot. The boys, all aged from about twelve to sixteen, took this opportunity to take the guns from their respective shooters and sit together on the ground under a tent with spray cans of oil and rags to take the firearms down to the last part, cleaning and oiling them, much to the amazement of the shooters, many of whom had never seen their guns taken apart before or had never learned to strip their guns themselves.

Other boys rapidly breasted birds out during lunchtime. Some were later taken back to the hotel in Cali for the restaurant grill, but

The AyA — no finer gun exists

most were given away to the boys or locals, including those of us who stayed in camp that night to prepare for the next day.

We had our own chance to shoot, at times, after shoots and as we got better acquainted with shooters who often invited us to shoot a few birds with them. This often came to some joking and wagering. It was quite a surprise to many that

Gravity My Enemy

my being in a wheelchair did not hamper me from shooting reasonably well, but I often liked to bet against them before taking a shot, in hopes of amicably hustling them out of five or ten bucks. George and I both consistently shot around sixty, but more often eighty percent when the birds were flying in good numbers and afforded us selective angles, which is the secret to good scores. Early in our shooting careers, after the first good year of guiding, we both rewarded ourselves with custom-made Spanish side-by-side sidelock doubles with hand-detachable sidelocks. These fancy shotguns were ordered on the encouragement of ex-president and close friend Guillermo Leon Valencia, himself an avid hunter. He had become close friends with the owners of the famous Basque gun-making company Aguirre y Aranzabal of Eibar. The guns took a full two years to make by hand, and these were top of the line, with engraving, gold inlays and personal measurements. They came in handsome, felt-lined leather trunk cases with brass corners and a large emblem proudly displayed inside the cover:

Aguirre y Aranzabal
Fábrica de Armas
Eibar

As we took the guns out after some friendly wagering, the U.S. shooters were both impressed and suddenly leery that they had been possibly suckered into a small competition. But all was in good fun and we enjoyed friendly, casual shooting with many of our clients. (And we did get them for a few bucks.)

As much fun as this and the local gun club competitions were, the most enjoyable and relaxing of all were our own hunts which involved no work or competition, and between us. These were usually

Doves

accomplished from an idyllic tent camp at a favorite site where we slept over an entire weekend to get away from the activities of town, do a little shooting and get some rest. We usually brought along our helper, Oscar Mosquera, and a superb yellow Labrador and friend, Mike. (Mike often retrieved over a hundred birds a day, two days per weekend, for maybe half the year. Over a four-year period, this amounted to an astonishing record for a single dog. Not surprisingly, he won first place nationally and possibly due to his fame, was stolen later and never seen again.) We had specially-chosen spots for these outings, which were each a pastoral paradise, under big, tropical shade trees loaded with tropical bird life, the branches overhead festooned with bromeliads and mossy epiphytes. The general rule we made for ourselves was we had to have a minimum of a hundred rounds each per day. We reloaded our own ammo and were not dependent on the local army battalion, which was the only source of "store" ammo, so we usually had enough to justify a trip. In a country with so many firearms restrictions, we strangely were able to buy bags of shot in a local hardware store.

The camps were always cool and comfortable, well thought-out and attractive.

We set up a big yellow Eureka umbrella tent with a front awning, and staked a heavy, iron grill nearby, that ingeniously swung on the single stake to control cooking with the mere kick of a foot. We carried a cleverly designed chop box with drawers of utensils, pots and pans, and usually took little food other than staples like salt, pepper, sugar and coffee, and an ice chest with butter, mayonnaise, drinks and ice. Our shotguns provided all the rest.

One time, we set out for one such hunt on a Friday afternoon and got a late start. To

Gravity My Enemy

complicate matters further, we got a flat tire on the way. By the time we arrived to the area and pulled off the Pan American Highway near the town of Santander de Quilichao and into the cattle ranch called Venecia, a huge spread with lakes, wooded areas and abundant game, it was already getting dark. By the time we set up camp, and despite doing so quickly as experts who spent almost half the year out under the stars, it was too dark to do any shooting and we were about to sack out hungry that night.

However, while setting up the camp, I was sitting in my wheelchair, light-headed from blowing up air mattresses and getting the campfire ready, (some of the few things I can do to contribute) I heard a lot of birds fluttering in two trees about sixty yards away. The trees were rounded with full foliage at the top. I asked Oscar, our helper, to get out a flashlight and carefully go under the trees to see what all the commotion was. He came back a moment later, excited, and said, "*Torcasas!* They're doves! Lots of them!" They had chosen this spot as their roost that night.

I asked him to get my shotgun out of the tent with a couple of shells, and push me toward the trees as I quickly cracked the gun open and loaded it. At about thirty-five yards' distance from the trees, I stopped and took aim into the dark center of treetops, and let fly with both shots in quick succession, one to the right and the other to the left, in the thickest part of the vegetation. There was a thunderous roar from the twin blast, as orange flame spit from the muzzles, and pandemonium broke out in the trees. Wings flapped in the tree branches and all around us in the night.

Doves

When everything was finally quiet, George and Oscar took flashlights, and ran over to the trees, searching. They collected twenty-four birds! We ate well that night.

Another time, we went on a morning hunt with six Colombian sportsmen who were dove-shooting fanatics. The spot was a freshly cut sorghum field, alive with doves. We began shooting at about eight o'clock or so, as Colombian doves are not early risers. We spread out in a firing line. The grain had very recently been harvested and much was spilled on the ground. The birds were flying in vast numbers and this particular day we were blessed with a good supply of ammo. Most carried an entire case apiece. When we finally quit at around eleven, the eight of us had over two thousand birds on the ground.

We packed them in gunnysacks and gave them all to a local hospital.

On another occasion, we got to the campsite in plenty of time to hunt but discovered we had forgotten to pack our guns! Home was a return trip of an hour and a half. I stayed in camp while George and Oscar made the tedious journey all the way back to Popayán to retrieve the guns. They also stopped by a small store in town to buy a couple cans of Carne del Diablo (appropriately called Devil Meat, as it was identical to stateside Spam, but came in big round cans.) I fell asleep in the tent while they were gone and when the headlights of the Jeep truck lit up the tent hours later, I awoke to hear doors slam and George exclaim, "Wow, look at that!"

I had no idea of the reason for his exclamation, until he came over and started beating violently on the tent roof. I quickly crawled out and saw that the entire tent was covered and sagging under the weight of thousands of June bugs.

Gravity My Enemy

Smoke from the campfire, combined with vigorously shaking the tent, finally rid us of them. We had no idea why this had happened and in many years, never saw it happen again.

Top — a morning's bag of doves (on fence)
Bottom — a shooter from the south (1.) & author

Our supper that night was Devil Meat.

Doves

Generally, we ate like kings on these outings. Dove breasts roasted on the grill, mashed potatoes and dove gravy with butter, with even a pie or cake, or a big can of peaches for after supper with coffee. (Most modern citizens don't know it, but it's faster and easier to cook and even bake over a wood fire than with a thousand-dollar stove.) A second, late-night coffee, drunk from old, chipped porcelain cups, was accompanied with a small, maple-flavored cheroot common in Colombia, as we put our feet up and exchanged lies or just remained quiet and listened to tropical night sounds and gazed into the dying embers.

Some people in the world may enjoy special, magic moments of spiritual insight as they contemplate the universe around them, but none did more than we did at times like this.

9 The Amazon

As a young boy I was always fascinated with movies about the jungle. Having no television beyond Howdy Doody, the movie theater was a rare treat for birthdays and special occasions.

My favorite was Tarzan. Little did I know that the Tarzan movies featuring swimming champion Johnny Weissmuller were filmed in a tiny pocket of rain forest in Mexico near Puerto Vallarta called Mismaloya, which I was to visit decades later. It disappointed me terribly.

But the Amazon did not.

In the final months of 1964 I was living and teaching in the colonial town of Popayán in southern Colombia. I had some vacation time coming in December, so I wrote a letter to the commandant of the Colombian air force and simply asked if I could obtain a free ticket on Satena airlines to Leticia. Satena was run by the air force at a big discount to encourage people to develop remote regions of the country. Their aircraft were military versions of transports and piloted by Colombian Air Force pilots in uniform. Seating in these planes consisted of canvas benches running the length of the fuselage, leaving the center available to strap down cargo.

The southernmost part of Colombia is a trapezoid located below the equator. It provides Colombia about seventy miles of access to the Amazon River. Leticia is a tiny village that sits on the north bank of the river and from this sleepy town one can see a wall of forest almost a mile distant across the river on the other side, which is Peru. Brazil is only a short boat ride down the river from Leticia, thus the town has an international flavor of sorts and both

Gravity My Enemy

Spanish and Portuguese, as well as native Indian dialects, are spoken interchangeably.

To my delight one day in early December of 1964, a very kind letter arrived from a brigadier general of the Colombian Air Force (called "La FAC"). Enclosed with the letter were four round-trip tickets from Bogotá to Leticia "in case I wished to bring along friends," he stated. At the time I lived at a *pensión,* as did several students from the Universidad del Cauca in Popayán who had become casual friends. I picked out three who were studying civil engineering. They were very excited, and we quickly planned our trip. One named Luis planned to take along his father's 16-gauge single shot shotgun. Another friend lent me a vintage rolling block Remington in 7 mm. They agreed to meet me several days later when classes let out. I had no idea that this caliber was prohibited in Colombia, as being the official military caliber used in the armed forces, so when I reached the capital, I naively strolled into the Ministry of Defense to ask for ammunition for this rifle. After patiently explaining this prohibition, an officer later appeared with a manila envelope full of 7 mm ammunition. *"Un obsequio,"* a gift, he explained, with a warm smile. With an effusive expression of thanks, as much for sparing me confiscation of the rifle as for the gift, I left the ministry with keen anticipation of my first visit to the famous Amazon. The flight was scheduled for the following morning at five a.m. My partners had not yet arrived to Bogotá but were expected in several days in Leticia. As it turned out, only two showed.

The following morning I got up in the dark and checked out of our cheap hotel, caught a taxi and drove out in the pre-dawn cold to the military sector of the airport of El Dorado, almost an hour from the city.

The Amazon

A sleepy-eyed civilian routinely checked my flight tickets without uttering a word, and gestured me to the tarmac where a large DC-4 (I was quickly corrected in military nomenclature — this was a C-54) waited in the darkness.

Several military mechanics in overalls effortlessly hoisted me up the steps of the ramp into the bowels of the plane and I transferred onto a canvas bench on the starboard side. The seat belt was a wide, heavy-duty version with the hook-and-snap latch. My companions, Luis and Alberto, who were scheduled to meet me several days hence, were civil engineering students at the Universidad del Cauca in Popayán. Two Indians climbed tentatively into the plane. They picked some space across from me and strapped themselves in after seeing me do so. Though they were scared, the hour was too early to lend itself to much conversation.

Free ticket to the Amazon

In about twenty minutes, three sharply dressed Air Force officers in short-sleeved, pressed khaki uniforms entered the plane. They exuded an air of confident authority as they shook

Gravity My Enemy

hands with us and wove their way past the stacked pile of cargo that was fastened in the center of the fuselage with rings embedded in the aluminum floor. As they disappeared into the cabin up front, I looked out through the Plexiglas porthole next to my face and could barely see the mountain of Monserrate near the city, its lights dimly flickering in the rarified atmosphere. Closer, I saw rows of blue lights marking the runway. Moments later, we were startled by the whine of the starter as it slowly turned an engine, which coughed and then spun freely without catching for a few seconds, but then was followed by another cough and the reciprocal engine slowly growled in a steady rhythm and crescendo. A second, then a third and finally the fourth engine coughed to life in a cacophony that precluded any conversation. The airframe vibrated reassuringly as the pilot ran up the rpm's in all four engines. The wonderful smell of burnt high-octane aviation gas permeated the cabin as we began to inch forward on our way to the rows of blue lights.

The C-54 rolled out onto the runway, made an about-face and locked its brakes as the engines roared. Three Indians seated nearby sat in wide-eyed terror as the ponderous plane slowly picked up speed and was finally airborne and banking sharply to the left.

After gaining altitude and watching the grids of Bogotá street lights disappear into the distance, we started to descend. In less than an hour, as it was getting light, we landed in the Llanos city of Villavicencio at the very edge of the beginning of the Amazon Basin. The arrival to this dusty town, which was unexpected, turned out to be an anticlimax. They pulled the plane up near a dirty, white building and shut off the engines. It was beginning to get hot as the

The Amazon

tropical sun rose. Outside I saw scruffy workers rolling 55-gallon drums under the wing.

One of the flight crew emerged from the cabin and I asked him why we had landed here. As he passed, he quickly explained, "A *tanquear,*" he said curtly — to gas up. This was puzzling to me. The workers outside were working a hand pump attached to a gas drum under the wing as one fellow standing atop the wing triggered the nozzle of a thick, black hose, fueling the plane. When the first drum was empty, the pump was rapidly attached to another drum and the process continued until they capped the tanks and briskly rolled away the empty barrels. The whole procedure did not take more than twenty minutes. As the Air Force officer returned, I asked why it was necessary to gas up after such a short flight. Without breaking his stride, he said it was to make this flight on full tanks from Villavicencio, as we had to cross hundreds of miles of *selva* or jungle without benefit of any emergency landing facility. In moments we were back in the air and flying at about eight thousand feet altitude, the terrain below us rolling, grassy plains interspersed with long, thin rows of trees. I was to learn later that this was called "gallery forest." As we plied our way southeastward, the strings of forest gradually became thicker and more frequent as the galleries of grasslands diminished in size until we were soon over solid forest.

I was fascinated with the scene below. What and who was down there, I pondered? The jungle was a solid mass of rounded treetops and seemed to form into shallow clefts with slightly convex topography between. A slight glint here and there revealed that the clefts were small rivers. Some trees were brilliantly flowered in hues of purple, yellow and orange. At one point, about an

Gravity My Enemy

hour into the flight, I saw a small clearing and peered at it intently. It had a cluster of round thatch huts. My heart pounded in excitement. I strained my eyes to try to detect further signs of life, but we were too high and the Plexiglas was badly scratched. This miniature Indian village was, I realized, quite out of reach of modern civilization. They had probably never seen a white man. What did they think our plane was? What would it be like to arrive at this village for the first time? What did these people look like? How would they treat us? How did they spend their day? My mind raced. This is what my dreams were made of, the final fulfillment of years of boyhood fantasizing. I had arrived.

The little village passed underneath us without ceremony. We continued on our lofty journey into the heartland of the largest forest on the planet, engines throbbing dutifully and reliably. These DC-4's had once been used by the U.S. military to serve in the Berlin Airlift in 1945 when the Russians blockaded the city following the war. They were used around the clock to fly in every conceivable need for the people of Berlin, even coal for heating. How they eventually found their way to Colombia, I did not know, but it was clear that they were real workhorses and obviously well maintained to be flying over the vast jungle routinely. In the years that followed, I came to have a healthy respect for Colombian mechanics and FAC pilots, admitting they did not fit the negative stereotype we so often read in books intended to amuse more than inform.

The Amazon River is arguably the longest river in the world, depending on how it is measured. For a certainty, it is the most voluminous river in the world. For pure volume it has no equal, as brown, fresh water is expelled from this monstrous

The Amazon

river out to two hundred miles into the Atlantic. Its mouth is two hundred miles across, and it has twelve tributaries the size of the Mississippi. In actuality, the Amazon is a giant ocean of fresh water with forest growing in it. According to season, the vast basin is flooded hundreds of miles from the main course of the river, and then alternately drained, creating a schedule of planting and fertilization, and controlling the culture and lifestyle of its people. The Amazon is extremely deep, serving as home to more species of fish than the entire Atlantic Ocean, many of them feeding and functioning by virtue of sophisticated sensory equipment that does not require eyesight, due to the dark depths and the opaque water as it drains off tons of soil from higher ground every minute. The Amazon is a world of superlatives, many of them seeming lies, but true. Early and even recent explorers come back from the Amazon with tales that defy the wildest imagination. Scientists have emerged from this river system with drugs without which we cannot survive in the modern world, most gleaned from tribes of errant Indians. Today, it is estimated that we have discovered only a small percentage of the drugs it still offers, and have catalogued only small percentage of the infinitesimal number of plant species. To the surprise of many, the soil in the Amazon Basin is virtually devoid of nutrients, and has little agricultural value. Cleared forest provides only two to three years of relatively little fertility and then more must be cleared later to make way for more crops or the raising of livestock. Almost all of the nutrients are found in the treetops. In fact, most non-aquatic life in the Amazon dwells in the treetops, which are a world unto themselves and the Amazon rain forest is a giant living, breathing organism of the greatest complexity,

Gravity My Enemy

producing most of the oxygen on the earth. Animal and vegetable matter falling to the ground is quickly consumed and disappears back up into the canopy to feed the forest and more animals in an endless recycling plan.

My daydreaming ended with the cutting back of the engines. We were approaching Leticia and the culmination of all my dreams, the Amazon.

10 Leticia

**The mighty Amazon — Peru on other
side is a mile away across the river**

It was becoming late morning when the C-54
transport plane reduced the revolutions of
its four Pratt and Whitney's and the noise
level in the aluminum tube where I was sitting
dropped dramatically. I felt the sudden emptiness
in my stomach as the huge plane nosed downward
toward the green canopy of the jungle, beginning
its glide path to the runway located a short
distance from the mighty Amazon River.

Gravity My Enemy

In only a minute, I could already feel the difference in temperature as we entered the muggy layer of humidity rising from the verdant mass below, as though an invisible cloud. The plane swung sluggishly to the left in a wide turn and I could see for the first time the wide band of the river itself as it rotated into the view of my Plexiglas porthole. It was well over a mile wide and the color of coffee with cream. I noticed a small dugout canoe plying its way toward us, hugging the near shoreline, its paddler sitting in the bow unlike the manner in which North American canoeists paddle. Both shores were blanketed with an uninterrupted, tall forest of giant trees. The jungle looked much like an unending group of clusters of broccoli from our vantage point high above.

Just as I was eagerly peering out at the scene below and spotted the small, white houses and thatched-roof bungalows of Leticia laid out like a diorama, another abrupt bank of the plane took the view from me and we entered the final approach to the Leticia runway. In seconds the pilot descended just above the treetops as we raced within mere feet of the billowing mass of vegetation, speeding intently for the runway ahead, unseen by me as I began sweltering in the rapidly changing climate. A tentative bounce as the tires kissed the runway, a momentary smoothness of air again and then finally, we were down on the rough ground, roaring as we slowed to the end of the runway.

The landing was quick and unceremonious. The hatch was popped open and the heavy, fetid air rushed in at me and a small stepped ramp was wheeled up to the plane as the four big propellers whirled their last revolutions. The crew emerged from the cabin in front, their khaki uniforms darkly stained under their arms in testimony of the effort of landing the plane on a steel-grated

Leticia

runway, too short for the aircraft they piloted. One of them brought my wheelchair, into which I transferred quickly, and I was lowered down the steps outside into the bright sunlight. A rusty jeep pulled up near us and I was helped into the front passenger's seat. The air force crew were eager to see their plane unloaded and return to the thinner, cooler air of Bogotá, so I thanked them as friends, shook hands, and the jeep, my duffel and two other passengers in back with their luggage, pulled off the tarmac around the small, moss-coated building serving as a terminal, and we headed for Leticia over a rutted, dry clay road.

Leticia was added to the Colombian map in 1933, after winning a brief war with Peru. A trapezoidal swallow tail extends from the main body of the country and juts down to touch the Amazon, affording the country access to the river, essentially a third coast which was navigable by ocean-going vessels another seven hundred miles above Leticia. The sleepy town with its mud streets was laid out in a grid a hundred yards from and along the fast-flowing river, which was now about thirty feet lower than the level of the streets. The only evidence of any remaining military presence was a small, rust-streaked gunboat moored on the nearby shore, abandoned, and a couple of ratty-looking army soldiers with vintage bolt-action Mauser rifles. The distant shore across the river was Peru. Its wall of green showed no sign of human habitation. River traffic was limited to occasional, sleekly shaped wooden canoes as they slipped by close to the shore, out of the current if they were going against the stream, or farther out if going down stream, to hitch a ride on the swift current. It was a rare event to see a wood plank boat, powered by an outboard motor.

157

Gravity My Enemy

Since virtually all visitors to Leticia need Mike Tsalickis for any number of things like lodging, information, guiding and transportation, the jeep deposited me with my duffel in front of his house, located on a prominent corner behind a cluster of shady bamboo. The house was so public, the front door stood open all day, the concrete walk entrance to it shiny and worn from use. I wheeled up to the door and shouted a greeting.

A skinny, rather attractive young girl appeared from inside and said in what I gathered was Portuguese, "Mike's in the zoo."

She seemed rather impatient and ill tempered, but I prodded further by asking in Spanish where the zoo was. She jerked her thumb over her shoulder to indicate behind the house and I said "Gracias." She smiled briefly, revealing rotted front teeth, destroying the impression of an otherwise attractive face. I left my duffel in his living room and wheeled around the back of the house to find a complex of cages and concrete pools with several animals, all under a corrugated zinc roof.

"Mike?" I shouted.

From around the corner came a small, wiry dark-haired fellow in his mid-thirties, wearing a tee shirt that depicted a crude drawing of an alligator on the front and said:

Tarpon Zoo
Tarpon Springs, Florida

"Are you Mike?" I asked, unnecessarily. "Sure am," he said affably, as he came over to shake hands. "What can I do for you?" Thus began a friendship that lasted many years. I explained that I was down on a visit of curiosity, on very limited funds, as I was teaching for the government

158

Leticia

in the town of Popayán. My interest was just to see the Amazon, some Indians of possible, do some hunting and look around the area.

"Well, if you want to save some money and aren't too particular about comfort, you can stay here at my place back in the shed," he offered. When I nodded assent, he motioned me to follow and we went around the corner where he led me to a large, screened, empty building with a wooden floor and screened all around. As we entered, I noticed it was basically empty with wood posts supporting a metallic roof far overhead and what passed for an office area in back. It had a well-used desk cluttered with piles of papers and unopened letters with stamps from different parts of the world. In the back of the office was a cot. He made a gesture at this, saying, "If you want a mattress, there's that — or if you like a hammock, I have a nice, big Yagua one you can use," he smiled. "Once you get used to them, they're better than anything else. The Indians make whole families in them. Later they sleep the whole family in one!" I laughed with him.

I later brought in my duffel and set it next to the cot. Mike offered to have me stop by for lunch in a while, after I got settled, and I gladly accepted. As we sat down at the table later, and dishes of deep-fried brown chunks of meat were served to us by the same girl I had earlier met, Mike said, "Caiman."

I raised my eyebrows in inquiry. I had never heard the term. "It's like alligator. See if you like it," he motioned to the plate. Surprised, I stuck my fork in a piece and took a bite. It was delicious, a firm, white meat that tasted much like lobster tail without the stringiness. I told him so.

"Some tourists don't like it when they hear what it is," as he started eating with me.

Gravity My Enemy

"We go out to get them once in a while, a fun hunt," he went on. "Maybe you'll be interested in going. I have these German tourists here who want to go on a caiman hunt." I shook hands with them around the table.

"Maybe we can go one of these nights," Mike offered. I said I would, with a show of enthusiasm and gratitude. He asked if I had done any shooting. I said I had, but never for alligators.

"I thought they were scarce," I commented.

"Not the caiman here," he explained.

"Some places down the river in Brazil they've shot them out for hides, but we just take a few for lunch. Maybe you'd like to try it," he offered, "not hard, but you gotta shoot quick."

I was starting to understand why Mike Tsalickis was so popular, and was getting to like him myself. He told me his story over lunch. At the table the three tourists from Germany understood most of what he said.

From a Greek-American family of sponge divers in Tarpon Springs, Florida where he grew up, Mike was an energetic, enterprising man willing to engage in the most risky endeavors. While he was planning a trip for adventure to the Amazon in his early twenties around 1947, he met a woman named Trudy Jerkins who was starting a small zoo and she offered to bankroll his Amazon adventure. All he had to do was investigate the possibility of collecting and sending animals to the United States.

In those early days, Leticia was a frontier town with no more than a few Indian huts and a small, military outpost. The only way to reach it was boating down the Putumayo River from the village of Mocoa far to the west, a risky journey of several weeks, or hitch a ride with the military on a big, twin-engine amphibian called a PBY Catalina, and land on the river. This in itself was

Leticia

dangerous during times of flooding, as there were heavy tree trunks and obstructions floating down the river, often unseen just under the surface.

After a time, Mike developed a system of collection of animals with the local Indian tribes, most notably the Ticunas and the Yaguas. Relations with the Indians were tenuous at best, as there had been a long history of enslavement and abuse by early Hispanic settlers and catholic clergy. Most tribes were fearful, hostile and distant. Mostly, they were very distrustful of any whites, made worse by the presence of soldiers who were known to take potshots at the Indians for diversion. Mike Tsalickis not only gained their trust over time but also became known throughout the territory as a savior. He took young children sick with yellow fever to Leticia to have them flown out for treatment. In later years, he was to build a small hospital on the shores of the Amazon to treat the Indian populace from the many maladies common to the rain forest. He did this with his own resources.

After much cajoling and many years, he was finally able to persuade Colombian politicians that Leticia had a great future for the country. With help from the U.S. military, the Colombian government finally hacked out space and built a runway for heavy transport aircraft, and Satena, the Colombian Air Force-sponsored airline, made flights operational out of Bogotá. The flight took well over four hours over some of the most inhospitable country in the world, but it opened up a frontier to tourism and other exploitation that has grown monumentally since. This service, of course, played into the hands of Tsalickis and his partner in Tarpon Springs, where they not only had a small zoo but a supply house for animals used for medical research and sale on the

Gravity My Enemy

open market. Mike's "zoo" behind his house served as a collection point for animal shipment to the United States.

Public awareness of declining numbers caused by animal exploitation plus animal rights activist movements gradually put a halt to the shipping of animals and Mike's business was altered as a consequence but did not reduce his high level of activity in other areas, primarily ecotourism. He built a lodge near Leticia called Monkey Island (which had a large population of squirrel monkeys) and a hotel in town, boat trips and sightseeing.

When I was there, however, everything Mike did had more than one purpose. We went out the following night to hunt caiman just after dark. His motorista and one helper lowered me down the steep, muddy bank in my wheelchair to the waiting, flat-bottom boat. The tourists were already waiting in eager anticipation when Mike arrived carrying a single-shot Stevens 12 gauge shotgun, and a headlamp held to his forehead with an elastic band. He greeted everyone and took his place in the front seat at the bow. As the motorista pushed off from shore and started the motor, Mike broke open a full box of flashlight batteries and loaded the box to his headlamp, which he then strapped to his waist.

As we headed out into the river, pointed upstream against the current, I noticed we did not go far from shore. Mike soon turned on the headlamp and shone its beam along the shore, up and down, at the juncture where water meets land. We plodded along rather slowly. The evening was cooler than the day, and the breeze off the river brought the primeval aromas of aquatic vegetation, mud and fish.

As I watched this lithe man with the light and shotgun in front of me, I wondered what he had

Leticia

seen in his lifetime, what he was now thinking, and how this evening would develop. Nonchalantly, he brought up the palm of his hand and flashed it in the beam of light in front of him, angling it to point to a spot on the shore where he had the light focused. The man at the helm, I later learned, was named Beleño, a full-blooded Ticuna whom Mike had taken in and saved years earlier when Beleño was a boy, half-dead from arrow wounds inflicted during a tribal vendetta. They had become as brothers over the years, as he was fiercely devoted to Mike. He swung the boat toward shore, following the light beam.

Just as we neared the shore, Beleño cut the motor, and boat coasted rapidly ahead. Mike had the gun shouldered firmly, pointed to one side, and with a violent blast and orange muzzle flash, sent water high in the air, dropped the gun hastily at his side and lunged over the gunwale to grab something in the water. He let out a grunt of exertion as he pulled the weight up to the boat, and in the dim light of the headlamp we could see him drape the glistening, wet form of an alligator over the side of the boat. All the tourists and I as well, had our heads up in curiosity, watching this spectacle.

"Tomorrow's lunch," Mike said. There was a titter of laughter and animated conversation in German. "That's a caiman," he explained, as he held up the front part of the animal for all to view. He dropped it in the bottom of the boat near my feet. I hoped it was dead.

We continued up the river. After no more than a brief moment, Mike again signaled that he had seen another caiman, and we turned in. He held the gun firmly again to make a shot, and suddenly discarded it at his side and reached over the bow in a lurch of his body, reaching into

Gravity My Enemy

the water. As he pulled himself up, he sat upright and extended his hand upward over his head for all to see. In it he grasped a small caiman of about eighteen inches in length, very much alive. People again commented in German excitedly, as Mike pulled out a gunny sack and reached the tiny caiman into the inside, flipped over the opening to prevent escape, and put it at his feet.

"What do you do with one that small?" I asked.

"Going to the states," Mike answered over his shoulder. "Collectors up there buy them." After a half hour of no activity, Mike once again signaled Beleño to turn into the shore, and as we rapidly approached, Mike again quickly discarded his shotgun at his side. To our collective surprise, he this time leapt overboard into the muck in a big splash. People let out cries of astonishment. I wondered if there was perhaps an emergency, as I saw Mike rolling and turning in the muddy water alongside the boat, uttering gasps of air and profanities in the process. I reached forward and

Caimán

picked up the headlamp he had thrown on the floor, still turned on, and shined it in the direction of all the commotion. Mike was rolling over and over in the water, wrestling a caiman! He shouted at Beleño, who leaned over me to reach him a rope, already tied in a noose. Mike grabbed it and deftly slipped it over the snout of the caiman as Beleño pulled it tight. Mike threw a

164

Leticia

couple half-hitches on the rope and Beleño pulled it toward the boat as Mike grabbed the tail and hefted the animal over the side of the boat, thrashing and threatening to knock the planks loose from the bottom of the boat. Sopping wet, Mike heaved himself over into the boat, dripping water, his hair hanging in his face, and they both secured the six-foot caiman under the seat on which I was sitting.

"Don't worry," Mike said to me (somewhat unconvincingly, I thought), "he won't hurt you."

This fellow was full of surprises, I thought to myself. The German tourists obviously agreed, as their conversation became much more animated.

11 River Life

In following days I alternately spent time with Mike and explored the environs of Leticia. This was a small town of only several blocks set back from the river about three hundred yards. Only the main street was paved. The space between the main street and the river was an open field, so from the vantage point of a small café, one could gaze out to the river and see Peru on the opposite side a mile away. The rest of the streets were dried mud and potholes. Being December, the water level of the river was about twenty feet or more below the banks, which were red mud and difficult to negotiate in a wheelchair. There was a small, hot hotel that seemed empty, an army post consisting only of a few offices. A bored sentry stood in front. A few small stores selling batteries, canned goods, bright blue pants for the Indians and a small selection of locally made sodas made up the total of this small, sleepy town. Most structures were wood frame or masonry. There was only one car, a jeep, and this busily ran up and down the street throughout the day. Occasionally, there were Ticuna Indians in twos and threes, dressed in brightly colored shirts and pants, in town for iron harpoon points, fishhooks, aluminum pots and salt. Money was derived from the sale of monkeys and dried fish.

The river had a very fast current. Any canoe traffic had to stay very close to shore while going upriver, to escape this force.

Paddlers sat in the bow. Going down river, they used the current more in the center and swept by swiftly. On rare occasions, a large boat chugged upriver. These interesting river craft traveled long distances at times and were cluttered with hanging hammocks to accommodate local passengers under the roof. Fighting the current, they made agonizingly slow progress. I was told that the Amazon was navigable to ocean-going vessels six or seven hundred miles further up, to Iquitos, Peru, but never saw anything that size in several months.

I found it enjoyable and interesting to while away my time at the river's edge and watch canoe traffic and people bringing in fish and animals of all descriptions. While down at the river one day I was surprised to see small dolphins surfacing some distance from shore. They were no more than about five feet in length and light pink in color. I couldn't believe my eyes. I asked Mike later about this. He confirmed that indeed the Amazon had dolphins, two different types in fact. The other was gray. On a later visit to the shoreline I saw a small wooden dugout pulled up to the shore, tied to its own canoe paddle which was thrust into the mud of the bank in an upright position. Amazonian Indian canoe paddles are often shaped like a heart with a pointed tip for this purpose. The canoes typically have a small fin on the underside to serve as a keel. What was interesting about this particular canoe, which was no more than fourteen feet long, is that it had a live, pink dolphin tied in the bottom, weakly struggling. I watched it in pity and fascination for some time, wondering what its fate was. Out of the water with its skin dry and in the sun, I knew its future could not be good. No one was nearby to ask, so I never learned why it had been brought in.

One day I was passing by the army post and struck up a meaningless conversation with the sentry in front. He was particularly non-verbal. He wore a plastic helmet liner and a wrinkled uniform about two sizes too big for his diminutive

River Life

frame. Part of his shirttail hung out. He wore a worn, web cartridge belt and black boots, scuffed and also two sizes too big. His entire get-up was U.S. Army surplus, and few American soldiers are five feet four inches tall with size six shoes, like this fellow.

This soldier had all his hair skin-cut like a freshly shorn sheep, with only a tuft of straight, black hair left in the very front. He was fiddling with the muzzle of his Mauser rifle, which had long since lost all its bluing in the tropics, but it was shiny from constant cleaning. The stock was black from the soaked-in oil of decades.

"What are you doing with the muzzle?" I asked idly. He said he had something stuck there and was trying to dislodge it. I looked to discover he had jammed a bullet in the muzzle. It was only the projectile, evidently removed from the cartridge out of curiosity of what was inside, and the tight fit made it difficult to remove. I asked what would happen if he had to use his rifle. He said he did not carry ammunition anyway. I could guess why. More worrisome to him was being discovered by his superior with the muzzle blocked. I went on down the street to let him work at solving his problem.

Several days later I had occasion to be inside the army post, talking to a lieutenant about buying some shotgun shells for hunting. Even sport ammunition is sold only through the military in Colombia, and the paperwork is horrendous. As we were talking, a deafening blast shook the dust off the light fixtures over the officer's desk. He jumped up and ran to the window and peered out through the rusty screen. I looked around bewildered, wondering what had happened. A soldier came to the door and said something I could not hear.

Gravity My Enemy

"What happened?" I asked him as he made a motion that our conversation was finished.

"The sentry in front, playing with his *fusil*. It went off," *Se le disparó,* he explained, agitated.

I rolled out the door. "Was he hurt?" I asked. "I thought they didn't carry live ammo," I added.

"No, but he's going to wish he was," he said cryptically, his jaw tense.

As I left the wooden building, I saw it was the same sentry I had seen days before with the plugged muzzle. Perhaps he had it coming.

Evidently, he had access to some ammunition, I mused. I wondered what his fate would be, thinking perhaps not much better than the pink dolphin's. Latin American military is a bad place to be for a buck private.

Every day at midday, on Mike's invitation, I went to his house to eat lunch, which was usually alligator, or more correctly caiman, tail. This was a beautiful, pure-white meat not much unlike lobster tail but less stringy in consistency. It had a bone in the middle of each chunk and was fried golden brown. I enjoyed it very much. It was wonderful and I came to encourage Mike to hunt caiman frequently, just to have these delicious lunches. His wife, a slightly overweight but handsome Brazilian woman, called the shots in the kitchen while the skinny girl I met on the first day sullenly served us. Mike's son, Mike Jr., a thin boy of about six, hung around the house playing. The table often had visiting tourists and in time I became a fixture in his place and was regarded by the visitors as a local resident who had settled in Leticia. I slept in Mike's warehouse in back, a large wooden building that was screened in all around. He had a small, cluttered office where I

River Life

worked daily to pay my keep, answering letters he had received months previous. I typed these on a black vintage Remington typewriter that had a ribbon so worn that the words were pale on the page. But Mike was happy to see that I cranked out volumes of correspondence for him in exchange for his hospitality.

Whenever he had a group of tourists to take or send somewhere, he sent me with them, acting like he needed me to help out but I knew in truth he was just providing me a means of seeing the surrounding area without cost.

I learned over time that Mike Tsalickis was the primary town father. Wiry and highly active, very friendly and against all odds, he had come to Leticia in the 1940's when it was only a military outpost. He was solely responsible for the construction of the airport, which opened up Colombia's Amazon frontier. Military surplus steel grating from the Second World War was used for the runway. Mike rescued countless Indians from the area who were dying of yellow fever and malaria, and brought them in to Leticia for medical treatment. In time, he built a small hospital, equipped with machines he brought from the United States. In order to operate a tourist business and collect animals for the Tarpon Zoo and medical research, he was forced to heavily bribe corrupt officials from three different countries. Bribes were not a trifle. They included cases of Scotch and outboard motors. The authorities knew the importance of his activities. Despite this system, Mike was always kind-hearted and accommodating to everyone who came to his open door, from small, sick children in the arms of desperate mothers to ambassadors down for an adventure tour.

We visited a local Ticuna Indian village one day, located down the river a short distance from

Gravity My Enemy

town, near or just across the Brazilian border. Beleño was his usual *motorista*. Between them, they always kindly got my wheelchair out of the boat, lifted me out, and hauled me up and down steep mud banks to our destination and back to the boat. In the Ticuna village, I was surprised to see Mike treat them with considerable deference. I thought he must know them well after so many years, but obviously there was a large cultural gap still between them, as he handed out Pielroja cigarettes one by one. Mostly, the Indians were a solemn people, the women often scurrying off in shyness at our approach, but when one man finally smiled, I was taken aback to see he teeth filed to points.

"They revere the piranha," Mike explained, "and file their teeth to look like one."

Their houses were small, up off the ground about three feet on posts, with a thatch roof. One-half of the houses was enclosed with cane or bamboo, which had been cut open and flattened, and this was their sleeping and cooking area. Typically, the kitchen consisted of a mud stove raised off the floor to table height where they cooked in blackened aluminum pots over stones surrounding the fire. The smoke simply went up into the roof, leaving the inside with a shiny tar coating. This had a function in preventing animals like lizards, spiders and snakes from taking up residence in the roof. From the outside, the smoke simply filtered out between the palm fronds. Hanging from an occasional tree branch outside the house was a narrow basket, about four feet in length and as thick as a man's arm. It hung from a loop, where the basket was open at the top. There was another loop at the bottom where there was no opening. The women loaded this with wild cassava, which was toxic, and squeezed out the toxin by placing a lever through the loop below, attaching

River Life

one end to the tree, and pushing the lever down to squeeze the basket's contents. When finished, they pounded the potato-like tuber in a mortar and pestle resulting with a hard, granulated meal they called *farinha*. It was crunchy to eat and after a time, I acquired a taste for this staple of the Amazon, taking my small basket of *farinha* with me as a lunch box daily as we went out to hunt, with chunks of caiman or peccary meat thrown in.

One day, as we were going into a very small Ticuna village on a pathway through the bush, we ran across a huge boa constrictor that was lethargically ambling across our path. Mike stopped everyone and gave quick instructions. He and several other men pounced on the snake, Mike grasping it behind the cantaloupe-sized head. It twisted and thrashed powerfully, causing the men at times to lose their footing, but was overcome as each man was spaced apart from the other. We

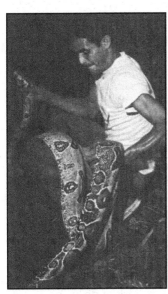

Mike with Boa

took the snake back with us that day to Leticia. It measured almost fourteen feet. On another occasion while living with the Yagua tribe, I had occasion to eat a similar boa and found it delicious and meaty. Finally, the day came to load the 16-foot boat for a lengthy river trip. It was very stable but heavy, powered by an antique outboard motor with an exposed flywheel on the top, around which Beleño had to wrap a cord to start it. We carried barrels of gasoline and empty cages

Gravity My Enemy

and boxes to collect animals. Canned goods and cases of pop were stacked amidships. Mike insisted I take the pop to avoid drinking river water, which microscopically was a veritable zoo. Beleño brought a small steel toolbox with spare propeller and shear pins, sparkplugs and an assortment of tools, including wire, sandpaper and files, obviously assembled after many years of experience on the Amazon waterways. We set off early the next morning downstream and before long reached the Brazilian village of Benjamin Constant. This small town was built entirely on stilts, with a wooden plank walkway running through the middle. The river ran underneath, the oily water visible between the cracks, and serving as the village's sewage system. We stopped for some lunch and had turtle soup. The place was seedy and uninteresting, and we moved on with no further delay. I did notice that the Brazilian girls were unusually attractive and coquettish.

With us were the two university students from the Universidad del Cauca in Popayán, who had arrived a few days earlier. They were named Alberto Montealegre and Luis López. Alberto, I later discovered, was a serious Communist agitator. Luis was somewhat ill tempered. Neither had any experience in the bush and I came to soon regret getting involved with them. Their immaturity and fussiness about native food, as well as their abusive nature with Indians irritated me and I hoped we would not have any problems. What worried me most was their inexperience and clumsy ineptness with guns, which is usually coupled with an eagerness to handle and shoot them.

Down river from Benjamin a few hours, we were motoring along in the heat far from shore and thus unable to see any of the wildlife we had expected. The heat made us drowsy and I found myself nodding

River Life

off as I sat on the front seat. Amazon travel becomes very monotonous in time and is soporific. Alberto sat on the wood bilge grate between my feet in front. Off in the distance ahead, I saw a white cattle egret on a low mud bar and motioned for someone to pass me a single-shot sixteen gauge shotgun Luis had brought, with a shell. We needed some excitement very badly. I motioned for Beleño to head toward the egret, cracked open and loaded the shotgun and handed it to Alberto, showing him where the safety was located. He eagerly took it. We began approaching the egret, which seemed to be feeding on something at its feet.

As we came within range, Beleño cut the motor and we drifted rapidly toward the bird. I said quietly to Alberto, "Shoot."

He aimed at the egret but did nothing. "Shoot," I repeated. Nothing. We were coming close enough to flush the bird.

"Shoot! Shoot!" I whispered urgently. As often happened with beginners, he probably forgot to release the safety and was pulling a blocked trigger.

The boat got too close and the egret lazily winged off, its neck folded back in an "S." The boat bumped the mud bank softly. I swore under my breath.

Uttering a pathetic-sounding moan, Alberto dropped the shotgun clattering to the floor and his legs stiffened out front, trembling. He threw his head back in a spasmodic reflex. At the same instant, I saw that the egret had been feeding upon a dead electric eel, washed up on the bank. My immediate, gut reaction was that Alberto somehow had his hand dragging overboard in the water and had received a jolt from the eel's companion, which had lingered nearby. Alberto then began to kick violently and throw his body around, moaning,

Gravity My Enemy

and it dawned on me that he was having a grand mall seizure.

Pushing the gun aside in fear of it firing in the confines of the boat with such thrashing about, I pulled Alberto's head back to make sure he had a clear breathing passage, and had to physically restrain him from pitching out of the boat. In a moment he was calm and, checking once again to make sure he was all right, I simply let him lay back off to my side where I could watch him, and let him sleep.

After a couple hours of river travel, he awoke slowly and I asked him if he was epileptic. He said he was. He was still quiet and in a daze from the effects of the seizure. "Don't you take medication to prevent attacks?" I asked and he said he did but in recent days he had become so interested in his new whereabouts, he had forgotten to take it.

"Did you feel the attack coming?" I asked, and he said he did. He said he felt a strange aura just prior to the attack. This was the first seizure I had ever seen and it struck me as dangerous.

River Life

"You could've fallen overboard. If you sensed it coming, why didn't you warn me?"

"*No tuve tiempo, talvez,*" he answered simply. I didn't have time, I guess.

Several years later, I learned that Alberto was more a revolutionary than I had suspected. He had flunked out of the university and went to Bogotá. One evening he was placing a bomb in an oil refinery jointly owned by the United States and the Colombian governments, called Ecopetrol. In the excitement of the moment, after setting the timing device, he evidently suffered another epileptic seizure and dropped the bomb, which later exploded and killed him.

He rested the remainder of the afternoon as we continued down the vast river, and stopped at a small house at the end of the day to ask for lodging. We were happy to be welcomed by some friendly *Caboclos,* a blood-cross between Indian and Portuguese Brazilian. The head of the house, named José, was a diminutive man with a whale of a wife. She stood over him and easily doubled his weight, with ponderous breasts and an angry demeanor. Despite this, he seemed very relaxed and of good humor. We asked if he had anything to eat that we could buy and I was delighted to see him bring out a huge smoked fish called a *pacu.* It weighed at least fifteen pounds, was slab-sided and golden from smoke. I pulled off the skin of one side right in the boat, as we were ravenously hungry. The skin was as stiff as cardboard and, other than noting a two-inch long brown cockroach scurrying out from beneath the skin, the meat seemed healthy and in perfect condition. We each pulled off handfuls of the smoked meat and it was wonderful in flavor. We filled up, ate stale bread and drank hot beer from worn, brown bottles to wash it down. It was one of the best meals I had in the Amazon.

Gravity My Enemy

Later, we climbed the steep bank and went into José's house to string up our hammocks for the night. As darkness quickly descended, as it does in the tropics, they lit small pitch lamps, fashioned from tin cans, with a wick and set them on several little shelves on the wall for the purpose. We sat in the flickering light and joked as bats lazily fluttered around the room in front of our faces, catching mosquitoes.

The people of this area spoke a combination of Portuguese and Tipu, a widespread Indian language used throughout the Amazon. José wasn't much more than five feet in stature, and very active, walked with the gait of a simian and exhibited the facial expression of a mischievous schoolboy. He was obviously very proud of his huge wife. As she lumbered by between us, he made graphic, lewd gestures behind her for our benefit. As she entered the kitchen area, he reached over to the table and picked up a tiny, flat pink pillow with white ruffles, and gestured how it was good to put this under his wife's ass during sex. We all chortled as I wondered what advantage such a small pillow could afford such an elephantine woman, when she suddenly exploded from the kitchen, huffing like a bull and cuffed José sharply over the head. She was very angry and repeatedly hit him with ham-sized fists until he slid to the floor, visibly hurt and flinching. Our uncontrolled mirth made her even angrier, as she kicked him heavily in the ribs before storming out of the room.

The following day, after a night made miserable by mosquitoes, we were back on the river and it was late afternoon. As usual, we were in a stupor from the heat and boredom of traveling along the endless waterways. The foliage on the shores was too distant to appreciate sightseeing and we

River Life

had long ago learned that wildlife is rarely seen on the Amazon as we had seen in the movies, with the exception of birds and the occasional splash of a fish. There was a throbbing noise I noticed only gradually as we proceeded and, as soon as I became aware of it, I felt alarmed that perhaps something was wrong with the outboard. This was certainly no place to have mechanical troubles. We hadn't seen a single motorized boat in days. I turned to gesture at Beleño about the motor but his bored countenance made no response. Yet the rhythmic throbbing continued.

A minute later, we came to a narrow opening from the main river, to our right, and turned in. The noise was now louder. Perhaps he noticed it all along, I thought, and was pulling in a safe harbor to look at the problem. We came into a small, placid lagoon that was idyllic in its loveliness. Thick, tall forest surrounded us as we gaped in wonder, and to our left were three small, tan houses with thatched roofs. As we approached, he cut the motor and I realized for the first time that the throbbing noise came from the houses, now quite loud. Inside, some fiesta was in process. We could hear the pounding of drums and strumming of guitars in a strange, haunting melody that had primeval jungle origins, as does much Brazilian music. The prow of the boat bumped the shore where steps had been cut out of the bank, and we got out.

Two lanky *Caboclos* arrived with beaming smiles and gestured us in. When we entered the gloom of the house from which the noise came, we could see two, wildly gyrating male dancers going around the room in synch to the beat of the drums and the guitars. They were leaping from one footfall to another, stomping their feet loudly on the wooden floor and coming within

179

Gravity My Enemy

inches of colliding with spectators sitting on wooden benches around the room. It was a scene unlike anything I had seen. I sat in the doorway entranced and slightly fearful of the violence of the dance. There could not have been more than a dozen people present but they were happy and totally engrossed. I learned that this had been going on, non-stop, for two days. The music was wonderful, with typical Brazilian rhythm, imitating sounds of the jungle with the percussion of rasping night insects, along with the tones from the stringed instruments. My first thought was that of regret that this was not being recorded.

During a short lull, I was invited to pass through the room and back to the kitchen area. One fellow, with a broad smile, handed me a tiny nutshell the size of a golf ball and poured from a gourd a spoonful of dark liquid into it. I thanked him as best I could and swallowed it down. It was hot in temperature and tasted a little like chocolate dissolved in water, rather pleasant-tasting. I was mildly surprised that the serving had been so Spartan and playfully held out my cup and motioned for more. They all wagged their forefinger side-to-side so as to say no. Curious, I insisted in a joking manner. Once again, they emphatically refused, while laughing amicably. With equal jocularity, I again insisted. This time, amid hysterical laughter, they served me another spoonful, which I tossed down.

That was the last thing I remembered.

Much later, I awoke with a grogginess and stupor I had rarely felt in my life. I was lying diagonally in a broad hammock and all was now quiet, the party over. Beleño in time came up to me, smiling his dirty teeth, and said, *"Al fin se despierta!"* Awake at last. I asked how long I had

180

River Life

been out and he held up two fingers in my face and said, incredulously,

"*Dos dias!*"

Could this be? I had no recollection of falling asleep or passing out, or of a hangover or any ill effect, but it became obvious to me why those follows had refused me the second drink. I to this day do not know what it was I drank, but it did not seem alcoholic or fermented, so I have to assume is was some narcotic.

These were extremely friendly and happy people, living as they did in utter isolation and total self-sufficiency. They had found ways to lead a happy life, did no harm to anyone or their environment and seemed very healthy. All were kind and light-hearted, and it was with some sadness that we left.

Coming out onto the Amazon from the protected lagoon gave us a rude awakening, as the water was quite rough and we almost swamped. Shortly after emerging onto the river, we violently ran aground on a hidden sandbar and I was thrown into the water. It was fairly shallow and my companions fished me out in a moment, choking, but glad I didn't drown.

A few hours later we reached the little village of Santa Rita.

It was like arriving to a modern country. Much to our surprise, sitting atop tall mud banks was a cluster of clapboard houses painted white, with zinc roofs, surrounded by a carefully groomed lawn. We climbed the bank and were greeted by a Canadian missionary, who was a physician. He put us up in cots with comfortable mattresses. I spent the afternoon talking with him about the local Indians and the area. He explained his mission was primarily that of doctoring, with a Christian message. He had a small line of Indians he was

Gravity My Enemy

injecting with penicillin for a disease called
pinta, which causes a loss of pigment, leaving
large, pink splotches on the skin, mostly the
hands and face. That night, under an oil lamp,
I read for hours from books he had collected on
the Amazon, and learned that the Amazon Basin
was really a very poor area with surprisingly
infertile soil. In fact, the area had suffered
severe famine throughout history, which was
responsible for their custom of developing food,
like cassava, from ordinarily toxic plants. I also
learned that the trees, as gigantic as they were,
had very shallow root systems, which explained
why we occasionally heard a huge tropical giant
crashing to the jungle floor in the night, despite
no wind.

The next morning, the missionary's wife
served us American-style pancakes with maple
syrup, in sharp contrast to what we had been
eating, and a delightful change.

As we loaded the boat to leave and waved
good-byes, we changed our course to return to
Leticia. Alberto and Luis had to return to start
classes. The trip upriver was lengthy and arduous,
and after what seemed an interminable journey,
we finally arrived in Leticia. We found a small
sleeping facility, had supper silently, and went to
sleep. They had a plane to catch the next morning.
I was staying, as I had hopes of visiting the Yagua
tribe without these kids, who had become a real
aggravation. The next morning I awoke to an empty
room. They had already departed, stole most of my
belongings and left me with the hotel bill.

Glad to be free despite the trickery, I saw
Mike later and asked him about the possibility
of visiting the Yaguas. They lived in scattered
communities far north for the most part, not a
frequent destination for his forays, but he felt

182

River Life

he could perhaps justify a trip the following week if I was willing to hang around. I was excited and accepted, as these Indians were virtually untouched by civilization, living out of the influence of whites.

In the meantime, I spent my time in Leticia and made occasional trips with Mike to surrounding areas. One day, we were hunting and he showed me some huge water lilies that measured about five feet across.

"They can support the weight of a small child," he said.

On another day, some photographers had come from a newspaper and some United States magazine publication to take pictures of the Amazon. They accompanied Mike on a caiman hunt one night and he dutifully leapt overboard to capture a large caiman for their cameras but they were unable, we found later, to get good pictures of the fray in the water at night. Since they were disappointed, Mike offered to give them a picture-taking opportunity with him wrestling a large anaconda.

They were very excited as they set out the following morning. So was I. The anaconda is a water boa, a constrictor, reported to be the largest snake in the world. For the purpose, Mike took along a large snake he had in his zoo, loaded it and one helper and all of us in the town's jeep. We headed out to the outskirts of town and pulled up to a small mud flat and got out. The fight was to be staged, but I was still anxious to see the event. The photographers got their cameras ready.

Mike waded out into the mud, which reached to just below his knees, with the snake and the helper. They carried the anaconda in a large bag and then, noticing the newsmen were ready, dumped it out heavily into the mud. It immediately

Gravity My Enemy

started to slither away and Mike jumped on it. As he did so, it began wrapping around his body with thick, glistening coils. He made to fight with it as it coiled around him more. The photographers were snapping pictures. Mike and the snake were totally covered with slime. One coil wrapped around Mike's face. The photographers were busily snapping away but something seemed wrong. Mike was pinned down by the snake, unable to move, and made a muffled noise. His helper soon realized that Mike was genuinely in trouble, and jumped in to pry the coil off his face. This was quite a task, as the strength of a sixteen-foot anaconda is beyond belief. They can easily kill a deer or a large pig, by tightening their coils each time the luckless victim lets out air, essentially suffocating the animal. Mike prevented this with his arms (and having a helper nearby) but one coil had gotten one of his arms and another across his face would not let him breathe. As this thick coil was finally pried off his face, he gasped in desperation, and finally escaped. He said later, laughing and covered with mud, that he was suffocating as he could see the photographers happily snapping away.

"At least it was realistic," he said, as they bagged the snake and we headed back to town.

12 The Yaguas

The day finally came to head out for the Yaguas. I was beside myself with excitement. It would be the first time in my life I would see a totally primitive people, the fulfillment of a dream from boyhood. We were about to enter virtually uncharted country. The boat was loaded to the gunwales with cages, several 55-gallon drums of gasoline, cardboard boxes of canned goods and a

stack of cases of pop. We carefully packed a large supply of trade items such as harpoon points, fish hooks and monofilament, glass beads, mirrors,

Gravity My Enemy

pots and other sundry items. I asked Mike how long the trip would take and he said it would be about two days. He had an airboat, Everglades style, with a Lycoming engine that almost flew at sixty miles per hour and it took him well over an hour with that, just to reach the first of several settlements.

This time, happily, Beleño and I set out alone. I had no trouble averting boredom on this particular journey. My mind was alive with visions of what I was about to see. The river we traveled was so narrow that the trees met at the middle and formed a tunnel, making it so bird life was virtually on top of us. On the shore in the small clearings we spotted several large mammals, mostly the capybara with its characteristic Chinese face.

Nearing the end of the first day, on the dark, placid river, we spotted two large canoes loaded with Indians, all furiously paddling to outdistance us. The outboard proved too much for them, however, and after much gesturing, they reluctantly heaved to as we pulled alongside one canoe. I had told Beleño previously that much beyond hunting, I was very interested in collecting Indian artifacts. As we held onto the gunwale of the canoe, Beleño told them what I was after in their dialect. They were extremely fearful of us, showing it in their faces. Little children cried. Beleño's demeanor with them was threatening and abusive. I asked him to ease up, but he used his authority as representing the White Guy to be imposing. It occurred to me the irony that he also was Indian. Most of the Indians in both canoes had necklaces made of little black shells ranging in size from a marble to the size of a golf ball. These were beautifully carved to depict different animals — alligators, turtles, beetles and monkeys. The necklaces also had monkey

The Yaguas

jaws with teeth, iridescent green beetle wings and small balsawood plugs wrapped with bright yellow and red feathers. They were breathtakingly beautiful. The Indians stripped their women and children of all the bracelets and necklaces. One little girl, perhaps five years old, was fearfully hiding a little necklace she wore with her hands. A man next to her pulled her hands away to reveal a lovely miniature of those they had already given me, and took it from her as she cried. This was too much for me. I did not come here to add to the many abuses these people had suffered over the centuries at the hands of whites. I was tempted to return all the booty I already had and, in fact, made a gesture to do so, but everyone protested and insisted I keep everything. One man even handed me a small, beautifully carved canoe paddle, which I gratefully accepted. I then told Beleño to get into our supplies and give them whatever they most needed and wanted. He got bags of salt and handed out small breads. I uncapped sodas and handed them all around, noticing they kept the empty bottles.

I grasped hands all around with a smile, and we pushed off and left the canoes behind. I looked back after a few moments and saw them, paddling once again in the distance and they soon disappeared behind a bend in the river. I think I was more shaken by the experience than they were. They had been "wild" Ticunas, living far from white towns and influence, much as they had done for centuries.

I learned that this tribe was noted for producing the best-quality curare in the area, the dart poison used for hunting. Their curare was so valued that it was actually used as currency in that area of the Amazon, and came in different strengths or values, much like coins of different

Gravity My Enemy

denominations. In their language, these strengths were called "One-tree curare," "Two-tree curare," "Three-tree curare," and so on, referring to how quickly a monkey would fall out of a tree after being hit. Blowgun darts are no bigger than knitting needles, fashioned from the center vein of a palm frond. They of themselves inflict little instant damage. Since the rain forest is so dense, it is important to be able to retrieve game without a lot of searching, thus the need for poison. Surprisingly, the poison that kills animals to eat has no effect on the person later eating it, as I found out from personal experience after eating many birds and monkeys killed with curare. Curare functions as a muscle relaxant and paralyzes the diaphragm, leading to asphyxiation. I had many occasions later to be with Indians of different tribes in the Amazon as they hunted with curare, and even saw it made. Monkeys shot with poison arrows often required several darts to bring them down, while birds usually dropped out of the canopy like ripe fruit. Curare has been synthesized by the scientific community to use in heart and eye surgery, and plays an important part in modern-day medicine, as do many drugs that have been derived from Amazon peoples. Some curares evidently have different recipes but the type I witnessed made came from the bark scrapings of a thick, twisted vine of the genus *Strychnos*. This is scraped onto an open banana leaf and then wrapped into a funnel, which is tied to two spears thrust into the ground so the funnel is placed above a small pot. Spitting water into the funnel begins a percolation process and the dark fluid drips slowly into the pot. This is later boiled and thickened in viscosity. The skin at the top is used to coat the dart tips, which are stacked crisscross in the smoke of the fire

The Yaguas

to dry. During the entire procedure, the Indians sing incantations to give power to the concoction. The scum used on the darts is often applied first to a piece of broken ceramic in which monkey meat has been boiled.

I once asked a Huaorani from Ecuador if curare could kill a man. He said it probably could but in the strength they commonly used for hunting, an accidental prick would merely make someone sick. Whether true or not, I made a special effort to always stay clear of the poisoned darts, which are distinguishable as having about an inch or so of the tip a shiny, dark varnished appearance.

We plied our way up the river towards the Yaguas as the waterway became ever smaller and more interesting, the trees towering overhead and providing a deep shade that added mystery and great beauty to the area. The water surface was now like a mirror and quite beautiful. Fish shot out into the air in groups, trying to escape unseen predators in the depths below. Now, unlike the hot, open Amazon, we began to see much more wildlife. Groups of black howler monkeys bent branches over as they sought fruits, while white-bibbed toco toucans flew from one tree to the other in succession, their big yellow bills thrust out in front. Beleño pointed out several things to me I usually could not see and could not discern what he was referring to. Once, however, a small disturbance on the water surface revealed a huge fish, perhaps the length of a person. This was the huge *pirarucu*. Several times we saw a line of capybara heads crossing the river. They had a face like a giant chipmunk with odd, oriental eyes.

As it became almost completely dark, we pulled over to the shore and tied the boat to an overhanging tree next to the muddy bank. The river seemed to be higher than the Amazon for

Gravity My Enemy

some reason, or the banks lower. We each ate a
can of sardines in tomato sauce with a couple
pieces of bread, and drank a warm, syrupy pop
with flavor I could not describe. All was done
under a flashlight. Beleño strung up a mosquito
bar for each of us with saplings cut from the
overhead tree and we spread duffels underneath to
serve as padding for mattresses. Shortly, we were
both asleep amid night calls.

I awoke very early the next morning while
Beleño was still snoring loudly, his head thrown
back and his mouth agape, revealing rotted teeth.
I picked up an empty sardine can from the bottom
of the boat and attached a short length of light
monofilament to the curled lid, and tossed the
can into the water alongside the boat. I held it
just below the surface to observe what it might
attract. Within seconds, a myriad of tiny, colorful
fish were wiggling inside to get at the miniscule
morsels of sardine, and I pulled it out to see
them up close. I recognized a species I had once
bought in pet stores in the United States for an
aquarium I had at the time in the college dorm.
They were neon tetras, rather expensive, as I
recall, and stunningly beautiful, blue and red —
almost electric in intensity, as the name implies.
My companion finally awoke and, with no hesitation,
stood up to take a leak over the side and quickly
started the motor to continue our journey.

We traveled almost the entire next day,
stopping occasionally only to fill the gas tank.
Though the trip itself was uneventful, I found
it extremely exciting and more fulfilling of my
dreams of adventure than traveling on the Amazon
itself. There was virtually no boat traffic other
than an occasional small canoe quietly paddled
by a brown Indian or two and no houses. The bird

The Yaguas

and animal life was far more frequently witnessed and the narrow breadth of the waterway, with the giant, towering trees overhead, many adorned with electric-hued flowers, was a constant source of wonder to me. It was like traveling through a huge cathedral. My only regret was the need to use a noisy outboard, which precluded hearing the natural sounds of animals and warned them and, everybody else, of our approach long before we were seen. All along the river, I was also surprised that the water continued to be a coffee-au-lait color. I had always imagined the rivers of the Amazon to be clear, but this turned out to be the exception. Making the serpentine twists and turns as we proceeded north was always intriguing, revealing new, unseen landscapes as we came around each bend.

There was at least some element of danger. Though we told Mike of our destination, it would be many days before he realized we were in any kind of trouble, should there be a mechanical breakdown or snakebite. Though very capable in my young years, as handicapped as I was, I doubted I could start the motor, refuel and handle such a trip by myself if anything were to happen to Beleño, and I had no illusions about getting such help from an Indian.

The Indians themselves in some regions were suspected as being hostile to outsiders.

One tribe south of Leticia and very close had lived for decades undetected, as they lived away from the river (the Yavarí, in this case, which I later explored, which formed the border between Brazil and Peru) and out of sight. When an occasional white or *caboclo* disappeared, it was never attributed to any action from any tribe until they were later discovered in 1965, a year after this particular story took place. The Yaguas had been reported to be friendly but at this time were still

Gravity My Enemy

mostly unknown. No one knew for sure what their conduct would be under different circumstances, and I was deeply troubled by Beleño's coarseness and insensitivity with the Ticunas down river. It was not only an issue of cultural decency, I mused as we motored along the dark river, but a matter of our very survival. Beleño had become arrogant from his experience with whites and, as happens even among Native Americans in the United States, those most abused become the most abusive to their own people once they feel they have the authority. His meekness while in the company of whites became overbearing when with his own people, as he had shown so clearly. One misstep with an entire village far from white dominance could result in a tragedy for us. Intertribal revenge killings were common among many Amazonian tribes, such as the Yanomami and Huaorani, and earlier, the Ashuaras (Jívaros as they are known to modern society), the famed headhunters of the Pastaza River region in Eastern Ecuador. In my limited experience and readings, I was of the firm belief that we had much to learn from these people and the only approach was to show humility and respect, rather than trying to impress them with the technology of our culture. They may be impressed with the sounds from a tape recorder or a radio, or the light produced from a flashlight in the night, but virtually none of us in our society could ever produce one of these implements with our own hands. So claiming some sort of ownership or proudly acting as the inventor really made no sense and was not fair, when one considered that virtually every single thing these people have and use is of their own making. If we were ever to find ourselves in a life-threatening situation, it was these people who would be our only salvation. We could never lose sight of that, I thought to myself as we passed under the canopy of the dark trees. Never.

192

The Yaguas

It was getting darker as we came to a spot in the river where there were several canoes pulled up onto the shore. This was our destination, it was revealed, as Beleño slowed and nosed the boat over amongst the canoes and cut the motor. After two days of travel we had finally reached the Yaguas. The silence was deafening.

Standing above us on a tangle of worn tree roots were six Yaguas. My heart jumped involuntarily. They showed no friendliness. The noise of our motor had obviously alerted them to our presence long before this moment, which obviously had brought them to where they presently were standing. In the shadow, they appeared darker in the face than other Indians I had seen. The men wore orange-colored grass skirts. Some had a similar grass piece hanging below their necks as a large necklace of sorts. They were quite muscular and of short stature, and all had Buster Brown haircuts, cut evenly at ear level. They looked upon us quietly. It occurred to me at that moment that I was the only white man present, and I felt a slight involuntary shudder go through my body. All carried a cluster of spears, bows and harpoons.

Beleño unceremoniously jumped out of the boat and grabbed my folded wheelchair, unfolding it on the bank, and gesturing that he needed help to get me out. This was the moment of truth, I realized. With an audible sigh of relief, I noticed that they all approached, waded into the water and between them hefted me to the shore into the wheelchair.

This was incredible. They had no idea what a wheelchair was, I was sure, or of my affliction, but pitched in naturally as though they had an instinctive desire to come to the aid of someone in need. That had to be one of the most revealing

Gravity My Enemy

and incredible moments of my life, regarding human nature in its simplest form.

More incredible still was the help I received from them to get into their village, which was several hundred yards inland. The whole route was a mass of heavy roots over water. They each grabbed hold of a different part of my wheelchair and literally carried me to their village as a litter as they traversed the root system, stepping nimbly from one to another without missing a step.

Another thing I quickly learned was that stealing, as we know it, is impossible among such people, in a manner of speaking. I soon found that everything is community property in the simplest definition of Communism. Each person produces and does his or her share, and each uses whatever is needed to maintain life. If the hunter kills a paca, it belongs to the community as a whole and no one asks or is invited to eat. If another needs a bow or harpoon, he simply takes it from the bow or harpoon maker, though he just as often makes his own. Thus there is no jealousy or envy, no stinginess or selfishness.

I found out that all our pop belonged to everybody, no matter how I objected, and after a taste for the sweet stuff had been acquired, the entire stack of cases I had brought in order to avoid drinking river water was gone in the first two or three days. In the days that followed, I found myself enjoying drinking river water, loaded with parasites, right out of the split gourds we used to bail the boat. And loving its flavor. (In months to follow, I would find myself engaged in a desperate medical effort to overcome a severe protozoa infection that almost cost me my life.)

Life with the Yaguas was as in a paradise. I lay each day, sleepy-eyed, in a hammock, gazing

The Yaguas

out below the thatched roof which was dripping
with rain at the eave, and watching children
play outside. A young girl might bring me chunks
of browned caiman, steaming hot and pure-white,
incredibly flavorful, with extremely sweet coffee.
The bread was long-gone but we ate granulated
farinha and liked it. Tiny wild bananas picked
from the forest were sweet and delicious, no more
than three inches long. Smoked monkey meat was
tough and stringy but tasty, though when whole it
looked like a small baby. Fish was abundant and
we ate big slabs of it in all forms. Incredible,
strange, exotic fruits with unbelievable flavors
were brought in daily and I thoroughly enjoyed them
all, with few exceptions. We ate turtle, snakes,
big lizards and animals I could not identify, many
of them simply tossed into the fire with the hair
on and the innards not removed. We broke them
open and picked out the meat. We ate, but I could
never accept, fat, white wood grubs the size of
a man's thumb, roasted in the fire and somewhat
resembling in taste a chunk of semi-raw bacon.
We laughed and joked and gesticulated. Life was
simple and the language barrier was really no
barrier at all, since what we had to "talk" about
were things we already intimately knew — food,
animals, fish, rain, sex, thirst and sleepiness.
They were good people and I saw no signs of those
sentiments that clutter up a more complicated
society like animosity, lusting, coveting, greed
or dishonesty, because there was no way these
feelings could exist under the circumstances.

Despite my vow to hide modern implements,
they knew what a shotgun was and I used it
frequently to make life easier for everyone.
I also used a headlamp and we got into the
routine of going out in a canoe at night to
hunt. The canoe driven with paddles was far

Gravity My Enemy

more silent and our gasoline supply was limited. I had brought boxes of flashlight batteries and used the headlamp only for hunting, with me sitting in the bow as a friend or two in back paddled. In the daytime, we went out in canoes to harpoon fish and caiman. They made a strong bow from an ironwood palm called *chonta*, which also produced

The Yaguas

a red fruit they enjoyed. The black, fibrous wood was as tough as steel. They shot arrow-harpoons with the bow, nailing fish on the surface. These had detachable heads and were connected to the long cane shaft, wrapped with a long cord. When an animal or fish was harpooned, the head came off, unwound the cord, which was previously wrapped around the shaft, and off it would go. By paddling quickly, we caught up with the floating shaft and hauled the prize in hand over hand.

With the shotgun and also poison darts, we downed gorgeous blue and yellow macaws, worth thousands of dollars each in U.S. pet stores, and ate them. Though they were often very tough, the flavor was much like duck. Toucans of equal value were less appealing.

Throughout the Amazon, wild yucca or cassava is a staple. From this comes tapioca, but I have no idea how this is accomplished.

It's a tuber much like potato or sweet potato, but with fibers running through it and more transparent when cooked. To plant it, they simply poke pieces of cuttings from the plant into the ground and let them grow. In time, they rip the big tubers from the ground, peel them, cut them into pieces and do with them whatever they are making at the time. I never liked the tuber in a soup. The Indians of different tribes make the farinha to which I had become accustomed, a grainy, crunchy meal that is dry and rather flavorful once one acquires a taste for it. They also make with cassava a thin, large cake on a griddle. This, when cooled, is cut or broken into pieces and I enjoyed it browned and toasted over the fire. It is so hard one can break a tooth. Another widespread favorite of most Amazonian tribes is to cook cassava in pieces and, after cooled, the older women gather around much like a quilting bee, and chew it up

Gravity My Enemy

thoroughly and spit it into a pot. This is covered with a big banana leaf, which is firmly tied in place and set aside to ferment into a thick beer. Different tribes give it different names, the most common being *masato* or *nijimanche.* Nearer white villages, it is called *chicha* but this term is also given to any type of home brew, be it from sugar cane or cassava. Psychologically, I could not deal with this, but it is very popular among all tribes of the Amazon.

I was never a witness to my knowledge, but was made to understand that the Yaguas burned the bones of their deceased and in ash form mixed it with a banana drink. This they would drink in a spiritual gesture of ingesting ancestors to perpetuate the positive characteristics of the people. Of course, my understanding of the details of much of what they did was cloudy and no doubt inaccurate.

The activities in which we engaged together, like hunting and fishing, were easy to understand. One day, we went out in several canoes with women and children and worked our way up a small, shallow river.

While the women went into the bush to cut some vines, the men fashioned a dam below us with branches. This was intended to block the passage of fish while allowing the water to flow through. When the women finished cutting pieces of this particular vine, they pounded them with rocks on a log in the stream. This released a milky substance into the water. Below, and after a time, everyone gathered at the dam with spears and bows with thin, reedy harpoons. Fish started to appear, floating belly-up and otherwise appearing to be ailing, and as they feebly finned on the surface, the people gathered them with the harpoons and even by hand, and tossed them into baskets and

The Yaguas

the canoes. They collected several dozen fish, each up to a foot long.

Evidently, the substance produced from the vine was a poison. Though I cannot recall the name used by the Yaguas, I later heard it called *barbasco*. If it is a poison, it like curare, has no ill effect on the consumer, perhaps due to being neutralized by stomach enzymes.

It always amazed me how these people had learned over the millennia to derive all their needs so efficiently from their surroundings.

How did they learn of these things? Was it by accident, an incredible amount of experimentation, observing animals? They had no predecessors and their history does not exceed twenty thousand years as cultures in other parts of the world, so who and what could they learn from? How many perished in the process? I wondered how much we could really learn from these people if we took the time and had the patience to do so, without arriving with a mission, to impose our ways on them, or evangelize them with our beliefs. How much had we cheated our own society by cheating these people over the last few hundred years? How much longer were they as a culture going to endure under the onslaught of exploitation and tourism?

Years later, living in Lake Geneva, Wisconsin, I met a lady who claimed to have gone to the Amazon and brought back Indian artifacts. Curious, I asked her if she would show me her collection and tell me about her experiences. She invited me to her home. It turns out she owned a tourist business and was given an "inside tour" of Amazonia given to tourist agents so they would later sell tour packages.

One item she brought out to show me was a blowgun. It was crude and unused, shorter than the usual eight feet. The blowguns of different tribes in the Amazon are often distinguishable in that they have different shapes and styles of mouthpiece, which is often carved from wood. The Yagua use a mouthpiece shaped like an hourglass, which is very distinctive from other tribes. I immediately recognized this blowgun she brought out as being Yagua. How had she gotten it? I asked. While touring several villages near Leticia, they went to one village and were offered a large assortment of artifacts made for tourists. She bought it with local cash. I felt physically sick in my stomach. Had these remote, previously unknown people been reduced to this kind of existence? I was afraid of the answer. This red-haired woman had donned Eddie Bauer khakis and entered this sanctuary with a gang of other tourist agents. How devastated I felt! How lucky I felt to have lived with these people before white contact.

Back at the Yagua village one day, a man from the house I was living in gathered a coil of rope with a huge shark hook attached to a heavy chain. This, in turn, had an old, rusty car gear attached to add weight. The night before, I had shot two or three black caiman and after cleaning, had left the legs outside the house. He cut off a large hind leg and thrust the point of the hook into the meaty part, and walked off toward the river. I asked for help from a couple nearby fellows to follow him. When we finally arrived at the shore, my friend was casually paddling his small canoe out into the middle of the river. When he got there, he tossed the baited hook into the depths, and began paddling back, the rope unwinding and playing out as he came. Once he heaved the canoe up on the shore, he brought the remaining coil up on the bank. To the end was attached a short

The Yaguas

length of log about eight inches thick, and this
aided him in securing the end to a tree of about
equal size. With little concern, he returned to
the village. I sat with my helpers, anxiously
watching. Hours passed. I fell asleep. There is
a lethargy that invades one's body and psyche in
the Amazon, and time stops as we know it. After
weeks, one soon finds himself absently staring off
into space, thinking of nothing, doing nothing,
planning nothing, much as though this were an
illness or subtle fever.

After some time, I awoke or became aware of
some quiet talk, and raised my gaze to notice the
men gesturing to the tree to which the rope was
lashed. At first, I could see nothing. In a moment,
I noticed an almost imperceptible movement and
I realized that the rope was taught! The tree
shuddered more, and another soon joined the two
men. With muscles bulging, they hauled in unison,
like sailors on an ancient deck, and gradually
brought the fish to the shore. Finally, much to my
excitement, they hauled a big, black catfish onto
the shore and quickly dispatched it with a club.
It had a reddish hue on the belly and I figured it
to weigh at least a hundred and fifty pounds. This
must be the *valentón* I had heard so much about,
reported to swallow small children caught playing
on the shoreline. But, like much in the Amazon,
there was an abundance of fantastic tales, and it
was hard to separate truth from legend.

When we arrived back to Leticia weeks later,
I felt I was entering a totally different, unclean
world of disease, corruption, filth and stink.
Everything was abhorrent to me. It was amazing to
me how, only a few short weeks earlier I had arrived
here, excited, and considered Leticia the most
primitive outpost of my life's experience. Now, it
was like the Big City without the conveniences.

Gravity My Enemy

People greeted us with some alarm, asking if we had seen a group of men from a German lumber prospecting company while we were with the Yaguas. I said we had not.

A small group was surveying tree species, evidently just north of our location with the Yaguas and three of them had been killed, five others wounded, in an Indian attack. The prospectors had no doubt passed our village late in the night without our noticing. The Indians were reported to have been Yaguas, although this to me seemed incredible, given the peacefulness and friendliness we had experienced. (Beleño, much to my relief, had behaved himself admirably.)

How had this happened? My only guess was, from the way I had seen grizzled, white tourists behave with locals, some disrespectful lumber prospector, no doubt with a bellyful of local *chicha,* got abusive with one of the Yagua women and the men later took revenge.

I was very upset to hear that the Brazilians intended to send a boatload of soldiers to the spot — to do what, I could only guess, but for sure it was not going to be even as well-intended as fundamentalist evangelism. Even in the Twentieth Century, after all we have learned, all our history and self-righteous proclamations, history repeats itself. *De nobis fabula narratur.*

13 Takeoff

I t was getting late and I feared I might miss the plane back to Bogotá. I had been in the Amazon area at the juncture between Colombia, Brazil and Peru for over two months and as much as I loved it, I now desperately wanted to get back to air conditioning and the modern world. There would not be another flight for almost a week.

I sat in the passenger's seat of the vintage jeep. There was no door and, in fact, the seat was fashioned with boards and a folded blanket as a cushion. The rusty jeep sped along the dirt road, raising billows of dust behind it. The driver slammed on the brakes suddenly and we careened into the airport. This was a single concrete block building that had once been white but now had green rain streaks on the walls, from the flat roof to ground level. Most of the windows were broken and, as far as I could tell from my limited experience there, the building itself served no purpose as I never saw it used. Most ticketing and delivery of cargo was done right on the tarmac in the glare of the sun, next to the plane.

The aircraft was painted with the colors of the Colombian air force, FAC, the rudder representing the colors of the flag: the top half of the rudder yellow, and the bottom half blue with red on the bottom. The rest of the plane was silver, with the letters Fuerza Aérea Colombiana painted in black above the windows. It was a C-54, to civilians, a DC-4. I earlier learned that it was used as part of the Berlin Airlift that made history when it hauled virtually everything, including coal, into Berlin after the Russians blockaded the city following the Second World War.

Gravity My Enemy

Its tired radial engines dripped black oil on the pavement below them but otherwise, the craft looked sturdy enough and seemed to possess all its parts. It gave an almost-animal sense of poised power, awaiting the deft hand that would make it roar into the sky.

The jeep pulled right up to the boarding ladder, and the driver, a worker for friend Mike Tsalickis who was a resident in Leticia, yanked out my folded wheelchair from the back and helped me into it. As always in Colombia, there were several willing fellows in soiled overall jumpsuits willing to hoist me up into the plane. Once seated, I maneuvered my way past a pile of cargo that was strapped down in the center aisle. I quickly transferred over onto a canvas-and-aluminum bench seat on the starboard side that ran the length of the inside fuselage. The interior was hot as an oven.

In time, several other passengers warily climbed in through the door, looking inside in some confusion and sweaty fear, and timidly found a place to sit. Almost all of them were full-blooded Indians of short stature, with straight, black hair. My guess was that not a single one of them had ever flown in an airplane before. Little did they know it, but they had good reason for fear.

It was suffocating inside. The outer aluminum skin of the huge plane pinged and popped in the sun, and inside we sweltered as we waited.

Finally, the jeep pulled up outside and the silhouette of a man in a tropical khaki air force uniform appeared in the opening through which I had entered moments before. From his bearing of authority and Ray Ban sunglasses, it was obvious he was the pilot. He wore a neatly pressed short-sleeved khaki shirt that already

Takeoff

had dark sweat stains in the armpits, an envelope cap smartly cocked on his head sporting a shiny air force insignia.

Following close behind were his co-pilot and a rather dumpy man who was definitely not military, with food-stained, wrinkled pants that looked like they had been slept in for many days, his shirttail hanging out, and a growth of dark beard about four days' old.

"What's all this?" the pilot waved his arm at the long pile of cargo. It was about two feet high and ran from the back door where they stood almost to the bulkhead behind the cabin, with barely enough space to pass into the cabin. The pilot was indignant and obviously irritated, as one is who discovers people trying to pull a fast one.

In mute response, the disheveled man handed him a clipboard, as though it carried some authority in and of itself.

The pilot held it up to the light, squinting at the ledger momentarily, following with his finger down to the bottom of the page and, in a sudden outburst, exploded, "What?! You expect us to carry all this?!"

He was incredulous. He walked forward in the passenger compartment, scrutinizing the multi-shaped mountain of dried, bound fish, caiman skins, crated machinery and vast quantities of twined cardboard boxes. The dumpy man followed close on the pilot's heels as he urgently jabbered and gesticulated.

"From this point back," the pilot now shouted, "I want all this removed. His hand was palm open in a chopping motion at the point in the pile he indicated. He was accustomed to having his orders followed without hesitation, as are most officers, especially in the Latin American military.

Gravity My Enemy

When the dispatcher hesitated, he barked, "All of it! Quickly! We have to get going!" He made hand motions for the agent to move into action.

The sweaty agent was unabashed — he was the dispatcher for the air force line called SATENA at the Leticia airport, and as such, was also used to giving orders and being surrounded by people, pleading for help. He protested, naming names of people who were supposed to sound important, "El Doctor So-and-So" and "El Señor Enrique González" (obviously someone of importance) and La Compañía are expecting this, and (he waved the clipboard in the pilot's face as proof) "this is machinery for repair — they have been waiting for it since last month, *Mi teniente,* we cannot delay this anymore!!"

"No!" responded the pilot emphatically.

"Our capacity is just so many kilos." he explained, probably for the tenth time, "and this exceeds that by far more than what is safe in this heat and density altitude," giving technical terms. "Don't even dream of sending all this on this flight!" he said with surprising calm. "Out with it!" and he made a sweeping motion with his palm.

To my astonishment, the dispatcher persisted. He either was too stupid to understand weight and balance rules in aircraft or he felt that he could persuade the pilot to overlook them. He was red-faced and sweating heavily, his hair hanging in his face. Could he have a personal, vested interest in getting this load to the capital? He was waving his arms, arguing and gesturing.

"The plane cannot take such a load," the pilot said evenly, as though talking to a child. "It'll be unstable. It'll crash!" he said the word that is never even whispered aboard any plane, any more than one says "bomb" in a U.S. airport. All of us were horrified, thinking to ourselves,

Takeoff

"Let's stop this! Get it off the plane! Get US off the plane!"

The pilot stood there patiently. And calmly in a low tone said, "It can't be done. Get them to offload it. Quickly — we can't afford to waste more time. It'll be dark before we get to Bogotá.

"I'm not in the mood to fly in the mountains after dark! Now, move!"

But the sweaty man stood his ground. It was getting disconcerting even to me to see the man continue to argue and gesture stubbornly, as though the pilot had said nothing. I was seriously considering entering into the verbal fray myself. Had I been physically able, I might very well have un-strapped and unloaded the cargo myself. I thought for a moment the pilot was going to begin unloading it himself as well, with help from his co-pilot, but the co-pilot joined in the exchange in a tone of ridicule, laughing at the preposterous weight the dispatcher insisted they accept in the plane. Finally, the dispatcher displayed the clipboard in front of the pilot's face and began flipping dog-eared greasy pages, pointing to individual entries, jabbing them with his finger for emphasis.

Then, to my utter disbelief, the pilot, resigned and weary, said in a defeated tone the words I never expected:

"Oh, all right."

He turned and plodded forward to the cabin, squeezing between my knees and the pile of cargo he wanted off the plane, with his crew, and the swarthy dispatcher, beaming in triumph, backed out the door and it locked shut. I was tempted to intervene, to grab the pilot by the knees as he passed and plead with him to stop this insanity, but lacked the nerve. SATENA had kindly given me free tickets.

Gravity My Enemy

I could not make a scene, even if I was about to die.

As they flipped switches and checked instruments, one engine started to turn sluggishly, coughed a plume of white smoke, spun by itself momentarily, and gradually coughed some more and growled into action. A cloud of smoke sped by my window. At the same instant, another choked into a spin and roared to life. Then the others. The flight crew left the door open between the cabin and the cargo/passenger area and we could view their activity, arms reaching, heads now wearing headphones turning to peer out the side windows. They accelerated the engines and we slowly edged out into a wide turning arch on the tarmac and plodded slowly onto the runway. It was an interlocking steel grate, a gift from the U.S. military Seabees.

When we reached the end of the runway, the pilot deftly peddled the nose-wheel and swung the huge tail out over the fence, so that only the forward portion of the aircraft and the main landing gear sat inside the fence. The plane then jerked sharply as he set the brakes hard, and the co-pilot put the cluster of four throttles to the firewall. The roar was deafening. The plane crept forward slightly in anticipation, and the entire metal frame vibrated.

I clutched the seat in preparation for a rocket thrust, and gritted my teeth. The plane still roared. I feared that something would explode, but the pilot forced the plane to sit at the ready for several long moments.

When he released the brakes, it was an anti-climax. The plane just inched ahead sluggishly. Any child on a tricycle could have gotten the advantage. It rolled forward gaining ever so slightly in speed, but still a far cry

Takeoff

from what is called a take-off. It seemed that minutes passed, and we simply rolled forward, now at car speed, eating up precious yards of runway. It swayed back and forth as he worked the nose wheel and gained a little speed, but there had to come a time when he would abort. There was not enough runway left to achieve takeoff speed.

But we lumbered forward, the engines roared, throbbing rhythmically until I was sure a piston or a connecting rod would come flying right through the engine nacelle. I watched for the big cloud of black smoke and fire, marveling at how this ancient machinery could hold up. Finally, he eased the nose up, and the aft section of the plane dipped close to the ground, and it hung there, refusing to take off.

He quickly lowered the nose to gain more speed and we now raced along the runway, clicketty-clack on the interlocking grates. We were going to crash into the trees at the end, and die in a fireball.

Again the pilot raised the nose and, once again, had to level out to claw for more speed. The third time he raised the nose, I felt the wheels leave the ground, and the smoothness of air under the wings, leaving the iron-grate runway behind.

In panic, I realized that he once again leveled out the plane, and we were not climbing to the safety of altitude. We continued our headlong dash to death, as I felt the landing gears thump, signaling our point of no return. Craning my neck, I could barely discern the row of trees just ahead — tall tropical trees like kapok and cinnamon and cedar, reaching 250 feet and more to the clouds. We could never manage to leap over such a hedge in the short distance available.

When I was sure we were going to plunge into the forest, the pilot hauled back on the

Gravity My Enemy

wheel and the heavy aircraft, still straining its engines beyond capacity, groaned audibly as it mushed for altitude.

We passed over the trees. As I looked down, I could literally see the veins in individual leaves. As soon as we reached the trees, we left them, and empty space yawned below us, revealing the wide coffee-and-cream expanse of the Amazon River. We cruised down the river for several moments without seeking more altitude, but not giving a second's relief to the straining engines, either. Brusquely, the pilot yanked the plane into a sharp bank. It appeared as though the wingtip would actually touch the water. He then pulled it into a gradual climb out of the river basin and over the billowing, green tree tops of the rain forest.

It was beautiful. Every tree canopy crowded next to another in an unending carpet of green broccoli-like treetops. Occasionally, flowered trees punctuated the beautiful monotony with blazing yellow, orange and purple cotton balls of splendor, as though in a fantasy world. The air quickly got cooler inside the plane, He throttled back the tired engines, and we continued climbing comfortably. I surveyed the faces of my fellow passengers. The Indians were terror-stricken, wide-eyed. One had vomited on the aluminum sheet floor, the rancid stench reaching my nostrils combined with the putrid odor of dried fish and animal hides. Nevertheless, I was joyful. After weeks in the humid, musty-sweet, sticky rain forest, and weeks of wet, incurable, itchy foot and crotch fungus, I was heading back to the cool city, a place I never thought I would like but realized now as my true home.

I also had severe dysentery, the first time ever, as I discovered the infliction far out in

Takeoff

the bush, miles from a cure, medicines or medical advice. It was no longer a small inconvenience, but actually very urgent aggravation, and now I was about to get rid of that as well. The need to dash off in the bushes three or four times each hour to relieve myself was more than a mere inconvenience: It was chronic. I later learned amoebic dysentery could become fatal as the parasites invaded the liver and even the brain.

We got to an altitude of about 8,000 feet, and were dodging fair-weather cumulus clouds. The pilot came back to me and showed a friendly smile. His facial expression said, "That was a close one!" but it remained unsaid. Instead, he asked me if I would like to come up in the cabin with the crew. I nodded eagerly, and two of them carried me up front bodily, sat me on the floor temporarily while one returned back to fetch my chair. They hefted me into it, and I sat inside the starboard wall across from the navigator, whom I did not recall seeing during the cargo dispute. The pilot and co-pilot turned back facing me as they sat on the armrests of their seats and we spent some while talking, while the plane carried on in auto pilot mode. There was a small scope mounted on the floor near me and I spent time entertaining myself by looking straight down at the ground through this scope, which was evidently for ground survey or map-making. I saw the thick vegetation extending for miles, and during literally hours of flying without interruption. The forest was interspersed by the cleft of invisible rivers, seen only in brief moments when light glinted off the water's surface through the dense treetops.

More exciting to me was the occasional sight of an Indian Village. These occasionally appeared in tiny clearings in the deep forest, completely surrounded by impenetrable miles of jungle, with

Gravity My Enemy

no river or road access, meaning simply that the people down there, looking up at this silver bird, had never once seen us, nor we them. What did they think we were? How would they react if they saw us up close? Would they run from us or attack? First-time anthropologists had experienced both reactions from different tribes. What were they doing at this moment? What were they eating? What were they thinking? I had some vague idea of the answers to some of these questions, as I was just returning from weeks of living with similar people, almost equally remote and out of reach. But the thoughts still intrigued me, and do to this day.

After some daydreaming through the scope, we began talking together again, the air force crew as amicable and brotherly as any friends I ever had. We laughed, joked, told stories. It seemed incredible they made these flights as routinely as Americans go to a fast food restaurant. As we were talking, I glanced forward through the windscreen and noticed a huge, looming cumulonimbus, or storm cloud, right in front of us. It was billowing, gorgeous, shining white. I knew from flying small planes it was wise to keep away from such clouds with their violent up-drafts and downdrafts. They could literally tear the wings off a light plane.

But, perhaps, this monster C-54 was oblivious to these weather disturbances. I waited for a break in the conversation to ask if we could fly into such a cloud, but it was hard to get a word in. Finally, as the cloud towered over us so close it filled the entire windshield, I was finally able to ask.

I gestured ahead. "Can you actually fly through that cloud with this plane?"

Takeoff

They turned and, in an instant, disconnected all the autopilot buttons with great urgency, and, grunting in effort, tried to veer the plane away just as we entered the thick cloud. In a second, the plane slammed up against something that felt as solid as the ground. It hit so hard, I thought there must be structural damage.

Then, just as suddenly, we went weightless, and I lifted up right out of the wheelchair. I was in the air so long, I was able to actually reach down in an attempt to make sure it was still under me when I came back down, but I could not reach it and fell hard to the deck, the navigator and wheelchair on top of me. The plane pounded and bucked, creaked and hammered, and finally we emerged out into smooth air.

We got untangled, the chair and navigator off me, and they collectively hoisted me up into the wheelchair once again. The pilot gave me a sheepish smile, and I knew all was well. My question on flying into a cumulonimbus was answered.

In time, we flew through the gap in the Andes to reach Bogotá and, still daylight, the pilot handily landed the plane as though it were a kite.

In the years to follow, he and I became close friends, flying often together to distant, wild places as SATENA fulfilled its promise to fly to frontier destinations no commercial line could afford to fly, to expand Colombia's boundaries. Many years after I left the country, I received a letter from an old friend in the Colombian air force, who was now a general. He told me, sadly, that Osorio had been killed when he was flying a C-130 Hercules on the same flight on which we had met, out of Leticia to Bogotá. There had been a fire on board in the front of the plane. Handled routinely without serious danger, this

Gravity My Enemy

was not a major threat, as they had automatic fire extinguishers. But the passengers had panicked and ran as a large group to the back of the plane. This so seriously changed the center of gravity that he lost control of the plane and it crashed in the jungle, killing him and everyone else on board.

The C-54

14 A New Paradise

A good friend named Guillermo Cajiao was an intelligent and talented fellow, dedicated to a myriad of exciting projects throughout his life. One was professional filming. He came to the Centro Colombo-Americano on several occasions to show his thrilling films. One that caught my interest especially was about fishing in a region on the Pacific Coast of Colombia called Cabo Marzo. It was a beautiful, totally unspoiled area with fishing most anglers could only dream about.

After watching this film in utter fascination, I grilled Guillermo about how we could go there. The only practical way was by air. If one did not have the resources for a charter flight, the only other alternative was to fly via *Satena*, the airline run by the Colombian Air Force intended to open up frontier areas of the country at low cost.

The route flown by *Satena* started in Bogotá in the wee hours two mornings each week.

Uniformed air force pilots arrived to the military sector of El Dorado airport, wiped the dew off the windscreen of a C-47, better known in civilian terms as a DC-3 or fondly referred to as the "Gooney Bird," an extremely reliable twin-engine transport designed in the 1930's but durable and unbeatable for bad runways, lousy weather and hinterland flying. It was endowed with a tremendous range. The first leg of the journey was from Bogotá at 8,700 feet altitude to Cali, 3,400 feet altitude. There, it stopped to load cargo and frightened passengers. The cargo was strapped down in the center aisle of the aircraft while the passengers sat along the sides on military web benches with their backs to the

Gravity My Enemy

portholes. It was in Cali that George and I first boarded the flight to the coast.

The second leg went from Cali down to the coastal port of Buenaventura at sea level, a hot, squalid airport consisting of a gravel runway in the middle of the jungle. More cargo was off-loaded and on-loaded, sweaty passengers gratefully disembarked while new, scared ones queued up to climb in the creaking, aluminum hull. The rudder towered over the small line of passengers, painted in yellow, blue and red, to depict the Colombian flag, and marked with *Fuerza Aérea Colombiana FAC* and a number with the Colombian registration beginning with "HK". The air force pilots, usually lieutenants and captains, had to be patient by nature to put up with the confusion and delays inherent in dispatching passengers and cargo in remote territories.

From Buenaventura, the plane headed out over savage country. The low cloud cover almost always dictated flying at no more than four hundred feet above sea level, just barely under a carpet of thick, gray cloud ceiling. With triple canopy rainforest below, and giant tropical trees towering as much as two hundred feet or more, this left a very small corridor for the plane, and the treetops below were like clumps of broccoli racing by at 200 mph. The next stop was the tiny jungle village of Condoto, its strip hacked out of the forest just barely wide enough to accommodate the wingtips with a few yards to spare. The pilots threaded the needle as they slipped down onto the graded runway, the large tires of the plane spewing gravel as it landed and they stood on the brakes to stop inside the allotted space. Just as the plane reached taxi speed and could turn around 180 degrees, the wall of forest lie just a stone's throw in front of the nose. Finished

A New Paradise

there, the pilots once again cranked up the twin Pratt and Whitney's, taxied to the very end, locked the brakes and ran up the rpm's until the huge engines were about to throw a connecting rod, then released for the dash down the runway, pulling back on the yoke in just enough time to clear the billowing green vegetation at the end. Then a hard bank, with the wingtip almost touching the leafy canopy below, and we were on our way to Quibdó, the capital of the department of Chocó, one of the wildest regions of all of South America, a land where the forest Indians used poison secretions from little, colorful poison arrow frogs, from which they got their name, for blowgun darts. Quibdó was a quaint, diminutive village constructed entirely of wood, propped up on stilts on the shores of the Atrato River. The village on market day bustled with *Cholo* Indians from the jungle villages. One day when I had time to get out of the plane and run into town, we saw numbers of these Indians as they arrived in the dugouts. One girl about age ten stood shyly near me and her belly was distended from parasites. She was painted black with juice from a plant called *jipapa*, from her earlobes and jaw line down to her feet. I noticed others down near the river were similarly painted. Their necklaces and bracelets were extremely colorful, made of dried seed beads and parrot feathers. Otherwise, they were completely naked.

Quibdó was a true frontier town, far from any other, disconnected from larger cities except by air, Medellín being the closest. The area was famous for platinum and many of the people of the surrounding area dedicated their days to panning this valuable ore and gold from the Atrato. In the 1960's the entire town burnt to the ground, or to the river, as it were, leaving its populace

Gravity My Enemy

without a single roof. At roughly the same time, a violent earthquake destroyed most of the town again, making the department of Chocó a habitual welfare state for years.

The last leg of the journey, if one is going only one way (the weary pilots must return to Bogotá before nightfall), is to the coastal village of Bahía Solano, which, as the name implies, lies at the bottom of a large bay on the Pacific. As we left Quibdó and headed out over the endless jungle, the plane went into a sharp dive. I had been invited by our pilot friends on this particular flight to sit up front in the cabin with them. Alarmed and curious as to why we were going into such an abrupt descent, I leaned forward and peered out the windscreen ahead. Below and in front of us lay a small clearing in the forest. The pilots brought the plane into a steep dive, just clearing the treetops as we came over the clearing. They then brought the plane slowly around and prepared for another steep dive, accelerating the engines, and came precariously close to the treetops once again. As we passed the clearing, I now noticed a grouping of small, thatched huts and chanced to see a couple of dark brown bodies racing across the clearing and into the huts. As we pulled out, the plane groaning to gain altitude, I asked the pilots what was going on. They were laughing, much to my relief. I thought we were in the middle of some emergency.

"*Los Indios*," the pilot pointed below us. We were diving on the Indian village to frighten them. I was incredulous.

"What do they do?" I asked.

"*Entran! Se tiran adentro!*" They dive inside, he responded, guffawing. I still found it hard to believe we were engaged in a simulated air attack on an Indian village. It certainly felt

A New Paradise

much different from inside the plane than what I had seen in the movies.

Flying over Bahía Solano a while later, we passed it and headed out to sea as we descended and made a gradual turn back to the town, which was right on the beach. The runway could be seen inland somewhat between two steep walls of low mountains. Both sides of the valley were eroded in red earth from landslides caused by earthquakes.

Coming only a hundred feet over the zinc rooftops of the town, we fast approached the dirt runway, dropped and thumped down on the ground, quickly reversed pitch and roared to a stop. Thus went the trip to the coast, to visit the paradise of Cabo Marzo. From the airport, we made the jolting trip into town in an incredibly dilapidated truck with a wooden bench seat in front, through two streambeds, coughing smoke, and limping to the Hotel Rodríguez. That the truck made it at all was a miracle in itself. It had no brakes, and the owner, Rodrigo Rodríguez, a portly, well-disposed fellow, simply let it coast the last few yards to a stop.

From Bahía Solano, we had to take a sea canoe north to Cabo Marzo, a journey of 42 miles out the bay, past the huge rocks called *Los Vidales* guarding the mouth of the bay, past a lovely cove called Nabugá and on across the open sea, to Piñas and on to Cabo Marzo. The trip usually took four hours. We saw incredible marine life along the way — birds, dolphins, sailfish finning out on the surface, rays flipping out of the water like pancakes, flying fish shooting out from under our bow and many other signs of the abundant sea life of the area.

Thus began a series of exciting trips to this beautiful corner of the world, virtually uninhabited and un-fished. We got large wooden

Gravity My Enemy

sea canoes hollowed from giant trees called *jijuanegro* and *jenené* and had the gunwales built up to handle the seas of the area, decks built to store things, and powered with outboards.

At first we camped on the beach and fished to our hearts' content, catching everything the Pacific had to offer, from small, delicious Spanish mackerel to huge black marlin. An hour or two's fishing was usually sufficient to provide us and our entire camp with enough fish for the day, or more, and often give away large quantities to the people of the nearby cluster of houses called *Aguacate* (meaning avocado).

The seas were beautiful and calm from January through August, and got rough in October through the end of the year, each season bringing us a set of different, delectable species of fish. In February through May we got dolphin fish, called *Dorado* for their golden color when caught. In all months we caught yellowfin tuna, but their flavor in March was like the most tender tenderloin steak. At night we fished needlefish and small sharks, as well as a small jack the locals called *cojinúa*. Rainbow runners abounded, as did muscular amberjacks and roosterfish. The fishing was astonishingly close to shore, never requiring more than a minute or two from the beach to get into big pelagic varieties. The whole experience was a graduate course in salt-water fishing, knot-tying, techniques, learning weather, seasons and the encyclopedia of species. We ate fish in every possible way, smoked, fried, battered, and boiled. A nearby beach provided buckets of clams, which we steamed and devoured with saffron rice by the pot-full. We roasted lobsters on the grill and dipped the white meat in buttered, spicy fondue sauce until we could eat no more. The climate was perfect, never hot but always comfortably

A New Paradise

warm. There were no mosquitoes or sand flies,
and we slept on the beach in complete comfort.
It rarely rained. The entire area was festooned
with a rainbow of flowers, monkeys roared in the
trees on the ridge behind us, parrots flew all
over and large formations of pelicans revealed
the abundant fishing the area had to offer. Huge
colonies of boobies populated the string of rocky
islands nearby. Tiny coves near us were as clear
as swimming pools, revealing colorful coral and
fish life. A single person could fill a bucket
with red snappers right from the rocks next to
camp in a few minutes. It was a dream-come-true,
and we finally decided we had to buy some property
in this Land of Oz of the sea.

15 The Perils

A year or so later, the Colombian Air Force acquired a new plane for these frontier flights, a British Hawker-Sidley Avro, which was a mid-high wing turboprop with power to spare. It had rubber de-icing boots on the leading edges of its wings and horizontal stabilizer. It was equipped with radar and was state of the art. It had the capacity to carry about thirty passengers.

To reach our destination of Bahía Solano on the northern Pacific coast, we departed from the old familiar city of Cali, took a short hop over the western Andes range and down to the hot, humid coastal city-port of Buenaventura. The airport was a grass strip, the most common in the country. The pilot, an old friend from my frequent flying of these routes, was sitting in the co-pilot's seat to train the crew on the new plane. He had invited me up front with them, as he was prone to do with friends. The new pilot, sitting in the left seat, seemed concerned he couldn't find the airport, as we got lower near the coast, leaning forward and gripping the top of the instrument panel and peering out much like a small child looking out a window. The cloud cover was very thick and unusually low. We had descended to a mere two hundred feet in search of the airport, nervous that many tropical trees in the surrounding jungle exceeded that height, but still without even discerning the treetops.

Suddenly, the green, rounded tops of the trees suddenly emerged from the thick clouds below the belly of the plane and we were flying right over them at an exhilarating 180 miles per hour. No sooner did we make visual contact with the ground than we immediately spotted a tall, thin antenna directly in front of the plane.

Gravity My Enemy

The novice pilot rapidly yanked the yoke back to clear the antenna but was unable to pass completely over it. We felt a mild thump on the right wing as we sailed over it at high speed. A look out the right cabin window revealed aluminum sheet peeling back in the wind from the leading edge, and we knew we were wounded.

The pilot banked hard to the left and swung around to make his approach to the field, and we were soon on the ground, the wheels noisily racing across loose gravel and the young pilot, with a pumping motion, intermittently braking the plane to stop before reaching the tall dark forest at the end. He abruptly swung it around to taxi to the small, white, single-room terminal building located halfway down the runway, where the ADF antenna could be seen broken at the top, and its top-most section dangling from the main mast of the structure. In the past, we had often gotten out to stop and eat a delicious, cold seafood *ceviche*, which they stored in a big crock in an antique refrigerator that had a coil on top. This time, however, our new pilot was obviously in deep trouble, knitting his brow, so we spent only enough time on the ground to quickly survey the damage, and the few passengers on board were unceremoniously dumped onto the tarmac and told to wait, while we made a quick return flight to Cali for repairs. The military crew chief back at the base Marco Fidel Suárez was an older vet and he spared no words of insult as he riveted on a new patch, alluding to the pilot's mother and his lack of intelligence with equal fluency.

After the repair, the pilots sheepishly climbed back aboard, their tails figuratively between their legs, and we returned to Buenaventura, where we picked up the passengers and continued

The Perils

our flight to the north. We first stopped in the little jungle town of Condoto.

This was the most primitive strip I had witnessed in all of Colombia, and I had a yearning some day to get out there and spend some time at the place. The strip was hacked right out of triple-canopy rainforest, just wide enough for clearance at both wingtips. The surface of the runway didn't even boast the luxury of gravel, but was mud, splashing up on the undersides of the silver wings. It must have been short in length as well, since the pilot before takeoff taxied to the last available foot, swung around and revved the engines to the breaking point before releasing the brakes. As it was, we had the thrill of watching the tall trees at the end approach very quickly, higher than we were, and then pass in a flash directly underneath us, with no more than a few feet of clearance. There were a couple forested ridges to cross over and then, flying just under the 400-foot cloud level as though we were ducking under a low ceiling, we proceeded to Quibdó, the capital of the Department of Chocó, a cluster of wooden houses on stilts above the water on the brown Atrato River. As we banked steeply to make the runway, we could see small, wooden dugout canoes paddled by dark-skinned *Cholo* Indians. After exchanging a few passengers and some misshapen cardboard boxes wrapped in twine, we continued out to the coastal village of Bahía Solano next to the ocean.

Typical of many small coastal villages on the Pacific, it was nestled between two steep ridges that showed red earthen scars from recent landslides caused by the frequent earth tremors of the region. Bahía Solano was a decaying, fetid town populated by interesting characters and miscreants, refugees from past lives in other places, fugitives of problems and bad reputations.

Gravity My Enemy

The stench of sewage draining onto the beach was alleviated each day after high tide. This was a place that had once, but no longer, captivated the interest of foreign governments and entrepreneurs who viewed the area as the place of the future. But, once disillusionment set in after being frustrated with unsuccessful attempts to get the locals to do any work, the projects soon became rusted machinery covered with vines, abandoned forever, too unwieldy to consider recovering.

As we approached Bahía Solano, we passed low over the town, which looked infinitely tidier from the air than it did up close, swung out over the ocean where we could see the jutting black rocks of *Los Vidales* at the mouth of the bay, and made a gradual turn back toward the coastline. The young pilot cut back on the throttles and began to descend toward the town. We passed over it at about three hundred feet, the wooden shacks blurring by as we did so, and we headed straight for the red earthen runway located between the two steep forested ridges rising inland on either side.

As we approached the small red clay runway ahead, the captain directed the young pilot from the right seat, raising his hand palm up to indicate that he should pull back to decrease the descent, palm down to increase the slope of descent. The young uniformed pilot watched these signals out of the corner of his eye, applying gentle pressure on the yoke accordingly as the sight picture of the small, fastly-approaching runway bobbed and weaved back and forth in the windscreen of the airplane.

At the last instant, when the runway was almost right in front of the nose of the plane, the pilot in the right seat turned his palm up, then started raising it more vehemently, and finally

The Perils

resorting to urgent voice commands, *"suba, suba, suba . . . SUBA!"* Go up!

The runway had been bulldozed flat years before in its creation, leaving mounds of dirt piled at both ends. One mound loomed before us at the last split-second, and the novice pilot yanked abruptly on the yoke. We thumped sickeningly on the obstruction, sailed almost gliding down the runway for a moment of hesitation, and bellied onto the gravel surface in a screeching, agonizing tearing of metal, racing down the runway almost as low as though we were sitting on the ground. We had lost our entire landing gear. As the plane skidded like a toboggan down an icy hill, it turned slightly sideways, as we were completely out of control. After what seemed an eternity, we finally scraped to a halt.

Then there was silence. Smoke came out from below in small wisps. After seeing this scene repeatedly in the movies, I fully expected the plane to explode in a fireball, throwing pieces of metal everywhere, while we perished inside, screaming in our last moments of life as we were fried in the inferno. But nothing happened. The captain went to the passenger area and opened the hatch. People clamored in desperation for the door and hurriedly jumped out onto the ground and ran from the plane in all directions, expecting a blast any moment. I, of course, couldn't move until help came, so I resigned myself to whatever was to happen. I looked forward. The novice pilot stared out the windscreen with no expression. It was anyone's guess what his thoughts were at the time, but I had a feeling it may have had something to do with the fate of his career. Finally, the captain came back to the cabin and, with the help of the pilot and civilians grouped outside, got me out of the plane in the wheelchair. I never felt quite so impatient to get

Gravity My Enemy

out of a plane before, but showed an outward calm. As I cleared the plane I pushed my wheelchair a distance away and turned to look at it.

The silver bird was lying crooked on the runway, one wing drooped to the ground like a glider. The wheels and undercarriage were gone.

Weeks later I returned to Bahía Solano and the same aircraft was still lying like a giant wounded bird on the runway. The thought crossed my mind that it was now going to be one of the wrecked derelicts so often seen behind old Quonset hangars in Latin America, engine nacelles empty, windows broken. But on a subsequent trip I was surprised to see it gone, the runway yawning at me in emptiness. Like a Phoenix raised from the ashes, it must have been repaired and flown out, as there was no other practical way to move it. Colombian mechanics, both auto and aircraft, despite all their faults, are probably the most resourceful on the planet. With a smile, I wondered if the same angry crew chief from Cali had been brought down to do the job, cussing at the pilots and the mosquitoes for the many days he must have been there. I heard later that the young pilot who crashed it quit the Colombian Air Force, and wondered if he quit as result of crashing a million-dollar aircraft or to escape the scathing comments of the mechanic.

Those were the incidents that affected me directly. I felt fortunate to have "walked away from" them.

Others with which I was in close contact did not have such happy endings.

***

My brother Tim came down to visit once and we decided to go fishing on the northern Pacific Coast at Cabo Marzo, where we had made

The Perils

so many flights in the past. Fishing in this region forty-two miles north of Bahía Solano was fabulous, if one could go through the sacrifices of getting there. We took the same route from Cali to Bahía Solano.

Too many Avro's had been destroyed or damaged on these primitive runways. I recall seeing the rubber de-icing boot on the leading edge of the horizontal stabilizers in the tail section completely shredded from the gravel kicked up by the main landing gear. So, the Colombian Air Force went back to the tried-and-true Gooney Bird and I, for one, was greatly relieved.

The DC-3 is a very noisy aircraft. Rivets on the wings vibrate and rotate loosely as one watches. Being a tail-dragger, it had a wheel in back rather than the more modern configuration of a tricycle gear. As such, it wagged back and forth on the runway during take-off, felt dramatically by passengers in back, who are tossed side to side. The small side windows of the aging and scratched Plexiglas did not offer much of a view, adding to one's apprehension as the plane roared forward. Tim was having the first, true white-knuckle flight of his life, and I was enjoying every minute of it, adding to his terror by telling him horror crash stories. The parts and wrecked planes on the sides of the desolate runways gave mute testimony to the veracity of my tales, and he eyed them warily as we passed.

The flight northward was exciting but uneventful. The approach to Condoto is potentially very dangerous in heavy clouds, as the plane must usually fly at a thrilling four hundred feet altitude, just under a solid ceiling of clouds, and then cross two heavily-treed ridges before dropping down suddenly to the hidden landing strip, tucked between the tall tropical trees of a

Gravity My Enemy

dense rain forest. To cross over each lofty ridge, which disappears into the clouds, it is often necessary to rise up into the clouds momentarily to cross them, blind, guided only by an altimeter and the knowledge of the height of the ridges, and then drop back down into clear air and dump the heavy plane into the mud of the runway.

We finished the air portion of the journey, then traveled by sea canoe forty-two miles across the open sea to get to our camp, and spent a very exciting week of world-class salt-water fishing. After our trip back south across the sea to Bahía Solano to catch the air force flight back, we finally boarded the vintage aluminum C-47 (DC-3) and I was delighted to discover that the flight crew on board this time were close friends. The pilot, Lt. Nelson Sarria, was an especially close friend, as we had spent many evenings of debauchery out together in Cali nightspots. He came back and gave me the customary Latin embrace of friendship. I introduced him to my brother, who got an embrace as well, and Tim was promptly marched up to the flight deck as a dignitary, where they strapped him into the copilot's seat for the return flight. Naturally, he was delighted to get this front seat view.

Between hops, Tim came back to visit with me in the passenger section and informed me that he didn't feel the danger up front as he did sitting in back, since visibility of where they were going did much to improve his confidence.

I assured him that, though these military aviators were the best in the world for this type of flying, there were many risks. The flight we were on made its run on Tuesdays and Fridays. We returned on the Tuesday flight and Tim was back in Illinois by late Thursday.

The Perils

The Friday evening news in Colombia announced the crash of the same aircraft while on its approach to Condoto.

Reports the following day indicated that it had the same flight crew and preliminary speculation from pilots who had often made the same flight was that our pilot friend had misjudged the first ridge he had to cross as the second, before reaching the Condoto airstrip. He began his descent and flew right into the side of the second ridge. There were no survivors.

I sent the newspaper clipping to Tim on Monday. No comment was necessary.

***

On a visit years later to Jaqué, Panama, to buy a boat, we got up one rainy morning to hear a light plane approaching. We had slept in the police station, where we were kindly offered quarters. As George and I left the small wooden building, we noticed the plane was circling around us at a very low altitude through low cloud cover, then swung back over near the airstrip and suddenly went silent. We thought nothing of it at the time, as we thought the plane had cut its engine down on its final approach to the grass runway. Five minutes later people came running, shouting excitedly, claiming the plane had crashed. Being a very tiny coastal town, George and I dashed out to the airport on foot and arrived in a few moments. We learned that the plane was a Cessna 180 piloted by a local American missionary and carrying three Indians. They had gone down in the mangroves adjoining the strip and there was a search party out to rescue them at that moment. We waited anxiously, hoping that the low altitude had allowed them to escape uninjured.

Gravity My Enemy

In perhaps a half hour, they brought one Indian in to the runway, using a small canoe as a litter. He was agonizing in pain and had evidently broken his back and was paralyzed. This struck home to me as I sat next to him in my wheelchair, myself never to walk again. He was in such pain he was oblivious to my presence. In a few moments, they brought in the missionary. His face was covered with blood and his head was double the normal size from swelling. Someone commented that he had hit his head on the control yoke of the plane, actually breaking it. The other two fortunately had only comparatively minor injuries, one a broken arm and the other just badly shaken and cut.

As the missionary was arriving from Panama City and approached the runway, he cut the throttle and the engine quit on final. The plane lost immediate lift in the hot, humid air and went into the trees, shearing off both wings and ending up in the water. A U.S. Army helicopter arrived less than an hour later, and the rescue crew was very professional, putting in IV's on the ground and warning the flight crew of the need to take the injured at a very low altitude back to Panama City to avoid problems caused by head injuries. We never learned the ultimate fate of these unfortunate people, but I was impressed with the good fortune the Panamanians had, unlike most other Latin Americans, with the presence of the U.S. military.

***

A couple years later, a group of Colombian air force pilots went up to the United States to take delivery on a bunch of new Cessna 182's that had been painted up as military trainers and called T-41's. The group flew back together across Mexico and Central America in a loose gaggle, their planes

The Perils

loaded with television sets and stereos for their families. These pilots came down through Panama and into Chocó. They talked back and forth excitedly over the radio informally, as they were on their final leg of the journey to their homeland. Suddenly, the engine quit on one of the planes. The pilot tried repeatedly to restart it, but to no avail. His companions frantically offered suggestions and the radio waves were congested with shouts. They were flying over a region where a crash landing was certain death. All was deep rain forest with no clearings or even open swamp.

After several moments, watching their close buddy lose altitude to his eventual death, they one by one bid tearful, emotional farewells. As the plane was about to hit the treetops, the doomed pilot tried once again to start the engine, and it coughed to life. He accelerated and recovered altitude, to continue to the Marco Fidel Suárez air base in Cali without further incident.

Friend José Manual Sandoval, who was one of the pilots in this gaggle and a lieutenant at the time, came to Popayán a couple weeks later to visit me in one of these same aircraft to take me for a little ride. As we were taxiing on the runway, the engine quit and it was only with great difficulty that he was able to start it. It was evident that there was some serious flaw with the injection in these aircraft, but I learned later that the problem had been solved.

***

At another time some years earlier, the binational center I directed received a large book display from the State Department. Foggy Bottom in Washington is often replete with people who have hot ideas about what we should do in

Gravity My Enemy

foreign countries to impress Third World people, without knowing them or having been there. Thus, according to their thinking, all the little brown and black people of the world would become little Americans. This collection of a couple thousand books was entirely in English and thus held no interest whatsoever for the people of Popayán but being of a sound cultural nature, they dutifully came to the BNC in great numbers to thumb through these meaningless tomes. Some fool back in Washington probably sat back in proud satisfaction that he had made some contribution to the cultural development of the Colombian people. Such is the manner in which U.S. foreign policy is determined.

Equally bored, I sat around looking proud and important, thumbing through the same silly books, when one, alas, caught my eye. It was about competitive international aerobatics, with speeds, diagrams and all. How this could hold any interest to the average Colombian citizen was something only some State Department functionary could explain, but I stole it and took it home. The fact that no one ever later asked me about this missing book substantiated my belief that all this was pretty foolish.

I later presented it as a gift to my friend, Lt. José Manuel Sandoval, explaining the truth behind the "acquisition." He showed a lot of enthusiasm, quite naturally. The fact that my little theft ended up in the hands of the man who was later to become an air force general, and the strong pro-U.S. commander of the entire Colombian air force, I like to think was partially due to my quick thinking in absconding with the purloined book.

I had long forgotten this twisted act of generosity when the phone on my desk rang one morning. It was José Manuel. He was at our airport

The Perils

in Popayán, called Machángara, and would I like to go for a little airplane ride? he asked. In minutes, I was in a car headed for the airport. Far better to fly than to run silly State Department programs, I thought. As I pulled up, he stood on the tarmac in his handsome khaki uniform with his arms crossed, his plane parked behind him. I went up and shook hands, as with all close friends. Behind him was a perky Mentor T-34 trainer made by Beechcraft, silver with the military markings of the Colombian air force. It was a low-wing tandem plane with a powerful engine capable of high-performance maneuvers. It looked very much like a World War II fighter plane without the guns.

"I've read the book you gave me," he explained in Spanish, "and have been working on some of those maneuvers. Want to give some a try?"

I eagerly accepted. Some workers at the airport hoisted me up onto the wing of the trainer, and then into the front seat of the cockpit. It was very austere inside, as can be expected of a military plane. For a seat cushion there was a parachute, and I was strapped into that. Standing on the wing outside, José Manuel put earphones on my head, adjusted the boom mike, slid my canopy forward into its locked position, gave me a thumbs up, and climbed into the back. In seconds, the engine was started and we were climbing rather steeply into the Wild Blue. It was exhilarating. He started with loops, "just for starters" he said, and we progressed to snap rolls, pull-ups and Immelmann's. I loved every minute of it. Then he did a hammerhead in which he drives the plane straight up vertically, and then lets it fall on its tail haphazardly. This was getting to be pretty rough, and I was becoming disoriented. Forces on my body did not coincide with the scenery outside the Plexiglas and I was

235

Gravity My Enemy

starting to feel stressed. He asked if I was okay, and I said yes.

He then headed for a large rice field some distance away. It looked like a smooth, flat, green carpet as it lay in view in front of us. He brought the nose down as though in a strafing attack, and the plane was screaming. As we came very close to the ground at red line speed, no higher than the treetops, he suddenly flipped it over, turning the horizon into a ceiling above our heads. Then he brought it down to within about twenty feet of the ground! We were going over 200 mph, but I didn't dare even look at the instrument panel. I was grasping the seat in front of me in a painful death grip, holding my breath and awaiting being torn to pieces. Then, still upside-down, he pulled away from the earth, pulling us strongly in such negative G's I feared going right through the canopy. I was glad he remembered to reverse the controls to pull out. Then, he violently flipped it back upright.

That was it. I had had all the thrills I had ever wanted, and more.

"*Cómo te sientes?*" He asked. I said I felt a bit disoriented, and not real good. He chuckled over the intercom.

"I took my brother Camilo up once and he threw up all over the inside of the cockpit — just flying normal. So, you've done pretty good!" I didn't ask him how they ever managed to clean up that mess for fear I might repeat. When we landed, the helpers at the airport came out with big grins and asked me how my kidneys felt. So, by that comment at least they were impressed with the aerobatics we did. On one occasion I remember seeing the control tower fly by right outside the cockpit.

As I got out, rather shakily, I sat back and admired the plane. It had a big 312 painted on the

The Perils

side of the nacelle. He explained to my horror that this plane was not truly aerobatic for long-lasting or extremely difficult maneuvers, as it had no "inverted system" which prevented the engine from cutting out while upside-down for long periods. He added that the flight manual stipulates a maximum of nine seconds of inverted flight.

"How do you count them?" I asked.

"We just make a best guess."

That was a Saturday. Two days later, on Monday, a promotional film team showed up at his base in Cali to film some aerobatic flying to make a recruiting film for new cadets. Another more distant friend, Lt. Osorio, was assigned the flying duties. Using the same No. 312 trainer we had used, he was doing an inverted pass over the Air Base runway when his engine cut out and he was killed. I understand it happened in less than nine seconds.

To this day, if one ever visits the Marco Fidel Suárez military airfield in Cali, the monument can be seen, with a twisted propeller mounted on the front, and a bronze plaque below commemorating the death of Lt. Osorio.

It was during the trip to Jaqué in Panama that we had occasion to taste our first shark fin soup. Tulio Mong was of Chinese stock and born in Panama. A nicer fellow could not be found. He was jovial, intelligent and a dear friend.

Sharks stink. When lying in the sun, their odor after a while is downright obnoxious. The fins are made of a fiber and resemble plastic Styrofoam packing. I told Tulio I could not for the life of me understand how anyone could bring himself to eat a soup made from such a revolting piece of fish anatomy. He admitted to liking it, but I chalked it up to his ancestry.

Gravity My Enemy

One afternoon, he asked me if we could stop by his house for dinner. We gratefully accepted. His maid served up soup, which was very common throughout Latin America, so I thought nothing of it. After some time, he asked what we thought of the soup. I remarked that it was unusually tasty. It truly was. It had a flavor unlike any I had tried and was terrific.

"That's shark fin soup," he said with a big smile.

I was incredulous. I had expected to see a triangular fin floating around in broth, and told him so, asking where the fin was.

"See those thin fibers in the soup that look like tiny noodles? That's the fin," he explained.

Now I can understand why it costs a small fortune to have shark fin soup in a Chinese restaurant.

A lot of concern was going around in those days about sharks. Though dangerous, I personally felt there were many exaggerations. We had seen lots of sharks, caught many and suffered no mishap. I felt they were over-rated. One day while the work crew was busily engaged in building our house in Cabo Marzo, one worker let out a yell, pointing to the beach in front of the house. Incredibly close to the actual shore could be seen a very large dorsal fin of a hammerhead, so close in fact, it seemed impossible it could even swim in such shallow water. One fellow had a harpoon nearby and he made a dash for it, but the shark was gone before the worker could get there.

We had been working on the project for weeks and the only easy way to feed more than twenty workers was to go out fishing every morning. Cleaning all these fish in the little fresh water stream in front of the house, we conveniently disposed of all the guts and heads as the current

The Perils

washed it all out into the bay. Over time, it was
not surprising that this attracted sharks, but
this was the only incident that made us aware
of them.

Our preferred means of fishing was trolling.
The local fellows, however, without benefit
of outboard motors, were accustomed to bottom
fishing, and they consequently enjoyed this much
more — not only the style but the type of fish.
Their favorite was *bravo*, the powerful amberjack.
The preferred portion was the head, which we
discovered was loaded with tender meat in the
shape of cones where the body meets the head.
These fish often came in sizes of ninety pounds
or more and fought with a power and tenacity
that most anglers could handle only with great
difficulty. We soon discovered that most fish
species could be identified before seeing them
come to the surface. Wahoo, for example, took off
like a marine rocket at first strike and took
line off the spool so rapidly one had to take
care to keep hands clear of the line for fear
of being cut. After the first run, the Wahoo
would often leave the clutch in the reel smoking!
Yellowfin tuna were the species we most often
caught and they invariably ran among porpoises.
In fact, we liked to put out lines when we saw
porpoises with the certainty of getting tuna. The
porpoises, of course, were too smart to ever take
any fishing lure. Yellowfins were very strong
but jerked the line out in spurts, the distance
determined by the size, but most averaged fifteen
to twenty pounds. Dolphin fish were among the
fastest and most beautiful. They quickly revealed
their identity with a series of jumps. Sharks were
usually avoided because of the time it took to
bring them in. They were like being connected to
a cow when hooked.

Gravity My Enemy

George with amberjack

Occasionally, the line pulled equally as hard as an amberjack but in a circular motion, and this signaled they had a shark, which fights by going around in underwater loops. Disgusted, they swore, realizing they had to bring this huge fish to the boat before being able to recover an

The Perils

expensive stainless hook and resume their quest for more useful fish. The shark was like being snagged on a rock. It was neither exciting nor very desirable for its flesh, though we ate them frequently. The smaller ones were tastier but the white-tip reef sharks had a fibrous meat that left one with a wad of fiber much like chewing gum in the mouth. They usually got white-tips, black-tips, bulls, hammerheads, and sloppy nurse sharks. In the bay during certain seasons, we spotted sleek blue sharks, an occasional mako and lemon. Hammerheads were very common and we often saw them in the classic feeding frenzy, chasing rainbow runners and amberjacks, which leapt clear out of the water to escape. Tulio Mong of Jaqué in Panama nearby once caught a giant tiger shark that was robbing "smaller," 200-pound sharks he was catching for liver oil. It was so huge, they were unable to even bring it on the deck of a very large boat with a crane, as it caused the boat to list so much.

We heard reports often of people killed near the mouths of rivers north of us in Jaqué and to the south near Piñas Bay and the idyllic grass shack village of Nabugá, but never saw evidence of these attacks. Other than this, we were unconcerned with any dangers.

The black fellows in Aguacate, the cluster of little houses near our lodge, enjoyed going out together at night to fish *jurelillos*, a panfish-size jack. Each paddled his own ten- or twelve-foot dugout called a *panga*, and they headed in a group over near the rocky string of islands jutting off the point, perhaps a half-mile from shore. Nights were often very calm and quiet, and the fellows carried on conversations amongst themselves even though separated by a hundred yards or so.

On the particular night in question, our hearty mariner, Rómulo Aragón, was out with his

Gravity My Enemy

buddies and it was pitch dark. This region of Cabo Marzo had a type of plankton, which was very phosphorescent, leaving patches of bioluminescence in the water after each paddle stroke, and in the wake of a powerboat. In fact, the fish themselves glowed. Rómulo was working a couple of light lines and suddenly noticed a very large luminescent shape pass directly under his little canoe. He knew immediately it was a large hammerhead shark. Without paying further attention, he continued bobbing his lines and hoping for a bite. Without warning, the little canoe took a sudden jolt and almost tipped Rómulo overboard as water rushed in over the gunwale. His heart jumped as he realized it had been the shark that slammed the canoe, trying to spill him overboard. Righting the boat quickly, he frantically bailed water out of the bottom with his split gourd shell. Again, the shark hit the *panga*, and again, he had to hold tightly to avoid falling in the inky black waters. This time, he saw the shark pass below and he caught his breath at the size. He figured it to be over twelve feet, larger than his fragile little craft, which only had a freeboard at the gunwale of about two inches.

Rómulo bailed as fast as he could move. He had seen sharks all his life along the Pacific Coast of Colombia, from Tumaco near Ecuador to Panama, but he never considered them a threat. This time, however, out at sea at night and with help too far to quickly reach him, he was genuinely scared. It was the first time he had been attacked. He saw the hammerhead make a wide circle around him, just below the surface, its dorsal fin slicing the water with a hissing noise. It came at him again in a quick dash, hitting the canoe and once again almost tipping it completely over. Rómulo bailed in frantic desperation, as the canoe was totally

The Perils

awash. He knew instinctively that if he ever lost the protection of its hull underneath him and got separated from it, he would most surely die in a cloud of bloody water.

Now, the shark tried a different tactic.

It slowly got its head under one end of the canoe and raised it up in the air. Water rushed in from the other end. Rómulo kept bailing like a madman. The shark obviously saw and went after his movement, so Rómulo tried something different. He lay down in the water of the bilge and tried to remain still. This was taking a major risk, because a single impact from the shark could now dump him out, as the canoe was so full of water as to be unstable. But, disciplining himself to lie still, not even attempting to bail, he felt small waves washing over the gunwales. Only the natural buoyancy of the wood kept him afloat. He lay in the water in a state of stark terror, unable to even mark the time. Minutes passed and the shark still had not returned. He waited more. Nothing. Did he dare raise his head to see if he could spot the shark nearby? No, he decided. He would wait some more, fully aware that one more impact from the shark would most likely spell the man's last moment alive. More time passed.

His partners, hearing some commotion and then silence, called over to him but he was unable to answer. Finally, after what he guessed to be about a half hour, he sat up, holding himself upright by grasping the gunwale. He found his Pielroja cigarettes floating near his gnarled feet, still dry and tightly wrapped in a small plastic bag. He fetched one out and put it in his mouth, let go of the gunwale to strike a match, and pitched forward on his face in the water, as fear from the ordeal had robbed him of the strength needed to sit upright. He then started to shake uncontrollably. He looked around in the dark waters with a feeling of dread, but there was no sign of the shark. He had survived the only shark attack of his life.

Rómulo was not a terrific mariner in the sense of understanding weather, currents or boat handling, but he was a superb fisherman. Watching him fish with just a hand line was a thing to behold. He used 120-pound line and kept it wound on a net float. As he became accustomed to our style of fishing, he often let out what is called a flat line behind the boat, trolling a baitfish or a one-ounce feather jig, white or yellow being the most effective. When the bait was far enough behind the boat, skipping happily in the wake, Rómulo would then give the line a turn around his big toe to hold the distance, and run the motor at the same time. This to us seemed awfully dangerous. A powerful strike could literally rip his toe out by the roots. Yet, as always happened when he got a strike, the line would somehow zip

The Perils

off his toe, whistle in the air and the net buoy would sail overhead, spinning like a top. He would cut the motor, somehow grab the line and begin his battle with the fish. These contests were of great entertainment to us. He would talk to the fish as though to a person, shout obscenities at them as he carried on the tug-o'-war. He would pull the fish toward him with great effort, his powerful arms and shoulders straining as an Olympic weightlifter, then suddenly lose line, almost being pulled overboard, then gain the upper hand once again and finally bring it closer, leaving large coils of line in the bilge at his feet. As he brought the fish close to the boat, it usually made a last, valiant effort to yank out line, but by now Rómulo was in charge and the fish was totally played out. Since many saltwater fish have very sharp teeth, once in the boat they can bite like a dog, so it was customary to use a club before boating them. With sharks, we had a steel lance, which was used to kill them before hauling them aboard.

"There are fish out there that just are never gonna be caught," an old salt-water angler once told me. We were out trolling jap feather jigs and had caught several smaller fish in the twenty-pound class. I was resting my weary arms. George was using fifty-pound tackle, sitting back relaxed and enjoying the sun and the breeze. Wham! He got a terrific strike. At first we thought it was a large tuna because it was not season for the huge, fast Wahoo's of the area. Tuna, however, yanked out line in spurts, zing-zing-zing, then hesitated and did it again. This did not seem to be a tuna.

Others, like sailfish, no matter how big they are, invariably jump high into the air and show themselves in spectacular fashion, playing themselves out with their acrobatics. But this

Gravity My Enemy

pulled out line as though George were attached to a freight train, almost as if the fish himself were unaware of being hooked. The worst thing the angler can do under such circumstances is to tighten the star drag. The line will always snap and the fish lost.

Once while measuring the length of our beach, we used regular monofilament fishing line to take the measurement. It was then that I realized what a tremendous drag line had in the water, all by itself. After six hundred yards or so, I was totally unable to hold onto it as it dragged straight behind the boat. So it was then I came to have faith in just leaving the drag on the reel alone, and trusting that the fish will kill himself in the Herculean effort needed to pull line off a hefty reel, like a Penn, and a stiff boat rod. With three or four hundred yards of line, there is hardly a fish that can endure, and so George just hung on and let him strip out line. The boat was stopped. We sat back and watched. This was no doubt a very large fish. It would be interesting to see what it turned out to be. George's ropey muscles were strained but he held on patiently. The line kept going out and the stack on the spool gradually grew smaller and smaller. The fish had to give up the ghost any moment.

But it didn't. Line kept going out, inexorably. We began feeling a little anxious, glancing at the spool, wondering when all this would end, when we could finally see what kind of unbelievable fish this was. I glanced again at George's heavy, black reel and could see the beginning of bright chrome showing beneath the wraps of line. George looked and gasped. All the line was now off the spool. He quickly stood up and leaned into the line. Rómulo threw the motor

The Perils

into reverse and followed the line, but it was pulling George over the back seat.

The boat sped up and water started gushing over the transom. George was leaning so precariously over the seat I thought he was going to fall, and then, Ping! The line was gone.

We never saw the fish, or any sign of it.

To this day, we cannot even guess what manner of monster that fish must have been.

Once while bottom fishing off the rocks near the point, Rómulo caught a roosterfish.

This is a type of jack found only in the Pacific, and named for its dorsal fin, which forms a lovely crest that opens like a big fan. There was nothing particularly remarkable about his catching this fish, as he often got them off the bottom, but this day the sun was setting orange and shone off his bulging muscles as he fought the fish, making for a rather memorable mental picture. As the fish was hoisted into the air, only about eighteen pounds, it glistened bright silver in the red sun, its dorsal fan outstretched as it turned in the air on the end of the line. The breeze had calmed, the swells were smooth and the air was pleasantly cool. The point in the distance was covered in thick jungle, a line of pelicans flew over it, and boobies were wheeling in the air overhead. This was the Cabo Marzo I came to love.

Chile

16 Cabo Marzo

I n 1972 we bought a lovely piece of property with a large beach. It was located on our favorite beach in Cabo Marzo on the Pacific coast of Colombia, equidistant between Bahía Solano and the Colombia-Panama border, about forty-two miles from each. The phallic-shaped peninsula of Cabo Marzo first juts out westward and abruptly droops southward to form a protected bay. Our property was located on the inside, or west side of the bay and the shoreline of the property was the shape of a rounded W, measuring six hundred and sixty meters from rocky point to point. The middle lobe of the W was created from eons of flowage from a small, fresh-water creek that tumbled down a circuitous route from the low-forested mountain behind the beachfront. The creek provided cool, clear, potable water and measured about fifteen feet across where it reached the beach. Its faster-flowing portion further up the slope measured only about five feet across. This lovely stream gave us a refreshing, fresh water dip after a day out fishing under the tropical sun, when we arrived encrusted with salt spray. We used it also to flush the salt water from our outboards each day, mounting them on a false transom we had devised for the purpose.

Above all, it was our source of clean drinking water. We laid a pipe into it and pumped water to a large tank embedded in the steep earthen slope that rose behind the house.

This Godsend also was our source of electricity. We built a concrete dam about five hundred meters back in the forest on a high ridge, and ran a high-pressure pipe down from this blockage to a Pelton wheel which powered a heavy, gray, ten-kilowatt generator, which for our house was a

Gravity My Enemy

limitless source of free electricity, allowing even the use of a large electric stove in the kitchen and the luxury of a water heater for the bathroom, as well as the aforementioned water pump.

We built an attractive varnished wood house on the level ground at the foot of the jungled mountain, back about fifty feet from the highest tide and on safe ground even in a storm, with the little stream crossing in front between the house and the beach. This was in turn crossed by a quaint little wooden bridge we made for the purpose. The entire area around and behind the house was heavily forested with giant tropical hardwoods from which two local wood cutters provided almost all the planking for the house construction, except for some specialty lumber we brought up on the Yellowfin from Buenaventura. The footings were posts made from an extremely dense wood called *guayacán negro*, which is so dense it sinks in water and, as its name implies, is as black as ebony and so tough that a nail cannot be driven into it without drilling first. Early steamships used this wood to provide the main bearings in their huge steam engines. The more time *guayacán* is in the ground, the harder it gets. Rather than rotting, it becomes as hard as steel and is totally impervious to bugs.

The woodcutters used a huge, twelve-foot handsaw with wooden handles at each end. To watch their operation was a lesson in industry and old-fashioned ingenuity of leverage, not to mention sheer bravery. They first picked a hefty, straight tree called *jijuanegro* that produced a yellow, pine-like wood. I insisted that nothing be cut near the house, as I did not want to deplete or affect the appearance of the nearby forest. After several hours of laborious cross cutting at the base, the huge tree would gradually lean and then topple,

Cabo Marzo

coming crashing to the ground with a thunderous reverberation that could be heard and felt from a long distance. Its trunk was usually six to eight feet in diameter at the base. The next step was to remove all the upper limbs and branches, many of them the size of a tree themselves, leaving only the main ponderous trunk. With great care and planning, the two woodcutters would then construct a solid wood frame they called a *troque* onto which they would later roll the giant trunk with levers and pulleys. The process of doing this, and the actual levering of the multi-ton tree trunk, was miraculous and got our highest admiration. How only two small-statured men could manipulate and totally master such a massive log was nothing short of incredible. A man could die instantly from a single mistake.

Once in place on top of the *troque* structure, one man stood on top of the log, the other underneath, and they began cutting planks lengthwise with the precision of a mechanical sawmill, a mere one inch thick and perfectly straight. They in turn cut the planks to slightly more than eight-foot lengths and six inches in width, and these we purchased by the dozen for a fixed price, which was so low as to embarrass me as I write these words today decades later. These we stored alternately on edge at a forty-five degree angle, leaning on a beam, to dry out before using them to form the siding of the house.

The roof structure was made from a stout, dark-gray wood called *chanul*, and was in turn covered with corrugated sheets of aluminum, very light in weight, waterproof and producing a wonderful sound in the rain.

The floors and furniture in the house were made of two-inch stock mahogany that was contraband. Some woodcutters north of us in a small

Gravity My Enemy

coastal town named Juradó had felled a number of mahogany trees without permission from, or payment of bribes to, the Colombian conservation office, INDERENA, and piles of beautiful, straight blocks measuring four inches thick by eight inches wide were laying there confiscated, going to waste in the rain and sun. Upon hearing of this, we made a trip to Juradó late one afternoon, deviously to 'have a few beers and talk about fishing' but in truth to ascertain the possibility of getting some nice mahogany. Over a beer and under the table, we negotiated a ridiculously low price from the woodcutters for the lot, provided we took upon ourselves the responsibility and risk of spiriting it away right under the noses and the watchful eyes of the authorities, and they provided the muscle to help us load it. We felt we had two aces in the whole. The first and most important was the fact that the INDERENA guys had to sleep. The second was that a lot of time had passed with no attempt at removing the lumber and their vigil was consequently lax. Parenthetically, they were quite corrupt themselves and their only intention was to sell it, pocketing the money for themselves. So we felt little remorse. When our chartered ship, the Yellowfin, was anchored off the shores of our property in Cabo Marzo miles distant and we thus had a means of transport, we made our plans.

We had three wooden sea canoes of about twenty-eight-foot length and about five feet in beam that were very stable and seaworthy. These were powered with outboards. Once we cut the deal, we arrived to Juradó with these late in the day, some money changed hands, and posing as fishermen, to draw no attention, we waited till late evening. Later in the night, we started loading the sea canoes under cover of darkness (and, I might add, drunkenness of the INDERENA functionaries,

Cabo Marzo

who at this outpost level commanded little more respect than government laggards brought in off the street). They certainly had virtually nothing to do but spend their paychecks on prostitutes and beer. The boats were soon loaded and we sped off southward to our home base over calm tropical night waters and were soon safe at our landing, where we quickly off-loaded our illicit cargo. No sooner was it unloaded and safely on the ship than we turned around again and sped northward for another load. We did this all night long and by dawn had almost the entire lot of mahogany — large enough to build our floor and furniture, plus a sizable load to take back to Buenaventura for sale to help defray the costs of the charter. To our added satisfaction, a small fortune in mahogany had disappeared from under the noses of corrupt officials, who would later only find the woodcutters sound asleep, albeit with a possible smile on their faces and a stash of money secreted away.

And vampire bats.

The weather in Cabo Marzo was sunny almost all year around, except from August through October or November when it rained occasionally and the sea became rough and leaden in color. The breeze was comparatively cool, usually with temperatures in the low eighties and we never saw a single mosquito. In fact, while building the house, we often slept on the beach in the open. The only pests we experienced were land crabs that liked to share our warm sleeping bags (often a very rude, fearsome awakening in the middle of the night).

None of us Americans ever got bit by a bat during the entire period of construction, but the workers often awoke in the morning with ulcer-like bites on the backs of their hands and fingers or on the bridge of their noses.

Gravity My Enemy

A nice Wahoo

We had hired a local woman to cook for the twenty-some workers. Her five-year old daughter was bitten repeatedly by bats, usually on her face and nose. This may have contributed to her mother's habitual crabbiness.

After a time, realizing we had no reason to fear rabies, the bats were simply a nuisance. The wounds they caused involved no pain — in fact were accomplished without the victim's awareness — and the only thing we had to do was administer some antiseptic to prevent infection and try to take precautions against further bites.

The preventative for bat bites comes so close to Medieval legends that it is almost embarrassing to make mention of it. First, just like in the movies, the bats could not tolerate light, either sunlight or man-made, so we often tried to keep a small pitch lamp lit at our side during the night. Secondly, wearing garlic on a necklace prevented bites, so Bram Stoker's legend is undoubtedly based in some degree on fact. The only thing we never tried was a crucifix!

Sleeping on the beach in the open air was very restful and my little tin pitch lamp, called a *candila*, often flickered out from the sea breeze after I fell asleep. I was awakened several times by the fluttering of a bat over my face, hovering mere inches away. I fortunately awoke each time as I sensed the fluttering and was spared a bite by sheer luck, but most of the workers got bitten at one time or another, some awaking the next morning with a gooey-black regurgitation from the bat on the front of their shirts. Why the bats vomited the blood was a mystery to us but we were always repulsed by the sight.

Just as mysteriously as the bats became a problem when we started construction, one day they simply disappeared as strangely as they had arrived. For reasons still unknown, the day came when they no longer troubled us.

With the exception of finding one harmless boa constrictor about two hundred yards behind the house while building the dam for the Pelton wheel, and the sighting of a venomous but lazy and non-aggressive *verrugosa* snake (named for its rough, pebbly skin), no one ever had a single run-in with the local terrestrial fauna that could have been considered a threat. The location, in fact, was thoroughly benevolent and as beautiful as an Eden.

Feeding that number of people in the bush and without benefit of commercial food sources was quite a challenge, and we spent several hours each day fishing and collecting fruits such as coconuts, plantains, lemons and avocados to keep

Gravity My Enemy

everyone well fed and happy. A woman who lived nearby occasionally prepared hot chocolate for us from the wild cacao fruit, using a carved wooden spindle as an egg beater to bring it to a frothy drink superior to any chocolate I had ever tasted. All the fish we caught daily to feed the crew were cleaned at the mouth of the little stream, and the current carried the refuse out into the bay, evidently attracting some sharks in time. One day, a worker yelled out, urgently pointing to the unusually large dorsal fin of a hammerhead very close to shore in front of the house. It fact, it was so large I was amazed it could approach as close as it did, which seemed only about four feet from the actual shore. One of the workers ran to get a harpoon he had stored nearby, and ran with it top speed to spear the shark, but it disappeared too quickly beneath the surface and the excitement quickly was over, leaving us with a lesson and a warning about swimming at the beach nearby, at least during the construction period.

Despite that, neighbors often came to visit, some swimming alongside their shapely little hand-hewn *pangas* — small wooden canoes. Two fellows in particular were good snorkel divers and we came to depend upon them to provide us with an unending supply of scrumptious spiny lobsters from the rocks located at the extremes of our property. These they speared with homemade sharpened steel rods. We usually ordered thirty or forty lobsters for a good meal. The price was a peso apiece, about three cents of a dollar. The divers soon learned that bringing me more than I ordered got the money out of me anyway, so we often had over a hundred lobsters to cook. We ate lobster for breakfast, lunch and supper. We snacked on cold lobster while out fishing.

Cabo Marzo

Our favorite way of preparing them was on the grill with firewood. The boys would twist the heads off from the tails and, with a heavy shears we had in camp, we cut out the transparent "belly" from under the tail, painted its underside with margarine spiced with salt and fresh-ground black pepper and threw them on the grill till the "feathers" were charred black. The cook then pulled out the meat with a fork, cut it into bite-sized pieces and replaced it into the red tail shell and served these with a potato salad and fried plantains. We dipped the lobster chunks into a hot butter sauce and ate till we could eat no more. Ever since, it has been impossible for me to lay out huge sums of money for a lobster as in any restaurant, where it is neither as delicious or as abundant and cheap, nor could it be eaten in such a paradise as we did, as our Cabo Marzo lobsters.

Across the bay we discovered another delight, which was clams. We filled buckets with these, dug from the wet sand of the beach, cooked them in brine and scraped them out into a saffron rice made with onion, diced green and red pepper and garlic. It was a wonderful dish.

About a half-mile from the property was a small cluster of about eight houses, too small to call a "town." Its name was Aguacate (meaning avocado). The people, though friendly in great part, tended to be troublesome and demanding by nature and we thus limited our contact with them to a necessary minimum. There were some exceptions, of course. Rómulo Aragón was one. In time he became our main man in camp, accompanied by his pal, the one-eyed Genaro, who served as his deputy owing to his angling skills and a terrific man at rigging end-tackle and baits. Both were black, and very muscular and powerful. Rómulo was a fair *motorista*, and ran the outboards, a good seaman and an excellent fisherman. He understood the fish and their habits, how they behaved and fed under different conditions, what bait and fishing technique to use, the best hours to fish, and he carried on a personal conversation with the fish as he fished for them, talking to them as though old friends. We preferred to troll, pushing the boat at about twelve miles per hour. Our feather jigs skipped and splashed in the wake behind the boat, and a strike was always exciting and often involved extreme physical exertion to land the fish, which we usually did with a gaff, plunging it into the side of the fish and hauling it out, flapping powerfully in the bottom of the boat.

Rómulo, not having use of a motor when we were not there, preferred bottom fishing and, instead of the rod and reel we used, had his line wrapped around a net float. He let out line behind the boat as he handled the motor. After reaching the proper distance by letting out line, he looped the monofilament around his big toe to hold it, a practice that I always felt was risky and foolhardy, and given the power and speed of some fish we encountered every day. I always feared he would get his toe ripped out by the roots some day, leaving a bloody stump. Even using the standard boat rods we did, we were often cut or burned by the line as it was torn off the reel at over fifty miles per hour. But, somehow, when Rómulo got a strike, the line would fly harmlessly off his toe and his melon-sized net float would spin like a top in the air, as he hurriedly throttled down to fight the fish. He would grab the line with his gnarled hands, shouting insults or encouragement to the fish all the time, the line stretched like a guitar string and singing in the air. He was often cut but just swore at the fish and made a different purchase on the

Cabo Marzo

line, sometimes releasing line as the fish fought too hard and other times, sensing the fish was weakening, laboriously pulling it in with muscular back and arms. At times the tug of war was a draw, and Rómulo refused to let go and came close to being pulled over the gunwale into the water. But inexorably he won out and soon was bringing the fish in hand-over-hand in a groaning contest of titans. As the fish approached the boat it often made its last and most valiant effort, wetting us all down thoroughly, Rómulo swearing mightily over our laughter, line tangled everywhere as he searched for a paddle or a club to pound the fish into submission as soon as its head cleared the water. After a moment of cussing, blood and brutality, cut fingers and almost tipping the sea canoe over, we inevitably saw him hefting a large fish over the side into the sopping bilge of the boat. It was always a spectacular sight and we enjoyed watching him land a heavy fish far more than we enjoyed catching them ourselves. His most exciting battles were against sharks of three- to four hundred pounds or, his favorite fish of all, the *Bravo* (meaning "angry"), the local term for amberjack, usually going seventy to ninety pounds. An amberjack of that size caught on a hand-line is something to behold. Another very exciting fish, for him as well as for us, was the Wahoo, which came in when the weather was foul, the water ominously gray in color and the waves nasty. These often reached ninety pounds and we felt were the fastest fish in the ocean, shooting straight through lofty swells like a bullet through the walls of a tent, and coming out the other side of the swell, totally airborne. The first run made by a Wahoo made the reel scream, often leaving the clutch smoking. We used a leather harness to fish bigger fish and one Wahoo once violently

Gravity My Enemy

pulled me off the seat onto the deck. After all these years, I can now readily confess that the Wahoo scared me to death. If the line were to loop around one's neck, a Wahoo could decapitate the person as quickly as a French Revolution.

During the hot, sunny days of March and April, we got dolphin fish we called *Dorado*, the blunt-headed, slab-sided fish that shares its name with Flipper, but fights like a crazed scrapper, jumps and races with dashes that seem impossible in speed. They like to lie in the shade out at sea under a floating log or flotsam, waiting to ambush baitfish. Once, as we passed such a log closely one day, trolling at our standard twelve miles per hour, we noticed the wake of some fish as it shot from the log away from us out to about a hundred yards. In no more than a second or two, our baits were racing past the same log as we quickly sped past it and the very same fish hit! How it covered all that distance in what seemed no more than perhaps two or three seconds was nothing short of astonishing. It almost ripped the pole from George's hands and instantly, a silver-blue dolphin rocketed out of the water, yanked many yards of line from the reel, jumping again and again. George fought till he reached a stage of arm-fatigue and exhaustion, and when Rómulo was finally able to plunge the point of the gaff into its side and muscle it aboard, it flopped all over wickedly, throwing tackle and hooks dangerously in all directions. You cannot keep a big dolphin alive inside the boat. He must be clubbed till he is stone dead or he'll destroy everything. This one weighed fifty-seven pounds and, as they do, immediately turned yellow-green with tiny blue and red spots like a brook trout. Soon after they are dead they turn to a very dead-looking gray. Only the sailfish fights as

Cabo Marzo

spectacularly and gallantly, and with such color, but pound for pound, the dolphin or the Wahoo are greater adversaries in the muscle department.

Rainbow runners and yellowfin tuna were common every day, all year long. The tuna always ran among schools of porpoises. When we saw porpoises, we knew we were going to fight yellowfin tuna.

We once witnessed the famed "feeding frenzy" of some unusually large, twelve-foot hammerhead sharks chasing rainbow runners, which are beautifully yellow and blue in color and about three or four feet long. Any notions we ever had about the veracity of the common Hollywood scene where some swimmer is trying to out-swim the attacking shark, with people back in the boat yelling in a state of hysteria to hurry up as the dorsal fin of the shark wagged lazily back and forth behind the swimmer, we quickly realized was pure bunk. These hammerheads zigzagged back and forth like falcons amid a flock of pigeons, their dorsal fins slicing the water with a hiss, the spray shooting skyward. Even the swift rainbow runners could not outrun them at speeds we guessed well over thirty miles an hour. The conclusion: If the shark really and truly wants you, you belong to him. The happy fact is the shark probably regards eating you or me about the same as we regard eating a can of dog food.

Yellowfin tuna, as mentioned, are always found among dolphins. On the Pacific in this region, porpoises are seen daily and we always were thrilled to see them as old friends, as it seemed they were to see us. It may be my imagination but it seemed if we yelled and whistled at them as they jumped in the air nearby, they could be enticed to approach quite closely, putting on a bigger show for us if we goaded them on, waving our arms and expressing our delight. Sometimes, they even jumped

Gravity My Enemy

across the boat at the bow, but this was rare. Amongst them, we invariably caught yellowfin tuna in the fifteen-pound range. The tuna, when caught, yank-yank-yanks the line in powerful thrusts of strength and is always recognizable by this trait. We were not overly fond of tunas for eating, as it is a heavy, rich, red meat, but in the month of March they tasted exactly like super-tender filet mignon. With some butter, a little salt and black pepper and hot from a skillet, they were terrific. When they were not, they were the baitfish preferred by the locals for amberjack.

We always came to regard the dolphin or porpoise as a friend, as did the people of the coast. There were many accounts of people having been saved from shark attack by them on the Pacific coast of Colombia, either by being pulled to shore or by attacking the sharks themselves. In fact, some areas, especially near Jaqué in Panama and a little to the south of us near Piñas Point and the village of Cupica, were notorious for shark attacks, undoubtedly all such incidents officially un-reported due to lack of communication with authorities or news sources. For this reason I have always felt that recorded shark attacks worldwide are under-reported. In the heavily populated areas and big beaches where the news reporters live and work, sharks tend to establish non-human eating habits unless they are in the few areas in the world where they at times confuse humans with seals. Normally, sharks are naturally timid especially in the presence of heavy human activity, such as a public beach. Tiny tropical villages on the coast, on the other hand, evidence little public swimming activity and many have recent tales to tell of shark attacks.

In Jaqué, Panama, just north of the border shared with Colombia in what is called the Darien

Cabo Marzo

area (and coincidentally the only region that has been so rugged that it has defied completion of the Pan-American Highway), a Chinese-Panamanian friend by the name of Tulio Mong had a castor oil business in which he had the objectionable practice of putting out porpoise meat baits on huge shark hooks buoyed with empty fifty-five gallon oil drums. As much as the porpoise is revered throughout Latin America, it is believed that sharks prefer porpoise meat over any other and thus it is common to harpoon porpoises for this purpose. To make the oil, they remove the livers from the shark and put them in a drum and cover them with a layer of salt. After a time, the oil comes to the surface, is skimmed off and sold for a good price.

Tulio told us once that some years earlier, many sharks were being robbed from his hooks, presumably by a larger shark. We considered this quite amazing, since the sharks he caught averaged two- to three hundred pounds. Surely it would take quite a large shark to attack these as bait! Finally one day Tulio was out in his forty-ton ship collecting sharks he had snared. He did this by hoisting them onto the deck with an electric winch and boom. As he approached one empty oil drum, he noticed it was still moving but did not consider this unusual, so his crew attached the cable hook to the drum float and began cranking it up with the winch. As they wound in the cable, rather than raising the drum float and the shark from the water, its weight caused the ship to list dangerously to port. Once the cable was taught, Tulio and his crew gathered on the low side to witness a catch so heavy as to make the ship list, realizing that they might have finally caught the culprit of the stolen sharks. The edge of the deck was awash. In open-mouthed astonishment they saw, still very much alive, a huge tiger shark

Gravity My Enemy

swimming just below the surface. Determined to catch this monster, not only for its liver and fins for the famous Chinese shark fin soup, but also to put an end to the thievery, they ballasted the ship as well as they could on the starboard side, anchored it securely and continued cranking the winch. It only pulled the ship deeper to port until the deck was deeper awash. Nothing they could devise was sufficient to bring their catch on deck. They had no weapon aboard to kill it and it was so unmanageable that they had to discard ideas of bringing it into Jaqué submerged. So they finally unhooked the winch cable from the barrel and let it go in hopes it would eventually disgorge the hook and let their rig go to be picked up another day.

We never did learn how big the tiger shark really was and Tulio, not being a boastful sort, refused to speculate. But he did invite us one night to a wonderful dinner of shark fin soup, one of the best soups I ever tasted. I fully expected to find a triangular fin floating in the soup but Tulio explained that the fin had been skinned and shredded to a yellowish fiber resembling tiny strands of spaghetti. In years since, I have looked in many restaurants for shark fin soup. Where it is rarely to be found, the price is prohibitive.

Another interesting story came from night fishing. We occasionally went out at night near camp to fish with a gas lamp, which seemed to attract fish. Rómulo and the other workers had a particular fondness for small sharks, which they called *tollos*. It was quiet on this particular night and we had caught few small fish, when George turned abruptly in anger and punched me in the arm, shouting, 'Cut it out!'

Dismayed, I asked why he hit me. As it turned out, a needlefish about two feet in length

Cabo Marzo

was flapping on the deck behind him. It had jumped to the light and smacked him in the back of the neck, and he thought I had hit him with the fish as horseplay.

Sea snakes were quite common in the Cabo Marzo area. They are extremely venomous but tend to be slow to strike. In fact locals at times would quickly grab one as it approached the boat and toss it away.

George once got one tangled on his feather jig, quite by accident, and it was a delicate task removing it, but jigs and stainless steel hooks were imported and too costly to discard.

The yellow-and-brown snakes were rather pretty, with their typically flat, spatula tails.

On another occasion, he caught a pelican as it dived for the bait. Getting the frightened bird in the boat and removing the hook without causing damage took some careful work.

Our primary interest in the Cabo Marzo region was taking tourists fishing, and we needed a small lodge for that, so we hired an architectural draftsman in Popayán to do blueprints for the ideal lodge. It was modest in size but comfortable, with four bedrooms, a bath, a large working kitchen of all stainless steel and a wrap-around porch to serve as a dining and lounge area.

Sitting on the expansive front porch under a gentle southerly breeze and gazing out over the lovely bay was a wonderful experience.

17 Cabo Marzo — Adrift

We awoke late the next day, sore and stiff from an entire night of hauling contraband wood. We got aboard the Yellowfin in some haste to vacate the region on the off chance that the INDERENA people should come looking in our direction. It was already past noon and we were disgusted with ourselves for sleeping so late. Captain Lopera took no time in cranking up the diesel below decks and it wasn't long before we were plying our way out of the broad bay and gradually distancing ourselves from our lovely paradise at the foot of the steep jungle.

This was always a very emotional moment for me, as I had never known such a pristine, beautiful spot in my life, and over the few years we had been visiting and dreaming of building a fishing lodge there, I had become very attached to the place. As it receded in the distance, I choked back my customary welling up of feeling, and took in the wonderful sight. The entire point of Cabo Marzo jutted out about two miles from the mainland. It was steep and dark green with towering trees. Small, sandy coves backed with leaning palms punctuated the cape, the sandy beaches in the distance now only thin yellow lines. Threadlike cascades of water plummeted from rocky heights amid a riot of vines and electrically hued flowers, and pairs of macaws occasionally flew in formation over the lofty treetops. Protruding from the cape itself was a string of cone-shaped rocky islands, which eons ago had once been a peninsula but was now eroded away to individual rocky islands, habitable only to vast colonies of sea birds who gave strong testimony to the abundance of fish in the area. Most of these were boobies, but there were also many herring gulls

Gravity My Enemy

that tipped us off when a feeding spree among fish was taking place, and on rare occasions we spotted an osprey that hung out among the dead branches of trees at the very tip of the cape. Long lines of pelicans drifted frequently over the point as bombers going out on a mission. The view was so wonderful it was intoxicating and I always feared that the day might come when it would be our last visit.

Buenaventura was two days and nights distant. This raunchy town is Colombia's principal cargo port and often rated as the world's sleaziest, but I always felt a fondness for the small, dirty city. It had a smell that combined the odors of sweet, fresh-cut lumber with raw sewage, spilled petroleum with fish, and the salt air with the odor of humanity in its basest form. Sailors from the world over roamed its streets in pairs and small groups. Local vendors, hawking their wares in the dirty streets, along with surprisingly attractive prostitutes, vied for the opportunity to exploit the sailors' personal needs and loneliness.

On the street pavement there were patches of dried blood from last night's fights, couples huddled on worn park benches giving evidence of transient love affairs of great passion, and the cacophony of commerce, the frenzy and roar of trucks and warehousing goods, cranes off-loading huge vessels with rust-streaked hulls from long voyages out of Wilhelmshaven, Hong Kong, and New Orleans. Hefty winches hoisting house-sized loads of wares trucked along big I-beams. In the background there was the perpetual rhythmic Latin beat of music emanating from open bars that reeked of cheap *aguardiente* and Ron Viejo de Caldas rum, urine and rancid vomit.

Buenaventura did not intimidate me, as I was careful to remain an observer and most of the

Cabo Marzo — Adrift

ambience was house dressing and non-aggressive by day. I felt at home in it, intrigued by its baseness and international flavor, the different faces a mosaic of interesting characters, the excitement and its symphony of strange sounds and smells. Yet it offered a comfort, had a personality and character that somehow felt friendly and warm, like an aged, over-weight prostitute who had become trustworthy and warm of heart.

Buenaventura was the homeport of the Yellowfin, a sixty-ton ship that had once been a hard-working fishing boat out of New Orleans, with booms that swung out to the sides for nets and a powerful winch behind the cabin. But the Yellowfin was now semi-retired to rust in the tropics, doing odd jobs between tiny banana ports along the Colombian Pacific coast, from the tepid mangrove and jungle shores of Tumaco near Ecuador, to the rocky, mountainous northern coast near Panama and Bahía Solano, where huge seabird colonies nested in the rocky shores. The Yellowfin was as austere and muscular as any working vessel with no extras for comfort, had Spartan quarters and dank, oily innards. She was steel-hulled and powered by a thundering Caterpillar diesel that vibrated reassuringly beneath one's feet on the deck, kept in perfect condition by crack Buenaventura diesel mechanics, for her captain was a stickler for seaworthiness and safety, if not good looks.

Marco Lopera was an ex-Colombian navy captain, and knew his job as well as he knew every mile of the Colombian coastline, both on the Pacific as well as the Caribbean, each port an intimate and veritable home for him. His function, as was the Colombian navy's occupation before drug interdiction, was more that of coast guard patrol and rescue than national defense, as Colombia had enjoyed good relations and respect

Gravity My Enemy

from her neighbors throughout most of her history, with the exception of the independence of Panama encouraged by president Teddy Roosevelt to gain the canal at the turn of the century, and a border conflict with Peru in the Amazon in the 1930's.

In appearance, Captain Lopera looked like the spittin' image of James Mason as Captain Nemo on the Nautilus in 20,000 Leagues Under the Sea, and was every bit as eccentric and autocratic. He was well read and universally knowledgeable but dictatorial and despotic, which an effective sea captain must be when dealing with rowdy and undisciplined sea rabble found at random in the world's ports, possessing doubtful personal histories. He had a dark, furrowed brow, a broad forehead, a heavy mop of black hair and a swarthy appearance, and was built stocky and low to the ground, his arms protruding out to the sides, suggesting he was once a weight lifter. His gait was purposeful, his head thrust forward in determination.

We had contracted his boat to haul everything we needed to build a fishing lodge in Cabo Marzo far to the north, forty nautical miles from the Panamanian border, and I spent two busy weeks getting refrigerator, water heater, lumber, light bulbs, bricks, electrical and plumbing supplies, a two-cylinder Petter diesel engine with a ponderous ten-kilowatt generator and even a dump truck load of clean sand to mix with cement for construction (beach sand was salty), all accumulated in Lopera's warehouse at dockside where the Yellowfin rested and awaited orders to come to life for our journey north. A greasy, ill-tempered mechanic finally emerged from the bowels of the ship and announced to the anxious captain that she was ready for sea. Eventually, all was loaded and secured, the decks cleared and Captain Lopera stood at the helm and

270

Cabo Marzo — Adrift

brought the Yellowfin to a low rumble, we edged
away from the warehouse and began our tedious
exit from the serpentine, oily river of the port,
and we headed north in low, gentle swells.

Now many days later, we had totally unloaded
our cargo in Cabo Marzo by anchoring the Yellowfin
three hundred feet off the beach and bringing
28-foot wooden sea canoes alongside in relays. The
workers loaded the canoes all day long, as they
shuttled tons of cargo to the beach and unloaded
kitchen appliances, bags of cement, pipe, aluminum
roofing panels, shovels and lumber in organized
piles, stored safely under a 30-foot shed roof of
palm-frond thatch on the beach. The job was done
after two fourteen-hour days of hard work and we
were now headed south in a moderate swell, laden
with our mahogany treasure.

Captain Lopera set a course out of the bay
of Cabo Marzo to the southwest toward the point
called Piñas and, as the red sun was setting off
to our right over the vast, heaving Pacific Ocean.
Captain Lopera entered his cabin and closed the
door to get some rest. We gradually neared Piñas
Point and were about to set out onto the open
seas toward Buenaventura, two days distant. The
cook had been below even while we were anchored,
preparing a surprisingly tasty beef stew and one
of the crew soon brought me a chipped China soup
bowl full to the brim with stew which I eagerly
accepted and ate while on the deck next to the
wheel house watching the sun set. I had not eaten
all day and was exhausted. The beef stew had an
orange color of tomato and *achiote*, with globules
of beef fat floating on the surface. It smelled and
tasted terrific. I ate hungrily and anticipated
turning in for a good night's sleep at sea.

We came abreast of Piñas Point and began
to pass it, about one mile off to our left. There

suddenly ensued some shouting between crew in the stern and the pilot at the wheel. Their urgency gave me reason for some concern. Captain Lopera exited from his cabin and ran aft. After a few moments, he came briefly to me.

"We've lost our rudder." *Perdimos el timón.*

I felt a cold wave run through my chest.

In the distance, Piñas was a cluster of huge, cathedral-sized black volcanic rocks jutting two hundred feet into the dark, evening sky like grotesque inverted cones. At their bases where rock met sea, huge white plumes of foam and spray exploded into the air as the waves came crashing thunderously against the first solid obstacle they met in thousands of miles. The captain made a quick assessment of wind direction and we realized to our horror that we had a westerly, on-shore wind that may soon blow the ship onto the rocks. The distance of a mile no longer seemed as much as I had previously felt. I asked him about the current.

"The current in these parts is slightly northward but since we've passed the point somewhat, I'm afraid I calculate our trajectory right into the middle of the rocks," he said soberly.

"How much time do you figure we've got?"

"We have several hours, but remedies also take hours when out at sea," he responded. I was relieved to hear him say the word 'remedies.' "We've put down the anchor but the cable is too short for this depth. This is one of the deepest trenches along this coast, which probably explains why you people get such good fishing here. You're essentially fishing far out to sea without need of venturing far from the actual coast."

"What can you do?" I was getting quite alarmed. A big steel hull on those rocks spelled certain disaster.

Cabo Marzo — Adrift

"They're adding a second cable now to the anchor. We'll know in a few minutes if it reaches bottom," he said.

"And if not?" I asked.

"If not, we just leave it hanging and hope that the anchor catches before we reach the rocks."

"It has to," I insisted. "How can it not?"

I still felt some hope, or at least in my mind was trying to create a sense of hope.

"Not necessarily!" Lopera quickly warned.

"The charts show an extremely deep trench going very close to shore. We could hit the rocks before the anchor is firm. The bottom may also be sandy and the anchor could drag. Besides, the cable doesn't go straight down but at an angle behind us."

My heart was pounding. When he turned away to attend to the problem, I searched for an air mattress I was using for sleep and industriously inflated it, getting lightheaded in my haste. Captain Lopera then returned to the wheelhouse and entered. He reached up to a switch and flashed our running lights three times, then repeated the series again and again. It was now getting dark enough to use lights.

"Who could possibly see us?" I asked him. "There's a ship out there," he nodded his head, as he looked out to sea.

I, too, looked in the same direction but saw nothing at first. I kept searching from one side to the other and finally noticed a small, black shape on the far horizon and could make out its faint lights. It was a ship — I could not distinguish its size — but I could see it was heading towards Panama, possibly the canal.

The captain flashed our running lights again.

"Why doesn't he acknowledge? Can't he see us?" I asked in exasperation.

Gravity My Enemy

"Oh, he sees us. He just doesn't want to come in," he said, matter-of-fact.

"But why? Aren't there rules at sea?" This was preposterous. We sent a distress signal and were being ignored.

"There's no obligation. He might have a schedule to keep, maybe doesn't want to get involved. Sometimes there's piracy in these waters and he may think our signal's a trap. *Quién sabe?* Who knows?"

After a short time, we could no longer see the ship and I felt more desperate and lonely than ever. The air mattress was inflated at my side on the deck and I tried to imagine what it would be like to be lying on it, floating by myself among the white maelstrom near shore and I felt an involuntary shudder.

Captain Lopera came to me again and said, "Of course, the rudder isn't totally lost but hanging by a chain connected to the hull." He explained that the big nut or whatever it was that secured the rudder's shaft inside a tube, had sheared off and the rudder had dropped out of the tube housing and was hanging underneath the ship.

"Can't somebody recover it?" I was now hopeful, and imagined they could pass a rope down the shaft housing from the top and someone could dive below and fasten it to the end of the rudder shaft, to be pulled up again in place.

"We could, but in the dark and in these waters that are known for having many sharks, I can't persuade anyone to go!"

"If we survive, could someone do it tomorrow?" I asked hopefully.

"Perhaps," he replied, "but I doubt it.

"Too many sharks, and I don't have a good diver on board. If we survive, we'll think of something," he said, rather wistfully, I thought.

Cabo Marzo — Adrift

The exhaustion of the day and the stress of the emergency must have had its effect on me, as I fell asleep on a cot on which I had reclined to rest. When I awoke, it was getting light in the early morning and, as I gathered my senses, I felt jubilant to realize we were still afloat and alive, and astonished that I had slept for hours while in jeopardy of a shipwreck. I got up into my wheelchair quickly and looked around. We were about two hundred yards from the rocks. The surf crashed against them in a thunderous roar, and shot explosively skyward in huge plumes, soaking the black rock. High above, hundreds of brown boobies squawked among their nest colony, while others flew purposefully overhead towards the sea in their search for sardines. Obviously, the anchor had caught and we were safe, at least for the time being.

I was anxious to get a report on our state of affairs. The ship heaved up and down in the huge swells that had grown in size as they reached the shallower waters near the rocks. I glanced toward the stern and saw the captain working with the crew near the winch. They had two fifty-five gallon drums upright on the deck aft of the winch. Some men were filling them with seawater while others were lashing them with heavy ropes. In time, they opened a section of the scuppers on each side and rolled them overboard, one on each side, and suspended by the heavy rope to the booms, which were now swung out abeam. They had adjusted this arrangement so that one barrel was in the water while the other was raised above the surface. The captain ran the winch back and forth, testing his invention, and when satisfied, gave the order to start the engine and engage the propeller in gear forward. Slowly, the ship began making headway away from the perilous rocks, as they raised the

anchor and, when further out to sea and safely
away from the rocks, Captain Lopera worked the
winch so that the portside barrel dragged in the
water and the starboard barrel was lifted free
of the water into the air. Sluggishly, the boat
responded and swung its bows toward the south as
they raised the port-side barrel barely clear of
the water and lowered the one on the starboard to
an equal level, barely clear as well. Far ahead
on the horizon we could see another point with
some rocks to the right and the captain set a
course for that. Since steerage was not constant,
the heading often drifted and required continual
adjustments by lowering and raising the oil drums,
an aggravating exercise but it did the job.

Captain Lopera's expression revealed
satisfaction with his ingenious steering
arrangement and after two hours we found ourselves
abreast of the very point that had earlier been
our target heading. The huge rocks, called Los
Vidales, heralded our entrance into the bay of
Bahía Solano, the largest Colombian town north
of Buenaventura. In another hour, we reached the
proximities of the town itself, nestled between
two tall mountain ridges whose red earth scars
gave evidence of recent landslides caused by the
earth tremors that were frequent in the region.

We rested at anchor off the town as the
captain, accompanied by two of his crew, ran into
town in the ship's launch to talk with the local
welder. I sat in the warm sun and read a novel. I
felt no inclination to run into Bahía Solano. I had
been there many times on the way to Cabo Marzo.
It was a mosquito-infested town where I once got a
bad case of scabies, the people were a troublesome
sort and the place smelled of raw sewage.

The captain returned after a couple of hours
and seemed cheerful and energetic. Evidently he

Cabo Marzo — Adrift

had located a good welder with adequate equipment to affect a repair.

The tides on the Pacific side of Colombia fluctuate about twelve to fifteen feet. In the shallow bay of Bahía Solano, this variation represented several hundred yards of beach between high and low tides. The shoreline to the south of town was more abrupt, forming almost a cliff with a road on top of it. The captain, obviously consulting tide tables he kept in his cabin, timed the operation so as to be next to this steep shoreline at high tide — so close, in fact, that the belly of the ship's hull chafed against the shoreline with the light wave action of the sea. The ship was securely lashed broadside to the shore with heavy lines. We had then waited while Captain Lopera was in town and, during his absence, the ship began to noticeably list to port. After two or three more hours, I found myself trying to get properly situated in my wheelchair so as not to roll into the scuppers. A sailor finally came to my aid and lashed the wheelchair in a reclining position against a bulkhead of the wheelhouse, and I resumed reading *Run For the Trees* by James S. Rand while the crew of the Yellowfin worked to detach the rudder. The jeep in which they had come from town waited alongside. Its seats were made of wood into a single bench, the hood and fenders were missing and what remained of the body was so rusted and dilapidated, it seemed unbelievable that it could run at all. Its driver, Rodrigo Rodríguez, waited as they finally loaded the rudder onto the open back of the jeep. He was the owner of the only hotel in town and one of the few fellows for which I had a high regard. He caught sight of me on the deck and yelled over to me. *"Ola, Edmundo!"*

Gravity My Enemy

I smiled and waved in response. The sailors and captain got behind the jeep and pushed to start it. When it finally coughed to life in a roar, belching a cloud of smoke, they leaped aboard and drove away. The engine quit again, they jumped out and pushed as it quickly caught and they finally sped away, the engine hiccupping on two cylinders.

In what seemed hours later, as I was beginning to get sleepy and the book was slipping from my hands, I was startled into wakefulness by the roar of an unmuffled engine and looked up to see the captain and his men drive up next to the ship and triumphantly jump out of the vintage jeep. They collectively hefted out the big rudder, now repaired. I waved farewell to Rodrigo as he bumped away in a cloud of blue smoke.

The crew rapidly began re-installing the rudder in its original tubular housing. As high tide approached, Lopera sent into town for the remaining wayward seamen and we made ready to resume our journey homeward. Bahía Solano was a sleepy, smelly town with little to offer. Unlike Cabo Marzo, it had no comforting breeze, the stench of sewage was overwhelming at low tide and at night it literally hummed with large, stinging mosquitoes. Yet, it seemed that sailors anywhere were content to visit the worst of ports.

Captain Lopera came to me after the rudder had been installed and high tide righted the ship, which now had its Caterpillar trembling rhythmically below in readiness. We pushed off from shore and slowly eased our way out toward the mouth of the bay.

"It's not a permanent job like we'd get in Buenaventura, but it should hold till we get home," he said, "save for any rough weather!"

Cabo Marzo — Adrift

We gradually made our way out of the big bay and were out on the open sea in less than two hours. It was good to be on our way again. I shook my head in amazement over the genius and cool head of Captain Marco Lopera, and felt thankful to be on board ship with such a capable man.

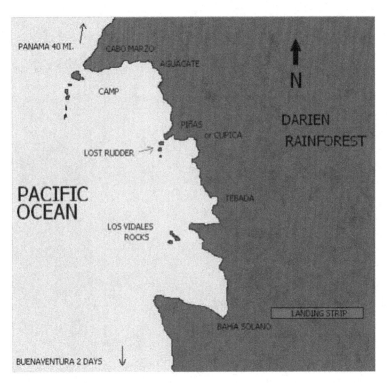

18 Cabo Marzo — High Seas

B y the time we emerged from the bay of Bahía Solano and onto the familiar, rolling Pacific swells, it was late afternoon and the sun's bright yellow orb was quickly approaching the jagged watery horizon in the west.

The cook once again served up his old standby, the hot beef soup we had been eating since we left Cabo Marzo eons ago. I had to admit it was still quite tasty, perhaps even tastier than before, despite or because of its vintage, as older soups and stews tend to improve with time, like wine. I have always been a firm believer in never eating a soup on the same day it was made, and for the same reason, I cannot enjoy a spaghetti sauce concocted an hour before dinner. In spite of this fact, and the cook's stalwart efforts with little at hand, I had a real hankering for some good seafood — certainly not an unfair desire given the fact I had been living on the sea for several weeks — and I expressed this to the captain during an idle moment prior to reaching Bahía Solano, in hopes there would be time to pay a short visit to the local hotel for a plate of fried fish. But Captain Lopera felt we should make our visit as short as possible. Knowing Bahía Solano as I did, I could not blame him.

No sooner were we out on the high seas after rounding the south point of the bay than Captain Lopera, now in a more jovial mood after the repair and overcoming seemingly insurmountable dangers and problems, walked by me on his way out of his cabin and casually said, "I've got a little surprise for you."

Gravity My Enemy

"You do?" I countered, but he left the wheelhouse without giving me an explanation. I was in dire need of some pleasant news, anything to get my spirits up, as I was weary and overwhelmed with recent frights and problems. But he left me sitting there next to the bored pilot who was standing at the wheel, and I had no clue to the mystery of his remark.

As the sky began to turn red and reflect its hue on the heaving sea and, looking in the opposite direction, the eastward sky over the coast darkened to a deep purple, one of the crewmen asked me if I wanted to go back on the poop deck behind the winch and watch some television. As evening was approaching, this seemed a super idea and I eagerly shook my head, whereupon he grasped the handles of my wheelchair and hefted me up on the pile of mahogany on the deck outside the cabin, and deftly maneuvered me around to the back, where I was greeted by several young men sitting in folding chairs and lying in hammocks.

The breeze was cooler outside and rather pleasant, and the scenery far more interesting. We were riding up and down broad swells as though on a gentle roller coaster, the diesel's muffled roar was felt more than heard below decks, and I could barely discern the tall mountains of the coastline about five miles off our port beam. It was very pleasant to be out on the deck. Our wake extended far to the stern and was straight as an arrow. The steel booms, earlier used to raise and lower the oil drums for steerage to port in an emergency, had been stowed vertically once again and the crew had rigged a large brown tarp over the poop deck to offer a shaded area during the day. At present, with the sun almost out of sight, it served merely as a roof enclosure and availed a rather homey atmosphere with the small cluster of folding

Cabo Marzo — High Seas

chairs and hammocks assembled as a small theater for watching television. The subject of everyone's attention was a very modest black-and-white Sharp TV which rested on a makeshift shelf over the winch, commanding the rapt attention of everyone present. They were watching some Colombian soap, and had obviously gotten very caught up in the plot, making frequent vociferous comments and exclamations as the story progressed. I found it hard to become engaged in this drama myself, and derived more pleasure from watching my companions' reactions and emotional involvement with this corny drama taking place before them.

After about an hour, the TV's picture began getting snowy. Several crew members grumbled and one lanky fellow in blue jeans and a tank-top soccer shirt that proclaimed *"Millionarios"* reluctantly got up and sauntered forward to the cabin, reached up and grasped the edge of the roof above his head and nimbly swung himself up onto the roof, as a monkey in a tree, and disappeared from sight. In a moment, the whole crew watching the image let out a yell, *"Ahí!"* — "Right there!" expressing satisfaction as the picture on the screen gradually became clear again, as our unseen friend above physically twisted the mast of the TV antenna.

A moment later, the skinny sailor swung down, much in the same manner as trapeze artists in a circus let themselves down from the edge of the safety net after an act, upside-down and onto the rail and then the deck. He ambled back to resume his viewing of the low-budget soap, without a comment. With his greater height, he was obviously the one designated to climb up onto the roof of the wheelhouse to twist the mast of the antenna to aim at the relay tower far inland, after our progress down the coast had caused it

Gravity My Enemy

to wander off target. This procedure was repeated two more times during the early evening, each time the lithe fellow climbing precariously up on the roof to serve as a human antenna rotor, and then swinging down onto the rail and inboard to the deck each time with practiced ease. When one soap ended, another soon began, some story about the abuses of an American fruit company on the Colombian Caribbean coast near Santa Marta featuring a pallid actor faking an English accent as he spoke Spanish, in an effort to play the part of the abusive American, equally boring to my mind but far better than sitting by myself in the unlit wheelhouse in silence.

But, in time my eyelids became heavy during the third soap and I asked a couple of sailors if they would kindly help me back to the cabin, where I had a cot waiting. I was soon sound asleep, rocked by the smooth swells of the Pacific.

Some time later, I was awoken as Captain Lopera exited his cabin behind me at the back of the wheelhouse, carrying a large compass in a wooden box in his gnarled hands. He talked somewhat angrily with the young man at the wheel, pointing to the compass, and I gathered that the captain customarily slept with the compass on the deck next to his cot and often woke to consult our heading with a flashlight. Evidently he noticed we were off course and came forward to make an issue of the pilot's carelessness.

The ocean was also kicking up. Instead of the comfortable, easy swell of before, the ship had taken on a jerky motion and a wind had kicked up and was blowing in gusts into the cabin. In the distance, flashes of lightening could be seen and it seemed we were about to encounter a storm. The captain, with a short nod to me in the gloom of the cabin as he passed, returned to his cabin,

Cabo Marzo — High Seas

and the young pilot at the wheel had a demeanor of chastised renewed alertness. I soon fell back asleep, but was awakened again before long by shouting and thumping footfalls on the deck.

The captain exploded out of his cabin and ran to the poop deck. More shouting ensued and I soon saw the bright shaft of a searchlight on the roof, shooting out in different directions. The captain arrived back to the wheelhouse, breathless, and shouted orders to the pilot to change course abruptly. He spun the wheel in response and the ship ponderously listed over to one side as it made the turn at top speed. It seemed we had turned completely around 180° and were now heading north. The powerful searchlight on top of the cabin shot its blue-white beam forward overhead and wandered back and forth, left to right, as though seeking something on the water.

"What's going on?!" I shouted to the pilot.

"Man overboard!" he yelled back, visibly upset and peering forward intently.

The Yellowfin went first in one direction and the pilot then spun the wheel on the captain's command to change our heading in another, and then another. The beam of the spotlight burned through the misty air as a white-hot shaft. Spray from the bow was illuminated momentarily. Other sailors on foot lit smaller, powerful hand-held lamps to search the rough, black waters off on all sides of the boat but with each passing moment there was an air of increasing desperation and hopelessness.

We circled the area round and round, fruitlessly, for over three hours. No one spotted even a sign of the man overboard.

He had evidently fallen when routinely climbing up on the roof to rotate the antenna. A slip, a slight mistake, a lost grip, a rogue wave in the worsening weather, and he was gone.

Gravity My Enemy

The very contemplation of what he must have gone through, the desperation, the frantic unheard shouting, the noise of the diesel and increasing wind, the fatigue of trying to remain afloat treading water, watching the ship recede in the black night... I shuddered and choked back a sob. And soon I felt hot tears flowing down my cheeks. I didn't even know the guy but we had developed a small common bond over the last few days and I shared his desperation, his fight for life, his tragedy.

In the dark, other members of the crew became more morose and soon sullenly quiet, and I knew they felt at least as bad as I did.

The same two crew members that helped me came to the cabin and confirmed to me it was Saavedra, the same lanky fellow that had so ably climbed up on the roof the first time. They thought he was from Pereira- Colombian coffee country. He had been in the Colombian navy in his earlier years and joined up with Lopera when the captain retired and bought the Yellowfin. They had been together for several years. Soon, the captain returned and, even in the darkness I could see the heavy lines in his face and sense the heaviness of spirit. I felt a deep sympathy for what he must be experiencing. In a low voice, he finally gave a new heading to the pilot, with an audible sigh, and we resumed our southbound journey. There was obviously no hope of rescue after all this time and the searchlight was shut off, as a statement of finality. Captain Lopera returned to his cabin, and I lay down once again in hopes of getting some badly-needed sleep, but could not get the image out of my mind of a young man struggling in the dark waves miles from land, choking as he swallowed water, renewing his frantic struggle to remain alive, but gradually

Cabo Marzo — High Seas

being sapped of strength, inexorably losing to the tomb of the sea. Then unconscious, relaxation and peace as his body sank slowly down into the dark depths of the Pacific, adding to the many thousands, millions, of souls who had preceded him in similar death struggles.

My own struggle with sleep finally ceased and I found peace finally, temporarily secure on a little damp cot on a small ship tossed by huge swells on the black Pacific Ocean, the thin line between life and death a frail one at best.

***

I fell off the cot and rolled in the sawdust on the deck, rudely awakened, utterly exhausted, spitting sawdust from my mouth, confused and scared. I sat up with difficulty and dragged myself to the cot and tried to hoist myself up onto it but was too weak and exhausted, and the deck was heaving violently.

The captain stood patiently next to the wheel and the young pilot, both peering ahead. Flashes of lightening illuminated the mountainous seas around us like split-second flickering strobe lights in a horror movie. I glanced out the side door of the cabin as I sat on the wet, sawdust-covered deck, bracing myself against the rolling of the ship, and another quick flash of lightening lit the swells to our starboard side where I watched and I gasped in horror at the sight. Never had I seen such seas! The ship was literally dwarfed in a deep canyon of water around us, the howling wind blowing the tops off the gigantic waves above in a horizontal spray that I could not distinguish from heavy rain. The doors of the cabin swung open violently and slammed shut repeatedly with a loud bang.

Gravity My Enemy

As the storm had worsened in my sleep, the crew members had spread sawdust on the decks to improve their footing in the relative protection of the cabin, as waves were crashing over the sides of the ship. We had already lost some of our precious cargo of mahogany. With some help from a nearby crewmember, I got back onto the cot and held on as though on a roller coaster off its tracks and out of control.

"*Un poco de marejada*," Captain said casually, as though he were telling me that a slight breeze had kicked up. "A little bit of rough seas." I was scared to death.

"Dangerous?" I asked in a shout to his back.

"*No mucho,*" he said with a calm that amazed me. "The only thing that worries me is the *timón*, the rudder."

He went on to explain, "Those tiny port welders are not well-trained. Self-taught. *Autodidactos* was the term he used in Spanish.

"Only good for fixing door hinges in *casas de cita,* in whorehouses," he shouted contemptuously.

The ship heaved violently, as though alive. The stress on the rudder must have been terrific. I found myself doing something I never would have imagined in my life: I prayed for that rudder, pleaded for its survival as a man would pray at the bedside of an ailing relative. "Please give it strength! Please, God, extend Your power into the rust of that old shaft and make it hold!"

I must have fallen asleep again, for I found myself once again awoken abruptly and lying on the hard, wet deck, caked in a layer of sawdust as a fish rolled in bread crumbs before being thrown into the hot fat. I struggled again to the cot and the pilot left the wheel for a moment to help me back up. I fell asleep again — how, in such as state of terror, I cannot understand to this day

Cabo Marzo — High Seas

but my exhaustion must have reached new depths. I awoke a third time (or was it the fourth?) on the deck, covered in sawdust, but this time I simply avoided struggle and let sleep take over, now oblivious to discomfort, rolling back and forth like loose cargo, and caring about it as much.

The next morning dawned gray and misty. The sky was gloomy, as though in mourning, the air heavy, hot and laden with moisture. As I lifted my head, I realized I was still lying on the deck of the wheelhouse from the night before, and my hair was caked with sawdust. My shirt was full of sawdust and I felt my body covered inside my clothing. I had pungent-tasting acrid sawdust in my mouth. My body ached everywhere from bruises and exertion, and it was almost impossible to make any movement. I lay my head back down on the hard, wet deck, closed my eyes again and tried to survey my situation mentally. The ship was still heaving mightily but I sensed less abruptness, more of a rolling motion. No more did it shudder and tremble in the steep waves. I could barely detect the reassuring vibration of the engine below decks, so figured we must be still moving southward toward Buenaventura. A crewmember passed by occasionally, so I surmised everything was normal and we had suffered no important mishaps during the stormy night.

Then I was suddenly jolted into reality as I realized that we had lost a man overboard. I felt a dull nausea in the pit of my stomach at the thought, and tears welled up again at the memory of what he must have gone through.

Even having accomplished so much, hauling so many important things to the construction site, the triumph of getting tons of mahogany at a steal, outwitting corrupt officials, the money we would be getting to defray the costs of

Gravity My Enemy

the ship, overcoming the near-death situation of the lost rudder so close to the rocky coast and the ingenious rigging by the captain to defeat overwhelming odds — it all paled into stupid folly, silliness and frivolous endeavor in comparison to the loss of that man. It was a fitting memorial for this day to dawn gray so sadly, so gloomily. Our hearts were heavy and it even seemed the ship rode slightly deeper in the water as we plodded home through the swells.

Cabo Corrientes was a large, broad point stabbing out into the Pacific from the Colombian mainland and a primary landmark north of Buenaventura. We had passed it in the night, unseen, hours ago, and I had hopes of soon reaching Buenaventura and putting this whole debacle behind us. The sea was still rough and very angry, the waves in a nasty chop that threw spray and looked ominous. How the Pacific attained its name was baffling to me, as I had never seen it flat calm. There was no sign of life anywhere, no porpoises, no flying fish rocketing out from under our bows as usual, not even the ubiquitous sea birds. We were traveling in relatively shallower waters and that caused the steeper chop, though I could never understand how the bottom hundreds of feet down could affect wave action so far above. My sides ached from the rolling and pitching of the ship, as I tried to maintain my balance with the weary, aching muscles of my trunk. I needed some sleep badly. I needed a bath and a change of clothes. I needed something to eat and had to figure out a way of relieving myself though, luckily, I was constipated.

Hours added to endless hours and the sea did not change, no feature changed far off on the horizon where I could barely see the dark gray coastline. The engine throbbed endlessly.

Cabo Marzo — High Seas

We saw not a boat, not a town and, were it not for the unmoving statue of the tireless pilot at the wheel, I easily could have believed I was a passenger on an abandoned derelict ghost ship, heading nowhere on unknown seas. I fell back asleep in a dreamless sleep.

***

I felt someone shaking my shoulder. I blinked my eyes open to see the face of the captain, smiling.

"Time to wake up — *despiértese*," he said. "*Estamos casi en puerto*," he announced. We were approaching port!

I smiled in return, sat up and brushed off as much sawdust as I could and hand-brushed my hair.

"Remember the surprise I told you about?" He asked. I said I did.

"We had too much excitement and I forgot to show you," he said grimly, but he held out a chipped bowl. It had two lobsters in it, bright red in color and steaming. I was taken aback.

"You might not be in the appropriate mood to enjoy these, but it's eat them now or never, and perhaps they will help." He had gotten them in Bahía Solano as a gesture of friendship, perhaps in apology for all our rudder troubles, or maybe it was in recognition of the monotony of the Yellowfin's galley, tolerable to working sailors but possibly tiresome to a visiting passenger. I could not guess the reason, but it was a welcome surprise. Captain Lopera was quite a nice fellow. They were hot to the touch but I cracked them open and did what I could to enjoy them for breakfast, accompanied by hot black, syrupy-sweet coffee. Rather than relief, I felt slightly nauseous. Either it was from the tragedy or the fatigue, or maybe

Gravity My Enemy

it was my first real experience with seasickness after many hours of rough seas. I tried not to let it trouble me, and put it out of my mind. Even Captain Horatio Hornblower, I remembered from my boyhood reading, suffered severe seasickness during his first days out at sea, so much so, he even hid in his cabin from his crew, or so said C.S. Forrester. I loved the savage beauty of the sea, and always would, I was sure. But the sea deeply scared me, especially as I thought about it late into the night while secure in my bed on the mainland, high in the Andes. It was a primordial fear I could not conquer intellectually. Man was so small and powerless, even in his big ships and protected by modern technology. We always felt safer in bigger ships but ran to small boats when these foundered. Why did the sailors in the days of sail usually not know how to swim? Was this an expression of resignation and futility? The ocean was a giant of immeasurable force, a mind of its own, a Goliath for which there was no David. As much as I loved the sea and would always be lured back to it, a seafaring man I was not, and after recent events, I admitted I had little chance of ever becoming one. I would prefer its edible bounty over all others, would be entranced with sea stories, marvel at watercolor paintings of the sea, would love its smell, breathe deeply in its breeze and feel my heart pound at its wild savagery, but it would always scare me to death.

We entered a broad inland watercourse as we entered Buenaventura, and plodded along on this broad waterway interminably. Small, gray shacks with rusted corrugated zinc roofs lined its shores, alongside little overturned canoes and larger, damaged fishing boats with streaks of rust painted down from its rotten bolts. The smell of land was different, putrid, reeking, a

Cabo Marzo — High Seas

mixture of rotted garbage, excrement, dried fish and wood smoke. I was anxious to reach port and actually feel the ship belly up to a wharf, and feel my feet on dry land.

It would be many days on dry land before I would get rid of the feeling of perpetual ocean movement from my guts, especially while lying in bed at night, but it was nice to contemplate a return home.

It seemed many, interminable hours to navigate the labyrinthine water course to port but finally we started seeing the larger building structures of warehouses and the anatomy of other, rust-streaked ships with names on their sterns like Amsterdam and Hong Kong, and before long, we even saw people and automobiles.

Captain Lopera had been inside his cabin and finally emerged, decked out in the very handsome white uniform of a sea captain, shined shoes, fresh shave and combed hair. He was actually quite a handsome fellow and showed the pride of his station in life as we approached the dock and he gave out orders from the rail to the helmsman to carefully maneuver up to the concrete dock. We finally edged up to it quite softly, lines were tossed ashore from bow and stern and we were made fast. We were home.

***

Many months later, friend George and I had occasion to be in Buenaventura on some errand or another, and decided to stop in on Captain Marco Lopera.

We found his house quite easily, perched high on a hill on the outskirts of Buenaventura. As we drove up the winding driveway to his house, it seemed strange and rather incongruous to think

Gravity My Enemy

he actually lived and slept in a house, for his abode to me in my mind would always be a little cabin in the back of a wheelhouse, his private inner sanctum, on the Yellowfin.

George got my wheelchair out of the back of the Land Rover as dogs barked around us hysterically, and lifted me out just as Marco Lopera — no longer a captain to me, as I saw him in these surroundings — came out to greet us. His small, mousy wife accompanied him, her hair a wispy gray and there were small wrinkles around her mouth and crow's feet at the corners of her eyes. She was a handsome woman despite her age, which perhaps came more from being the wife of a sea captain than her years.

He walked up to us in confident strides and stretched out his hand with a big smile, and we shook hands firmly as we greeted each other and I introduced him to George.

We sat and drank a tea together at a white metal table outside under the sun in his somewhat cluttered back yard. Cats slunk along the base of his house as we talked small talk. As I looked at him, he somehow seemed smaller in stature, more narrow-shouldered, than the sea captain I had known on board the Yellowfin. But I guess he indeed was a man of lesser stature, less heroic in my eyes than the man I had known on the Pacific so long ago.

19 The Llanos

During my tenure in Colombia I learned that the real political and military leaders in the country were quite accessible and genuine. Over the years, I had the privilege to cultivate friendships with people who were actually making history, something unheard of in my own country as regards common people, much less common people of foreign stock as I was.

A man who became one of my dearest friends was ex-president Guillermo Leon Valencia. When he retired from politics he returned to live in his hometown of Popayán, a city that had produced fifteen presidents despite its relatively small size and colonial aspect. I had met Valencia when he was still in the presidency through influential friends, and he struck me as a very angry man at the time, which intimidated me considerably.

When we later became close friends, I confessed this fact to him, much to his amusement. His response surprised me.

"Amigo Edmundo," he said, "the happiest day of my entire life was the day I left the presidency."

His career had been illustrious and, though I had no clue at the time, he was to go down in Colombian history as one of its top presidents. The violence that started with the assassination of Jorge Eliécer Gaitán and the resultant Bogotazo had set off an epidemic conflagration of violence throughout the country, leading to uncountable deaths that numbered in the tens of thousands. Bandit splinter groups formed consequently and ravaged the countryside. Political strife led to more violence, primarily between the two main parties, Liberals and Conservatives, and this was further complicated by the dictatorship of General

Gravity My Enemy

Gustavo Rojas Pinilla, which in turn led to a military junta that governed the country, led by General Paris. (His son, Gabriel, a U.S.-educated geologist, became a close friend of mine as well.) The country spent record years under martial law.

Guillermo León Valencia was one of the principal authors in the development of a political coalition called the *Frente Nacional,* or National Front, which in essence was a system whereby the two political parties shared and alternated governance, involving four four-year term presidencies of alternating parties, for a span of sixteen years. Valencia, a Conservative, was one of these four presidents.

Although guerrilla activity was soon eradicated for the most part under this system and determined military counter-insurgence, lingering animosity between the parties provoked mud slinging and scandal intended to degrade the prestige and authority of a given leader. Guillermo León Valencia was not immune to being victimized by dirty politics. Things got especially nasty during the last year of his presidency, thus his frank expression of relief upon exiting politics.

When he later died in 1971, I was invited by his family as an honored guest at his funeral ceremony, and sat with ex-Presidents Carlos Lleras Restrepo and Misael Pastrana.

Valencia had just gone to the Mayo Clinic for a check-up with his son, then Senator Ignacio Valencia. After the check-up (in which he, according to Ignacio, had gotten an encouraging bill of health) they were walking the streets of downtown New York together, visiting sports shops and looking at hunting equipment. Valencia was having a fine time. He had just had a dinner of frog legs in a fancy restaurant and was walking down Lexington Avenue when he suddenly felt very

The Llanos

ill. Ignacio checked them into a nearby hotel and, as they were entering their room, President Valencia collapsed to the floor and said *"Me muero"* (I'm dying.) and passed away on the spot.

At the funeral ceremony, held at the huge palatial Valencia home in Popayán that had been the residence of his father, the famous Colombian poet, Guillermo Valencia, he was hailed as "The President of Peace" for his successes in putting an end to the rampant violence in the country. Only small vestiges of Cuban-financed guerrilla groups survived, among them the ELN (National Liberation Army) and the FARC (Revolutionary Armed Forces of Colombia) headed by the same Manuel Marulanda or *Tiro Fijo* I had almost encountered while hunting Pudu deer in the mountains outside Popayán.

During his life, Valencia was a memorable character. His command of classic Spanish was eloquent and at times supremely hilarious. He was a master of the double *entender* and his ability to lay bare some of the traits of famous people in humor was popular among friends.

During a period when it was expedient in Colombian politics to remove him from the leadership scenario, he was sent as Colombian Ambassador to Spain while *Generalísimo* Franco was leader. They became fast acquaintances, if not fond friends, (Valencia used to refer to Franco as a *pendejo*, the vulgar equivalent of "damned fool") and Valencia spent many outings with Franco hunting driven partridge and large wild boar hunts. During many evenings we spent at Valencia's house in later years in Popayán, we were entertained late into the night with his humorous and fascinating tales.

On one particular occasion during a visit to his home in November of 1970, I mentioned to President Valencia that I was planning a hunting

Gravity My Enemy

trip to the *Llanos Orientales* the next month, and my younger brother was coming down from the U.S. to accompany us.

Valencia knitted his brow in concern. "Edmundo, I don't think a trip to those parts would be advisable."

When I asked why, he detailed a recent situation in which some non-Indian malcontent rebel was agitating the Indian tribes for some obscure political purpose. This was taking place in the eastern sector of the country adjoining Venezuela, where I was planning to go, and there had been some killings. He asked what area I planned to hunt and I described the region near the Planas River. He was intimately familiar with it, as he himself had hunted the region many years past.

I argued that we were careful and avoided problems effectively but he insisted I make plans for a different area.

After going back and forth on the subject for a few minutes, he finally picked up the telephone and made a call. It was to the home of the Minister of Defense, General Gerardo Ayerbe Chaux, a close friend of his.

After effusive greetings, expressions of surprise and exchanging of news, he told General Ayerbe he had me sitting next to him.

Ayerbe said he and I had met and he knew who I was. Valencia explained where I planned to hunt and asked for a report concerning the safety in the area. Valencia listened for some few minutes, thanked him, made a small parting joke, laughed and hung up the phone.

"That was the Minister of Defense. He sends you his greetings. He reports that this area you plan to visit is the very place where they have been having trouble and some Army troops have been sent there to quell the disturbance. He

The Llanos

recommends that you stay away from there," he warned.

I knew the area well from past trips, I argued, and insisted that we could avoid trouble. We disagreed, but I was determined to go. He finally shook his head in resignation, made a comment about my stubbornness, and finally succumbed to my persistence.

"I have an idea," he finally said, standing up, "but it may not have any value." He went into a back room in his house and came out moments later with a bolt-action Mauser rifle, and laid it on the table carefully.

"Only part of the danger will come from the Indians. What you really have to watch out for are stupid, over-zealous soldiers from the military that have been sent there to curb the violence. If they search you and find you have guns, it will mean nothing to them that you are an American and they won't make the distinction between hunting equipment and that used in a rebellion. You could be shot on the spot," he told me ominously.

"These are stupid people, looking for promotion. They shoot you and are then credited with killing agitators." He went back into his bedroom and returned with a small business card. He wrote on it briefly and handed it to me.

It simply said,

Guillermo Leon Valencia
Presidente

and he had written a short note saying I was a friend and to be treated with respect. He was lending his rifle to me, given to him when he was in the presidency.

He handed me the rifle. It was a rather ordinary model 98 Mauser in 7 mm but I noticed it was unusually tidy. The stock was finely finished in hand-rubbed oil, and the bluing was impeccable. It showed no use. On the top of the receiver was a stamp of the seal of the presidency of the Republic of Colombia.

"The Colombian Armed Forces presented this to me as a gift when I was in the presidency," he explained. "You take this and use it as your own. This card will serve as your permit, and if you have any trouble with military out there, ask for the commanding officer and show him this card and the rifle." He sat back in his chair.

"At least that will solve any problems you have with the military." he said, "As to the Indians, you will have to use your own resourcefulness. If they are angry with past injustices, killing a friend of an ex-president will only bring attention to their cause. Now, let's eat some black bread and honey. The bread is made especially for me this afternoon and the honey's still in the comb. This is a real special treat. We may not see each other again!" And he smiled to imply a joke.

***

We started the trip in the early morning. My brother Tim had arrived two days earlier. A friend of Popayán, who was also a hunting companion but not going on this trip, insisted we take two deer hounds he had. He explained that the dogs would not only serve as a benefit to the hunting itself but would aid in identifying us as hunters to any military we might encounter. When we went for the hounds to his small nearby farm, the place was in pandemonium.

There must have been at least thirty hounds there, all howling and yelping hysterically. Some seemed pure blood black-and-tan hunting hounds but

The Llanos

others looked as though they had wandered in right off the street. He claimed they were all proven, blooded dogs. I was reluctant to take them, as it was a long trip and the confines of the Volkswagen bus we were using were pretty tight.

Forming the party were Ray, George, our ever-present helper, Oscar, my brother Tim and I. Now two hound dogs, which are not noted for their amiability, were added. They had absolutely no discipline and slobbered all over everything.

"You see for yourself," Roberto said. "They will make all the difference in the world!"

So, I accepted, wondering what I was getting myself into. Roberto selected out two lanky, rather skeletal black-and-tans, legitimate-looking and eager enough in appearance, but we were going to be literally sleeping together in a tightly-packed car.

The trip was grueling. The car was underpowered for the load we carried and the mountains we had to travel were some of the most rugged in the world. After two and a half hours we reached Cali to the north and continued further north over relatively flat lands till we reached the road that would take us over the central *cordillera* of the Andes. As we climbed the mountains, snaking around steep "S" curves, the little van labored away in first gear, we watched the temperature gauge carefully, and every time it started to overheat, we pulled off to the side to let it cool.

After several hours crossing the mountains we reached the summit at a point called *La Línea*, a divide that was a rocky, barren, cold and windy area. We then began a snaking descent that really tested our nerves and the quality of our brakes. The downward slope combined with the weight of our vehicle caused it to accelerate rapidly and it was necessary to slow it continually to

Gravity My Enemy

negotiate the sharp curves at the end of each stretch, beyond which was open space and a scene thousands of feet below. Rusted axles with wheels still attached, multicolored fenders and pieces of car body adorning the roadside served as grim reminders of the penalty for poor brakes.

The weaving, undulating line of vehicles preceding us, mostly heavy trucks with canvas tarps covering the back cargo areas, left in its trail a constant odor of burning asbestos brake linings. It was difficult for us to detect if the smell came from ours or from the others. Ray expertly used the gears, downshifting to minimize the use of the brakes. Before long we came out of the cold mountains and reached a town called Girardot, where we stopped for something to eat and a little rest to settle our nerves.

The rest of the trip to Bogotá took us up again into the mountains but the climb was not as steep and we were rewarded with beautiful scenery and lovely vegetation. There was a lot of eucalyptus. The air was fragrant with the smell of trees and high-altitude flowers. The area approaching the capital city became more populated. Small cacti were planted on top of ancient stone walls surrounding the *latifundios*, or large land holdings of the old aristocracy, as an impediment to trespassers. The side of the road was sheer rock, many times with tiny waterfalls and springs of sweet, pure water, where we stopped for a refreshing drink and to replenish the depleted water in our water cans. From the rocky walls, people had carved out little chapels that were indented out of the reach of rain, featuring a small statue of the Virgin Mary. It was customary for truck drivers to place used headlights in front of the small statue inside, as a sort of offering to assure protection while on the perilous journey.

The Llanos

On the darker side, the edge of the road through the mountains was frequently adorned with little painted metal crosses, to show the spot where some unwary or unlucky driver had gone over the side into the void below. The number of crosses was virtually uncountable. My brother Tim became very upset with this constant reminder of tragedy, combined with our own overloaded car and the smell of worn brake linings.

At one point, we could not avoid some uncontrolled mirth, laughing hysterically when we noticed that the yellow painted stripe dividing the lanes on the road started first to waver, then snaked more dramatically and ended by careening off the road altogether, pointing at a spot on a sheer rock wall where the vehicle had collided. Either the brakes had failed or the painters had indulged in too much *guarapo*.

In Bogotá, we rested for a day in a cheap hotel room, letting the dogs sleep in the car and guard our belongings.

It had taken us eighteen hours to reach the city.

The next morning, feeling refreshed in the chilly mountain air of the huge Andes, we headed out of town through dark, pre-dawn streets and got on the road to Villavicencio, the capital of the *Llanos Orientales*.

Traveling by land to the Llanos from the populated interior of the country is a major trek, often involving several days of hot, dusty perseverance and a very reliable vehicle, since any means of repair and parts is left hundreds of miles behind. Driving from the starting point of Bogotá down to Villavicencio is like riding a giant, four-hour roller coaster with no respite. In that short time, the altitude plummets from a lofty 8,700 feet all the way down almost to sea

Gravity My Enemy

level, and the temperature inversely soars from the low 40's F. in the pre-dawn Capital city to the high 90's or more as one nears the plains.

The winding road through the gargantuan, green Andes to the *llanos* is paved for the most part but is narrow, and since the mountains dictate road direction, there is rarely a straight stretch.

The car swings around one tight curve downward on screeching tires to another, tossing its passengers first hard to the right and then to the left as the car careens around each switchback.

Much of the road runs along sheer mountain cliffs on a shelf carved and blasted out of pure rock, with a drop at the verge of the road that falls dizzily into oblivion. Occasional reminders of the reality of possible disaster are seen along the entire trip in the form of battered and rusted fenders laying in the gorge below. Shiny, detached bumpers glint in the sunlight through the lush vegetation, and whole truck cabs with shattered windows lie at the bottom after having been violently separated from their chassis as they tear a path through the trees in a headlong, tumbling free-fall to their final resting place far below.

Giant black, rusting axles with pumpkin-shaped differentials populate the steep mountainsides, marking where distracted drivers paid the ultimate price for a moment's inattention while lighting a cigarette, or from brakes worn from the heat of constant use on many miles of decline, giving the hapless driver no other option than to leap out of the truck and helplessly watch their ponderous vehicle sail over the precipice in an acrobatic free-fall.

At several points, even the hewn rock ledge road was missing and gave way to a gap that was

The Llanos

spanned with a creaky, rustic single-lane plank
shelf to replace the slippery but solid rock.
The groaning wooden shelves were barely wide
enough to accommodate a single vehicle and lacked
the illusory security of a barrier. Underneath
the old, dry-rotted shelves were jury-rigged
triangular supports held together with rusty
bolts and spikes. Occasionally, planks were
missing altogether, and the driver of a vehicle
had to be vigilant to avoid dropping a wheel
into the void as he crossed. With no barrier, the
precarious crossing required the full attention
of the driver and nerves of steel. As passengers,
we just hung on and prayed.

As is the case too often in Colombia, several
good, stiff drinks provided the necessary courage
for many of the other drivers on the road.

The bridge groaned and swayed under our
weight as the car crossed to the relative safe
firmness of the other side. Someday, we privately
mused, dry rot would obviously cause it to fail.
Would it be today?

We breathed a collective, audible sigh of
relief each time as we reached the far side,
wiped the sweat from our brows, and proceeded,
hoping there would be no more of these wooden
shelves. When we had journeyed about halfway, the
road leveled out temporarily and we stopped for a
short respite in the small town of Cáqueza. This
was a truck stop of sorts, where they served tall,
cold glasses of wonderful, fresh orange juice and
generous slabs of roast pork. It was delicious.
George also found a store where they sold our
favorite small, maple-flavored cheroot that made
for an enjoyable smoke around a campfire at night.
They came in small, cellophane packets of sixteen,
and we stocked up with a good supply.

Gravity My Enemy

After an hour and a half more of mountain driving, the road leveled out and we reached Villavicencio.

"*Villao*," as the locals call it, is a sprawling, dusty, hot town that attracted us little, so after gassing up the car and filling the 55-gallon drums we had in back to provide for our needs the rest of the trip, we quickly threaded our way to the other side of town and got out on a straight, loose gravel road toward Puerto López, two hours distant.

As we picked up speed on the straight stretch, billows of dust rose behind us, and if any other car was headed in the same direction we either had to pass it quickly to escape the choking dust plume or slow our speed to fall behind enough to avoid the fine, white coating of dust over everything and everybody. Fortunately, the traffic was almost non-existent that time of day. The road was crowned sharply to shed rain during the rainy season. This caused a washboard effect on all but the very center of the road, and it was narrow, so passing another car involved some risk and presence of mind, or the car would spin out of control in the gravel and end up in one of the numerous, swampy drainage ditches along the side of the road, populated with jacanas and white cattle egrets.

After two hours, we finally reached Puerto López in the heat of the midday. It was a sleepy town right out of an old Western movie, except it had many shade trees.

Clapboard houses lined dusty, pot-holed streets, which were shaded with scrubby acacias. Open-windowed bars were everywhere, with hostile-looking cowboys leaning against doorframes, smoking stubby cigarettes. Prostitutes

The Llanos

peered out windows and stood in doorways as they spit contemptuously in the dust.

After a short eating stop in Puerto López, we drove down to the river, which bisects the town. This was the Meta River, a major flowage that crossed the plains in an easterly direction and eventually joined the huge Orinoco of Venezuela, flowing north and ultimately into the Caribbean, a river first seen by Columbus in 1502 and one of the wildest jungle regions on the Earth to this day.

There was no bridge. To cross the river in the few vehicles that ventured beyond this outpost, they used a rusted steel barge called a *planchón* to ferry them across. This craft could accommodate two large cattle trucks or four cars our size. When our turn came to drive onto the barge, which had just returned from the other side of the river, the sleepy captain snugged it up to a well-worn, muddy part of the shore and dragged out thick metal plates and tossed them contemptuously on the shore in a loud clatter to serve as a ramp over which to drive onto the barge. They were slightly bent from use by heavy vehicles and Ray deftly drove the van onto the barge, which rolled in the water from our weight. A big, empty cattle truck joined us on one side, and the barge rolled in the opposite direction, rather a scary experience. The captain came by to charge us a fee, and in a few moments, he released the square, rusty craft from the shore and we began to cross out into the center of the turbid waters of the Meta.

A one-inch cable extended from shore to shore, and the ferry was attached to it by means of a heavy pulley. Evidently an invisible rudder underneath in the water served as a vane so the current propelled us across. It was a tense crossing. The barge was definitely not very seaworthy or

Gravity My Enemy

stable, as its rolling motion indicated as each vehicle was loaded. Its steel construction would no doubt send it to the bottom like a brick if ever there were a mishap. To emphasize our concern, the captain ordered us out of the car before embarking. I explained I could not easily get out and he walked off with a shrug.

Much to our collective relief, the *planchón* bumped gently on the far shore and, after again clattering the steel plates, the boss motioned us to drive off onto the churned up, muddy shore. There was a big bump as we reached *terra firma* but we were very glad to be off the river monster. I was tempted to ask the man if there had ever been a tragedy, but since we had to return the same way and he didn't seem very conversational, I chose to remain quiet.

There was virtually no human habitation on the other side of the river, as we drove through the trees toward the open plains area we were soon to reach. We followed a deeply rutted dirt road and soon were out on the open plains, as though exiting a tight harbor into the sea.

Colombia's eastern portion has two huge river basins, one flowing south and easterly called the Amazon. The other flowing east and eventually north is the Orinoco.

Both of these massive basins combined form the largest wilderness on the planet. The Amazon Basin is characterized by increasingly dense forest as one flies south, while the Orinoco Basin consists of undulating plains. These plains, or *llanos*, as they are called, are low and rolling folds with humid clefts between them. In these low areas grow strips of thick, tropical vegetation called "gallery forest." This tends to grow in miles of meandering rows that divide the higher knobs and form open galleries of a

The Llanos

sort. The open areas between consist of windy grasslands. As one travels down through these galleries with tall forest on each side, there is the impression of going down giant hallways, thus the name "gallery" forest.

On the western extreme of this expanse, embracing the base of the Andes was the city of Villavicencio, the unofficial capital of the *Llanos Orientales*, now lying two hours behind us to the west. It sits on the very edge of civilization and is the last outpost before venturing out onto the vast, hot, wind-blown, plains.

The combination of open plains and wooded cover makes an ideal habitat for large game animals the world over, and the Eastern Plains of Colombia is a textbook example of this.

Birdlife and reptiles abound.

The Colombian Llanos look almost identical to the plains of East Africa, with roaming herds of animals, flat-topped acacias and birds of prey wheeling overhead on the thermals created by the heat rising from the hot grasslands. Rivers are common, and the open plains are studded with tall anthills in colonies. These reach as much as ten feet in height and extend over several acres.

These were true *llanos*. The mud road was no longer rutted but instead was packed dry and broad. The grass on both sides was wild, yellow and waving in the wind. The *llanos* were quite undulating, making it difficult to see beyond the next hill several hundred yards distant. Over the top of each hill were several alternate dirt roads or paths fanning out over the horizon. We found there was little difference in the quality of each and decided that they must have been formed during the rainy season when one particular path became too muddy and another, new one was forged to avoid getting bogged down. After some time, in

Gravity My Enemy

fact, we experimented by venturing off the beaten path altogether into the grasslands and found that the terrain was almost equally drivable, with only a slight increase in bumpiness. We commented that this must have been very much like the early pioneers traveling the Bozeman Trail, only at a slower speed, Indians and all.

While glancing to the side we could often see distant expanses. In the lower areas were thin stretches of tall palms, obviously capitalizing on the greater humidity in these lower clefts, forming at times meandering lines of thin gallery forest that extended for miles.

It was very windy, a saving grace as the heat from the pounding, constant sun was penetrating. A thermometer we carried among the baggage was fished out and showed 112° F. Yet we felt relaxed and exhilarated. The car was running well and not overheating and we were going at an astonishingly fast pace despite traveling on a provisional path through the wilderness. At times we saw far-off grass fires that produced a wall of smoke that reached the heavens. The flames themselves were invisible but a constant feature of grass fires was a large number of many different species of hawks wheeling overhead. These were attracted to the smaller animals fleeing the fire. The heat of the plains produced updrafts particularly useful to soaring birds, which explained why most of the hawks were of the *buteo* genus with big, rounded wings and broad tails. Also common was the *caracara*, a falcon-like bird the size of a crow that had red skin on its face. Tiny, four-inch burrowing owls were often seen standing a vigil from a small mound of earth on the side of the road. The plains were a fascinating place and we enjoyed it immensely. The reports of danger seemed impossibly remote and far from

The Llanos

our concern. We had not seen a single human, much
less marauding Indians or surly soldiers.

In about three and a half hours out of
Puerto López, we started to enter a territory
that gradually appeared different. It became more
wooded as strips of gallery forest converged,
less hilly and the baked earthen path narrowed
into only two or three alternatives, some deeply
rutted but sufficiently firm to transverse without
difficulty. Occasionally there were vast groups
of tall, black anthills forming colonies off to
each side. Some of these anthills were eight or
ten feet tall and about five feet in thickness
at the base. We soon spotted some small houses
of mud-and-stick wattle walls and thatched roofs,
and before long we were entering a small inhabited
area that we knew had to be Puerto Gaitán.

20 Indian Uprising

The streets were packed dust, laid out in an orderly grid in the small town. Children playing in the streets stopped to watch us pass slowly by.

The apparent center of town was located within sight of the river. This was the Manacacías, about one-fourth the breadth of the Meta where we had crossed it. The main road ended down at the sloping bank and parked at the shore was another, smaller, rusty planchón.

We got out to stretch our legs. It had been a long trip. George dragged out my chair, unlimbered it and hoisted me out into it. Oscar took the dogs nearby and tied them to a tree, where they alternately howled and relieved themselves. We felt fortunate that they had not done so while in the car for so many hours.

We wandered over to what seemed like a place to eat. To call it a restaurant would have been a gross exaggeration. A woman came out and we asked if there was anything to eat. She had common fare: some crusty *pan de yuca*, thin, cheesy-flavored bread the shape of a doughnut, some canned meat that was the Colombian version of Spam aptly called *Carne de Diablo* on the label, Devil Meat. And the ubiquitous soda pop, fortunately cold. Their electricity came from a giant diesel generator that we learned ran during the day hours until seven at night. We bought a can of sardines, one of "Devil Meat" and some *pan de yuca* as well as regular bread. George and Ray each ordered a Club Colombia beer and Oscar and I had a local soda, which was obnoxious-flavored carbonated sugar water the color of dark urine.

The town itself did not seem very interesting and its people were evidently all

Gravity My Enemy

off doing something else and were unavailable
for any conversation or information so, once we
had eaten and gotten a little rest, we decided
to cross the Manacacías on the unstable *planchón*
and make camp off in the bush someplace, away
from possible problems with dogs or their owners.
Small towns like this offered little to entertain
their people and drinking was often prevalent.
The added novelty of *gringos* camping near them
spelled a sleepless night.

The crossing of the Manacacías on the iron
barge seemed more precarious, as it was smaller
and less stable. Luckily, we were the only ones
to cross, other than a man with a horse, and we
made it to the other side in a few minutes without
mishap. As we were crossing, we saw a two-foot
coral snake swimming in the muddy water alongside
the barge. The climb up the bank was steep but as
we bucked the car over the muddy hump and came
out on top, we could see a large expanse of plains
before us, with the dirt road we were about to
travel bisecting the grasslands in a southerly
curve, to more or less follow the course of the
river southward.

It was getting late and we did not want to
set up camp after dark, so we were constantly
on the lookout for an acceptable campsite as we
made the turn in the road. Not seeing anything
particularly special or attractive, we simply
settled for pulling off the road to be out of
sight of any passers-by, and after about a quarter
mile, pulled over to stop under a single tree.

We decided to dispense with the tent, since
it did not look like it was going to rain, and
there were apparently no mosquitoes.

In a half hour, air mattresses were inflated
and laid out next to the car and George was
boiling some package soup on the tiny gas stove.

Indian Uprising

We were too exhausted to eat much and were all asleep soon after dark.

***

I awoke to the hee-hawing of a donkey. I thought I was dreaming, but there was another urgent hee-haw nearby and the thumping of hooves on the ground.

I listened more intently, still disbelieving what I heard. We were far from any human habitation. What were donkeys doing out here?

The hoof beats became louder and ever closer. They seemed to be approaching us. I opened my eyes but as I stared upward, all I saw was a black sky with a million diamond chips of stars from horizon to horizon. The hoof beats were very close now, several animals.

Suddenly the sound was a crescendo and they were upon us, literally. Two or three large animals came galloping right across the top of us, missing us on our air mattresses by pure chance. I felt the wind of the hoofs as they passed inches over my body and the realization of how narrowly we had escaped injury struck us only afterwards.

"What the hell was that?" Ray gasped. "Jesus!" Ray shouted. "They went right over the top of us!"

After our nerves gradually got settled, having miraculously escaped being trampled by a pack of donkeys, we fell back to a fitful sleep, suffering only minor disturbances at times from the dogs, who refused to sleep outside the car. Fleas were bothering them. One dog would begin yelping at low volume and increased his yelping and volume in urgency as the flea entered his ear. Then later, another would do a rendition of the same. Oscar, who was the only person sleeping in

315

Gravity My Enemy

the car, seemed strangely oblivious to them. We were barely aware of them ourselves and eventually were sleeping soundly.

"POW!!" The explosion jerked us violently out of our sleep and we all sat up, wondering what we had heard that woke us.

"Pow! Pow-P-Pow-Pow! Pow! BOOM!!"

The sky lit up across the river with multi-colored stars and bright flashes, followed by more staccato percussions.

"What the hell is going on?!" Ray shouted in exasperation. We were all puzzled, still in a semi-stupor and confused.

"It's Christmas Eve!" I shouted, after a moment's thought. It had just dawned on me that this was December. We had completely lost track of time. More rockets shot up in a trail of orange sparks from Puerto Gaitán across the river, as though to confirm my assertion, some showering colored stars after a dull "pop" and others with reverberating concussions, felt more than heard, preceded by a blinding white flash. We sat there on our air mattresses and enjoyed the brief show. After several minutes the display subsided as the revelers exhausted their meager supply of pyrotechnics, all no doubt imported for the occasion from the far-away capital city. Some few strings of crackling firecrackers followed intermittently and then all was quiet.

"They celebrate Christmas with fireworks in the southern states, too," Tim said. We were all Yankees, Ray and George from Connecticut and we were from Wisconsin.

"Yeah, I guess they do," Ray answered wearily.

We lay back with a sigh and were soon asleep again. George was already snoring.

As the morning dawned, we slowly got up.

Indian Uprising

Oscar, who had been through the camp routine with us for several years and knew our tastes, got to work on a pot of coffee and was toasting chunks of bread on the grill to disguise the fact that it was getting stale. We paused briefly for this light breakfast of toast and jam with a small piece of white "mountain" cheese, drank black coffee mixed with chunks of brown *canela*, a block of unrefined sugar with a distinctive flavor, and soon the car was packed and we were ready to go.

We resumed our journey southward, out of sight of the river, which lie west off to our right, and following a clearly cut dirt road.

The terrain was rolling, with low, gentle rises and dips. Fingers of gallery forest and wet lowland protruded out toward the road on occasion but never quite reached it, so the road was dry and passable. We progressed at a reasonable rate. The ubiquitous hawks and vultures wheeled overhead in the cobalt sky. In about two hours, we reached an area referred to as "*Bengala*." A small, wooden sign nailed to a fence post signaled the location, with a little red arrow pointing left. This was probably the name of the old, abandoned ranch far in the distance. As we neared it, at the top of a long rise, we noticed rusted barb-wire fencing hung down into the tall yellow grass, stapled to rotten, leaning posts. A small, unused path veered toward a dilapidated concrete house. Standing to one side was an old windmill, long in disuse, with a rusted angle-iron frame and some of the blades missing.

As we approached, we could see the house had probably been unoccupied for years. The original white paint was black-streaked down the outer walls from rain. The old paint was flaking off the woodwork. A gray, weathered door in the front entrance swung weakly back and forth in the wind,

Gravity My Enemy

on squeaking hinges. We cautiously passed through a narrow, open gate leading to the back and, as we came around the corner, Ray stopped the car abruptly.

"Quail!" he said urgently under his breath.

My heart jumped. I had Indians on my mind, and was expecting a nasty surprise at every turn in these close quarters. Ahead of us was a scattered bunch of quail, picking grit from the road.

"Quick! La *escopeta*! The shotgun!" George whispered urgently to Oscar, who was already sliding a gun out from the piles of baggage in back of the car, pulling it out of its protective canvas case. George frantically rummaged in the metal military ammo box for shotgun shells, grabbed two and palmed them into the open breech. He then slipped noiselessly out the side door of the van and aimed steadily at the covey, which was now bunching up in alarm at the sight of the car, their heads sticking up like wooden pegs, and heading off in the direction of the tall grass on the opposite side of the compound.

Boom! The shotgun roared and kicked George in the shoulder. The cluster of pellets swept across the covey in a cloud of dust, leaving several stone dead and others crippled and fluttering on the ground. George let loose a second blast to flatten the cripples that still had their heads up and showed signs of departing.

"Not very sporting, but we need some fare for supper," George admitted, and walked over to the quail and stooped over to pick them up one by one.

"Eight!" he yelled over to us. As he came our way, we saw they looked to be garden-variety bobwhites. Ray started the car and drove up to him and he got in back through the sliding door and tossed the load of ruffled quail on the floor.

Indian Uprising

We passed slowly through the farm complex and continued on the dirt road behind it heading eastward. The road ran on top of a broad, gently rounded ridge, the sides sloping gradually off to our right and left. In the distance at the bottom of the slopes were stretches of forest running parallel to the dirt road.

About three miles beyond the farmhouse down the ridge road, we gazed off to our left and noticed an attractive, small blue lake next to a large wooded area at the bottom of the slope. The jungle stretched northward to the left for many miles. Ray turned the car left off the road in that direction and we descended toward the lake through the open grasslands. The ground was dry and firm. Even off the old dirt road, it was equally smooth. An armadillo scurried off into the grass in front of us and disappeared. As we approached, we commented on the beauty of the area. It was like an Eden. The blue lake measured perhaps a hundred yards across, and was roughly round in shape. The forest surrounding it on three sides was deep green and lush. Vines and flowers hung from tree limbs near the shore into the water. Inside the forest itself, it was dark and mysterious. The tall trees cast a pleasant, cool shade onto the grass on our side and it looked very comfortable and inviting. A moist organic smell reached our nostrils. We pulled up in this area and began unloading our gear.

After about an hour, we had a very attractive and cozy campsite. In front of the big yellow tent, Oscar and George rigged a tarp as a porch as added space for a shady dining area, and slung a tent fly over the top of the main tent to reflect the sun and create an air space through which the ever-present breeze could flow, to give the interior additional coolness.

Gravity My Enemy

Ray, always interested in fishing, soon had his spinning rod out and was heading down toward the pond to see what fish lurked beneath its dark waters. After camp was ready and gear stowed, Ray could be seen on the other side of the lake tramping around the thickly vegetated shore and casting artificial lures toward the middle. We relaxed in the shade, drank a warm soda and discussed plans for later.

There were hundreds of very bothersome yellow deer flies around us. They had bright green eyes. They continually searched for the chance to suck our blood. A bite from one resulted in a severe, itching, painful welt, so we were intent on avoiding them. The word given them in Spanish was *tábano*, which is the local term for "electric cow prodder," giving some idea how it felt like to be bitten by one.

We decided to go out hunting later in the afternoon and got together some lunch and a big pot of Cool-Aide in the meantime.

Ray came in to camp with a couple small fish that looked like *piranha*. They were slab-sided and shiny bright silver like newly-minted coins.

Indian Uprising

As we ate, Oscar went off to the edge of the wooded area away from camp, carrying the quail and an empty pot and quickly cleaned them for supper and washed them out at the water's edge. We talked about going hunting in the late afternoon and Ray was in agreement. We decided to return back west through the farmhouse area to exit the corridor where we were presently, and go around from there to the left, further southward, and enter a large, open "bay" of grassland surrounded by gallery forest. We would hunt the edges of the forest in this bay.

Large game such as deer and tapir often came out into the open to graze and forage at night and we could often catch them at first light in the morning and very late afternoons. We especially liked to hunt sectors that had recently been burnt over, as the new grass was tender and attractive to wild game.

About mid-afternoon we pulled out our rifles and checked them over, donned some camouflage clothing for concealment and got in the car to go. Oscar would stay behind to tend camp and work on supper.

Our primary concern regarded the reports of hostilities with Indians in the area. We had seen no sign of anyone — not even military — on our way into this area and thus were not overly preoccupied as yet, but as a precaution, we made arrangements with Oscar to assure our safety. We instructed him to watch for us when we returned, and explained that our arrival would be after dark. We carefully told him that we would stop at the top of the ridge above camp about a half-mile distant from camp and flash the headlights of the car on and off toward the camp to announce our arrival. We would not approach the camp until he came to us on foot. This way, we could be

Gravity My Enemy

certain he was all right and no one had invaded the campsite. We did not want to blindly enter an ambush situation. Conversely, if he did not walk to us, we would know he was either being held captive or dead. We did not mention the second possibility to him. It was a rather cruel safety precaution but a necessary one under the circumstances. We repeated everything and asked if it was clear, reminding him again that we would not return until after dark. It was clear, he assured us. He seemed casual and unconcerned, rather upbeat, as was his usual nature.

We then motored up to the top of the ridge over the same tracks we had made coming in to the camp, to create a sort of instant roadway that would be easy to spot in the darkness, then turned onto the old dirt road at the top and took a heading toward the farmhouse. The view from the ridge was spectacular. We could see for miles around us. There was a slight haziness and heat shimmer. The thermometer back at camp read 118° F. Tim especially was having trouble enduring the heat and, having noticed that he rarely had soup on the trip and seemed to be consuming an inordinate amount of soda, I explained to him that his tolerance for the heat would improve if he ate things to restore the salts lost in sweating, as well as liquids. I suggested he eat more soup.

"Soup?" he said incredulously. "Soup? How can you eat soup in this heat?" He said he wanted a freezing cold Coke with crushed ice.

"You know that's impossible within five hundred miles of here," I said, amused. "You'll find that you'll start feeling better, not cooler but better physically, if you start consuming more salty liquids."

"Like soup," he sarcastically said.

Indian Uprising

"Like soup," I repeated with a smile. "You need salt." He turned away in disgust. In fairness, he seemed genuinely out of sorts, almost ill from the effects of the heat.

We finally could see the farmhouse in the distance, and his mind fortunately turned more to the business at hand.

After cutting through the old farm compound, we angled out on another dirt road that divided off the main path in a wide curve off to the left. This brought us into the broad opening of the "bay," which was perhaps a mile across at its mouth. We entered the bay on the closest, left side, and began skirting the long strip of gallery forest about one hundred yards from the actual group of trees. The terrain was lower than the top of the ridge we had been traveling, and we had to be very careful to avoid wet, low spots, as we had gotten stuck on past trips, once spending an entire day to get out. There were no tow trucks or nearby friendly neighbors out in the Llanos.

We ambled slowly along the edge, scanning the tree line, and aimed toward the back of the wide expanse, which seemed about three miles in depth.

I was the first to be dropped off. Tim and George helped me out at a spot that looked to have a good vantage point. They handed me my rifle, a canteen of water and some insect repellent, then got me positioned next to a low bush to break up my outline, got in the car and proceeded on.

The sound of the car faded in the distance and I was alone for the first time, waiting for the disturbance of our arrival to "wear off." I remained stock still, watching for any movement on the edge of the trees as the copper sun sank slowly and imperceptibly in the hot afternoon sky.

I literally didn't move a muscle for two hours and was getting stiff. Only my eyes moved,

Gravity My Enemy

keenly searching for any movement. My senses were keen. My rifle, a 6 mm Ruger bolt action with a variable-power scope, rested across the armrests of my chair at an almost-ready position. It would require little movement to shoulder and fire it. All my senses were as tight as guitar strings, and finely-tuned.

A small troop of toco toucans flew to the trees at my left. Their flight pattern was that of woodpeckers, swooping, then hurriedly beating their wings, then swooping again. Their huge beaks seemed ponderous, the same length as their bodies, but were actually feather-light and hollow. Their beaks were black with yellow borders. The exotic birds had snow-white bibs in front, thinly edged in scarlet, the rest of their bodies jet black with a red rump at the base of their long tails. Their "song" was a raucous, incongruous croaking, emitted as they jumped from branch to branch, searching for soft fruits. Despite the dangerous appearance of their huge beaks, they had little power to handle hard fruits, seeds and nuts, so their diet consisted of softer fruits and edibles they could handle. Oddly, they were known at times to swallow small nestlings of other birds in a single gulp.

They moved on after a time, leaving the trees still and quiet once again, and my eyes resumed the scrutiny of the border of the woods. I suddenly saw a slight movement out of the corner of my eye and my heart quickly pounded in reaction. I trained all my attention in the direction I had detected the movement and tightened my grip on the rifle, which was slippery with sweat. I slowly wiped the palms of my hands on my shirt, and then grasped the rifle again, placing my sweaty thumb on the tang safety.

Again, I saw the movement and finally a large shape emerged from behind the brush.

Indian Uprising

It was a jabiru stork, about five feet tall, the largest land bird in Colombia. Its sharply pointed beak was shaped like a sword, black and menacing. He stood on long legs and his body was black and white. I looked at him curiously through the scope of the rifle. Soon, he was gone behind the brush, and I took a deep breath and resumed my search along the forest.

The sun dipped down to the treetops and the air cooled perceptibly. This was the best hour, but still no sign of game. Soon it became harder to see in the failing light and, without warning, it was dark. In the tropics darkness comes like a falling curtain. I hunkered down in solitude and waited for the other fellows to arrive in the car, slightly disappointed that the day had ended without any luck hunting, and resigned that it would take some time for them to arrive. I had listened closely all afternoon but had heard no shots in the distance, so I knew their luck had been similar. It did not surprise me when the twin headlights of the car appeared in the distance, the beam bobbing up and down as the car traversed the undulating terrain, and they told me on arrival that they had seen nothing. They helped me in the front passenger seat of the car, tossed my folded chair in the back, and we following the path in the grass back toward the mouth of the bay.

"Strange that not one of us saw any game," Ray commented. But we had been skunked before and did not consider this unusual.

We continued traveling out of the bay and began making the curve toward the farmhouse.

"Guys, I hate to say this," George said slowly, "but look behind us."

His tone was ominous and somehow frightening. Ray stopped the car and we all craned our necks and looked back.

Gravity My Enemy

Small fires were spaced along the dark outline of the woods from where we had come, at rough intervals. There were perhaps five or six of them. Seeing them startled us almost physically. They were a sure sign that people were present. This was an area where there had been none.

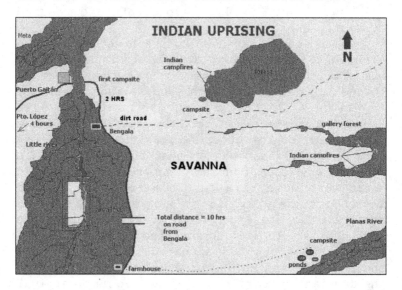

More startling than that was the realization that we had just come from that area and had, without a doubt, been observed. This perhaps explained our not having seen any game among four hunters spread out over a distance of pristine hunting habitat. An afternoon's hunt usually, but not always, availed at least some sightings.

"What do you think?" Ray asked shakily. "Well," I volunteered, "the fact that we saw no sign of people or human activity makes it an almost sure bet they're Indians. Don't you think so?"

"Yeah, I agree. If they were whites, we would've at least seen some dwellings and smoke

Indian Uprising

in the daytime — and they'd probably be grouped together." Ray said.

Ray moved the car forward along the path, aiming out of the bay, and toward the farmhouse. In five minutes the abandoned house showed pallid white in the darkness. When we reached it, we turned in and returned along the dirt road at the top of the ridge, back toward the campsite.

As we traveled slowly ahead, we were alarmed to discern more campfires at the border of the large woods to our left, the same woods where our camp was located but further north.

We counted three fires. They seemed to be small, cooking fires. Our hearts pounded in anticipation of what might come. It was a certainty that they could see our headlights at the top of the ridge, and they knew where we were headed. We continued on nevertheless, having no other option.

When we reached the turnoff we had made in the grass toward the campsite, Ray followed it for about a hundred yards and stopped, still on the flat on top, carefully aiming the car's headlights toward the camp. He flashed them on and off. The engine idled. We waited.

Ten minutes passed and Oscar did not appear. We were now genuinely alarmed. Ray again flashed the lights and honked the horn. Ten more minutes passed. No sign of Oscar.

"Pass me the side-by-side shotgun up here," Ray said, his voice grave. He loaded it with buckshot but kept the gun over his knee with the breech open for safety. As a second thought, he closed it and laid the shotgun across his lap. "What do you think?" he asked.

"I dunno," I replied warily. "Let's give him a few more minutes. Honk the horn again." Ray did so, but the horn sounded puny in such an open plains. He flashed the lights again. The engine was still idling quietly.

George said, "Shut off the engine — let's listen. Maybe we can hear the dogs or something. I'd hate to sit here blind looking down the light beam and get attacked from the side."

Tim kept quiet but I could hear his heavy breathing. This was not like life in high school in the States. He had entered a completely different world, almost as a step back in time when people worried about Indian attack and life was precarious on the frontier.

Oscar did not arrive.

We each pondered in our own minds what to do, all virtually scared to death.

"The way I see it, we've got two choices," I said.

"You're right." Ray was shaken. "We either go in now or we quickly get the hell outa here."

I agreed. "Okay, but let's decide quick." "We can't leave Oscar and all our stuff,"

George protested. Then he added, "Whether he's dead or alive."

"Right." I said.

"Right," Ray added his vote. Tim was too new and taken aback to even speak. George handed him an automatic Remington 1100 shotgun and a handful of shells.

"Are you giving him buckshot?" Ray asked. "At such close quarters, it doesn't matter if it's birdshot," George said, wisely.

"Tim, let's slide this back door open and you and I get positioned to shoot out the side. I'll hold a flashlight."

As an afterthought, he added, "Ed, you'd better limber up that Schmeisser."

I unhooked and pulled open the door panel on the passenger's side to reveal a secret

Indian Uprising

compartment in the door where we kept a small, World War II-vintage 9 mm German submachine gun. I unfastened it, and slammed a fully-loaded 32-shot clip in the underside and pulled the bolt back to ready, and put the safety on "fire."

"Okay, let's go," George said. "Let's not approach too slowly — kinda come in like gangbusters, and swing around to the left just before the camp so we'll have a clear range of fire."

Ray started the car, sighed audibly, and turned on the lights again, and we ran down steadily toward the camp. The tents soon appeared lightly in the beam of the lights ahead. I opened my door wide to get a free shot from my side to combine fire with George and Tim.

We raced up to the camp and Ray swung the car hard to the left about fifteen yards short of the tents. A cloud of dust followed and overtook us. The engine idled and we waited, watching the camp with nerves in a hair-trigger state, fingering the triggers of our weapons nervously. The camp was dark and still. George panned the area carefully with a flashlight. No one uttered a sound. We carefully examined the whole area for any sign. Nothing. George and Tim got out quietly, their guns at their hips, ready for the slightest sign of trouble. I pushed the door open wider and leveled the machine gun at the camp, feeling for the third time to make sure the bolt was cocked and ready to fire.

All was dead quiet.

"Oscar!" George yelled. I jumped.

"Oscar!!"

Something stirred inside the tent, and we heard the sound of a tent zipper. The two dogs finally barked.

Oscar finally emerged into the flashlight beam, squinting and bent over as he came out

.

329

Gravity My Enemy

under the tent awning. He smiled at us sheepishly, rubbing his eyes.

"*Qué pasa?*" What's happening, he asked.

"That's what we'd like to know," I said angrily in Spanish.

"*Me dormí!*" he said. "I fell asleep!" "Is everything okay?" I asked him.

"*Claro*," he said — of course.

"*Claro* your ass!" I said. We ought to shoot you right here and now."

"And the stupid dogs, too!" George added. We all got out in relief and Ray shut off the car. We got lanterns lit and the campsite finally emanated a welcome warm glow. Oscar stoked up the fire. At least he had not forgotten to make supper.

We all started dishing out supper, consisting of rice and fried quail. The breasts were browned nicely, and the meat white. It was delicious. We shared the small fish fillets and they were tender and flaked nicely. We poured coffee in dark-blue porcelain cups and sat around the fire, and even Tim, who had never smoked in his life, lit a cheroot with the rest of us. We were all still somewhat shaken.

"We escaped a tragedy this time," I said, "but the fires we saw were real and we were seen by those people, whoever they are. This may not be over yet."

All agreed, and we decided to keep guns loaded and post a watch for the night. Oscar got selected as first, "since he had already slept," we said sarcastically.

"Death penalty for sleeping on watch!" Ray said to Oscar in clear Spanish. He did not seem to be joking.

I think Oscar believed him.

Indian Uprising

Oscar

21 Camp at Bengala

The night was uneventful. We slept soundly despite taking turns on watch. Evidently, the people who had made the fires we saw the previous night were uninterested in us, at least during the night, and we felt more assured.

In the morning, Tim was sick and vomiting. I became very concerned. We had a good medical kit and an abundance of medications, but we were far from quality help and I hoped it was nothing of great importance. I talked with him as he lay inside the tent, holding his stomach. As it turned out, he admitted that he had foolishly taken a heaping tablespoonful of salt the night before in an attempt to restore salt he had lost from perspiration! In other words, he had taken my advice on eating soup and a big step further than mere soup, and now had a more serious ailment. I suggested he attempt to vomit all he could and drink copious amounts of water.

We used a few drops of bleach to purify water in the field, and then mixed it with packets of Cool-aide to eradicate the bleach taste. It worked well and tasted wonderful. Boiling water was a joke. In the heat of the tropics with no refrigerator, the water stays hot for hours.

We left Tim to suffer alone in the camp and drove out onto the dirt road on the ridge above us and headed east to see if we could find someone to talk to about the Indian problem and get some advice on a good spot to hunt ducks. About six miles distant, we came to a small shack with a corrugated zinc roof and mud-and-stick wattle walls. Smoke came from under the eaves, indicating habitation. Chimneys are an unnecessary appliance in most of the Latin American countryside and they simply cook over open fires inside the house

Gravity My Enemy

and let the smoke rise to the rafters, offering several advantages, the main one being mosquito abatement in the night. The underside of the roof becomes coated with creosote and treats the wood against woodborers while controlling the presence of other objectionable critters such as snakes and lizards.

We pulled up to the door of the house and greeted a young man who had come out. His name was Ernesto. He was about five foot four inches tall and had a Fu Manchu mustache. He wore a small-brimmed black Stetson with a fancy band of shiny medallions in the style of a Hollywood gunslinger. He had the hardened look of someone who lives a hard life on the frontier and seemed to be in his late twenties. The mustache unfairly gave him the impression of a scowl but he seemed friendly enough.

As we inquired about Indians, he informed us that several families of Indians had gradually entered the area over the past few months but his family had not been threatened by them. The Indians were camped along the edge between the wooded sectors and the plains. This confirmed our suspicions from seeing the campfires the night before.

We asked if he had heard any reports that they had been ornery or dangerous. Ernesto said that, to his knowledge, no one had been killed, but that he was unable to venture far from his house to find out and that, since he was poor, there was not much he had that could possibly interest the Indians. The assumption, of course, was that the only motives the Indians might have for violence would be stealing, and Ernesto obviously knew nothing about political issues. Yet, he said they showed little inclination toward friendliness and warned us that they may find reason to bother

Camp at Bengala

us, as we had guns and other wares that might interest them.

"If they come and demand something," he said in Spanish, "just give them what they want."

We had no problem with that policy, as it was our practice under ordinary circumstances with anybody living far from the conveniences of the city, to leave them all that we could. But, I explained to Ernesto, we had to limit our generosity to common, every-day items.

"They may demand your guns," he said.

"That's what I mean about limits," I clarified, and he said we could have problems if we refused.

"And they could have problems if they insist," I laughed.

The *llaneros* were a tough, independent people and further bravado was unnecessary.

The conversation turned to ducks. In the back of my mind, I wondered what Tim would do back at the camp if confronted with Indians demanding guns, and felt a slight urgency to return. Ernesto said there was a marshy area east of his house where there were *"muchos patos"* — lots of ducks. This piqued our interest, and we asked him if he would be willing to show us the way. He quickly agreed. I asked how far it was and he said,

"Not far." *Aquí no más*. "Right over here," and he pointed east.

Having been led on many wild goose chases that were *'aquí no más'* that turned out to be hours of taking locals on joyrides, I suggested to George and Ray we return to camp first and talk to Tim. They readily agreed and, as we pulled away, Ernesto jumped on the back bumper of the car, holding his small black cowboy hat so it would not blow off. He held a sharp machete in one hand.

Gravity My Enemy

Tim decided he felt well enough to go with us, but I suspect he did not relish staying in camp and having a possible confrontation with people he could not understand and who might be angry. Oscar once again drew guard duty and seemed pleased with the opportunity to stay in camp and probably go back to sleep.

We decided to remove most valuables from the camp, and loaded our guns and ammunition in the car as a safeguard.

The dogs stayed in camp as well, as an added deterrent. They seemed worthless as watchdogs, but the Indians did not know that.

As it turned out, Ernesto was true to his word regarding the distance, if not the ducks.

When we approached the marshy area he indicated, we saw it was open with little cover for ducks and not a typical spot in which one would expect to find them as it was too exposed. There were eight black ibises standing in the water, their heads straight up in alarm.

"Where are the ducks?" I asked Ernesto.

"*Allá!*" he exclaimed emphatically, pointing at the ibises. "Right there!"

We strained our eyes trying to locate the ducks he was showing us but could see none. Perhaps the grass was higher than we thought and they were well camouflaged.

"I don't see any ducks," Ray said.

"Where?" I repeated. *Dónde*?

"*Allí!*" he persisted, impatiently. Stupid *gringos*!

We finally realized he was calling the ibises "ducks." I said those weren't ducks, they were *coclís*, giving the word used in Colombia for ibises. Ernesto shook his head in disgust. Although probably edible, even delectable, we were not inclined to blast ibises for supper and

336

Camp at Bengala

I told him so, that we only shot real ducks. Then I went into a lengthy description of what we meant by *patos*, tried to imitate the whistling sound of tree ducks. Finally, he nodded enthusiastically and said he knew what I referred to, and those, too were *patos*, but a "different kind" of *patos*. Now, we were getting somewhere.

"Where are those kinds of *patos*?" I asked.

"I don't know," he confessed. "*Lejos*." Far away.

Thus ended our duck hunting with Ernesto. We found later that he was indeed an expert at chasing down and killing armadillos in the grass with his machete, and we had a tasty supper that evening of roasted armadillo. It resembled pork in flavor and we came to like it very much. Thereafter, we always kept our eyes open for armadillos in front of the car.

That afternoon we decided to head back to the same region we hunted the day before, and left earlier. Tim felt very ill but chose to go along for the ride. This time, we took the dogs, the strategy being to put them in the woods and hope they would strike a scent and put on a chase the length of the woods. We were not sure if deer from the *llanos* would stay in the cover and race along the length of the woods to jump out at right angles to the woods or make their escape over the open grasslands. Our biggest hope was not to see deer as much as flushing out a tapir or a jaguar.

We once again entered the "bay" and George was the first one out of the car this time. I got out about a quarter mile farther down the line, within sight of George. Ray, Tim, Ernesto and the dogs went on toward the bottom of the bay. They decided to not go as far as the day before, yet once out of sight and hearing, I resumed my old technique of freezing dead still and watching for any game movement along the vegetation, but

Gravity My Enemy

this time with greater expectations since I knew the dogs would be coming our way before long and possibly moving game before them.

I looked back at George. He was squatting next to a low bush. With his camouflage, it was hard to make him out. He was looking my way, and I gave him a slow wave. He waved back, being careful to keep movement to a minimum.

Some time passed and all was still. I glanced once again at George and he also was scanning the woods between us. I then saw him stand up slowly and peer intently at a spot near the woods. I could sense the tension in his posture. My heart started beating in anticipation. He had seen something — that much I knew. But what? I watched him nervously. He was the only indication I had that something was afoot.

He appeared even tenser, and then brought his rifle up, ready to shoulder. I saw three dark shapes of some animals running smoothly through the grass between us. I guessed they were very close to George. They were not deer, as their color was black and did not have the bounding gait that is characteristic of deer. What could they be? Capybara? Not enough water. Tapir? Too small, and tapir did not run in groups as far as I knew. They were passing between us toward the higher, open plains of the center of the bay.

Once past, George snapped his rifle to his shoulder and took aim, following their trajectory for an instant, and then I simultaneously saw his shoulder impact from the recoil of a shot, a faint smoke exit the muzzle and, to my left, one animal go over with all four feet in the air. Then a loud thud as the sound reached me.

I pumped my arm in the air and yelled "All right!" no longer having to take precautions with concealment.

Camp at Bengala

George looked over at me and raised his gun in the air in a gesture of triumph. He ran hastily over to the downed animal as I watched intently, desperate to know what he had shot. Whatever it was, George hit it perfectly, up-ending it as though it had been struck by lightning. He finally reached it and squatted down to look for a moment, and then turned the animal over. He stood up, shouldered his rifle and walked toward me.

"Damn feral pig!" he yelled as he neared me. "Nasty buggers! They came right at me at first and I was about to turn and run, but when I stood up, they veered off. I got my sights on the biggest one!" He was excited and breathing hard.

"Feral?" I asked, astonished.

Gravity My Enemy

"They sure looked like black barn pigs to me, only leaner. They had a nasty look on their faces!" He laughed nervously.

"That looked like quite a shot," I marveled.

"Pole-axed him! When I went to look, I couldn't even find a bullet hole, but then I looked real close and saw that the bullet went right in his ear. Where it exited, I don't have a clue — probably out his mouth!"

George was using a 6.5 x 55 mm Swedish Mauser with a 4-power scope.

"He never knew what hit him!" he said proudly.

We decided to stay together at my location and watch for any developments from Ray and the dogs. About an hour passed and everything was quiet. Then, far off in the distance, we heard a shot, then another. George and I nodded at each other silently, smiling.

Sometime later, still well before darkness set in, we heard the van chugging off in the distance and it finally emerged, its light blue roof looking like the back of a small whale, surfing the waves of blowing grass. They pulled up next to us and Ray got out followed by Tim and Ernesto.

"Man, you guys wouldn't ever believe what happened!" he said breathlessly.

"We got down to what looked like a good spot and got the dogs out. Damn stupid things didn't want to get outa the car!" Ray said, disgusted.

"Had to drag 'em out!" Tim interjected. "And they wouldn't stay out — they kept climbing back in the car!"

"Real hunters, these mangy dogs." Ray was angry.

Camp at Bengala

Tim laughed in amusement. "Brought 'em all the way from Popayán and they're scared to hunt!"

Ray continued, "Then when we shut the car doors and they couldn't get back in, they climbed under the car and we couldn't budge 'em. We ought to do Roberto a favor and blow them away right here, save the trip back."

"So, what happened? We heard some shots." "We just left the stupid mutts under the car. I went over and posted farther down the line, and Tim and Ernesto stayed in the car." Tim was obviously still feeling sick and Ray refused to take Ernesto with him, despite his protests. He had no gun and would simply contribute to more noise and movement. Ray got to a small tree that was standing alone in the open about fifty yards from the woods when a small herd of peccaries came out of the woods and attacked him.

"They actually attacked you?" I asked.

This seemed incredible.

"If I didn't shinny up that tree, I would've been mauled, and that's the God's truth!" We broke out laughing. This was unbelievable. Ray must have panicked.

"They were milling around under the tree below me. I damn near dropped my gun! They were actually snapping their teeth at me!" We could imagine Ray trying to pull his feet up out of their reach, while hanging desperately onto the tree and his gun, and we couldn't contain our laughter. Tim started laughing as well and so did Ernesto, although he could only guess at the reason.

"What were the shots?" I asked.

"Well, I got myself perched up in the tree, more or less secure after almost falling out

Gravity My Enemy

into the herd of pigs." We all broke out laughing again, uncontrollably.

"It's not funny!" Ray said, insulted. "Let me talk!"

We settled down and listened.

"They were still milling around below, snapping their teeth. I think they were white-lipped peccaries, not the collared type. They were mean bastards. The tree was just a little thing, only about twelve or fifteen feet high, and lucky for me, it had a couple of stiff branches I could hang on to."

"Did you see all this?" I asked Tim. He shook his head "no," not wanting to interrupt Ray's monologue.

"As soon as I felt I wouldn't fall, I just sat still, hoping they'd move off. I tried to aim the gun at one but I couldn't hold on and shoot at the same time," he explained. "But after sitting there a half-hour, with about twenty of these things snapping below," George again tittered. "I decided the only thing I could do was try to scare them off with a shot. I grabbed the rifle one-handed like a pistol and let off a shot in the middle of them! The kick damn near tore my thumb off!" And he illustrated the wound, holding up his hand. The web between the thumb and forefinger was cut and bleeding slightly.

"That did it," he continued. "They really bolted. I jacked in another round and let loose again, just to make sure. No way I was gonna get out of the tree without being pretty sure they wouldn't come back!"

Ray had waited a while in the tree, and then finally ventured down, and ran to the car. "Good thing the dogs didn't tangle with that herd," George said. "Probably would've torn those chicken-shit dogs to pieces!"

Camp at Bengala

"Yeah, and no loss!" Ray added.

We all got into the car, George driving, and, with a smug look, he drove over to the pig and got out.

"A hundred pesos says you can't see where I hit him," he challenged.

"I thought I heard a shot!" Ray said, "But with all the ruckus I couldn't be sure." Story telling is a major part of hunting, from prehistoric times to present, and George told his story in detail as we drove back to the camp. I added what I saw from my perspective, which was a very impressive shot. We stopped at the camp to make sure Oscar was okay and George got out and cut off a big ham from the pig and threw it on the floor of the car in back for Ernesto. We then took him home and said, "If you need any more meat than this, let us know." And he got out.

The trip had taken a good turn, and we were happy.

"You know, it's funny," I said to no one in particular at the camp, as Oscar was butchering the pig. "You can hunt all week, and if you don't get a deer, you say it was a lousy hunt. But, if you hunt all week, still don't see anything or get a shot, but with the exception that one deer appears and you shoot it, what happens? How long did the whole thing take? Ten seconds? A half-minute at most?" I asked. "Then you tell everybody, and remember that week for the rest of your life as A Good Hunt." I laughed. "What was the difference between the two hunts? Just a few seconds! The week was hours and hours, and seven whole days of nothing!"

"Except hope and anticipation," Ray said.

"That's the part that hunting is all about — not the shot or the kill."

Gravity My Enemy

"Plus the chance you'll get your ass shagged up a tree!" Tim said, and we all busted out laughing again. This time, Ray joined in.

It appeared also that Tim was feeling better.

We put a huge pork roast on the grill that afternoon, and ate like kings well into the night.

22 Río Planas

For some reason, we remained confident regarding any possible danger from the signs of incursion of strangers in the area, and decided to remain for another day to hunt the area, while taking the same precautions we had earlier, and remaining together at all times. Strangely, we had no encounters and, in fact, never laid eyes on these people. They were characteristically reclusive, as they had been in other parts of the country at other times and, despite some disturbances and news of killings, these people of which we had seen evidence nearby were probably the same.

A few years earlier in a region further east near Puerto Carreño and the Venezuelan border, an event took place that I could not erase from my mind.

Friend Roberto Ayerbe had been on a jaguar hunt with the writers of a well-known magazine from the United States. They had hired local guides who knew the area and once, while alone with one of these guides, Roberto had spotted some Indians across on the other side of a river. To his open-mouthed astonishment, the local guide took a pot shot at the Indians with his rifle, and they quickly vanished in the bush.

Outraged and taken aback, Roberto asked him what the hell he thought he was doing and the guide light-heartedly gave the rhetorical answer: "Shooting at Indians." Fortunately, none had been hit.

"How can you do such a thing?" he pressed the local.

With a casual gesture of dismissal, the guide said they did it all the time.

Gravity My Enemy

"It's commonplace," he said, as though he was commenting on shooting quail.

"And against the law!" Roberto was still outraged. "Have you ever killed anybody?" he asked, hoping for an answer in the negative.

"Oh, sure," he said, again tossing it off as though it were nothing of importance.

"How many?" He felt extremely irritated with the guide's cavalier attitude and no longer made a pretense of civility.

"Oh, I don't know," the guide answered, and added in illustration: "How many deer have you shot?"

I assumed these were the famous *Motilones* Indians.

With this still clear in my memory and having earlier related it to my companions on this trip, any defensive precautions we had taken were purely in a spirit of self-preservation and not antagonistic toward our presumed adversaries. In fact, we felt a deep sympathy for their plight and, if an encounter were to take place, we had agreed to carry out the intention to attempt dialog and offer some empathy and expression of support — without, of course, any gesture that would get us embroiled in an armed dispute.

A day later, Ray decided to take a walk in the woods to the east of the farmhouse, mostly to watch some howler monkeys he had seen there and to do some bird watching, a favorite pastime of his. He even carried a small pair of binoculars and a notebook, to hopefully add to his Life List of confirmed sightings, the ledger by which all bird watchers are judged. Mindful of his recent experience with the white-lipped peccaries, he also carried a 16-gauge shotgun and some shells loaded with birdshot. As it turned out, he was to have quite a hunt, without intending it.

Río Planas

As he was walking quietly through the thick brush, he spotted a deer standing quietly not more than twenty yards distant. Since Ray was a newcomer to hunting, it never occurred to him that a shotgun loaded with birdshot was far from the ideal weapon for deer but in his ignorance and excitement, he took aim and shot.

The deer went down, stone dead. The shock effect of many small pellets hitting at the same instant probably killed it as effectively as a high-powered rifle designed for the purpose. He was jubilant. Our hunt thus far had not been as productive as we had hoped and this was a major accomplishment, especially in the heat of the day when game was not habitually on the move.

Never having shot a deer before, he dragged it out of the trees onto the open grasslands without gutting it, and leaving it, he headed on foot toward camp in search of help. No sooner did he emerge from the woods than he happened to spot two large, black curassows, a big chicken-sized bird of the same family, giving a larger appearance with a crest of curly feathers on top of its head and a long, black tail. Somehow, he managed to shoot them both. They were heavy as he carried them out.

Luckily, Ray did not have to go far before he spotted us in the van nearby. We swung off the path to meet him and he breathlessly told us about the deer he had down at the edge of the woods. We were impressed with the two big curassows, as he climbed aboard, and he directed us to the deer and told us his story on the way. We were incredulous that he had shot the deer with a mere shotgun loaded with tiny birdshot. The only explanation we could conjure up for its effectiveness was the shock effect of many pellets over a large part of its body, even without the penetration of a larger, single bullet.

Gravity My Enemy

"I can't believe you shot that deer with a shotgun!" George exclaimed. I sensed some disapproval in his voice.

"Well, you know, it's funny sometimes," I remarked. "I consider myself a real expert when it comes to guns and hunting. And I think I'm justified, with years of experience and lots of shots fired, not just talk. But if I had seen that deer as Ray did, with a shotgun in my hands, loaded with birdshot, I never would've even pulled the trigger. Probably would've come outa the woods angry for not having the right gun. Ray knows little, blasts the deer with something I wouldn't use on anything bigger than doves or quail, maybe a duck — maybe! But Ray walks outa the woods with a big deer. Live and learn!"

When we arrived to the deer, George took a close look and could see little visible sign of any wound. Oscar was with us, as we had left the camp alone, in the care of the dogs, which we hoped would serve as a deterrent to any visitors while we were absent. Oscar got down on his knees and began deftly gutting the deer, and soon had the job done.

To our surprise and disgust, he cupped both his hands together and bent down and drank the fresh blood from the body cavity of the deer, claiming it was delicious. They hoisted the deer onto the roof rack of the car and we went back to camp, where Oscar hung the animal by its hocks and skinned it. It was at this time that the hide came off that we noticed the dozens of pellet holes in the hide, barely having penetrated to the muscle. Most of them fell out on the ground as he pulled the skin down off the carcass, like shucking a large corn on the cob.

We now had too much meat. We butchered off the choice parts of the pig and salted them

Río Planas

for later use. We likewise cut off the loins and hindquarters of the deer. We estimated its weight on the hoof to be about one hundred and thirty pounds. What we kept was probably half that. Oscar skinned the birds. Each was the size of a fat laying hen. Later that afternoon, we took the rest of the hog and the front part of the deer to Ernesto's house and offered it all to his family. They accepted the deer but only a small part of the hog, explaining their supply of salt was low. We gave them two pounds of salt, which was all we could spare, and left with a huge chunk of hog left and had no idea how we could save it in this heat.

"Maybe we'll run across someone that needs it," Tim said. He was feeling a little better after ingesting all the salt but not quite normal yet.

The dinner that night consisted of a big pot of venison stew and *curassows* roasted on the grill, which was a real treat. The stew was wonderful as well. We sat around the fire a while drinking coffee and smoking. There was just idle talk. As we were getting ready to turn in, Tim said, "What are we gonna do with that pig?"

By tomorrow it would probably be really ripe. I volunteered an idea.

"We've agreed to pack up and head south tomorrow. Why don't we load it on top and take it with us. If we don't run across anyone before it goes real bad, let's toss it in some water to see if it attracts some *piranhas*."

"Hey, that sounds great!" Tim said. "I've never seen those fish, but have always heard about them."

"Yeah," agreed Ray, "they say in the movies that those things can strip a cow to bones in a matter of minutes!"

Gravity My Enemy

We all enthusiastically agreed on this course of action and explained our intentions to Oscar, who seemed excited at the prospect as well. He had never even heard of *piranhas*, coming from a different part of the country to the west where there were none, but was fascinated when we told him exaggerated versions of the stories we had heard.

***

The following morning, we packed up early and headed out and back onto the main trail south, parallel to the Manacacias, which was still out of sight perhaps a mile or so beyond the trees. We were on fairly high ground and the trip was hot and dusty, with few features of any real interest besides an occasional colony of tall, black anthills or the sighting of an unusual bird.

The weather was clear and the sky a pale blue, with puffy fair-weather cumulus clouds that, we reminded ourselves, could quickly gather and give us a downpour that could bog us down in the mud for days. Traveling hundreds of miles from any significant population and its accompanying amenities always carried with it some risk, and this vast area of the Eastern Plains, which also formed part of Venezuela, had claimed many lives throughout history, the mainstream of life of comfort, and people in the cities totally oblivious to many solitary, white bones bleaching in the sun, each silent testimony to a desperate tragedy and story untold, without witnesses or compassion.

Nor were we haphazard or casual in our approach to being in such a hostile environment. We scrupulously cared for the mechanical condition of the car, responding with unified concern to

Río Planas

any subtle change in the sound or feel of the car, climbing underneath often to examine the carriage. Once, a brake line tube was broken and we repaired it. On another occasion we punctured the gas tank on a hidden, protruding rock. We sealed it by rubbing the puncture with a dry bar of soap, a technique we had heard once from the ever-resourceful Colombians. It worked only when there was no rain, of course. We carried abundant water, no longer concerning ourselves with the long-forgotten luxury of ice or cold beverages. We daily monitored our gasoline supply, and carried spare parts and filters, and a tire patch kit all in a heavy metal toolbox that George treated almost with affection. We took fanatic care of our guns and kept them and their respective ammunition within easy reach at all times. Back in "civilization," we mercilessly bothered doctor friends in our home town of Popayán for medical information, learned how to do sutures, take blood pressure, sanitize lacerations with hydrogen peroxide and iodine, how to use a tourniquet, give shots and diagnose the most severe ailments. We carried a veritable pharmacy with us for most contingencies.

The sun was hot, at its zenith, and we plodded along on the undulating, dusty road for two hours without seeing a single person or any habitation. The pig on top of the car was obviously ripe, as rancid odors wafted in our direction through the windows frequently, offending the nostrils. The dogs, too, literally stunk an offensive dog smell and living with them inside the car would have been more tolerable if they could somehow endear themselves unto us as friendly or intelligent, or even skilled at something, but they were cranky, cowardly and worthless excess baggage that smelled bad and had to be fed.

Gravity My Enemy

The road curved widely to the west and brought us closer to the forgotten Manacacías River. We were hot and needed a rest. We could see the refreshing sight of water to the west close by and decided to pull as close to the bank as possible. There was a very inviting shade tree as we neared the river and George swung the car under it and stopped in a cloud of dust. He shut off the tired engine. It was quiet and cool, and the relief from the engine noise and heat was welcome. We all breathed the fresh air deeply, and got out of the car, audibly glad to be stretching our legs. Oscar dragged the unwilling dogs out of the car and tied them to a scrub tree in the shade and took them a big plastic basin of water, from which they eagerly lapped together.

Ray walked down to the water's edge and looked around, probably thinking of fish. Tim, George and I slouched in the shade under the tree.

Ray came back several minutes later and announced, "There's a small pocket of water coming in this way from the river, forming a tiny bay somewhat isolated from the main body of water — a perfect place for *piranhas*," suggesting we offer the pig to them.

Piranhas are not usually as voracious as the stories make them out to be, but become hungry and aggressive when the water level has gone down and they have become isolated from the big water and their main source of food: other fish. When their food source diminishes over time and becomes scarce, they in turn become more desperate. We had no idea if this area even had *piranhas*, much less having any experience with their eating habits, so this was just a gamble; we were excited to see the results and were anxious to be rid of the source of the foul stench coming from the roof of the car. George got in the

352

Río Planas

driver's seat and slowly drove the car near the water where Ray had indicated. With Oscar's help, they untied the carcass and dragged the stinky hulk off the roof and it fell to the ground with a sickening "plop." Using the rope attached, they dragged it down to the water and unceremoniously rolled it into the water, where it disappeared under the oily surface.

We stood together at the shore, watching the nearby waters expectantly, as though they would soon erupt in boiling, seething activity, foam and blood splashing about.

But all was still. The water had not a ripple.

We waited. Minutes became a half hour.

Ray let out an audible sigh, and turned away and walked to the tree and its inviting shade.

The rest of us followed soon after him, resigned that, if there was going to be a response from these ravenous legendary fish, it would take some more time than what was shown in the movies.

When we got back to the car, I asked Oscar to dig out a bucket, a bar of soup and a towel and he wheeled me down to a different section of the shore from where we had tossed the pig, and I stripped down. Oscar brought up a bucket of water and dumped half of it over my head. It took my breath away. Sputtering, I lathered up in a state of relieved ecstasy and scrubbed myself vigorously, whereupon he dumped the remainder of the water over me to rinse. It was delightfully cool. Another bucket full of water felt unusually luxurious after the hot, dusty ride, and I was now soap-free and actually enjoying the warming sun. I decided to sit there in the wet wheelchair stark naked and allow the breeze and sun to dry me off as I gazed out over the water, sneaking an occasional furtive glance at the location of the pig bait to see if there was any sign of activity, but the water was still.

After drying completely and getting dressed, I summoned Oscar for a lift back to the shade tree, Tim came instead and, as he tilted the chair onto its back wheels to roll more easily over the rough ground, I asked him, "What do you think of all this?"

He replied, "The Llanos? It's like taking a time machine back in history. It's wild. It's beautiful and a little bit scary to be so far from civilization."

An hour passed as we rested. We decided to move on. We had been at the spot all this time and, as far as the *piranhas* were concerned, there did not seem to be any takers. Disappointed, but anxious to reach our destination before nightfall, we climbed back in the car. The roof had been scrubbed with an old broom we carried and it was clean of stench. We loaded in the dogs again, also scrubbed clean despite howls of protest. We renewed our journey.

About two hours passed when we finally reached a rusted fence line. A small white board was nailed to the corner post with the futile intent of designating the name of the property but long exposure to the sun had made it illegible. The road continued closely along the fence and we soon reached a modest house that lay off to our right. It was accompanied by several rustic, wooden outbuildings, the walls loosely boarded with spaces in between. They were all roofed with corrugated zinc. We stopped in front. The house was only thirty feet from the fence and it took only a moment for a very tough-looking man to appear on horseback, followed closely by two more.

They looked for all the world like characters from an Old Western movie, sporting worn, dusty

Río Planas

Stetsons, dirty leather boots. From the waist of
each hung an old, leather gun belt, slung low to
the side in the fashion of Hollywood gunslingers.
But these were no actors, we had to remind
ourselves. This was the real thing. All three had
the squint-eyed sun burnt countenance of genuine,
hard-working cowhands who tolerated no nonsense.
Their revolvers were big and heavy looking, the
metal buffed shiny from repeated rubbing and
removal of the tropical scourge of rust, and the
wooden grips on the handles were dark, oil-soaked
and worn. I could not help thinking that this
was like a revisit in time to a period in our
own history over one hundred years ago, when
people wore guns for a reason other than sport or
appearance. Strangers were viewed with suspicion
until their good intentions were proven beyond
the shadow of a doubt. This was where the only
justice came from: that wood and steel deterrent
hung from a belt, and where good behavior among
neighbors was in everyone's best interest. Despite
the obvious hardships of their life and daily
exposure to possible threat and danger, the three
men approached us with broad smiles, and reached
out to shake hands with knurled, callused hands
and a painfully firm grip. We were quick to explain
our presence, and showed the open, innocent
friendliness that wins confidence so readily in
a remote, hostile environment. We said we were
hunting just for sport, not commercially, and were
looking for the Planas River, which we expected
to find somewhere to the east. We explained that
we had been advised that this river region was a
good hunting area. They all nodded assent eagerly,
indicating that they understood what we were after
and, much to our relief, they said that Planas
was directly east of their ranch about forty-five
minutes distant. This was good news indeed!

355

Gravity My Enemy

The "Llanero"

We had practically reached our destination, after many days of travel and literally hundreds of miles.

When we asked for directions, however, they were vague and said there was no road or path we could follow to arrive there without getting lost.

I asked about landmarks or some other means of getting there, or even if there might be a

Río Planas

different hunting location that would be easier and closer to reach.

No, they said, Planas was the best, but one of them could accompany us to show us the way, if we could bring him back to the house that same day. It was still early enough in the afternoon and, if the time of forty-five minutes they stated was accurate, we could possibly make it, but the question remained, How could we get back to Planas alone after bringing him back?

"Your car will make tracks," one said.

We looked at each other as in question, and decided to go for it.

One of the men volunteered, got in the car, and we bid farewell to the two remaining, with a promise to return shortly. He said his name was Orlando as we drove off into a series of strange knob hills to the east. We each introduced ourselves. We had to carefully skirt each hill, as they were too steep to drive over. Luckily, it was not wet at their base and the ground was firm. The hills were almost perfectly rounded, as though from a cartoon fantasy or molded from mud by a huge child with an equally large tin cup. They were no more than twenty feet high and about sixty feet in diameter at the base. All of them seemed perfectly identical, and the general appearance and sameness was somewhat frightening, in its strangeness as though we were in an alien land where things looked different from the world we knew. The unchanging repeat topography was just that which lends itself to getting hopelessly lost. But, with certainty and self-assurance, our newly acquired friend guided us inexorably toward the Planas River, which we were happy to reach in the time predicted.

We arrived to a small group of lakes that, just as equally strange as the hills had been,

Gravity My Enemy

seemed also as though from a fantasyland. Each was perfectly round or egg-shaped in circumference and about sixty feet across. To add to their surrealism, they were of an opaque blue-green color and it was impossible to see even an inch below the still surface. We speculated that they might have been formed by some prehistoric meteor shower.

The gear was quickly unloaded in a pile. It was decided that George would drive Orlando back and I would accompany them, more to save time used in getting me out than for any purpose I might serve on the return trip.

Both George and I expressed some trepidation on returning alone, despite Orlando's assurances we could see our own tracks. As in confirmation of our worries we had noticed some areas where the ground surface was of a hard-packed fine gravel rather than grass and we feared losing our track. George and Orlando consequently got out near a wooded area and cut an armload of thin poles about six feet long each and cut them to a point at the bottoms, and quickly tied them to the rack on top of the roof, and we continued.

Most of the path was fairly visible, if we watched carefully but, as feared, there were indeed spots where we could not discern our path coming in. It was at these points that George and Orlando got out and securely thrust a stake in the ground. After a time, we finally reached the house, thanked Orlando sincerely, and told him we should be back out to the house within five days, information that is customary in remote areas to guarantee that help will arrive if we fail to reappear when we say.

As an afterthought, we asked him about Indians and in answer he shrugged his shoulders and, with a wistful look, finally patted his sidearm. These

Río Planas

were men of few words. His partners came out and greeted us again and we introduced ourselves. It turned out they were brothers, native *llaneros* and were taking care of the ranch, which raised tropical white Brahman cattle, and was owned by a man from Bogotá, who rarely came except to truck back some of the herd to market. The names of the remaining two were Luis Enrique and, of all things, Abigail, in an evident attempt by their parents at one time to give their child a foreign name without knowing its gender. He had skin the color of mahogany and, looking at him in his gun belt, looking like a very dangerous gunslinger, I doubted sincerely that he ever got any teasing as a schoolboy, if indeed he had ever gone to school.

It was getting late and nightfall drops like a curtain in the tropics, so we bid farewell and turned back to the Planas River area, secretly hoping we would experience no problems finding our way.

The return trip was uneventful. The marking stakes had served their purpose well and we were happy to finally pull into an already-erected campsite and our companions, who were just starting a small cooking fire with a pile of twisted firewood gathered from the woods next to the river. The Planas was not in sight but lay about one hundred yards distant, in back of the grouping of lakes and was marked by the thicket of trees that grew along its shores. The little campsite had a welcome feel to it. The main tent, however, was only about ten feet from the low, cliff-edge of the lake.

Ray looked at the proximity of the precipitous edge and said, "I hope nobody is a sleepwalker!"

23 Piranha!

The Planas River area had a strange feel about it from the start. The small, knob hills we witnessed on the way in gave us the first signal of its alien nature. These were so perfectly rounded as to make us wonder if they were possibly man-made — ancient burial mounds, sculpted by a people long-gone in our past, hiding within them the secrets of their culture and their ancestors. They had a screening effect, blocking off a view of any distance and giving us a claustrophobic feeling. This was very untypical of the rest of the Llanos and it had a confining effect on us. We felt a discomfort, a vulnerability that comes from being unable to forewarn oneself of a nearby, approaching menace. This new and strange world no longer had the openness for which the Llanos are famous and attractive. Despite it being our final destination of the trip, we felt uneasy.

The little lakes we encountered beyond the hills that surrounded us near the campsite were colorful and neatly laid out, their hue almost that of a swimming pool, but they, too, had a symmetry and perfection that was disconcerting. It was as though they had been crafted by a sinister, inhuman hand rather than the haphazard benevolence of Mother Nature. There seemed to lurk beneath their surface something unknown and vile, and we unconsciously stayed away from the sharp, low precipice that made their shores, in secret fear of accidentally falling into the milky waters to be swallowed by some ravenous, malevolent force.

The following morning, just as it was getting light, Tim and Ray wandered off toward the woods to still-hunt together, while George and I left in the van to check out a different area to the west.

Gravity My Enemy

Oscar stayed in camp with the two dogs, now long discarded by us as worthless, and probably slept an hour or two more after we disappeared from sight. George and I headed westward in the van, veering off toward the river, which was so small as to be non-existent in some stretches and only a trickle of water in others. Yet the entire stretch was lowland, thus wet and wooded. I got out and sat with my rifle laid horizontally across the armrests of the wheelchair, my outline broken up by a low piece of shrubbery. George continued off to my right with the car and went out of sight.

We agreed to limit the hunt until about nine or so. We were tired and our expectations were frankly low, as we had gotten a late start and already had plenty of meat in the larder.

After the sound of the disappearing car had long gone, I relaxed and settled down for a careful scrutiny of the wooded line spreading across in front of me. As soon as the sun came up, a breeze stirred from my left, much to my relief, as there was no better way to ruin a hunt than to be positioned upwind of game, which often trusted their olfactory ability far more than their vision.

I saw a big harpy eagle soaring ponderously just above the treetops. The trees looked like giant, green celery. The eagle was massive, probably the biggest bird I had seen so far in the Llanos, or anywhere else in South America, with the exception of the man-sized Jabiru stork. The harpy was dark gray with black markings and had a large crest.

Finally, the giant hawk-eagle landed heavily in front of me in a thickly leafed tree top about fifty yards away. I was very excited to see such a spectacular predator so closely, and abandoned all interest in searching for land game, just to savor this unique experience. His head was

Piranha!

the size of a cantaloupe and crested on top with big feathers loosely pointing up and backwards, giving him a fierce, streamlined appearance. His large beak was black and sharply hooked in a design to tear meat in large chunks. His body size was that of a large turkey and, through the branches I could discern one yellow foot. The thickness and length of the curved, black talons gave me goose bumps. They were so huge and powerful, I had no doubt that this monkey-killer could instantly kill the largest of monkeys in the forest, such as the howler or woolly monkeys, some going as big as thirty pounds or more and with canines resembling those of a medium-sized dog. Those talons could penetrate a skull in an instant. The dark, deep-set eyes of the harpy were menacing and intent, dangerous in demeanor. This bird looked to be straight out of the depths of hell, the Tyrannosaurus Rex of the present-day bird world.

Before landing, I noticed his wings were shorter and broader than those of an average bird that size, but more powerful. The tail was longer and less fanned in appearance than the soaring predators and carrion birds we commonly saw in the region, obviously designed for greater maneuverability among the branches of tall trees in the rain forest, as were the *accipiter* hawks that encompassed a family of savage

Ecuadorian Postage Stamp

363

Gravity My Enemy

hunters, this was a multiple of that in size, truly the Monarch of all flying predators of the world. I sat there utterly enraptured and in awe as I watched this magnificent bird.

Finally, after perhaps twenty minutes, the harpy leisurely took off with powerful wing beats and resumed his search for prey, disappearing in an instant. I felt limp and breathless, wanting to preserve this sight in my mind forever, and hoping frankly that no other event that morning would happen along to erase it.

I decided to simply relinquish my interest in hunting, took the rifle off the armrests and set it vertically butt-down on the ground under me, slid forward and slouched in the chair and cast my head back to breathe the fresh, warm air and soak up my surroundings.

I must have fallen asleep, for when I heard the car approach it startled me by its closeness. When George pulled up and jumped out, I feigned alertness but he said,

"What happened? D'ja fall asleep?"

I saw no point in denying it, said I guess I had, and told him about seeing the harpy eagle. He seemed fascinated and listened to my every word as I told him what I had seen. We talked about it on the way back to camp, which was very close, and we arrived in minutes. He explained he had seen nothing while out.

"But I did see some fresh tapir tracks going along the river on the other side," he said, "About six inches across and pretty deep-set. Must've been a good-sized animal. Probably from last night," he added.

This was good news. The tapir is a hefty, pig-like animal with a very movable, prehensile nose and is a good swimmer, though probably not as good as the capybara. They have an ancient

Piranha!

heritage. In size, they are the largest mammal in the Amazon region and an unusual prize on a hunt. Their big, three-toed tracks are distinctive and usually cause for some excitement.

Tim and Ray were back at the camp when we arrived, and Oscar was up and about, working on a campfire. They, too, had seen tapir tracks but no live game other that the white flag tail of a deer bounding away in the distance. I told Ray, the bird watcher of the party, about seeing the harpy eagle and his excitement was as though we had won the lottery, asking questions and expressing outright jealousy that I had made the sighting. He vowed to return to the spot where I had seen it that very afternoon.

"If you're not going back there, of course," he quickly added. I said I wasn't, as I knew how important it would be for him to make a sighting.

After a light breakfast, everybody turned in for a nap, while Oscar and I stayed up near the fire. Oscar took the aluminum pots and pie plates we used for dishes and scrubbed them out at the water's edge with sand. I pushed my wheelchair over near the edge of the small shore precipice and examined the pond next to the camp, as I idly smoked a Pielroja cigarette. The water was almost completely opaque and milky, calm as glass and a strange, blue-green color. There was no movement visible below the surface but, after a few minutes, a turtle stuck its head above the surface in front of me. I guessed its size to be slightly bigger than a foot in diameter, too small to make a dinner for us, so I just watched it for a moment, and it soon vanished beneath the surface, leaving a tiny ripple in its place. I never spotted him again, though my eyes searched intently all over the pond, which otherwise seemed devoid of life.

Gravity My Enemy

A bright yellow kiskadee flycatcher sat in a small tree near the pond off to my right, flitting out into the air nearby every few moments to pursue a flying insect, and returning to his perch to resume his vigilance and repeat his song, from which his name is derived, *"KISS-ka-dee, KISS-ka-dee."* In Colombia, this bird is called, for the same reason, *pichojué*, making the sound *"peech-o-WAY, peech-o-WAY."* This flycatcher is the size of a robin, has a lemon-yellow breast and a black-and-white striped cap.

I finished my cigarette and flipped the butt out into the water. I thought I noticed a slight swirl and the small, white butt disappeared beneath the surface. Strange!

I bent over and picked up a large pinch of fine gravel from below my chair, sat up and tossed it in the water in front of me, with some strands of grass and twigs included. Again, there occurred a swirl in the water right where the debris had hit the surface. The water was so opaque I could see nothing below its surface. Again, I threw some trash onto the surface and, once again, it swirled in a small eddy, with a slight splash. I pondered what to do as I lit another Pielroja, my favorite brand, what we called an "oval," loosely-packed cigarette that frequently burned holes in my pants as red-hot embers of small pieces of wood dropped from the ash. Its flavor was extremely rich and strong, making it impossible for me to ever after get any satisfaction from an American brand, even Luckies or Camels, which were flavorless in comparison. I drew the smoke deep down into my lungs and enjoyed the moment of the day. The idea that finally came to mind would have to wait.

Oscar finished washing dishes down at the shoreline and came back to organize the fireside

Piranha!

"kitchen" area. I sat smoking and intermittently read Robert Ruark's *The Old Man and the Boy* as I watched the pond.

Occasionally I looked over to check the kiskadee. After a short interval, my partners awoke and came out of the big yellow tent and discussed plans for the afternoon. Ray, of course, wanted George to show him where I had seen the harpy eagle. Tim decided to accompany them. I told them I opted to stick around camp and do some reading. In several minutes, they were gone and out of sight. I called to Oscar.

"Go in the back of the tent and bring me the twelve gauge," I said. "Bring just one shell," as I held up my finger. He brought them out after a minute and I loaded the shotgun and took aim at the kiskadee at the top of the ten-foot tree and, with some feelings of remorse, shot it. It dropped to the ground in a shower of feathers. I asked Oscar to bring it and hand me a knife. He was puzzled as to why I had shot a songbird. I roughly gutted the bird and put the intestines on the aluminum footrest of my wheelchair next to my worn loafer, and told him to bring me out the spinning rod and the tackle box of lures. When he returned, I searched in the tackle box and found a small, round plastic box of different-sized hooks, and snapped one on the end of a thin wire leader, which in turn I tied to the line, and bit on a small, lead split shot to add a little weight.

Taking aim at the area where I had tossed in the first cigarette butt, I cast out the hook loaded with a small cluster of kiskadee guts. No sooner did it hit the surface in a light splash than I felt a solid tug on the line and I yanked out a fish of about nine inches in length. I felt much like a Tom Sawyer with a straw hat and cane pole in a Norman Rockwell print.

Gravity My Enemy

Oscar looked on at me in casual interest.

I cranked in the line somewhat to raise the fish off the water and swung it to within my grasp and looked at it in the palm of my hand. It was a *piranha*.

"Look at this!" I showed Oscar. The sides were a beautiful metallic, silver-blue, brightly shining like a new silver dollar, with the same fine scales of a trout. Its belly was bright orange, and it had a fan tail that resembled a trout's but in body shape it was slab-sided like a bluegill or crappy of the north country.

"*Es bello!*" he exclaimed, "Really beautiful!"

"Watch this!" I said. I pulled out a clear plastic hexagon Bic ballpoint pen I had in my shirt pocket and, holding the fish firmly in my palm, I put the butt end of the ballpoint pen in its mouth. The teeth were incisors much like a human's but were sharply pointed. I forced the pen in the fish's mouth when I knew Oscar was watching, and the reflexive chattering, biting action that resulted snapped off one-half inch of the plastic pen with total ease in an instant.

"*La piranha!*" he said in awe.

"*Sí! La piraña,*" I confirmed. (family *Characidae, Serrasalmus Nattereri* — Piranha" is more common Portuguese spelling; "*Piraña*" is Spanish) I went on to explain that he did not want to go in that water, except maybe for a shore-side bath, and while handling these fish, he should be very careful to keep his fingers away from the mouth. He comprehended with great interest.

"Otherwise, they're like any other fish: Good eating!" I put another piece of bird gut on the hook and cast it out into the water and got another instantaneous strike. With the line taught, it fought briefly and I pulled out an exact replica of the first fish.

Piranha!

"Better bring a pot and put them in it," I said, re-baiting the hook for another cast. "And start cleaning them. No need to scale them — and you can leave the heads on.

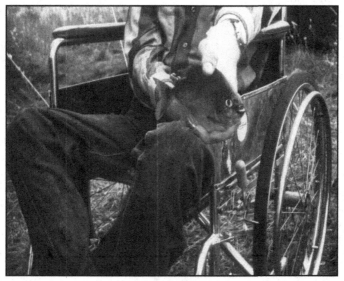

The *Piranha*

Just gut them and remove the gills."

I soon ran out of bird guts for bait and resorted to the entrails from the fish themselves, with no difference in the result. Each fish was almost exactly the same size as the others, and equally as beautiful. Unlike other panfish I had caught in the States, in addition to their vivid coloration, these were thicker and meatier in the back, promising very ample eating. In about an hour, I asked Oscar to make a count and he said we had thirty-three. The large pot was overflowing and I decided we had enough. Oscar added some water so they would not dry out or attract flies, and put a towel over them and moved the pot to the shade.

Gravity My Enemy

My partners returned early, well before dark, and said they had seen nothing but several more tapir tracks and lots of sign of deer. Ray was deeply disappointed that he had seen no sign of the harpy.

"How 'bout you? See anything nearby?" Ray asked.

I nodded for Oscar to bring out the heavy pot of fish, and said "No, just reading and relaxing." And I pulled the towel off the top of the pot.

Everyone stared in amazement.

"Where the hell did you get those?" Ray queried.

"Not a yard from where I sit!" I said proudly, gesturing at the water next to the camp.

"What did you catch them on?" he asked, still amazed. And I told them I had sacrificed our friendly neighbor, the kiskadee, to the cause, and shifted later to fish guts. Tim, on his first experience in South America, was especially incredulous, and took one out and looked at it carefully.

"They're beautiful," he said. "How are they for eating?"

"Looks like we'll soon find out," Ray said. "We're gonna turn the tables on the 'man-eater,'" he laughed.

Later in the afternoon, George got the fire going as Oscar got out the frying pan and some flour, salt and pepper. He mixed the ingredients and dusted them all with a coating of white.

"Sometimes," he said in Spanish, "the best way to cook is the simplest!"

"So true!" I said.

When the grease was smoking hot in the heavy frying pan, he carefully laid them in it, where they loudly sizzled and popped. In just seconds, he flipped them over. Ray ran for plates and Oscar

Piranha!

started dishing them out. They were golden brown and very appetizing in appearance, steaming hot on the plate. Without even bothering with a fork, George gingerly picked up a hot fish and, with his fingers, separated off the top fillet, which was snow-white and flaking.

"Wow! Somebody get me some salt!" he shouted in delight.

And thus we ate our fill of some of the finest-tasting fish we had ever had, all with our fingers.

"These are terrific!" Ray said.

"I don't think I've ever had any better," Tim said, and I added, "They eat good, too. The fillets come clean right off the bone. No bones to fuss with."

"How do you figure they got here?" someone asked.

"Probably from the river overflowing," Ray said. "Since they're separated from their food source, they're probably desperate by now."

"Well, they sure weren't hard to catch," I confirmed. "I could've kept going all afternoon."

The thirty-three fish was all we could eat. Each was quite hefty despite their small size in length.

We remained at this camp for three more days. Our approach to hunting was more casual than before, as we had plenty of salted meat and our newly found source of fish was right at our doorstep. We never saw a sign of Indians in all the days we were there. The last day there in the late afternoon, Tim shot a small deer with antlers the size of a small fruit basket. We dressed him out and hung him in the shade, and stretched cheesecloth over him to keep the flies out. When we finally packed up and left, we realized it was the end of our trip. Only the return remained, which was always tiresome.

Gravity My Enemy

When we reached the small farm, we decided to stop for a while and give some of our supplies to our hosts. We would no longer need many of the things we carried, and these fellows were far from commercial provisions.

They were glad to see us and greeted us with boyish exuberance. Tim hefted the bag of venison out of the back of the car and gave it to them. I explained it had not been salted, but we gave them almost all the salt we possessed. They were indeed very grateful. They lived at the farm alone. We learned that they had no families. They said they were all born in the town of Orocué to the northeast on the Meta River, and had grown up in the Llanos. Only Orlando had been out of the territory for a couple of years, when he tried married life in Villavicencio.

"I went to see Bogotá once," he laughed, "but that was too big — and too cold!"

They asked if we had seen any sign of Indians and we explained that we had seen several signs further north near Bengala, and they nodded to each other knowingly.

"*Y ustedes?*" I asked. "How about you?" and they said that Orlando had seen a few Indians on foot to the south of the ranch two days earlier, when we were camped on the Planas, but they vanished quickly. The brothers had seen only a few soldiers that arrived down at the river in a boat. They, too, asked about seeing Indians and made a report over a radio they carried.

We got out the medical supplies and I sat with the three brothers — their family name was Urrutia — in the shade and explained the different medications we had for them and how to use them. I was pleased that they listened attentively and once or twice made brief comments or asked questions. I wrote the names of the medications

372

Piranha!

in a notebook and made notations of what each was for and the dosage. I gave it to them and they took it all with elaborate gestures of gratitude. I was relieved that they were literate and could read from the page I had given them. Next, we asked about any food supplies or ammunition they might need. We took out some flour and a few aging potatoes and onions, and George brought them a box of shotgun shells, as they had showed us a worn single-shot that had all the bluing polished off. The stock was attached to the frame with tight wraps of wire.

Orlando held up one hand and dashed quickly into the house and came out with a gift of a red monkey skin. In his other hand he held a roll that was the skin of a boa constrictor. It was rolled up like a newspaper and was about sixteen inches wide and hard as cardboard. I held one end tightly and gestured for him to unroll it, which he did by backing up. Everyone stood there amazed at its size. George got out a tape measure from his metal toolbox and stretched it out on the skin.

"Twelve feet, two inches!" he announced. "And there's about three feet missing from the tail," I added. The tail end was cut off square and still had a width of about eight inches. "And a foot from where the head used to be. That's a snake of over fifteen feet!"

"Jesus Christ!" someone exclaimed.

We all got back into the car, shook hands in genuine friendship. The Urrutia brothers seemed actually sad to see us go.

Three days later, we arrived in Bogotá. We checked into a cheap hotel, the San Francisco, which was once undoubtedly an elegant place but was now worn and run-down. The once-polished brass door handles were brown with corrosion. The wooden floors creaked and the bellboys wore threadbare maroon uniforms, in a show of resignation to the run-down condition of the old hotel.

We parked the car in front and took turns during the next two days walking and feeding the dogs, who by now considered the car their home, and it smelled like it. We all showered in turn as soon we were settled in the room, and put on clean clothes, and turned over a bag of dirty clothes to the hotel laundry woman, who promised to return them the following day.

We had two important things on the agenda. The first was to find ourselves a good "city" dinner, and the second, to find a newspaper and get caught up on the news. For both, we decided to walk down the main thoroughfare, Avenida Jimínez de Quesada. The city was noisy and cold, the weather overcast and threatening rain. Behind us in the distance we could see the mountain of El Monserrate that hung over the city. It had a white cathedral perched high on its summit, reached by a Swiss cable car called the "*teleférico*." Part of the peak was draped in gray wisps of cloud and the steep slope was forested in eucalyptus trees. Black vultures wheeled lazily over the city. We walked together on the wide sidewalk and passed the large building of the famous newspaper El Tiempo, and were thus reminded of our interest in getting some news. We crossed the street and decided to get some supper at the Monte Blanco on the second story of the drab corner building, and sit at a window to watch the pedestrians as we ate. We had been away from people for a long time. I got a newspaper before we entered the building, and we took the elevator to the second floor, which featured a large barbershop, a curio store and the restaurant.

It was not crowded in the restaurant and George led the way through the array of empty

Piranha!

tables to a table next to the big window looking out onto the street. The bored waitress took our orders and we sat and had a big pot of coffee and looked out the window as we waited to be served. It was like an alien world. It was good to be back, but we all admitted that the Llanos were a paradise in comparison.

I sipped strong, black coffee as I casually paged through the newspaper.

"Mother of God! Look at this!" I said. On the front page was a single-column article entitled:

Muerte en los Llanos

I read a translation to them, which said: "Death in the Llanos" by Luis Carlos Campo. Puerto Gaitán.

> *"An Army patrol on the Manacacías River discovered today three dead, presumably victims of the wave of violence that has been rampant in the region.*
>
> *"The perpetrators," Army Sergeant Alfonso Muñoz says, "are Indians from the Planas River area" but their leadership apparently comes from white leftists with origins in the FARC — Armed Revolutionary Forces of Colombia.*
>
> *"The dead were identified as brothers of the surname Urrutia of Orocué, Department of Boyacá, and were employees at the finca called El Guacamayo owned by Dr. Jorge Lozano of Bogotá. We were unable to reach Dr. Lozano for comment.*

Gravity My Enemy

"An interview with General Gerardo Ayerbe Chaux, commander of the Colombian Armed Forces, said clearly,

'This is not an issue with the Indian population. It is leftist agitation emanating from groups wishing to disturb the constitutional institutions of the Republic.

"General Ayerbe further stated that this problem was 'small and local in nature' and he was confident that the existing armed forces would bring it to a rapid end."

24 Return Home

We opted to take the back route home through Huila and avoid the grueling and frightening trip over the central mountain range of the Andes, where the road crosses at the point commonly called *La Línea*. As we descended from the lofty peaks and chilly, rarified air of the Bogotá flats of 8,700 feet altitude (often referred to as the *altiplano*) we entered a warmer and more welcome clime and turned south towards the city of Neiva in the Province of Huila, an area once notorious for a bloody period of guerrilla violence but fortunately now tranquil. The undulating stretch of low hills was long and boring. And extremely hot. The only vegetation was short desert scrub.

As we reached the top of a gradual slope, the car slow and laboring, we heard an alarming and unmistakable knocking in the engine, glanced behind us and were horrified to see a thick trail of blue smoke. The knocking got so bad we were forced to stop.

With the car now silent at the top of a large rise, we could see both behind and in front of us for many miles through the heat haze. Not a vehicle or town was in sight. We were marooned, it was very hot and our money supply was down to small change, just enough for gas to get back. We were still a day and a half from home. We entered an instant state of despair and hopelessness. On what we thought was the final stretch home, all was now to be recalculated.

After standing on the roadside under the baking sun in a silent state of depression for an hour, a truck could be seen dancing through the road mirage in the distance, as though floating above the hot pavement. We readied ourselves excitedly to try to hitch a ride. There had been

Gravity My Enemy

so much banditry in this area in recent years we were concerned that local paranoia would make it difficult to be picked up, so we quickly decided to elect Ray as a single hiker, in hopes that the truck driver would feel less intimidated. Ray was a true *"gringo"* in appearance and our fortune lay in that fact. He got out into the middle of the road and we were beginning to worry he would be run over but were soon deeply relieved when we heard the truck slow and finally stop.

Ray quickly explained that we were stranded, and showed a big diplomatic smile. The driver invited him up in the truck and he was off without even a parting word. We all silently conveyed our blessing to him as the old truck rambled off into the distance.

Two, and then three hours passed. It was the height of the early afternoon heat and our words were very limited among each other as we waited, not knowing precisely what to expect. Ray might not find help and be forced to stay in Neiva overnight, condemning us to an uncomfortable night of uncertainty. In fact, we were not even sure how distant Neiva was, how long we would be waiting or even if it was the next town. What fools we had been to not have asked the truck driver when we had the chance!

Almost in answer to that same doubt, a truck appeared as a speck in the distance ahead and gradually neared through the heat shimmer, and slowed as it approached. We rejoiced with shouts of jubilation as Ray jumped out of a tow truck, which turned around to get into position to tow our microbus. We were fearful of even negotiating a price, the reasoning being that what we did not have, he could not charge.

It took us a far shorter time to get to Neiva than we had thought, there being no intervening

Return Home

towns, and he towed us to the nearest Volkswagen repair shop. The fee was lower than we expected and we dispatched the driver with expressions of deep thanks.

While George and Oscar pushed the car near the big door entrance to the repair shop, I went in with Ray to talk with the owner and explain to him our financial predicament to see if he would help us with some credit for the repair. There were few credit cards and no wire transfers in Colombia in those days, but we encouraged him to call our banker in Popayán to get some assurance that we would soon have money to pay. Happily, the establishment turned out to be a Volkswagen dealership replete with parts. He was a very kindly man and showed understanding and a willingness to get us back on the road as quickly as possible. He merely asked that we sign an IOU for the cost of repair and parts.

Secondly, he asked that we help in providing the menial work on the repair to reduce the cost. We were very grateful, and eager to get started.

Oscar pitched our smaller tent across the street in the grass next to a small municipal park, through which ran a small stream. We could no longer afford a hotel or restaurant. Camping was virtually unknown in Colombia at the time and we attracted the attention of numerous passers-by, mostly children. Two very attractive girls in tight mini-skirts stopped to flirt, as Americans were often an alluring novelty in such out-of-the-way places, and came out and directly offered their services. We were, however, in no mood for fun and games and felt the weight of terrible finances. They seemed slightly offended to be curtly sent on their way. George went through all of our luggage and made an inventory of all available food, while I cajoled the mechanic to place a priority on our situation and get started as soon as possible.

The mechanic in the shop, named Joel, felt we could get the job done in four days if we pitched in on the work, as the boss suggested. George approached us after a time and said his inventory revealed that we had enough food but were cutting it very close. The mechanic agreed to get started that same afternoon and we were very pleased. We had the engine out and taken apart before nightfall.

The next two days were a dreary, tedious experience. We spent the first part of our time sitting together in a greasy, depressing shop piled all over with incredible clutter, scraping the carbon deposits off all the internal combustion parts using pieces of broken piston ring as a scraper. The job was endless and dirty and we were all sullen and disinclined to engage in any conversation. We labored desperately. We each periodically took a piece we were scraping to Joel for approval. Some he sent back to do better, others he accepted. Finally, he began reassembling the engine and we had hopes that he would mount it in back of the car before the day was out, but it was not ready until the following day. We were crushed and beside ourselves, irritable and fed up with spending all our time in this jumbled mess of broken axles, old tires and rusted chassis. It was hot, we were tired and hungry, and time dragged on interminably.

Finally, the engine was mounted and after hours of work, everything connected. Joel gave it a try and we held our collective breaths. It cranked over quickly and fired, coughed and then smoothed out. It ran fine!

It was late afternoon. Ray visited the owner again in his air-conditioned office and brought

Return Home

down the invoice which, fortunately, turned out to be slightly less than we expected. At least it was a known factor that we could deal with. We each signed the IOU. The owner came down and encouraged us to wait to travel till the following day, as the sun was about to set, and even offered to get us a very low rate at a friend's hotel, but we were so desperate to be out of that shop and on our way, we unanimously pressed to resume our trip then and there. We bid farewell and thanks to our host, shook hands and left.

Getting back on the road was wonderful. At first, we felt very worried about the condition of the car, wondering if it would hold up, and began imagining we heard small noises here and there, but in time we settled down and accepted the noises as normal and realized that the car was indeed going to probably get us back home, a trip over the mountains that we estimated would take about fourteen hours.

As it started getting dark, we began ascending the central mountain range, or *cordillera*. The road was unpaved and only had a surface of hard-packed gravel, but was not as steep as the other, northern route and the traffic was lighter, though the switchbacks were more frequent and serpentine. At times we encountered considerable delays as a result of getting stuck behind a procession of lumbering trucks and not being able to pass them on the curves and the narrow road, often sitting behind a groaning truck going through its gears and belching clouds of acrid, black diesel smoke. Since this climb not as abrupt as the roads over *La Linea* lighter traffic there was the advantage, however, and we were able to make better headway with these few exceptions. By the time darkness was upon us, we were well up into the mountains, and it started to rain. Then it began to really pour. Soon small rivulets were forming along the sides of the road and, in time, these formed into small raging torrents, throwing water high in the air over obstructions such as rocks and fallen trees. Our visibility was reduced to almost nothing as the tiny windshield wipers labored away in a futile attempt against the deluge and the inside of the windshield steamed up with thick condensation, obligating me to constantly wipe it with a cloth so Ray had a small porthole through which he could see the steep, winding road ahead. An occasional oncoming truck, with its lights on high beam, blinded us so badly we had to stop. Then, as is the custom in Colombia, he would shut his lights completely off as he barreled down the mountain grade, leaving everything in total darkness, were it not for our weak, yellowed headlights. Then, just as suddenly, his bright beams would turn back on, causing us to throw a forearm in front of our faces to shield our eyes from the blinding light.

Some gorges in the mountains produced small, raging rivers that could quickly wash out the road. To counter this, the road builders and designers had poured huge concrete slab wash-ways across the surface of the road at those points, rather than the customary large culverts underneath as seen elsewhere, so the water coming in a torrent down the mountainside flowed across on top of the road and we had to drive through it. Happily, so far these flows were only several inches deep, but finally, we came to one that was so deep and fast, Ray stopped the car momentarily to examine it before venturing across.

"What do you think?" he asked, nervously.

The rain pounded like thunder on the tin roof of the car. The water crossing the concrete

Return Home

washway seemed to be about a foot deep, but it was hard to ascertain for sure what contour or depth the washway really had. The speed of the flow was surprisingly rapid and rose up in violent crests of white water, producing a virtual roar. At the edge of the washway on our left it shot out several feet into the air before falling to the jumble of boulders below.

"I don't know," George said with some trepidation. "We could end up spending the night here," he added gloomily. For me, that did it.

"I think if you stay to the high side on the right, we'll be okay," I said. The concrete slab was about fifteen feet wide, from right to left, and perhaps thirty feet to the other side. I did not think the water was so deep as to cause the heavily laden car to lose its grip on the pavement, and I said so. Everyone reluctantly agreed. Tim was characteristically silent. The Colombian experience of the past several days had made him morose and withdrawn. Ray slowly released the brake and started easing the car across the current.

The rush of water slammed into the front of the car from the right and a wake shot six feet in the air, but the car remained steadfast as we slowly initiated the crossing. It seemed we would make it fine.

When we were about midway across, a higher, more violent wave hit us from the right and literally rocked the car, almost tipping it on two wheels. A flash flood!

The water came up the side of the car and washed up the window on my side and sloshed over the top of the car. I thought we were about to be swept down the rocky gorge below to the left. The engine conked out and we were stuck in the center of the most violent torrent imaginable, the car

Gravity My Enemy

rocking crazily. The brute force of the wave of water swept the front of the car sideways to the edge on the left, rotating the car and leaving us canted at a forty-five degree angle on the road.

"Whatever you do, don't open any door or window on the right!" George shouted over the roar of water. The level was now up to the seats of the car inside and I felt, with the added weight, we were about to go over the ledge. I recalled, from a wary glance before starting across, that the drop was a jumble of boulders on the left, descending steeply into dark oblivion and what appeared like certain death. If we went off the ledge, the car would tumble end over end in a maelstrom of raging river through giant boulders. It was doubtful we would ever survive such a fall.

"Oscar!" I yelled. "Start inflating air mattresses! Right now — as fast as you can!" I was so shaken and scared, I had no idea what I could do to save my life, other than grasp an air mattress and hope I could exit the car somehow. No one could swim in such a raging current, and I sincerely doubted we could even manage to exit the car, but I asked Ray in a shaky voice to please try to help me if we toppled over.

George rapidly searched for a heavy towing rope he had stowed in a coil in back. Thanks to his ever-present sense of organization, he knew exactly where to look and pulled it out.

"I'm getting out!" he shouted. "Ray, don't take your foot off that fuckin' brake! Maybe it'll do something to stop the car from moving over the edge! I'm going out this off-side window and see if I can get us attached to something on the far side."

And in an instant, he was out the window and gone, the rope slung over his shoulder.

Return Home

At first we could not see him and were not sure if he might have been swept down to his fate in the current below, but shortly we saw him carefully walking along the car on the off-side from the current, steadying himself as he went. The headlights, which had been left on, illuminated his upper body as he bent over in front of the car and actually disappeared under the fast-flowing water to get the rope fastened to the bumper support below. In a moment, visibly gasping for breath, he emerged from the rushing black water and tentatively began venturing out into the current alone and without any support, leaning against it. The water was up over his waist and flowing so fast, it splashed in the air over his head. How he kept his footing was a miracle, but he kept a wide stance and, in a moment, came out into shallower water and was soon on the shore on the far side, dripping, the coil of heavy rope still slung over his shoulder and bending crazily in the current between him and the car. He quickly looked around and spotted a heavy boulder right next to the concrete slab on the high side of the road. It was pointed at the top and approximately four feet tall and about three feet thick at the base, standing like an inverted ice cream cone. He rapidly whipped the rope around the base of it, strained hard and pulled it taught as a tightrope in the air above the surface of the raging water and lashed it quickly and repeatedly with a series of half-hitches. It was not much, but it afforded us an added degree of assurance we would not be totally washed down the gorge.

Within just a few minutes, we could see that the water level was slowly but measurably subsiding and before long, it was only a foot deep. The roar of the flash flood calmed as well and we all felt a reprieve in the comparative

Gravity My Enemy

quiet. Ray decided not to try to start the engine as yet for fear it might still be partially under water. A large truck appeared on the far side and stopped, blinding us with its headlights. We saw that George ran over and talked to the driver, and was soon untying the rope from the rock and lay down in the mud under the truck's bumper, fastening it to the truck with repeated knots.

"Let go the brake gradually," George yelled over to us, and the truck backed up, slowly tightening the rope. We could feel the car gradually being pulled out of the water to the shore on the opposite side. After untying the rope, the truck drove past us with a parting blast on his air horn and we shouted our thanks out the window.

Ray let the car drain for a few minutes, and tentatively gave the starter a try. It turned over and over. He waited and tried again. The engine finally coughed to life, missing roughly on one or two cylinders at first and then smoothing out. He put it in gear and we forged ahead. The relief and joy of finally being on our way after all we had been through was almost sensual. I glanced around at everyone's faces with a big smile.

We all had tears in our eyes from relief.

George had been utterly heroic.

We jabbered nervously as we resumed the trip in the dark mountains but exhaustion soon took over and we continued the trip in silence, except for the occasional whimpering of the dogs.

When it was almost dawning with a slight pink edge in the sky behind us, heralding clear skies, we finally limped into Popayán in an advanced state of exhaustion. I don't remember what we did with the dogs, or Oscar, or our pile of hunting and camping equipment that morning. It is now too long ago to remember, but I think we must have slept for the next two days.

25 The Llanos Revisited

After having made several arduous land trips through the *Llanos Orientales*, we became intrigued with the idea of making a river trip. Several fairly large rivers cut through the areas with which we were already familiar and the idea of traveling without the dust, the mechanical car problems, saving on gasoline and hunting in regions not trafficked by people gave us reason to give this idea a try.

George had some funds stashed away back in Connecticut and offered to pay the lion's share of a new outboard motor. At the time, the *Banco Popular* was offering outboards for business prospects such as tourism, in which we were engaged, at astonishingly low prices, so we one day got a spanking new Mercury 20 horsepower. George and I, anxious to give it a trial run, took it down to our favorite duck hunting area near Santander de Quilichao, on a ranch named San Julian, where they had several nice little ponds. We hauled a 14-foot boat we had earlier made ourselves in the garage, and tossed in our shotguns for good measure. Hooking up the shiny, black motor in excitement, we pushed off and cranked it up.

It started on the first pull and purred beautifully. I got in the bow with my side-by-side 12 gauge, and George twisted the throttle gradually as we sliced through the grassy passageways of the lake complex. Immediately, I spotted a small gaggle of black-bellied tree ducks ahead and before they could get up, I put a raking shot pattern through the middle of them, leaving four of them bottoms up with their white feet paddling aimlessly in the air. The remainder took flight and after a moment in the distance, swung around and headed in our direction, evidently hoping to

Gravity My Enemy

pick up their straggler brethren. George and I held dead still with our faces down. Out of the corner of our eye, we tensed as they came into range. Suddenly, both of us sat up with guns to our shoulders and let fly, first the right barrel and then the left as they passed overhead. A pair of ducks cart-wheeled out of the sky on the first quick volley, and the second pair tumbled on the second volley, splashing noisily into the water in front of us about thirty yards distant. We left not a duck from the original gaggle. We had a good dinner for that night, and our new motor was blooded, so to speak.

So, it was with great excitement when the day came to head for the *Llanos Orientales* and we packed the new motor into the back of the car. We decided we would make *Puerto López* our departure point, on the *Meta* River, and head down to its juncture with the *Manacacías* near *Puerto Gaitán*. This latter river was virtually unexplored. Large sections of aerial survey maps were still blank next to the *Manacacías*, which flowed northward into the *Meta*, to ultimately blend with the waters of the *Orinoco* in Venezuela, some of the wildest and most remote jungle on Earth.

After a horrendous trip from Popayán, north to Cali and over the mountains to Espinal and Bogotá, we took a well-deserved overnight rest in the comparatively frigid capital, splurging on one of the best steak dinners known at the famous restaurant *La Braza*. The Lord knew we were soon going to be on restricted jungle fare before long, so the expense was worth it. After dinner, we collapsed in our cold beds and slept like the dead.

The next morning, feeling refreshed in the chilly, rarified mountain air of 8,700 feet altitude, we headed out of town through dark, pre-dawn Bogotá streets and somehow found the

The Llanos Revisited

road to Villavicencio, the capital of the *Llanos Orientales*. We had made this trip several times before and were familiar with the single-lane wooden bridges that crossed over open chasms in the mountains along the way, creaking and swaying precariously, and did not relish the experience. We made our customary stop in Cáqueza for fresh orange juice and a generous portion of baked pork for an early lunch halfway down the mountain slope, and stocked up on our favorite maple cheroots for the trip.

Villavicencio, four hours of winding, descending roads from the capital, is a hot, dusty, uninteresting cattle town and we were anxious to be through it quickly and into the true *llanos*, or plains. I had made a brief stop here years before when on my way to the Amazon, but only saw the dirt strip airport runway.

We carried extra 22-gallon fuel drums and filled up these and the van itself, as this was our last opportunity to get gasoline at regular prices.

The road to Puerto López from "Villao," as Villavicencio is called, is graded and gravel, and raised the familiar, huge, choking plumes of dust we remembered from past trips. But we tolerated it in the knowledge that we were soon going to be traveling the tropical waterways of the Eastern Plains, in clean serenity. Most of the territory along the stretch from Villao to Puerto López is farmed and fenced for cattle and although the wildlife is interesting and represents a different climate range in the country, it is not as wild as the area farther east where we were headed. We were about to enter into a territory few modern men had ever seen.

In two hours, we were glad to be in Puerto López and out of the dust, at the virtual edge of wilderness. We were six hours out of Bogotá,

Gravity My Enemy

the last, true civilization, and on the verge of a large gallery forest region, which precedes the Amazon and Orinoco Basins.

Puerto López is not a large town. After downing a cold drink, we quickly found the Meta River, which flows right through the southern part of town, its shores shaded rather pleasantly with towering tropical kapok and mahogany trees. From their limbs in the canopy hung incredibly long nests made by the yellow-tailed oropendula, a weaver bird found throughout the tropics which makes a bubbling, wheezing sound that matches no other in the tropical forest.

We asked where we could rent a boat to continue the trip down the Meta toward the Manacacías River and the frontier town of Puerto Gaitán. After some directions from people lounging along the river, we located a boat, but somewhat to our chagrin, with it had to come Roberto, who the boat owner claimed was a good "guide." It seemed impossible to ever go on a hunting and fishing trip in Colombia without dragging along freeloaders who knew nothing of the area or hunting and fishing, and more often than not were a liability.

The owner of the boat was a round-bellied, swarthy man with a red face and a four-day growth of black beard, reminding us of Bruno from Popeye cartoons. His shirt was filthy and stained, several sizes too small. Buttons were missing, making the shirt ride halfway up his furry paunch to reveal his navel. His price was ridiculous. His insistence on our bringing the skinny old drunk, Roberto, made the deal worse. But there seemed to be a scarcity of riverboats for hire so, reluctantly, we accepted after negotiating the price down somewhat, more out of principle than economic expediency.

The Llanos Revisited

Taking along errant locals is always an aggravation but is a very common, necessary evil in Colombia. To make the distinction from real Colombian sportsmen who are knowledgeable and generous, these parasites usually hang out in some bar and know little to nothing of hunting or fishing. Though they refer to themselves as "guides," we usually discovered that they had rarely been out of town. While in the bush they had a liking for drink and abusing women. They made noise when we wanted stealth. Most irritating of all, they invariably insisted on using our guns without permission despite knowing nothing about them. Such was our Roberto.

The Mercury outboard we had brought along was securely clamped onto the transom and the contents of the car were loaded into the boat, which was about twenty-six feet long with a beam of about six feet, totally made of planking over a frame. It had a wooden roof that ran almost the entire length of the boat, thus affording us protection from the glaring sun and the rainstorms we were sure to encounter along the way.

Since it was getting late in the afternoon, once the boat was loaded, we opted to spend the night in Puerto López and get an early start the following morning. To guard our possessions, we decided to sleep on the sandbar next to the boat. It did not seem there were many people there to bother us and those that were there assured us that mosquitoes were not overly bothersome. We then looked for a place to keep the car locked up in our absence, and went out on the streets in search of supper and a cold beer. We asked the boat owner to keep an eye on our things in the boat, and felt assured he would. We settled on a nearby bar for lack of a restaurant in this frontier town and, aside from the ubiquitous drunk

391

Gravity My Enemy

who wanted to talk about Americans in a loud voice, we found the people to be rather friendly and self-reliant in a simple way. We came to like these *Llaneros* at first blush, who are known for their unique culture and lifestyle similar to that of our own Old West. Many packed sidearms — actual six-shooters — with the bluing worn off to a silvery shine. And most wore, to our surprise, a Colombian version of the Stetson.

We talked with the people in the bar, as we ate a couple large oval cans of sardines packed in hot tomato sauce, with little bread loaves, asked questions and told a few jokes as we bought some guys a couple rounds of a tasty beer called *Club Colombia*, for which Colombia is famous. The sun set and we wandered down to the river near the boat, and unrolled sleeping bags right on the sandbar.

The night was very pleasant, somewhat cool, and as we lay on the sand on our backs, we gazed up into the inky night sky, amazed at the clarity of the night. Millions of stars shown like a scattering of diamond chips. George had studied astronomy in school and gave us an interesting primer on different constellations seen at this latitude. I specifically recall Orion. Talk slacked off as we became sleepy. A river rat squawked raucously in the bush on the opposite side of the river a hundred yards distant, disturbed by some wandering predator.

It had been a very long day. We were sound asleep in minutes.

***

We slept soundly the entire night and awoke to birdcalls in the trees near the sand bar where we slept next to the boat. The edge of the horizon

The Llanos Revisited

was pink in the east and the air was humid but pleasantly cool. The Meta river thirty feet from where we slept gurgled quietly as its brown waters rapidly swept past numerous deadfalls.

From the direction of the *planchón* landing, two men plied their way towards us on foot and another two followed. I sat up to watch their progress.

As they neared, I noticed that the first two were connected together in tandem by a long pole across their shoulders, weighted in the middle by a huge fish. I called for Ray and George and they rolled over, blinking. It was barely getting light. The men approaching were returning from a night's fishing. I hailed them from a distance to come and show their catch. The first two men preceded the others by a hundred yards. As they approached, I was dumbfounded to see the size of the fish they carried between them. It was a gray catfish they called a *valentón*. It had to weigh at least a hundred pounds. We asked them to stop and Ray quickly shot a photograph. Since they were straining under their burden and probably wanted to get to the fish market quickly, we kept our curiosity in check and our questions to a minimum. It was a nightly activity for them. They used a large shark hook and a rusty gear from an old truck transmission for a sinker, and baited the hook with rancid meat. The "fishing line" was a light rope. When the catfish took the bait and swallowed the hook, it took the combined strength of both of them to bring it to the riverbank.

They continued on their way toward town, their catch swaying back and forth on the bent pole between them. A moment later, the other fishermen arrived carrying two different types of catfish. Although these were smaller than the *valentón*, they were huge in themselves, each well over three feet long and more slender. One was gray with white whiskers a full foot long, wide in configuration like the blade of a stiletto. They called it a *barbiancho* or "wide-whisker" for the shape of the barbs. The other fish closely resembled the

Valenton (left) and barbianchos

first except in coloration. It was black and white striped, and thus called a *rallado*. Both had sloped aerodynamic heads with a mouth like the wide air scoop seen on fighter jets. They were obviously swift swimmers and the size of their mouths suggested a predatory nature. Despite their sleek appearance, they were hefty and muscular. The men said that these catfish frequently jumped like sport fish when caught, and were in the habit of putting up quite a fight. After more picture taking, we thanked them and they went on their way to the market.

The Llanos Revisited

As we noticed the sun rising, we hurriedly loaded our sleeping gear in the boat, checked the gas level and began asking about Roberto, who was supposed to act as our guide.

He finally appeared, carrying a gunnysack containing his personal belongings.

We boarded and pushed off into the fast current, the new Mercury started on the first pull, and we swung out into the main stream of the river amid dead tree stumps and branches. The swift current swept the bow downstream and our journey was thus begun, soon leaving the lines of wooden shacks of Puerto López far behind and entering a territory with tall tropical rain forest on either side, occasionally interrupted by open stretches of grassy plains. Both riverbanks were vertical and about fifteen feet high at this season, and colored red.

The river itself was well-defined at first, the current guiding us down its main course, often ballooning up on its turbulent surface in high spots as it flowed over unseen obstacles and, in turn, showing low depressions of fierce whirlpools on the water's surface, a rather disconcerting thing to see for the first time, as we had always expected a river to be quite placid. This river almost seemed to be a living thing, a giant water serpent flowing and undulating on its long journey eastward to the Orinoco and eventually to the Caribbean Sea.

At the outset of a long river trip, one's attention is riveted everywhere. Our hearts went in our throats each time the boat rose up onto a crest of vertical current, fearing we would capsize, but each time the event passed without incident and we became accustomed to it, even exhilarated. Then, we sunk into deep whirlpools and depressions, with equal trepidation, only to exit without incident. The difference in these

Gravity My Enemy

levels was quite remarkable, possibly as much as six feet. At times, we saw a large tree trunk jutting from the water in the middle of the river at an angle, wobbling back and forth in the strong current, spraying a stream of water high into the air on both sides like the blunt bow of a huge steamer plying its way upriver.

We searched the shoreline for animal life but were disappointed for the most part. Usually, we found it faster and safer to travel

**Rallado & barbiancho catfish from Meta River —
Puerto Lopez**

The Llanos Revisited

the center of the fastest current, making our distance from the shore at times well over a hundred yards, so we were out of sight of most fauna on the Meta, other than birds that commuted across the river continually. Most notable among these were large, white egrets and their smaller cousins, the cattle egret. Common were bright red macaws on powerful wings overhead, their long tails streaming behind. We could hear their raucous calls even above the noise of the outboard. They almost always flew in pairs and, in silhouette against the bright cobalt sky it was often difficult to distinguish any color until they entered the shade of the shore vegetation.

Skimmers, vaguely resembling seagulls, were graceful as they flew up and down the river in small groups with their larger lower mandible slicing the water's surface for minute aquatic life. They were very lovely in flight and fed along the surface with a skill rarely exhibited in the wild.

Though the growl of the motor was muffled in good part, we were deprived of hearing the multitude of wild sounds associated with a jungle river, and could only imagine what it must have been like to travel by canoe with paddles. Likewise, our approaching sound must have alarmed much wildlife that we did not see due to lack of surprise.

One exception was the howler monkeys. Their throaty roar could easily be heard over the outboard, even at a great distance, a "huh-huh-huh . . . . oooooagh!" announcing their presence. They sounded every bit like huge lions from the veldt of Africa. Careful scrutiny often revealed them traversing through the upper canopy of the trees in search of fruits and succulent leaves. They were very black and surprisingly large in size, bending the branches down under their weight.

Gravity My Enemy

As we turned around the first big bend in the river, we noticed that there was a myriad of jungled islands in the middle. These were not apparent as separate pieces of land because they blended in with the shores and could not be distinguished until we got closer and the current often split around them, flowing on both sides and, in the process, creating some confusion as to the best course to take. At times we became quite worried, as we seemed to diverge so abruptly from what had been our original course. This river travel was not as simple as we had thought! We quite obviously ended up taking the long way around at times but soon relaxed when we realized that all the water was eventually going to the same destination.

Fortunately, though the water level was low this time of year, we experienced no problems running aground on sand bars, and were able to make good time.

As we came around one big turn in the river, we saw a large flock of roseate spoonbills in the distance, casting a shimmering red reflection off the sunlight as they turned in unison, then flashing pink as they made a different turn. It was breath-taking to watch.

River travel in the tropics is hot and, for the most part, uneventful. We often found ourselves feeling rather soporific. Ray was lounging across a pile of duffels toward the bow and was sound asleep, his head thrown back with his mouth wide open. Oscar was in a similar state, looking like a rag doll as he lay across another heap of supplies. Roberto's head was nodding under his rumpled black hat. Only George seemed alert and kept me company as I held the tiller of the motor, half-asleep myself.

The Llanos Revisited

Off near the shore the water was calmer and shown like a mirror, reflecting the trees and red mud bank in the background. Every once in a while, a fish made a large splash near the shore and we wondered what we would find when we later had the time to do some fishing. Ray was the angler in the group, George and I being more inclined and dedicated to hunting.

As it appeared past midday, George opened a couple of oblong cans of sardines and forked them out on chunks of bread we had brought from Puerto López. We all ate heartily, as there had been no breakfast before our departure. The sun was now well past its zenith in the hot, pale-blue sky. Small fair-weather cumulus clouds lay off to the south, white and puffy, and to the east where were headed floated a larger cloud of the same shape. A slanted shaft of rain protruded from its flat underside. Large bunches of screeching, green parakeets raced frantically overhead, fleeing wildly to the opposite shore. Placid white egrets sailed nonchalantly along just over the water, their necks bent back in a characteristic "S," their yellow feet trailing behind. Occasionally, to the south we saw a huge pillar of smoke rising above a large grass fire in the distance. A multitude of large hawks and vultures wheeled over the fire in their never-ending search for rodents and carrion.

On a rare occasion, over the treetops we saw the characteristic shape and wingbeat of a harpy eagle as it hunted monkeys in the leafy canopy.

Once, as we came unusually close to the shore, we saw a group of white-bibbed Toco toucans hurriedly flying from one tree to the next in their characteristic swooping flight pattern that is reminiscent of woodpeckers. Their huge beaks seemed over-proportioned to the size of their bodies.

Gravity My Enemy

As the shadows grew longer in the afternoon and the heat and throbbing motor brought us to a state of virtual stupor, we suddenly approached a high cliff to our right on the south side of the river. Perched atop it was a fairly large cane-and-wattle house with a thatched roof. It was the first sign of human habitation we had seen on the river all day. Little children were playing at the water's edge below. White and colored laundry hung outside the house on a line.

I swung the boat shoreward and throttled back on the motor. The change in vibrations and tone of the motor woke Ray instantly. Roberto's head came up and only Oscar continued to lie sound asleep amongst the luggage. I cut the motor as we came to the shore and the prow of the boat bumped the shore softly. The kids stopped their playing and shyly stared at us, keeping their distance while we sat in the boat, watching for some sign of life. Strangely, the children seemed rather light complected but we reminded ourselves that lighter hair is often a sign of malnutrition among dark-complected children. A short, stocky, surprisingly light-skinned man appeared above us on the bank overhead and waved a greeting.

He enthusiastically descended steps leading down to our position. These had been carved meticulously into the red mud embankment. He came down them swiftly and extended his hand to each of us and said hello in surprisingly cultured Spanish.

He asked if we would like to stay the night, as it was late in the day, offering hammocks and reassuring us that the mosquitoes were not a problem in the area.

We accepted and got out of the boat, stretching stiff joints and lashing the painter to a small tree overhanging the water. Our host

400

The Llanos Revisited

pitched in to help me up the embankment as soon as he saw George and Oscar struggling to get me out of the boat with the wheelchair.

"How far up the Manacacías is Puerto Gaitán?" George asked.

"Well, once you get to the Manacacías it is upstream and you must fight against the current. But it is a much smaller river and doesn't have the same strength of current as the Meta. Gaitán is not far. Probably two hours. It is on this side," and he held out his right hand.

In a few moments, arriving breathless from my weight, everyone was atop a flat plain above the river, surrounded by tall shade trees and enjoying its relative coolness. The panorama of the Meta River below in the late afternoon was splendid and pastoral.

Our host, with the unlikely Scandinavian name of Eric, to fit his physical appearance, engaged us with a friendliness and level of culture unbefitting the rustic surroundings. His hair was short-cropped and quite blond in color, and his eyes were a striking light blue-gray. Wrinkles around them revealed him to be a habitually happy and friendly man. Though age is hard to distinguish among many people in the tropics, I would have guessed him to be in his mid-thirties.

From the way his small children fondly kept in close contact with him, across his knees and hanging on his arms, it was obvious he was a very gentle, loving parent, and not the tyrant or strong disciplinarian one would expect in such harsh surroundings. Yet they were all well behaved and respectful. He occasionally sent them off to fetch things such as matches or a cigarette, and to serve black, syrup-sweet coffee made by his diminutive wife, who had just moments ago appeared as silently as a wraith from the

Gravity My Enemy

kitchen. The children scurried off quickly each time in response to his bidding. It was anybody's guess how they got any formal schooling in such a remote place, but they were perfect examples of good upbringing. And their father gave the immediate impression of intelligence and unusually good schooling. They lived as a family in a small, remote paradise in the middle of the eastern plains. It seemed he had about five small children.

Oscar and Ray fetched some necessities from the boat, brought up the guns, and we made ourselves at home. We asked about our general whereabouts, as serpentine river travel disorients the traveler, and we wanted some idea of how far along we had come on our way to Puerto Gaitán. We asked him how long it would take to reach the Manacacías River and Eric was hesitant to give an immediate answer but thought it would take a little over a half day with the outboard.

"Upriver back toward Puerto López," he said, "is a different matter. The current is swift. If you took a day to get here, it will take you almost two days to return. The current in this Meta River is very strong! And that boat is very heavy and water-logged," he added with a smile. Eric said we had reached more than our halfway point. That was a pleasant development. As it grew dark, we lounged around in hammocks, ate a light supper and drank coffee. We asked Eric about hunting. He said the best deer and capybara hunting was along the Manacacías River. He, like many who lived modestly far from population centers, did not hunt much with a firearm since guns were unavailable. His greatest enthusiasm was for fishing the behemoth catfish of the river. Our relaxed conversation came to be about fish and fauna.

The Llanos Revisited

Once the sun disappeared behind the black silhouette of the jungle wall across the broad muddy river, darkness fell quickly and the searing heat of the day rapidly was transformed to a pleasant coolness. All was quiet save for night crickets and the faint gurgling of the water against roots and other protrusions of the shore.

As seen from the outside, the little house glowed orange like a paper Japanese lantern seen at outdoor evening parties a world away, illuminated by small pitch lamps fashioned from discarded tin cans. These had small wicks and were placed carefully on small wooden shelves high on the walls that were designed for the purpose throughout the house. The main room glowed amber in the flickering flames of the lamps and we sat around the periphery of the room on wooden benches and talked quietly, as bats fluttered softly at eye level between us every few moments.

I noticed Roberto sat off by himself and made no comment. We had had no opportunity to talk with him during the entire day's trip down the river, primarily because of the interference from the motor noise, but despite that fact, he did not seem very inclined to be sociable. At the same time, we found he was simply quiet and generally agreeable to everything. And probably tired, as we all were.

Eric, in contrast, was very talkative and animated. Life was lonely out here in the *Llanos*, visitors scarce.

I asked if there were any caiman in the area.

"*Muchos!*" he said, enthusiastically.

Caiman are a relative of the alligator found throughout tropical rivers in Colombia. Unfortunately, their hides were in great demand like their cousins' and years later they became as endangered as the Florida alligator. We had

Gravity My Enemy

no inkling they were in danger at the time, and hunted them at every opportunity. The meat from the tail was white and firm, similar in many ways to lobster tail, and possibly superior. The assurance they were in abundance was good news indeed, and we all nodded approval among ourselves in the semi-darkness.

"What were you saying about jaguar?" I asked hopefully.

"*El tigre. Es otra cosa. Muy arisco.* That's a different story! He's very elusive. You can look for years and only see a track on the sandbar once in a while. That is in the daytime," Eric clarified. "At night is different. We cannot see them but they come and visit on rare occasions. We see their tracks nearby in the morning sometimes!"

We collectively tuned our senses to the darkness outside the house. Only cicadas and tree frogs chirred and hummed.

"Sometimes we hear them coughing across the river," Eric said. "But we never hunt them.

The *tigre* is much too smart. He is also a fisherman—not afraid of the water like house cats."

He told us that there was a hunter that lived down river, beyond the Manacacías who had been successful with jaguar. He employed a technique that capitalized on their territorial nature. Eric went into the kitchen area and returned with a plastic bucket. He sat down and bent over his knees with his face in the bucket and made a heaving noise, as though vomiting. The effect he created was identical to the sound made by the big cat. He said another way to call the jaguar was to attach a thin cord to the bottom of the bucket and wax it with beeswax, and grasp it tightly between your fingers and pull hard, slowly. As the

The Llanos Revisited

waxed string slid through the fingers, it emitted a sound much like that of a jaguar.

He turned to the subject of fishing. He told how they often caught the huge gray *valentón*, the big catfish we had seen on the sandbar near Puerto López.

"Some say the *valentón* eats children. We have never seen it but their mouth is big enough. We use a big hook if we can get one, the kind they use for sharks on the coast. And we bait it with any kind of meat, the more putrefied the better! That is what the *valentón* likes the best." He smiled. "If you get one, there is meat for many days, like getting the *danta*. The tapir. We salt it, and it lasts a long time."

As big as a tapir! That was quite a statement.

Eric kindly offered us supper but we declined gratefully. We had already eaten from cans in the boat before reaching his house.

"The coffee is enough for us," I said, explaining we had eaten in the boat before. Ray was already nodding off. Roberto had his head thrown back against the wall, snoring in loud gasps from his cavernous mouth, which displayed a treasure trove of gold teeth.

"I think we should better get some sleep," I told him. "It has been a very long trip!"

We each settled in our hammocks which Eric had helped sling to the main house posts in the central area, forming a crisscross maze that made it difficult for anyone to get through the room.

As my eyes were beginning to close, I could still see the red tip of George's cheroot in the dark. This, after a time, arched and hit the ground a distance away in a shower of sparks.

26 Puerto Gaitán

My eyes opened and I stared at the ceiling. It was morning and barely light enough to see. Up in the rafters above my head the entire underside of the roof structure was visible and shiny black, as though spray-painted with liquid tar. The roof was thatch, made skillfully from palm fronds, which were deftly lashed with strips of thin vine. Years of smoky cooking fires had coated the underside of the roof with tar-like creosote. With newer roofs, there was no black pitch yet accumulated and it would be home to colonies of scuttling critters such as scorpions, lizards and geckos, but the coating of tar protected the house's occupants below very well, and we had slept in relative peace.

Eric's wife was up and had evidently noticed I was awake, for she quietly brought me a cup of black coffee in a chipped mug that had long ago lost its handle.

"*Gracias, señora,*" I said, sitting up in the hammock, straddling it with both legs so as to convert it to a chaise lounge. Without a word of reply other than a shy smile, she weaved her way back into the kitchen. Soon, as I was sipping the hot, sweet coffee, Eric came in quietly and smiled.

"*Buenos dias,*" he said. "You slept well, I hope?" He had a very ingratiating smile.

"Very well, thank you. You have a very nice house," I said. The walls were made from thin cane, lashed so tightly together, they left not even a crack of light. No mosquitoes could get through it, though the main room where we had slept was open-air. The floor was made from a heavy green bamboo called *guadua*. This had been split open with a machete and its sections knocked out so as to form thin but resilient planking. The shiny

407

Gravity My Enemy

side was facing upward so sweeping the floor with a rustic grass broom was easy and the sand fell between the cracks into a crawl space below.

Everyone was now awaking and sitting up and Eric's timid wife and children were busily serving coffee and plates of smoked fish. I guessed it to be a large slab-sided fish called *cachama* or *pacu*. It was delicious.

We gathered our things, took down the hammocks and began taking everything down to the boat. I offered Eric some salt, bread and coffee, commodities hard to come by so far from civilization, which he gratefully accepted. I gave his wife a large oval can of tomato sardines and her eyes lit up in gratitude. Within a half hour, the men had collectively hauled me down the steps carved into the steep, red bank to the water's edge and loaded me into the boat. We were on our way once again, down river. Looking back, as we eased our way out into the current, we saw Eric and his family waving as they stood on top of the clay bank in front of their house, watching us go out of sight behind a bend in the river.

It was still rather cool in the early morning light and we felt a renewed vigor, each searching the shoreline and the treetops for signs of life. Bright red macaws flew across the river in stately pairs, fish splashed in the calm inlets, while skimmers raced along the shore, their lower mandibles delicately slicing the calm surface of the river, making tiny, straight lines on the mirrored reflection of the green forest background as they lazily winged their way down river, scooping up miniscule aquatic life that was their food.

We occasionally got a fleeting glimpse of howlers among the upper canopy of the trees as they acrobatically climbed around in search of

Puerto Gaitán

fruits and blossoms. This was a veritable paradise, untouched since the beginning of time. It felt good to be alive and part of it.

Navigating a jungle river is not as easy as we had originally surmised. The main channel was not always obvious. It snaked in different directions constantly, sometimes going west when the river on the map showed a generally easterly direction, or north, then south, as it snaked on its meandering course. We first had the sun in our face, only to notice after a time it was off to the left, then behind us. All we could do was try to stay in the main channel, but even this was frequently broken up with huge, forested islands in the center of the river or off to one side, confusing us continually as to which direction to take. Big bays opened on either side, some extending back more than a kilometer from the main course of the river. So, when we reached the mouth of the Manacacías, we were not sure if indeed it was our destination until we had traveled up it some distance and ascertained that it definitely was not a blind entrance.

After a half hour on this smaller river, we almost celebrated as we realized we were indeed on a different river altogether, heading approximately south. In another hour, we could see painted houses far ahead on the west bank to our right and we soon nosed the boat to the shore in Puerto Gaitán.

***

This remote, little village on the shore of the Manacacías was in the middle of Colombia's vast plain called the *Llanos Orientales*, or eastern plains. It was named after Jorge Eliécer Gaitán, Colombia's first Communist. In the late 1940's,

Gravity My Enemy

Gaitán had negotiated in behalf of the workers of the huge American-owned banana plantations of Santa Marta on the northern Caribbean coast. The fruit company, with the tacit approval of corrupt government officials, had been accused of unfair labor practices over the years but was so powerful and managed by such cruel local bosses that the workers were powerless to achieve anything better than an indentured slave status. In a surprise move, Gaitán took the fruit company to court and won. From that day, he was a celebrity among the downtrodden of Colombia and was nationally acclaimed as their savior. Many believed he was slated to become the first president to come from the common people.

Soon after the historic court decision, representatives of all the American countries were engaged in attending lengthy meetings in Bogotá to draw up the charter for the recently-founded Organization of American States (OAS). They invited Gaitán to address the group of OAS delegates on April 9, 1947.

As he was leaving the building after giving his speech, an unknown assassin approached him in the street outside and shot him. Gaitán died in a nearby clinic an hour later.

Although it was never proven, everyone suspected one of the established political parties as being responsible for the assassination. The disillusion of the populace was so bitter and instantaneous that the scene on the street quickly turned to bloody chaos. The assailant was literally torn limb from limb and so disfigured that it was many days before they were able to identify him. He was a nobody, and could not be linked to any political group.

The assassination touched off a powder keg of violence, called the *Bogotazo*. Great parts

Puerto Gaitán

of the city were in flames as embassies burned and liquor stores sacked, feeding the violence with a drunken frenzy unmatched in Latin American history.

This anarchy, later referred to as the period of *La Violencia*, spread throughout the country and lasted for many years, giving Colombia, which has always been a country of culture, a sharply contrasting and enduring historical reputation for brutality and bloodshed that had lasted to the 1960's. Foreign correspondents compared it to the Nazi blitzes that took place in London in the late 1930's. The violence spread like a dangerous epidemic. People in rage randomly hacked into crowds with machetes, and were seen to stop only to hone their weapons on the concrete sidewalks. The army was soon deployed that evening and began shooting into crowds. News of the assassination spread like wildfire and the violence spread in turn to all corners of the country. Thousands died within the first hours, and those numbers multiplied in following days. The killing mutated into a series of blood feuds and vendettas, as victims and their families identified individuals and groups responsible, real or imagined, for the deaths of their loved ones.

Politics was artificially mixed in the hatred and bloodletting. The two principal parties were identified by colors. The Liberals were red and the Conservatives blue, as a tradition. Splinter bandit groups formed and went on a rampage then and in years to follow. If a given group identified with the Liberals (red) they would kill anyone they found wearing a piece of blue clothing. Other pillagers and bandits victimized anyone wearing the opposing color. In time, they lost any understanding of the political origins of their rampage and killed anyone wearing either

411

color, as justification for a kind of violence they had come to enjoy.

This was exploited many years later in the early 1960's by Fidel Castro in his and Ernesto "Che" Guevara's efforts to create a Latin American Communist Revolution, and was only brought to a temporary halt by a group headed by President Guillermo León Valencia, *"El Presidente de la Paz"* — the President of Peace.

Gaitán nonetheless was still regarded as a hero in many corners of the republic and we had now arrived at his namesake, a river village located in the midst of the wild Eastern Plains. Most of the houses were clapboard walls with rusted zinc roofs. The total population was probably no more than a couple hundred souls and most seemed absent. Several dugout canoes were haphazardly parked at the water's edge and there was one 15-foot Alumicraft boat with no motor, pulled high up onto the shore and turned upside-down in disuse.

There did not seem to be much activity in Puerto Gaitán. It was hot and dusty, the sun glared unmercifully from its zenith, but we welcomed the opportunity to get out and stretch our legs. We found a very small restaurant that served as a combination eatery, coffee shop and bar. No one was present. We rapped loudly on a worn wooden table that had long since lost its lime-green paint and was worn smooth and greasy from uncountable spills. A middle-aged woman appeared from behind a curtain that hid the interior of the house.

She had black hair in wet ringlets, still dripping from a recent shower. Her hair was somewhat close-cropped and a large red plastic barrette arched across the top of her head. This was combined with far too much bright red lipstick and an exaggerated dusting of rouge on

Puerto Gaitán

her cheeks, in a hopeless effort to look young and attractive again, though her time had long passed. Her breasts were the size of sagging oranges in a loose, cheap blouse encrusted with patterns of sequins, and she wore a flared skirt, with stiff petticoats under a soiled white apron, which was tied over a round pot belly, swollen from years of intestinal parasites.

Typically, though we were young and reasonably comely Americans that she had probably not seen in many years, she feigned the boredom of a hash slinger.

We, on the other hand, did not have to disguise our lack of interest in her, but ordered a big breakfast of scrambled eggs mixed with tomato and onion, bread and a whole pot of coffee. Roberto and George ordered beers to go with the greasy but filling breakfast.

To hunt and fish, we knew we had to get a smaller boat to tow behind the larger boat and use for this, while using the larger boat as a base camp. We split up and started asking around and were delighted to find that the aluminum boat was available for a reasonable price. We decided to tie the big boat to the shore nearby and switched the motor to the smaller boat, readying it for hunting later in the day, as well as some exploring upriver in a more agile and swift craft.

27 Little River

In many parts of Colombia, people make their living fishing. Some of the means devised for doing this are nothing short of astonishing and many would drive conservationists to insanity if they could witness them.

One man by the name of Ricardo we met out on the Pacific coast was fond of visiting small inland ponds with a gas-powered water pump and virtually pumping them out one by one in their entirety, right down to the mud bottom, and then slopping around to his knees in muck collecting every fish he could lay his hands on. In time, the ponds probably recuperated as nature often mysteriously does in the tropics, and the fish probably re-populated the ponds to a state of normalcy.

In the Amazon region, the tribes I visited used an interesting and effective method of collecting fish. They cut pieces of a vine they

Gravity My Enemy

called *barbasco* and placed these on rocks in a small river and hammered them to a pulp with large clubs. Then, they washed the pieces of vine in the river water. This released a milky substance in the water, which was swept down in the current. Downstream, other Indians had prepared a rustic dam from shore to shore, blocking any fish from escaping. It was at this point that the Indians later collected, some with thin spears, others with bows made of a tough, black palm wood called *chonta* and long, thin arrows with barbed tips and no fletching. The poison worked by depriving the fish of oxygen, and they began coming to the surface where the waiting Indians impaled them. Like the famous *curare* used to kill monkeys and other animals, the poison had no effect on the flesh for eating. Indeed, I had eaten fish and small animals that had been collected thanks to these poisons. The *barbasco* was later studied and synthesized and became the only safe pesticide, rotenone, and *curare* has been used for years in a synthetic form for both eye surgery and heart surgery, as a muscle relaxant.

As one travels around many areas in western Colombia, many men are seen missing hands. At first, it is tempting, and justified, to attribute this to the natural Colombian tendency among the despondent toward alcoholism and violence. The poor man's weapon is the ubiquitous machete. When a man is angry, drunk and has nothing to lose but his life of misery, machetes clang in small, hot villages in the night, and the following morning bodies and body parts are often found strewn in the streets much like any other debris and litter found in any place in Latin America.

But the machete and drink are not totally responsible for lost limbs. The culprit is "fishing." Many small-town general stores sell a

Little River

homemade dynamite to get fish. These explosives are as long as a Roman candle and as thick as a summer sausage, tightly wrapped in brown paper and heavily laden with some home-brewed explosive inside. The fuse is a commercially made white waterproof fuse almost as thick as a pencil.

Upon seeing this giant firecracker for the first time, I was shocked to see the fuse was only a nubbin in length, just barely visible as it protruded from the end tie wrapping of the sausage. They evidently did not believe in much of a safety margin.

It is customary to tape the stick of dynamite to some weighty object like a lead pipe or a discarded car part or a beer bottle, then light the midget fuse with a lit cigarette and quickly toss the whole works into the middle of a small pond. After a loud underwater muffled "thump" and the resulting billowing of muddy water and shredded aquatic plant life comes to the surface accompanied by dead fish, the "fisherman" wades out and scoops up fish of all sizes with a net. The fact that the great majority of the fish killed are still on the bottom out of reach means nothing.

There is a hitch, however. The sun is usually very bright in the tropics, making it difficult or impossible to see when the fuse is actually lit. The result is that many men become southpaws.

Being young and adventurous, we bought a few of these devices to try them out, just for fun. The first we taped to a fence post near my house and we managed to cajole our worker, Oscar, to carefully set it off and run like hell. This he did. The concussion was more felt in the chest than an actual loud bang to the ears; it shattered one window on that side of the house and blew away a chunk of the post about the size of a grapefruit.

Gravity My Enemy

We were convinced of their power, and a couple of these deadly sausages consequently went in among our items packed for the *Llanos*, along with guns for hunting and ammunition, and a small, black German 9 mm Schmeisser submachine gun for problems we might encounter in the bush of the people variety on such a long journey. The latter went inside the door panel of the car when we traveled by land, well hidden, as authorities in Third World countries are understandably counter to the public having such weaponry.

As we slowly traveled up the Manacacías one day after reaching Puerto Gaitán, often stopping to take a few casts as we went, and catching many interesting and exotic fish, we came across a small river that emptied into the Manacacías from the right, or West. It was only a few feet wide at its mouth and almost invisible from the main river, due to the heavy brush that obscured its opening.

Upon entering, it was dark inside and intriguing, so we slowly headed upstream against its sluggish current, looking around us in wonder and delight. It was a veritable Garden of Eden. The stream widened a short distance after squeezing past its mouth, and formed a quiet pool of black water surrounded by huge overhanging trees that effectively blocked out the light so as to make it almost twilight. We shut off the motor to listen. All was dark and silent. Not even sounds of birds were evident. We looked for life in the dense canopy but everything was as still as a tomb. We coasted forward without a sound when the silence was suddenly shattered by the squawking of a small green heron we spooked off a tree trunk that was jutting out of the water in the center of the pool. It dashed off into the darkness and the gloom was again deadly silent. We sat in awe, mesmerized by the deep beauty, the primordial

Little River

mystery and solitude of our surroundings. I felt that we were probably the first humans to witness this tropical cathedral.

We paddled slowly and with utmost care to avoid making a disturbance, up into the depths of this sanctum, as silently as ancient hunters, looking alertly in all directions, holding our collective breath. The water's surface was black as tar, unmoving, not a ripple. We could only speculate at what might be below its surface. Another couple of hundred yards further up the little unnamed river, the shores pinched off the waterway and we had to pull ourselves by hand to get through, pulling on overhanging branches, ever wary of the possibility of a branch suddenly becoming a venomous snake in our hands. We ducked our heads to get under the tangle of lianas and lush vegetation.

After a few moments tunneling through this maze without uttering a word, our world gradually became more illuminated and we emerged into a lovely pond about fifty yards in breadth, half-covered with giant lily pads five feet in diameter, their borders turned upward abruptly at right angles to form a gunwale that kept the centers dry. These were so huge, they could have supported the weight of a small child. In the very center the sunlight shone like a stage light featuring a slanting, dead tree trunk, protruding out of the water about the height of a man, with moss hanging from it like a witch's gray hair. Its angle easily permitted it to be used as a type of seating. The stump was as thick as a man's thigh and as we pulled up to it, we saw that it seemed sturdy enough to support a person's weight, so Oscar daringly jumped from the boat onto it and straddled it like a horse, proudly beaming at us over his intrepidness.

Gravity My Enemy

It immediately dawned on both George and me that this was the ideal place and opportunity to try out our dynamite. Ray objected. The place was too pristine, he insisted, too quiet — a sanctuary of sorts that shouldn't be disturbed. We both agreed but the temptation to use the explosive and also discover the mysteries of what may lie beneath the dark waters was too much to resist.

We asked Oscar if he was game to light it. With his customary bravado, said, *Claro* — "of course" he was. George dug amongst our gear in the boat and a moment later found the sticks and held one up for all to see. Laying it on the seat of the boat, he looked around and finally located and grabbed a Coke bottle from the bilge, dried it off with his shirttail, and with some black electrical tape from the toolbox, rigged the explosive. I lit a cigarette and took a couple of deep puffs, and handed it to Oscar, who happily smoked from it as well, to show he wasn't the kid we thought he was.

I carefully and with great emphasis instructed him on how to light it and quickly toss it in the water below the ragged stump.

"Be damned sure it's lit before you throw it in the water — but don't sit there watching it burn! Get rid of it quick!" I cautioned.

Oscar had lived among people with missing hands, so he easily understood the risks to which I alluded.

We first told him to wait to allow us to get some distance from him, and I think this made him nervous. He was really getting serious now. It was obvious that his enthusiasm and bravado were quickly disappearing. Perhaps we had good reason to move away?

When we gave him a nod to go ahead and light it, he put the burning end of the cigarette

Little River

close to the fuse but hesitated and pulled it back. He took a deep breath. I could see that the bright shaft of sunlight on him could prevent him from seeing the burning wick. I sternly told him to make sure he lit the fuse in shadow so he could see when it was ignited.

"*Solo en la sombra!*" I warned him again to do this only in the shade. He seemed more nervous than ever, and we found ourselves actually goading him on for fear he would chicken out.

Suddenly, he touched the fuse with the cigarette for a split second and hastily pushed the bottle away from him and tossed it into the water, as though he were ridding himself of a snake.

Ker-plunk! The circles of the wake widened as we watched expectantly.

Seconds passed, and we waiting with bated breath.

Nothing.

After some moments, we finally realized Oscar actually did chicken out and discarded it as a muscular reaction to his tension. We ragged at him for it, half angry, half derisive. George went into the luggage for the second stick and pulled it out into full view.

"Here's your last chance!" he said to Oscar, suggesting he repeat, but by now Oscar's nerves were frazzled. He puffed nervously on the cigarette, and it teetered rapidly up and down between his lips. The ash dropped off and burnt his forearm, and he recoiled as though stung by a wasp and almost fell off the limb into the water. He regained his balance and lost the cigarette, which fell with a hiss in the water. His demeanor turned almost angry in its seriousness and it was clear he wanted no part of this anymore, and to get back into the boat. There was now no manner,

Gravity My Enemy

reward or accusation of cowardice that would persuade him to repeat the operation, and we finally had to give it up, secretly very relieved. The little river was too much like a church to defile it with our boyhood foolishness.

After exploring a while more, we found we could pass no farther upstream, as the tangled vegetation was too congested. We headed back down, deeply appreciating the beauty and solitude of the little river along the way and, in time, came out into the brightness of the main river.

We never returned to the spot. It was not even shown on any map, and thus remained without a name, as it probably should. We are still happy we never spoiled it.

28 Anhingas

After several days of hunting and exploring the surrounding river area near Puerto Gaitán, we decided to dispense with the light aluminum boat for a few days and load up the big boat to serve as a base for some serious exploration up the Manacacías River to the south. From what we had seen on quick trips an hour or so up the river, it seemed totally devoid of people. The area evidenced no sign of human habitation, so we hoped we were to find unexplored territory. A look at the large maps we carried in a waterproof tube seemed to confirm this. There were large blank areas on the maps and comparisons between maps showed major discrepancies, a sure indication that there had been few if any surveys, even from the air.

We did not leave Puerto Gaitán very early, as we wanted to have the full light of day to see the new terrain we were visiting, and always with an eye to hunting and fishing for the pot, though we knew full well that very early dawn and late dusk usually are the best hours for hunting the world over.

As we traveled up river, we noticed the characteristic patches of jungle interspersed with the openings of plains, as the river cut through the gallery forest of the *Llanos*, so this was not much different in appearance from what we had seen between Puerto López on the Meta down to the mouth of the Manacacías.

But notably different was the intimacy and the sense of excitement we felt from being on a much narrower river. Since it appeared the Manacacías was a bit slower, it tended to meander more, creating interesting curves and bends that opened out continually to reveal a new panorama with

Gravity My Enemy

delightful frequency, thus keeping our interest level much higher.

On the larger rivers such as the Putumayo and the Amazon, one tends to feel hot and lethargic after a time of traveling on them and river travel can become virtually boring and soporific. The Manacacías, in contrast, was exciting at every turn and made more so by the fact that this river was not a thoroughfare, as were the Amazon and its huge tributaries. It reminded me in many ways of the Yavarí, a beautiful river dividing Peru and Brazil on which I had spent some time years before. We were seeing uncharted country, what explorers' dreams are made of!

The flooding created widening bays of interest, yawning before us at times on either side, revealing small pockets of paradise, yet the water level was not so high as to obliterate the higher sandbars and little lovely beaches that occasionally jutted out into the mainstream. It was at these places that we stopped at times to escape the sound of the motor and listen to the wildlife around us.

We also noticed some schools of silver fish about a foot long, resembling in shape and habits of the bonefish seen on saltwater flats.

These always seemed to be near the shallows of the sandbars. As the boat passed over these schools, they burst violently out of the water in alarm, rocketing into the air with such speed that we enthusiastically welcomed the possibility of getting one on the end of a fishing line to experience the fight it would give us.

Reaching one particular sand bar, we approached it cautiously from very close to shore to avoid spooking them and bumped the prow of the boat on the beach and quietly got out.

Anhingas

Ray was the real angler amongst us. He limbered up a light spinning rod and dug through his tackle box for the right lure, tied it on and tightened the knot with his teeth, and crouched low to sneak up on the other side of the beach in hopes of making an attractive presentation to a school of these interesting fish.

After a half-hour, he returned, shaking his head.

"I saw them," he said quietly, "but I couldn't get their interest."

He resumed his search through the tackle box and pulled out another lure and tied it on. He then repeated his earlier attempt. We stayed near the boat in the shade, relaxing.

Roberto made one of his few comments.

"*Sólo con atarraya*," he said solemnly. Only with a cast net can you get those fish, he said.

When Ray returned, again skunked, we told him what Roberto had said.

"Do you want to try the cast net?" I asked.

"Bullshit!" Ray said disgustedly. "All fish eat. It's just a matter of casting something out there that looks like what they eat," he smiled. "Patience!"

He went back again but after some time, he plodded wearily back to the boat, explaining that the fish had moved off.

"I'll try them later. But for now, there are others I saw. And big!" He went back to his assortment and came up with a large Mepps spinner with a treble hook hidden by a thick tuft of bucktail. He then went back to the other side of the beach, and we followed some distance behind to watch. He began casting near some deadfalls that leaned out from the shore. On the second cast, he let out a whoop as he jerked his rod high in the air, setting the hook.

425

Gravity My Enemy

"Got him!" His rod bent almost double and he leaned back into it, a bit dramatically, I thought, but what the hell, this is what it was all about.

Ray went down the shore fighting the fish and thoroughly enjoying every minute. He worked the fish to the shore, bent down, and then stood up, triumphantly raising a large green and yellow bass high over his head, flashing a beaming smile. He held the bass by the gill cover. He came to us at my calling, because it was hard getting the wheelchair through the loose sand to see it, and we all gathered around to look. It was definitely some kind of bass, weighing perhaps seven pounds, very powerful and hefty in appearance. It was the most beautiful bass I had ever seen. The underbelly was light yellow and resplendent orange and the sides were striped vertically in broad bars with darker yellow from the belly and deep green from the back. On the tail was a big false "eye," a trick of nature to ward off larger predators. On the top of the back was an odd fleshy lump in front of the dorsal fin about the size of a silver dollar. It was a very handsome fish.

"I've heard of these," Ray exclaimed. "They're called Peacock Bass, or Butterfly Bass. I read somewhere that they go to thirty pounds!"

Excited, he ran back to the boat and put the fish on a wire stringer and let it back in the water. He then literally ran back to the area of the catch and resumed casting. I sent Oscar back to the boat to dig out some bread and a can of spicy sardines in tomato sauce. George opened the can deftly with his Swiss Army knife and we sat in the shade and ate while Ray could be seen in the distance casting and occasionally splashing in the shallow water with a bent rod. In an hour's

Anhingas

time, he had eight peacock bass on the stringer and called it quits. He came over to us.

"Got any more to eat? My arms are tired!

Can you believe it?" He was sweating profusely and beginning to burn a little pink.

"I've never seen anything like this!" He stammered. "Those bass really fight! I think we've got enough for a big dinner," he beamed proudly.

The spot was idyllic. The river was about fifty feet across at that point and there was low forest on both shores. Only the beach area was bright and sunny. It showed tracks of caiman, the South American cousin to the alligator, and what appeared to be the big, three-toed pugmark of a pig-like tapir, but it was too washed out for us to be sure. The water was calm as a black mirror and seemingly deep, seen from above as a dark green color. Birds of neon-electric colors of every imaginable hue flitted around us in the shrubbery, oblivious to our presence. We knew little of the names of any of them but one that was particularly attractive was a *mot-mot*, a blue-green beauty with a long tail that had a bare spot near the end, with it terminating in a round dot of plumage, appearing like a giant exclamation mark. Skimmers gracefully sailed by in front of us at intervals right on the top of the water, their longer, lower mandible of their beaks slicing through the water on the surface, collecting minute organisms as they lazily winged by. It was warm but not oppressively hot, and we were lounging in a beautiful shaded area of the sandy beach near the shore. It was late morning, we had eaten, and we felt contented. I swung away the footrests of the chair and carefully leaned forward and slid out onto the sand and stretched out. There were no flies or mosquitoes to bother

Gravity My Enemy

us at this hour and it was not long before most of us fell asleep.

I awoke first, feeling happy and almost as though drugged from the quiet satisfaction we all sensed in this little corner of paradise. I looked around and noticed the shadows were getting somewhat longer on the water of the opposite shore, and the sun had crept up on us, obliterating our protective shade. I rolled on my side and simply gazed across the river, enjoying this lovely, exotic world immensely and not feeling very inclined to do much of anything. I let my companions sleep, but after some minutes the sunlight began waking them as it had me, and everyone was up and looking around in wonder, not feeling conversational in the midst of such beauty.

Finally, I told Oscar and Roberto to start cleaning the fish, and asked Ray and George if they would be interested in staying the night at this very spot.

"It's pretty and all," George said, "but it's still kinda early. Why don't we move up river a little more, see what we can see?"

"What do you think?" I asked Ray.

"Sounds good to me. Let's go slow so I can make some casts along the way from the boat."

As soon as Oscar got to the fish stringer, he urgently called out. *"Miren ésto!"* Look at this, he shouted. Everyone ran over to look. I was still sitting in the sand, anchored to my position.

"Ed, you gotta see this!" Ray yelled over to me. They brought the heavy stringer over and one of the larger peacock bass was stiff dead and had lost its coloration to a duller gray. Hanging limply from its gill on one side was an eel, firmly attached and sickening in appearance, writhing weakly. The eel was about as thick as

Anhingas

my thumb and a foot long. We were all strangely appalled.

Ray carefully unclipped the dead bass from the stringer and, grasping the fish by the lower jaw, slung it out into the river with the eel attached, then shuddered.

"Gives me the creeps!" he said.

"Probably still good to eat," I admitted. "Probably the eel too, for that matter, but we're obviously not that desperate!"

"Yeah, let the slimy thing have his dinner," George said.

The guys started cleaning the fish on the front wooden deck of the boat, and Ray joined in to help. George went back to the transom and rattled around in his metal toolbox, unclamped the cover off the motor and did what seemed a little cleaning or minor adjustment on the outboard.

Within an hour, we were again aboard the boat and heading upriver. The boat itself was heavy and felt waterlogged. Some of the planks were punky but it did not leak overly much. We bailed it out once in a while with a split gourd. The shape of the hull was not the best but adequate for hauling cargo. A sharp turn caused it to roll dangerously but not to the point of allowing water over the thwarts. Roberto was at the helm.

Ray stood before the roof structure of the boat up front in the bow, spinning rod in hand, and scanned the water's surface slightly ahead as we progressed, looking for signs of fish. I sat in the wheelchair next to him in the bow but my interest lay more in hunting, and I was carefully eyeing the brush next to the shores ahead, primarily the edges of the occasional openings. My 6 mm bolt action Ruger lay next to me, propped up against the gunwale, loaded and ready. Coming around each bend in the river was

Gravity My Enemy

a new adventure in itself, opening up a distinct panorama each time, not only in landscape but also in wildlife.

Once far ahead I saw a line of almond-shaped heads swimming across the river, right to left. They looked like heads from giant chipmunks, tilted back to keep their noses out of the water. I counted seven, and they were swimming very rapidly. In curiosity, I picked up the rifle and checked to make sure the scope was turned to the highest power, and shouldered it to view the animals. They were capybara, the world's largest rodent. None of us was especially fond of their meat but in time of need, a good capybara provided abundance. A big one might exceed a hundred and fifty ponds. These were too distant to shoot, and we had Ray's catch as a promise for a good supper, so I put the rifle down.

As we passed the point where the capybara had crossed, I glanced to my left and in a small opening in the trees, I saw one reddish-brown capybara standing on the shore watching us through its characteristic oriental eyes. I jabbed Ray in the ribs and he turned, saw the rodent, and nodded with a smile. This animal was probably part of the bunch that had just crossed, but got left behind and separated as our boat approached. He did not seem alarmed at seeing and hearing us go by, a testimony to the remoteness of the area and lack of human activity. In other places in the country, and in Venezuela, these herding animals were being decimated, their meat salted and sold commercially in market places in larger towns, as were salted hides from caiman.

The sun was starting to touch the horizon and the sky turned red. We began looking for a campsite. Soon, we found a pretty little grassy glade among the trees by the shore on our left and

Anhingas

we motioned for Roberto to pull over. There was a small embankment next to the site and this served perfectly as a dock on which to unload the boat.

Oscar had been through this procedure before with us countless times and did not need to be told what to do. He unloaded the tents onto the shore, along with the grub box, grill and air mattresses, and began quickly raising the two tents. After getting hefted over the side onto the shore in the wheelchair, much like part of the luggage, I sat on the shore getting dizzy as I blew up air mattresses. Ray and George pounded in the heavy metal stake on which the grill hung and set up the kitchen. George soon had a fire crackling under the grill. Ray was bent over the table, salting and peppering bass fillets and greasing a big, heavy black cast iron skillet that was our favorite. Roberto sliced potatoes and onions. One pot was dedicated to cooking up the vegetables; another soon had water steaming from it for coffee. The ponderous frying pan was now smoking hot, awaiting the fish fillets, which Ray was flowered whitely.

They hissed and popped in the grease as Ray forked them into the skillet, turning them after just a minute. They were golden-brown and fluffy in no time, and we queued up to the table in eager anticipation.

We used pie tins for plates and each served himself generously. I mashed my potatoes on the plate and mixed in margarine and a sprinkling of salt and pepper. The fish fillets were thick, white as snow and looked wonderful, and were popping and bubbling in the grease. Ray took the honors of serving these to each of us, "Hey Oscar! Bring over your plate!" And he flopped a heavy fillet on each man's plate.

We were very impressed with the fish. The flesh was very tender and flaked easily, steaming

Gravity My Enemy

profusely even in the warm evening air. We all
agreed it was far better than our American black
bass. But then, we may have been hungrier than
usual. There had been seven fish we kept and each
was at least five pounds "on the hoof," so we
had enough to keep some left over for tomorrow's
breakfast. Eventually, we were all too full to eat
any more, and we poured sweet coffee in porcelain
metal cups. George, Ray and I each lit up a
tiny, maple-flavored cigar from the supply we had
obtained what seemed a century ago in Cáqueza
near Bogotá. We slouched back in comfort, sipped
hot coffee and smoked in contented luxury.

Little was said. We alternately nursed our
coffee, puffed on our cheroots and our eyelids
began to droop. Without a word, Oscar and Roberto
gathered dishes and pans and took them to the
water's edge, scrubbing each with sand and leaving
them shiny-clean.

As we smoked silently, we heard a strange
noise emanating from the gloomy darkness behind
the camp. It sounded exactly like a nursery of
crying babies. It seemed to come from all over
in the woods behind us. The number and volume
increased as the minutes passed.

"What the hell is that?" I pondered.

"Jeez! I've never heard anything like it,"
Ray said in amazement. He was the bird watcher in
our party. His puzzlement only served to augment
the mystery.

"Could it be birds?" I asked.

"Well, I hope so! It sounds like a maternity
ward," Ray mused. He went into a tent and brought
out a big flashlight.

"I'm gonna find out." He was determined.

"Better be careful! *Mucho cuidado!*" Roberto
warned. *"Hay culebras!"* Snakes in this part of
the world were a serious consideration. Rummaging

Anhingas

around in the bush at night was not a wise thing to do.

Ray sauntered off, and entered the bush behind the camp from which the sounds were originating. The flashlight beam bobbed up and down among the trees and finally was gone from sight.

"I wish you had gone with him," I said to George.

"He'll be all right. Ray doesn't like company when he's off in the bush."

We held our coffee mugs with both hands, alternately puffing on our dark cheroots. Ten minutes passed and a beam of light shot into camp and Ray emerged from the gloom and came into the circle of light from the campfire. "Mystery solved!" He shouted.

"Take a guess!" Neither George nor I had the slightest idea.

"*Anhingas!*" he said in glory.

"What? What's that?" George asked. "Snakebirds, you idiots. You know those black birds in the Florida swamps that look like egrets? They're famous for diving in the water when alarmed and poking their head and neck out to resemble a dead branch? Their feathers aren't waterproof, so they can jump in the water and just soak it up and sink."

George and I nodded at each other. We had heard of these birds but had never seen them.

We finished our coffee, dumped the grounds in the fire and tossed our cigar butts into the remaining orange embers and decided to turn in. Roberto found himself a comfortable spot in the boat and curled up there to sleep. Oscar stayed up near the fire.

We were exhausted, and sleep came in minutes.

29 Search for Capybara

Down at the waterfront on the river, I was sitting in the aluminum boat early in the morning, watching the flat, oily Manacacías River roll by when a rather gangly *campesino* came over the hump of the river bank from the village and approached me with a smile.

Accompanying him about ten steps behind was apparently his wife. She was dumpy, with downcast eyes; her straight black hair was tied in a ponytail. She was wearing the typically favorite of country girls: a cheap satiny dress in bright pink with the shoulders ballooned out. In her case, the waistline rode uncomfortably above her distended stomach. She was either pregnant or had a bad case of what we called "worm-belly," an advanced infestation of parasites. Unlike her garrulous partner, she was shy, withdrawn and unsmiling.

"Did you shoot a *chigüiro* — capybara — yesterday?" he asked.

I said we had been upriver some miles and had lost one I was sure I had hit on our return trip downriver the previous day.

"We found it," he said triumphantly. "It's hung up on a deadfall near the shore. He's is a very big one!"

His smile revealed several gold teeth in front.

I was very pleased and excited to hear this news.

"What condition was he in?" I asked, returning his friendliness. The tropics go to work on decomposition very quickly.

"I think he is in good condition. That was late yesterday and he had a wound in his head, but nothing was eating on him and he seemed to be fine." He showed the same pleasure as I felt,

435

Gravity My Enemy

and I asked him if he would be willing to show me the animal.

This was the news he was waiting for, as he eagerly accepted and asked if I could take him, his wife and their supplies to their house, which also was upstream several miles, near the capybara.

"How far is your house?" Colombians in the country often have a way of getting you involved in lengthy goose — or in this case, capybara — chases.

"It's just a little beyond the *chigüiro*. Not far at all!" he said with enthusiasm.

"How far," I persisted. "Ten minutes? Tell me exactly. We don't have much gasoline," I warned.

It was now very plain I was his only chance to get back to his house now instead of waiting several days for some boat that would head in his direction. There were no other settlements up river. The dead capybara was their ticket.

"Not far," he insisted, continuing to be typically vague. I knew getting a straight answer was hopeless, and I too had a vested interest, so I finally agreed.

"But I want to go quickly — only on that condition! No waiting around!"

"Oh, yes! We're all ready to go. Just let me get our things, right here close by!" And he dashed off, harrying his wife to come rapidly.

True to his word, he reappeared in less than five minutes with a heavy sack of rice over his shoulder. His wife also was carrying a hefty burden that seemed too much for a diminutive woman, much less a pregnant one, if indeed that was the reason for her bell-shaped appearance. They slung them into the middle of the boat, and he quickly departed again, reassuring me, "*Un momentico, no más!*" And he promptly returned with

Search for Capybara

more, showing a big smile. He helped his wife into the boat, more because of her shyness than because of her inability, and lifted the boat from the gunwale and heaved it out into the current.

I was beginning to like the man. He was not hesitant in putting his shoulder to work and his friendliness seemed genuine and infectious. He was tall and very thin, and wore a rumpled black hat that had no specific shape. He was pure Dogpatch. Being quadriplegic I lacked the strength to pull the starter, and asked him to do so, explaining to him I could not walk and was handicapped. He quickly came back and yanked on it with the expertise of someone who had spent their life around boats and motors, and the motor sputtered and then hummed to life. Since it was almost new, I had confidence in going out with it by myself. I put it in gear and swung the light boat, now heavily laden, out into the mainstream and headed against the current, southward.

The river was smooth and there were very few tree branches or logs floating downstream, as is common during the time of floods, which was the season at present.

The shores on both sides were open plains in some brief areas and tall rainforest in others, darkening our river passage as though going through a tunnel. There were occasional sand bars but these were few, since the water level was fairly high. In some areas, the water overflowed its banks and extended far back beyond the natural shore, forming forested lakes that measured a kilometer or more in distance from the main river flowage.

It was sunny and the sky bright blue. Puffy fair weather cumulus clouds hung shining whitely on the horizon and hawks and vultures wheeled overhead in their endless search for

Gravity My Enemy

prey and carrion, riding on hot air currents with motionless wings. A troop of black howler monkeys bent branches down in the trees off to our right, uncaring about our presence.

Skimmers winged in twos and threes just inches off the surface of the river, swinging widely out of our way as they warily passed us in their daily journey downstream. Some time passed and I was thoroughly enjoying the trip and the sights around us. Two prehistoric grouse-like hoatzins clamored in branches overhanging the water at the shore, using the unusual claws they possessed on the leading edge of their wings, and their feet, to grasp branches and vines, rarely choosing to use their wings for flight except when frightened, and only then for very short distances. I soon noticed several more. Their disproportionately small heads had blue skin, much like the guinea fowl of Africa, but with a crest of brown feathers, and they seemed as though from another eon in time.

The Manacacías was narrow at this point, spanning only about 75 yards. This was my favorite type of jungle river. The shores were close enough on either side to see wildlife frequently, and the light conditions also permitted us to see color, unlike the open, anonymous big rivers such as the Amazon, where one saw only distant tree lines and, if any wildlife was visible, it was in silhouette or almost totally obscured. Here, colors were not only visible but resplendent in the orange shafts of early morning sunlight. Flowered vines cascaded to the water in proud splendor, the blossoms brilliant reds, purples and yellows, casting a rainbow of petals onto the quiet surface of the river, and floating them downstream in a parade of secret festivity.

My *campesino* friend, sitting in the bow with his wife, finally turned and looked back in

Search for Capybara

my direction and signaled with his hand to the left ahead.

I slowed the motor and the bow dug deeply into the water as it slowed, and I swung it in toward the shore on his directions, scraping by overhangs and ducking our heads to avoid the tangle of vegetation in our search for the dead capybara. With a quick, frantic motion of his hand, he signaled me to stop and pointed finally to a brown-haired bulk barely protruding from the water surface among the tangle, its round shape looking like a semi-submerged submarine. I threw the gear of the motor in neutral, not wanting to shut it off, and peered curiously over the gunwale as we approached the shape.

It was indeed a large capybara and I could see the wound in the back of the head was whitening from being under the water for a prolonged period of time. My friend reached out and tried to roll the animal over in the water, preparing to haul it aboard. As he did so, we could see that piranhas had been eating away at the flank and the nose. A faint rotten smell reached my nose and the *campesino* also wrinkled his nose in disdain.

"*Ya está dañado*," he said sorrowfully. "It's already rotten." He turned up his palms to say "What can we do?" and I agreed there was nothing we could do except leave the hapless animal, an act that always bothered me deeply, as I had grown up to hunt only for a purpose. But, at least it would provide a good feast for the fish, I rationalized to myself.

I put the motor in gear and slowly pointed the bow toward the center of the river again, and we resumed our upstream journey.

After a short time, I was about to ask my friend how much further we had to go when, true to his word, he pointed to a spot on the shore off

Gravity My Enemy

to our left. I could see no house, and gestured the question to him: Where is the house?

He motioned for me to turn toward the shore, or what had been shore prior to the flood season. The entire area was flooded back as far as we could see, and we headed inland — more appropriately "overland" — very slowly and amongst the trees.

I throttled down and all was quiet.

"See the big bushes there on the left?" he pointed to some bushes about eight feet high that ran in a line inward. "Run the boat right next to them, almost touching, and stay very close or you will run aground. Be very careful!" He said this with some gravity.

We ran at the slowest pace possible, just enough for steerage, and I stayed close to the bushes as he urged. He continually warned me not to venture away from them. We traveled far into the backwaters, perhaps over a half-mile, before the terrain opened out onto a big, flat lake. On the far side and to the right, a half-mile across, his little brown thatched-roofed house emerged into view from between the trees, perched high on a small knob hill. He directed me to head straight for it. A moment later, we arrived and I cut the motor. The boat coasted forward and the bow softly bumped the shore below his house. He seemed very jubilant to be home once again as he hoisted the bow firmly onto the shore, stepped out into the water and hefted the biggest sack onto his shoulder. Without a word between them, his wife also swung a sack onto her shoulder, and then onto the top of her head with such ease I was amazed at her show of strength. She followed him up the hill with her burden, and they both returned as soon as they reached the top, without going all the way to the house.

Search for Capybara

I wondered how they had ever gotten through this swamp to get into Puerto Gaitán, but he was too busy for me to ask.

As he hoisted another sack to his shoulder, he said, "Some bad weather is coming. Perhaps it would be good if you left quickly."

He gestured at some black clouds in the distance and then headed up the hill again with his wife in tow. When he reached the top, he held up his hand in a gesture for me to wait.

"*Momentico*," he said, and disappeared, only to return seconds later with a beaming smile. Under his arm he carried a huge rooster, brought it to the boat and proudly said "For you!" as he tethered it to the front seat with a piece of plastic twine.

"*Muchas gracias*," I said with enthusiasm. This was no small gift among such modest people, and I showed sincere appreciation for his generosity. "I didn't expect you to pay me! I was happy to bring you home, and you were kind enough to show me the *chigüiro*."

"I'm sorry it was no longer good," he answered apologetically. "*Los caribes*, the piranhas, work very fast at times. In the dry season they are worse!"

"You live in a beautiful house," I said.

He climbed aboard the boat and came back to me to shake hands, reached for the starting cord and pulled. This was the last chance I had to have the motor running, and I sensed some feeling of trepidation as I backed the boat away from the shore.

"Remember," he reminded me gravely once again, now back on shore. "Do not get far from the bushes, stay very close to them!" I waved acknowledgment casually as I continued to back the boat out in reverse slowly, and turned to head out toward the

Gravity My Enemy

river. They both stood on the hill waving fondly and I turned away and headed steadily across the flood lake to the trees in the distance.

For some reason, I felt somewhat scared. This was really the first time I had been totally alone and far from any help in a wilderness of this dimension, and I knew there could be no mistakes. The deep tropics are very unforgiving. I was utterly dependent on the boat for my very survival.

I finally saw the line of bushes ahead and veered in their direction, and soon was skirting them closely as instructed. The boat bumped into them slightly and scraped by, the impact changing my direction away from them slightly. Not wanting to swing the transom and the lower unit of the motor out too far from the security of the deep water near the bushes, I pointed the bow toward them gradually as I put-putted along at the lowest speed possible.

As the boat swung away from the bushes, I felt the propeller thump the bottom underneath in a steady vibration. My heart jumped into my throat. I twisted the throttle to increase rpm's to gain an advantage but the propeller could not get a purchase on the water and the boat was dead in the water. The prop was severely fouled in grass.

Frantically, I threw the gear into neutral in fear of stalling the motor. My only salvation and hope was to keep the motor running.

Grasping for an oar, I held it vertically and plunged it downward into the water at the side of the boat and touched the bottom to measure the depth. I was shocked to realize I was in only about a foot of water. Since I could not get to a sitting position by myself from a reclined position without great effort, I got a secure hold on the

Search for Capybara

front of the seat I was sitting on and carefully, tentatively reached over the transom in back next to the motor to feel with my hand what the situation was, at the same time scared to death that the motor's neutral was not totally neutral and I might lose a hand in the spinning prop.

I was also very mindful of the big chunks of flesh missing from the capybara caused by piranha bites, which I had just seen earlier, and was very nervous about keeping my hand in the water very long.

I felt a knotted clump of grass tightly twisted around the propeller the size of a basketball. This was a bad situation indeed! I was out of sight and far from shouting distance from the people I had just left, had no food or water and the motor was running on a limited supply of gas. One stupid mistake had been made. I could not afford another, such as falling backwards or letting the motor quit. I readjusted my grip on the seat and carefully reached down into the dark water to the lower unit of the motor again, clawing at the tight cluster of grass and removing as much as would come loose in handfuls. I repeated this over and over, each time tossing the clump of grass I was able to tear loose, out of the way to the side. In straining to do this, I soon felt exhausted and my arms were getting very fatigued. "Take your time," I said to myself urgently. "Think it out! And be very, very careful!"

It must have taken at least a half hour before my fingers finally were able to touch the bare blades of the propeller. I carefully ran my fingers along the leading edge of each blade to make sure nothing was broken or missing. Fortunately, the Mercury did not use a sheer pin that would have broken under the circumstances, but a rubber bushing that merely slipped. I was

Gravity My Enemy

deeply relieved to find everything intact. Very tentatively, almost in dread, I popped the gear lever into forward and breathed a sigh of relief as I felt the boat pull forward slowly toward the bushes. I bumped it right against the bushes this time, softly, to make doubly sure there would be no more mishaps. I again pushed the gear lever into neutral and reached over the transom to remove any grass I might have entangled in the prop after moving the initial short distance. There were only a few strands and I cleared the prop again in just a brief effort.

Then I sat up straight, took a deep breath, and proceeded forward, rubbing the right gunwale against the bushes the entire way, until I was overjoyed almost to tears to finally see the river open out before me. I carefully pulled out into the main body of the river, feeling almost giddy with relief. I noticed I was shaking very badly, my lips were trembling, and I plodded along down river slowly as I recovered my composure emotionally.

After a few minutes, I was speeding along like a Sunday vacationer and planing out under full throttle in the now lighter weight boat. Remembering the occasional submerged log, I quickly slowed down and swore I would never be a fool again if only I could get back safely. Clouds were gathering darkly just ahead and I braced myself for a hard rain, which was just starting to pelt me with large, stinging drops. They felt good in the heat and I luxuriated in the coolness of the rain.

Cat's-paws of wind gusts appeared ahead on the water's surface, and I began to feel an occasional gust take the boat to one side or the other. I was in control and unconcerned.

Search for Capybara

Suddenly and without warning, a violent gust took the light bow of the boat and weathercocked it around to almost 180 degrees, facing backward. The boat made a vicious cut to the side, tipping precariously and water came over the gunwale. I cut the throttle instantly, and regained control. My heart was pounding almost audibly and I felt light-headed from the scare. Rain lashed at the boat, the blasts turning it in still another random direction. I slowly headed for the shore to seek protection from the storm, and advanced carefully down river. I was soaked to the skin, blinking away rain mixed with sweat in my eyes.

It rained hard for perhaps fifteen minutes, when the storm quit as quickly as it started, and all was calm. Within minutes, the sun was out brightly and the surrounding jungle was left steaming in the aftermath. Raindrops on the vegetation sparkled like jewels in the sunlight. I again headed for the center of the river and opened the throttle in jubilation. The strong resulting breeze helped me dry off. I took off my shirt first, then shoes and socks little by little as I kept traveling down river, and then, squirming back and forth on the aluminum seat, took off my wet pants and sat there speeding down the river totally naked. I spread my clothes on the seat in front of me to dry and, exhilarated, continued my journey, my naked feet stretched out in front in the exultation of the moment. My body was already dry and I felt good. The clothes would not take much longer.

I started to recognize the familiar terrain of the Puerto Gaitán area and throttled back so as to have time to get my pants on before arriving. In a few moments, partially dressed, I was pulling toward the shore next to the little town. Ray and George were there awaiting me. My

445

feet by now were bright red from sunburn, and starting to sting. They had been uncovered in the bottom of the aluminum boat, roasting in what essentially was a reflector oven.

"How did it go?" Ray asked, a worried expression on his face.

"Good," I replied. "The capybara's no good. But he was a big one. Where's the sunburn cream?"

I decided to save the capybara story for another day.

30 Night Hunt

Having the advantage of maneuverability and speed with the aluminum boat, George and I decided to go hunting caiman one evening, and left in the later afternoon as the sun was setting in orange splendor, to get some distance away from Puerto Gaitán and into a territory more likely to have an undisturbed caiman population.

The caiman is a member of the alligator and crocodile family. Their eyes seem to protrude higher on the head, like turrets, and the mouth is not as broad as the alligator's or as narrow and long as the croc's but their size is often the same, as is the danger in handling them. There are said to be black caiman and white caiman, as well as a South American croc, but I never could tell the difference.

My mentor in learning how to hunt them was Mike Tsalickis of Leticia down on the Colombian Amazon, right across from Peru, but that's another story, and many years earlier.

The technique is to motor slowly down the center of the river (except the Amazon, which is far too wide), one driving the boat and the other sitting in the bow with a shotgun and a headlamp. The driver or *motorista* watches for hand signals from the shooter, who with the headlamp scans the shoreline for the orange eyes of the caiman. Only the shooter can see them, being directly behind the beam of light, and the driver turns on the shooter's signal when one is seen, and aims the boat to the spot where the light beam illuminates the shore, making small, final adjustments based on hand signals being made in front of the light. When about twenty feet from the target, the *motorista* cuts the motor so as not to unduly alarm the caiman and the boat's momentum takes

Gravity My Enemy

it to the shore as the shooter quickly decides if the size of the caiman warrants shooting, makes his only shot, drops the gun and reaches over the side quickly to grasp the prey.

As can easily be guessed, this rapid sequence of events lends itself to sudden excitement and often no small hazard. The shooter must decide in a second if the caiman is big enough to take. The only purpose we had in shooting them was meat for the pot, as it were, so we usually limited our size needs to a minimum of around four or five feet. Smaller animals did not provide enough meat. Some ran to nine feet or more but, in my opinion, the meat in the tail, which we preferred, was so large in the very big ones as to have a ring of fat that to me was somewhat disagreeable, so I usually preferred the four- or five-footers for nice firm, white flesh very much resembling that of lobster tail. When fried golden brown in a hot pan, with a little salt and pepper, there was little fare tastier in the world. It wasn't as stringy as lobster but every bit as tender and snow-white, and it had the added advantage of a center bone for grasping while eating large, bite-sized chunks. It was a meal fit for a king, virtually without equal in the jungle. I frankly enjoyed the eating far more than the hunting — and I was a lifetime hunting fanatic.

Once the quick decision determined this particular caiman was of adequate size, based on the distance between the eyes, the shot was fired directly at the eyes at the top of the head, usually blowing the top of the head off and killing the sauropod instantly. This is harder than it may seem because the eyes themselves are about the same diameter on any sized animal and the shooter usually cannot see both eyes at once to measure the distance between them until the

Night Hunt

last second as the nearing boat reaches proximity at the correct angle.

If a shot is made, all is chaos. The shooter quickly discards his rusty shotgun to one side, usually a simple break-open single shot with an external hammer, and reaches far over the side of the boat as it slides over the top of the caiman. A dead caiman will usually start to sink, so it's important to grab it on the first try by any part of its body in reach — the front leg or snout being most common.

Then the caiman, usually quite heavy, is pulled over the gunwale into the boat, with the help of the *motorista*.

It may surprise many to know that the shot at such close quarters is more difficult that it would seem, and often does not completely do him in, and the caiman still has plenty of life left in him when the unlucky shooter grabs it to pull it aboard. The telling characteristic of a wounded caiman is that it floats, rather than gradually sinking like a dead one, but the shooter only has a brief second to notice this and usually does not notice at all, sometimes resulting in a hand torn by sharp teeth at the same instant of convulsive thrashing of the tail, which is exactly how the caiman dismembers its prey in the first place. Once while hunting in the Amazon years earlier, we avoided serious injury with a big wounded caiman but it was so violent after pulling it into the bottom of the boat that it knocked planks loose and we came close to sinking.

Another friend on a different occasion in Brazil was hauling a large nine-and-a-half-foot caiman up the bank from the boat at the conclusion of a night's hunt. It had been lying dead motionless in the bottom of the boat for perhaps two hours or so and we assumed it to be dead. He grasped it

449

Gravity My Enemy

by the "arm" and slung it up over his shoulder, tail dragging behind him on the ground. It was remarkable he could even carry such a monster but he was a strong man. A last convulsive tail slap came around the front of his body and broke most of his ribs on one side. He was in the hospital for several days.

Now George and I were hundreds of miles north of the Amazon in what could be termed the Orinoco Basin, to try our luck at what was usually an innocuous pursuit. The sun was beginning to hide behind the tropical trees on the shore; the intense heat of the day had become cooler and deliciously comfortable as we motored quietly south, the Manacacías River as still as a mirror and beautifully serene. We were thoroughly enjoying the riverside bird life and watching for large, more exciting animals such as capybara or a large boa.

(On one such occasion just like this, I spotted a huge boa in the brush on a rather steep bank and, as a reflex, took a shot at it with the rifle and hit it right in the head. It was huge, and I have the skin to this day, measuring exactly twelve feet. Considering that the head was completely cut off in the skinning, and measured about a foot, and three feet of tail, too thin to skin easily, was discarded as well, this was about 15 feet in length, the biggest boa I had ever seen with one exception, and it provided a lot of meat for the Yagua Indian village in Brazil where I was living at the time.)

When it became dark enough to use the light, George, who was in the bow, stretched the elastic band over his head and centered the light on his forehead, and clipped the battery box on the back of his belt, keeping the wire clear to handle the shotgun. He cracked open the Stevens

Night Hunt

single shot and dropped in a plastic shell of
7½'s — a trap load usually used for wingshooting
but packing a wallop with over an ounce of lead
at ten feet — enough for any caiman. He rested the
muzzle pointing outward and forward against the
gunwale next to him and began slowly scanning the
shoreline where water meets the land. I slowed
the boat to slightly above idle, cruising at about
five miles per hour. It was a pleasant evening and
we had good feelings about what it would bring.
I tried to look at the shore as well, but keeping
an eye out for deadfalls ahead. Insects buzzed
crazily into George's light beam.

An inordinate amount of time passed and I
was beginning to wonder if the night was going
to be a bust for the first time, when, to my
relief, George started frantically signaling with
the palm of his hand in the light beam so I could
see it. He had spotted a red-orange eye to his
right, and I swung the tiller without slowing,
and followed his beam to the shore forty yards
distant. As we got almost within shooting range,
he quickly waved me off, and I swerved the boat
away from shore and back out into open water.

George looked back at me and held his palms
apart about two feet, to indicate the caiman had
been too small.

We resumed our slow journey down the center
of the jungle river and George patiently continued
the scanning.

Not a minute passed before he again signaled
me to turn off. I followed the beam steadily,
he had his gun up and ready and this time and
at the last moment, quickly shouldered it and
fired into the brush next to the shore. There is
nothing quite as startling as a shotgun blast in
the tropical night. The orange flame licked out
of the muzzle angrily, George's shoulder jolted

Gravity My Enemy

back from the recoil and the blast was startling even though I expected it. The impact of the shot column kicked up a plume of white water and it shot up three feet in the air, its actual spot of impact out of my sight, blocked by the bow of the boat, so I had no idea if there was a hit. In the same motion, George discarded the gun at his side and reached deep over the left side. A heavy weight prevented him from sitting upright.

Since I was unable to assist him, as my legs didn't function, I put the motor in neutral and just gritted my teeth. George grunted in exertion and, pushing against the gunwale with his other, free hand, righted himself and pulled a caiman of about five feet in length half over the gunwale. It glistened wetly in the light. With another heave, it flopped into the bottom of the boat, splattering a small amount of blood in the bilge that was washing the bottom of the boat.

We had our first caiman, and it was a good one.

As the night progressed, George and I switched positions and I took my place in the bow as gunner. I spotted an orange eye on the shoreline and signaled George to make the turn. He aimed the boat toward the area I illuminated on the shore while I made finer adjustments with hand signals as we rapidly approached. When about ten feet from the sauropod, I pulled back the hammer of the shotgun in readiness and shouldered it firmly for a shot. It was a huge animal, I noticed, as just the top portion of its head protruded above the water level in a tangle of aquatic weeds. Just as I began squeezing the trigger, the caiman sank below the water like a submarine. The boat, the motor now silent, slid over the very spot where he had been, and softly bumped the shore to a stop. We remained quiet as

Night Hunt

I searched around us in all directions with the bright headlamp, but there was no movement.

Mike Tsalickis of Leticia, an old pro at this game, often made a grunting call to imitate the sound of a young caiman separated from its mother. Whether this could be heard or not from under the water was just speculation, but I started making the guttural grunts in a series, deep down in my throat.

I noticed a thin, vertical branch move slightly to one side in the water to my left about eight feet off our beam, moved from the ponderous weight of the caiman as he slid by the obstruction. My heart pounding in excitement, I again shouldered the 12 gauge and aimed in the general direction of the movement. Seconds later, the wet back of the head of the caiman surfaced to the left of the bow, and I quickly swung the muzzle and let loose a load of birdshot. The bright orange flame spat from the muzzle in a deafening bark and a geyser of water shot straight up in the air, rolling the caiman over in the water. I just caught a quick glimpse of his yellow underbelly as he rolled over and disappeared. George hauled out an oar and urgently pushed the boat in the animal's direction as I dropped the shotgun at my side and leaned over with the full extent of my arm in the water, searching for the caiman. I touched a clawed foot and grabbed it, pulling toward the boat, greatly relieved to sense no movement or resistance. This was the moment of truth regarding major injury, but it did not appear to show any life. I straightened my back with all my force, pushing with my left arm against the gunwale to aid me in sitting up, dragging the caiman closer to the boat.

It was far too heavy for me to handle and George came forward to lend a hand. I had the

Gravity My Enemy

caiman's arm clear of the water, and he grasped it and pulled its body halfway over the gunwale with a muscular heave. A second effort brought the caiman slithering completely into the bottom of the boat behind me. It was one of the largest we'd seen.

George figured him to be at least eight feet. I had to agree. It was a gigantic animal. I looked at the top of the head and was amazed at what a load of fine birdshot could do from close quarters.

We had three caiman and all the meat we could possibly need and it was getting late, so we decided to head back to Puerto Gaitán. The evening was beautiful and we had had a good hunt.

After several minutes of motoring along the river, I was astonished to begin seeing trees in the middle of the river. George swerved the boat to miss them and we realized we were in the middle of a flooded forest. Somehow, we had lost the mainstream of the river.

We wandered about aimlessly, searching for the main body of the river in vain. I suggested we stop for a moment and look down into the water under the boat to see if we could discern a current. We came to a dead stop, drove an oar into the mud bottom and shown the beam of the headlamp down into the water as we peered over the side. We could see grass under the boat, obviously from an area that was usually not flooded, but it revealed no current whatsoever. We moved on a few minutes and tried the same method, to no avail. As we wandered, casting about in different directions, it seemed we were entering into denser forest rather than emerging from our dilemma.

After about two hours we were totally frustrated and exhausted. There seemed to be no exit from the trap we sprung on ourselves.

Night Hunt

Finally, George said he thought the whole exercise was foolish, and only served to tire us more and use what little remained of our gasoline. We reluctantly agreed to wait out the night in the boat, and find our way in the morning.

I lit a cigarette and sat on the hard aluminum seat, hunched over, and neither of us felt inclined to say anything. All was dark gloom around us. We tied up to a tree. Though it was to our advantage to discover a current to find our way out, all it could do if we slept was gradually bring us against some standing brush or deadfall where it was likely that a venomous snake might be suspended to escape this watery world. I finished my cigarette and contemptuously flicked it into the water where it drowned in a hiss. As any cigarette addict does, I squeezed the pack and was alarmed to discover I had only four or five smokes left. It increased my desire for another but I held it in check and tried to lie down. The beam of the boat was far too narrow. I stretched my feet over the gunwale and rested my head on the other, but it was painfully uncomfortable. I tried stretching inside the boat but there was no room for my six-foot-three frame. I searched for something to use as a cushion but there was nothing. Even the large caiman was as hard as a log. I could tell George was also desperately uncomfortable, as he shifted in first one position and then another, emitting grunts of disgust.

Our only hope was that the time would pass quickly and dawn would guide us out. I turned on the light and quickly glanced at my watch. It was 10:25! Seven more hours of this!

Then it began to rain.

It was only a light sprinkle at first.

After a few minutes, it started raining in earnest. We hunched our shoulders and leaned

Gravity My Enemy

forward in total misery, the rain soaking our backs to the skin. I soon felt cold rivulets of water running around and down my ribs to my stomach. It started soaking into the waistband of my pants. I reached to safeguard my treasured pack of cigarettes under the seat, out of the rain, but the seat design allowed no space underneath due to enclosed flotation and I was forced to seek the only dry place I knew, in my crotch on the seat. I leaned further over to protect this last remaining bastion of dryness and warmth, but it was hopeless. It began raining with renewed vigor and in minutes I felt the icy seeping of water on the seat underneath me between my legs. The last sanctuary of comfort had been violated. In utter despair, I pulled out the cigarette pack and extracted one. I put it between my trembling, wet lips and flicked the lighter repeatedly until I got a weak flame. I held it to the soggy cigarette in a rush of expectation and warmth, but it would not light. It was too soaked. I tried again a second time and the cigarette crumbled between my dripping fingers, particles of tobacco falling at my feet in the flooded bilge. This was misery beyond anything I had ever known. I shifted position on the cold, hard seat and water squished under my buttocks. I was now totally wet and I began to involuntarily tremble around the abdomen. It was violent. Water shook off the tip of my nose and my chin. My hands were numb with cold. Could this actually be the tropics? I pondered to myself. We were both reduced to sullen silence. Every attempt to find a comfortable position rocked the boat.

How in hell could we have gotten ourselves in this mess? How could guys like us, the great adventurers, hunters and explorers that we were, be so incredibly stupid? What insults and ridicule

Night Hunt

would I lay on some other unfortunate in this
same predicament?

I looked again at my watch. 11:55. Shit!

It felt like four hours had passed. Are we
in some kind of time dilation as a punishment
from God for being idiots? When will it be
light enough to see our way out? My mind dimly
tried to remember what time was first light. I
couldn't even think straight. Was it four? Don't
be ridiculous, I said to myself. Of course not.
What about the false dawn they mention in books?
Is that a possibility? A hope? My whole body was
shivering uncontrollably. Can we possibly endure
for so many hours? Is there a choice? I looked at
George's back. It was shiny wet and black. He was
still. Could he possibly be asleep? I hoped so.
At least we'd have one person with his wits about
him when the time came to escape. What time would
that be? In four hours? More likely five — even
six. With it overcast from the rain, dawn would
take longer, I mused in despair.

You're on the wrong track, Old Ed. Think
positively. Imagine good things. Avoid thinking
about the time. Avoid guessing at the number of
hours. And, whatever you do, don't look at that
damned watch! It has no place here in the bush.
Nature has its own clock. Live with nature, not
man-made contraptions. Did Julius Caesar carry a
pocket watch to decide when to set off an attack
on Sextus Pompey? No, he most certainly did not.
But he did it with the precision of a clock,
because he was closer to nature. He was finely
attuned to all of nature's signals. You're here,
Ed, not in Chicago. Roll with the punches.

What will we feel, I forced myself to
imagine, when we first realize we can see well
enough to start the outboard? Excitement. Elation.
For sure, elation. And we definitely will feel

Gravity My Enemy

relief. It will come. No doubt about it. What will we feel when the boat starts moving? We will see the tree trunks pass by faster with each passing moment until we see the open river before us. All right! Open the throttle! We're free! Will we feel the sun on our backs? Think about these thoughts, Ed. People perish from feeling miserable, from seeing the dark side. Is there any doubt we'll make it out? Of course not! It'll be so obvious when the time comes, we'll feel foolish. It will happen. It will . . .

I jerked my head up. God, I was nodding off! What a revelation! My ass feels numb from the hard seat. I shift painfully. My bones ache. Jeez, it hurts to move. But it has to be done, as I've lost circulation in my legs. My useless legs. I turn my head and can see the stark black tree trunks around us. Actually, they were gray. Is it possible I can see a little more than earlier? Could that be? When was that? I brought up my wrist and fingered the headlamp switch. No! Don't look at the damn watch. Remember, that's the rule now. No more technology, just nature. You want science, go back to the city. I raised my head more and looked around carefully. My neck was stiff. And, God, I was cold. I don't think I've ever felt so cold. Even out ice fishing for bluegills in Wisconsin. January. Now that was cold! What month is this? I tried to think but could not guess what month it was. July maybe? No, you idiot! How can it be July when we were shooting off skyrockets just a few weeks ago, in celebration of New Year's? No, this is March. Definitely, it's March. I could see the horizon behind the mass of trees, off in the distance. How could I see that if it's still dark? Is it getting light?

It's getting light!

Hey, George. George! Listen!

Night Hunt

George moans.

It's light, man! George, d'you hear me? It's light. Goddammit, it's light! Now, he's awake, moving in his seat, more excitedly. He gets into position and yanks the starter cord of the motor and it putts to life. The smell of the oil and gas permeates our nostrils so richly. Thank God for a new motor. (Thank George. He's the one that had the money for it.)

I don't remember exactly what happened after that, but we emerged from the trees before long in the dim light of early dawn. Soon we were out in the main course of the river and motoring downriver toward Puerto Gaitán. We felt rather embarrassed within ourselves at having salvation so close at hand all night yet being inept at finding it. Or was that my dream?

The sun slowly rose and felt nicely warm on my back as we raced home. Or was that in my dream, too? I do remember that once we arrived to Puerto Gaitán and people came to the water's edge to marvel at our caiman, I looked at one fellow and said, *Regálame un cigarillo, hombre.*

Give me a cigarette, man.

31 Farewell

As I was doing routine paperwork in my office one day, a close friend stuck his head in the door and asked if he could have a private word with me. I greeted him with fondness and motioned him in. He entered and closed the door.

This must be pretty private, I thought to myself.

Alberto was a trusted friend of many years. He was the sub-commander of DAS, *Departamento Adminitrativo de Seguridad,* the Colombian equivalent of the FBI. This security organization was very professional, consisting of U.S.-trained technicians in criminal investigation, anti-terrorist techniques, state security and immigration issues. All were plainclothesmen. Over the years, he and I had taken each other into one another's confidence on political and police issues, sharing facts and street gossip, issuing warnings and seeking information. An ex-Korean War veteran, he was a tall, robust man with mutton-chop sideburns and a receding hairline. His smile was affable and genuine, and I trusted him unconditionally, as he evidently did me. We spent many pleasant afternoons practicing with weapons. DAS used a Danish Madsen submachine gun (SMG) and never had enough ammunition, so I reloaded 9 mm at home and supplied a means for their agents to practice, giving me the unique privilege of firing an SMG, as they are called.

With much conspiratorial ceremony, he took out of his pocket a very small paper wrapping and unfolded it in front of me on the desk. It contained a pinch of white powder. He sat back and proudly beamed at me.

"What's this?" I asked, puzzled.

Gravity My Enemy

"Put a little on the tip of your tongue," he answered.

I complied.

"Well?" he said, expectantly.

"The tip of my tongue has fallen asleep," I said, still naively confused.

"*Así es!*" he said in triumph. Exactly so! "Could this be . . . no! Not cocaine!" He nodded with a big smile of affirmation.

On several occasions, I had seen small, back street shops with a large assortment of marijuana for sale laid out in rustic bags and thought little of it. Colombia, after all, was the pot capital of the world. Colombia had recently undergone an invasion of bearded, very scuzzy-looking Americans we called Flower Children, often emaciated in appearance, seeking a little hovel in the mountains to grow pot and make brownies. Their Nirvana. Other than that, they were harmless. I thought nothing of that other than some limited embarrassment at calling them "fellow Americans." The police cared little, other than dragging one in on occasion and making me serve as court interpreter to assure that their legal rights were observed.

Colombian Indians of the Andes had chewed coca leaves for millennia before the arrival of Europeans. Activating it with a pinch of lime, they customarily carried a bag of coca leaves on their shoulder and labored the entire day owing to this stimulant. As a result, they felt little hunger and great energy, and no scientific studies ever revealed any adverse effect.[1]

Decorative shrubbery in front of posh homes in Cali often consisted of coca plants and nobody thought twice about it.

---

[1]   See Wade Davis' "One River" for legislative history.

Farewell

Yet, from my perspective, this moment in my office turned out to be the Genesis of a civil war in Colombia costing thousands of lives, not only in Colombia but also throughout the world, a literal change in the course of human history. It also marked the beginning of the end of my life in Colombia though I did not know it at the time.

I looked at the little snip of wrapping paper, commonly used to wrap bread in Colombia. This was still my period of innocence.

"What about it?" I asked. "It's interesting — the first time I've ever seen the stuff — but what's the deal?"

"Edmundo," he said, patiently, as someone does when they talk to a child, "you're beyond suspicion. You could go anywhere, cross any border, without being searched."

I nodded assent. Generally, this was true enough, though I explained I was not totally immune. I had been in and out of the U.S. and Colombia several times over the past decade without having a bag opened by customs. But I did not like the direction this conversation was going.

"We have about a kilo of this stuff, roughly," he explained, under his voice. 'A friend of mine from the F-2[1] confiscated it and told the guy to run. You're just the man we need. We'll let you have it for *doce mil pesos*." Twelve thousand pesos. That about four hundred American dollars.

I was more amused than anything. Me?

"I work for the U.S. government, for crissake," I said. "What are you trying to do to me, Alberto?"

"That's one of the reasons you're beyond suspicion."

In those early, fresh years, I was naïve enough to think this meant I was a saint. I laughed off

---

[1]   a plain-clothes apparatus of the regular police

Gravity My Enemy

his offer, said it had been interesting, but wryly thanked Alberto for thinking of me. Thanks but no thanks, I said with a friendly smile. He left.

In those days, I wore two hats. I worked during the week as the director of a bi-national center and also guided tourists on hunting and fishing trips. Mostly Americans.

A week or so after this incident, we had a group of young shooters down from Ft. Worth, Texas, to shoot doves. The hunting packages we offered were fairly expensive because they including hotel, ammunition, all meals, licenses and transportation. Usually, this precluded having sportsmen as young as these fellows were, but it was not customary to ask many questions.

While around the fireside after the first day's shoot, enjoying coffee and a cigarette after supper, we engaged in lively conversation. I happened to tell them this incredible story (at least to me) of being offered cocaine by a friend from local law enforcement.

"Imagine me!" I laughed. They all laughed. Yes, imagine you, they agreed.

The next night around the campfire after supper out under the stars, it was a lovely night. Coffee was served and we were relaxing. Some bantering took place between shooters about their shooting, then we all entered into conversation on various issues. Then, there was a pregnant moment of silence, when one of the shooters, a tall, very skinny fellow with a shock of hair in his face, cleared his throat.

"About that story you told us last night," he said. Uh-oh, I thought. Now I knew why they were here in Colombia. "Could you still get that stuff?" Only a week or so had passed since. I said I thought I could.

"Why?" I said, realizing how stupid the question was as soon as I had opened my mouth.

Farewell

"We have a proposition for you," he said eagerly. Here it comes, I thought. "We'll pay your round-trip to Miami. How often do you get to visit home?" he asked. I admitted that visits back to the States for me were rare, given my limited resources.

"So, a free trip sounds good to you. How about a new wheelchair? What do those cost? I'll bet you can't buy those down here."

It was true. Mine was very dilapidated with all my hunting and fishing trips. Salt water had played hell on the steel tubes.

"Well, that's true. They run about three hundred dollars," I admitted. Three hundred was an almost-impossible sum for me in those days.

"Here's what you do," he instructed, business-like, "Wrap the cocaine in long, plastic bags, carefully sealed, and stick them in the tubing of your wheelchair. We'll meet you in the Miami airport with a brand-new wheelchair with all the bells and whistles you want. You just switch over to the new one. We take the old one."

"We'll make a deposit of fourteen thousand dollars in any bank you say," this was the littler, blond guy who fancied horses.

"We'll send you a bank receipt along with the ticket, of course."

Wow. I astonished myself — I was getting vaguely interested. Fourteen grand, a new wheelchair, the first trip home in four years.

"And what happens if I get caught?"

"You won't," they both eagerly agreed.

"Well, what if I do?" I insisted. "Just for sake of conversation — what would happen? The worst-case scenario, of course."

They looked at each other thoughtfully. For a moment there was silence. "You'd get maybe seven years," the tall, skinny one finally said. "That's if things go really bad. But nothing will happen. Be sure of it."

Gravity My Enemy

I thought for a moment and finally said, "Everyone has his price. I'm not going to sit here and try to convince you I'm self-righteous, because you know that's a crock." They nodded.

"I will say I can do my arithmetic, and I suspect so can you. Seven years, you say. Divide that into fourteen grand and tell me what my yearly income would be. Add to that a loss of freedom and a criminal record. Then answer your own question."

One week after the Texan boys left, an article came out in the newspaper about an eighty-four year old woman caught in Boston's Logan Airport with cocaine in the tubes of her wheelchair. I wished I could have sent it to Ft. Worth.

This event to me marked the beginning of a new chapter in Colombia for me. The final chapter.

I had enjoyed, in reality, many years of privileged living in Colombia. I knew many people in high places, even to the presidency. When President Guillermo León died, I was given seating at his funeral at the Valencia mansion with other presidents Carlos Lleras Restrepo and Misael Pastrana. I routinely played a game of chess every Friday afternoon with Colonel Cárdenas of the National Police. Every governor of our province of Cauca had been a close friend. Judges and magistrates met with me as friends in the local Café Alcázar. Military leaders, newspaper people and the clergy had been on close terms with me for years. There was virtually no problem I could not solve with my friendships, not even of a medical nature.

When Colombia became famous for drug traffic, first with the Medellín cartel and later with the Cali cartel, it did not happen overnight but over several years. When the guerrilla organizations FARC and the ELN (National Liberation Army) began operating with impunity throughout Colombia, even

Farewell

to the extent of governing large territories, they both began buying a political role in the country's future. And this also did not take place overnight, but gradually. As these two forces — drugs and guerrillas — gained leverage, Colombian institutions lost leverage and credibility. The military and police became harried, and there were converts. Money does that to people. The leadership of Colombia was beset with insurmountable problems. People began sympathizing with the drug people because of the rewards involved. The general public lent support to the revolutionary forces because the only way the people could get jobs in public and private institutions was through patronage from these illicit forces which had long since taken control of utility companies, branches of government, banks and schools. In turn, the revolutionary forces assured that only their cronies got the jobs and owed them a debt of gratitude. Like a cancer, the country became infected over time.

The privilege I had previously received was too much of a distraction for those that had so kindly availed it. My life style gradually deteriorated and I was forgotten.

Senator Frank Church of Idaho publicly said that the United States had to put a stop to spying abroad and meddling in foreign governments, stating foolishly that many U.S. operatives functioned under the cloak of missionaries and workers in aid programs and the Foreign Service, even tourists. This hit the foreign press like a bomb. It created instant paranoia among the Colombian public. United States citizens, thanks to this senator's indiscretion and outright stupidity, suddenly were treated as *persona non grata*. The popularity and deep trust I had enjoyed over many years from functionaries of all levels and the

Gravity My Enemy

public in general disappeared like smoke in the breeze. I was now eyed with suspicion, and even began to receive threats. I had to vary my route to work, and my schedule, for safety. I had to send my little son, Chiqui, to and from school with an armed taxi driver. My house was broken into one late night by irate rabble, intent on killing me. I survived. When a student mob came down the street to my office with blood in their eye, rocks and Molotov cocktails, to target the center I directed, I called the governor as I always did, and asked for protection. For the first time, the protection did not arrive.

Late one night, a police at a barricade in my own city of Popayán ridiculously asked me for a receipt for my wheelchair before allowing me to pass. I told him to call the police commandant. I was told he was not available but managed to get by. One day a thief stole several typewriters from the center I directed and was followed into a house. Late in the night, I called a judge I knew to issue a search warrant, and my friend Alberto from the DAS to come and make the arrest. The judge refused to take my call and I was told Alberto had been transferred to another city. His replacement refused to talk to me.

All these people, I sensed, were less friendly. Many Colombians said outright that the only reason so much attention was focused on drug enforcement was because the United States sent money to do so; that in reality, Colombia did not suffer from an addiction to drugs as did many in the U.S. In fact, as a producer, Colombia only stood to improve its lifestyle, while the U.S. as the consumer, showed only sporadic and feeble efforts to solve its end of the problem. Any problems the FARC was causing, many intelligent and educated people asserted, was simply because the people as

Farewell

a whole were tired of seeing certain groups live in a state of privilege (as I was doing) and the revolutionaries wanted this injustice, which had been in place since the Spaniards, to end.

And so my life in Colombia came to an end. I could no longer work effectively, hunt, fish, travel freely or have adventures and deep friendships as before. Coca plantations under armed guard occupied a good portion of this territory and many Indians and heretofore-simple people were involved out of the need to produce cash crops. It became impossible to travel the backcountry, or even the highways, with guns in the car for hunting or for personal protection. The conservation department, INDERENA, no longer would issue hunting and fishing licenses. But that did not matter because tourists no longer had an interest in coming to Colombia.

On December 8, 1975 in the dark early dawn, I departed by car for Cali with a friend, and headed to Palmaseca Airport. By mid-morning I was aboard an Avianca Boeing 727. After a short 25-minute hop to El Dorado Airport in Bogotá, I would be on my way to the United States for good.

I did not get out of the plane when we landed at El Dorado, but simply waited for the flight to resume. As I sat quietly by myself in the reclined seat, gazing out the scratched Plexiglas at the nearby countryside, I clearly remembered the day, over a decade ago, that I had landed on this very same runway in a Lockheed Constellation. There was the same row of eucalyptus next to the runway. The same cement light posts lined the fence along the runway that I had seen years earlier. In fact, there were still dairy cows grazing practically under the wingtips of departing jets. Much looked exactly the same as I had seen it that early morning of September 16, 1964, only I sat in a

Gravity My Enemy

727 instead of a Lockheed Constellation, but the person I now was, looking out the porthole, was a very different person.

I had married twice and had two boys.

Bobby Kennedy and Martin Luther King had been assassinated while I was gone. The Kent State incident occurred. The entire Viet Nam War began and ended in my absence. I had seen wonders and experienced adventures never imagined as a youth in my wildest dreams. And I had learned. Between these flights, I had known love, enemies, thrills, danger, fear and great sadness. The flight down to Colombia in the piston plane took seven-and-a-half hours. This 727 flight would take a mere three-and-one-half.

I was relieved to be leaving the country, relieved to be escaping the recent persecution inspired by Idaho Senator Frank Church, and his commission, relieved to still be alive — relieved I would not witness what was coming in Colombia. I was thankful to have the coveted birthright I did, to the greatest country on the planet. My Colombian friends were now charged with forging Colombia's future with what remained of its goodness.

I had doubts it would be a good future. Like a careening heavy vehicle without a helmsman, Colombia seemed inexorably heading to disaster.

The turbines whined and the jet lumbered slowly out onto the runway. In a moment, the plane turned a one-eighty at the end and quickly went to full power as it headed down the runway. The rapid acceleration pressed me back against the seat. The concrete light posts raced by outside my porthole, the same cows I saw at my arrival in 1964 were placidly grazing on the verdant grass, almost under our wingtips. Then, we were off the ground and the landing gear bumped into place. The Avianca plane banked sharply through small

Farewell

wisps of cloud and I could see the city of Bogotá lying out to my side at an angle. I spotted the peak of Monserrate through the haze, its tiny, white chapel on the summit.

I felt a lump in my throat and tears welled up. I failed in an effort to compose myself. The beginning and end took place at this very spot. I had lived and loved a hundred condensed lifetimes in Colombia. I had acquired many friends as well as a few enemies and was to learn from all of them — the good people, the truly great people and the bad, in unforgettable lessons. I was the child of many cultural foster fathers, rosy-cheeked Andean deer hunters, Amazon canoe paddlers, presidents and statesmen. I had cheated death more times than I deserved. Green hilltops now floated below. The air was fresh and quite chilly. Large, black vultures wheeled in lazy circles over the city.

Colombia was such a beautiful country.

Photo by Liliana Vidal C.

471

Further Reading

Arciniegas, German, et. al. Secrets of El Dorado: Colombia. South America. Second Edition. 1990.

Bagnal, Nigel. The Punic Wars 264-146 BC. Oxford, Great Britain: Osprey Publishing, Ltd., 2002.

Bligh, William, et. al. The Bounty Mutiny. New York, N.Y.: Penguin Books. First Published in 1789.

Burroughs, Edgar Rice. Tarzan of the Apes. New York, N.Y.: New American Library (Penquin Group), First published in 1914.

Caesar, Julius. The Gallic War. Translated by Carolyn Hammond. New York, N.Y.: Oxford University Press, Inc., 1996.

Cooper, James Fennimore. Last of the Mohicans. New York, N.Y.: Penguin Books USA, Inc., 1986. First published in U.S.A. 1826.

Crane, Stephen. The Red Badge of Courage. Mineola, N.Y.: Dover Publications, Inc.

Dana, Richard Henry Jr. Two Years Before the Mast. New York: P.F. Collier & Son Company, 1909-14.

Davis, Wade. One River. New York, N.Y.: Touchstone, 1996.

Defoe, Daniel. Robinson Crusoe. Mineola, N.Y.: Dover Publications, Inc., 1990. First published by D. Appleton and Co., N.Y., 1895.

Forrester, C.S. The African Queen. New York, N.Y.: Random House, Inc. First published 1935.

Forester, C.S. Hornblower series. G.K. Hall, Sage Books, Sanford V. Sternlicht, revised edition, 1981.

Gilliver, Kate. Caesar's Gallic Wars. Oxford, Great Britain: Osprey Publishing, Ltd., 2002.

Graves, Robert. Suetonius. The Twelve Caesars. London, England: Penguin Books, 1957.

Haggard, H. Rider. King Solomon's Mines. New York, N.Y.: Oxford University Press, 1989.

Hemingway, Ernest. Big Two-Hearted River.

Heyerdahl, Thor. Kon-Tiki. New York, N.Y.: Simon and Shuster, Inc. 1950.

Lamb, Harold. Genghis Khan Or Emperor of All Men. Robert B. McBride & Co., 1927.

London, Jack. To Build a Fire. First published in The Century Magazine, v. 76, 1908.

Mails, Thomas. Fool's Crow. Originally published Garden City, N.Y.: Doubleday, 1979.

Marcus Aurelius. Meditations. (Originally To Himself.) London, England: Penguin Books, 1964.

Pressfield, Steven. Gates of Fire. New York, N.Y.: Doubleday, 1998.

Roberts, Kenneth. Rabble in Arms.

Ruark, Robert. The Old Man & the Boy. New York, N.Y.: Henry Holt and Company, LLC. 1953.

Sabatini, Rafael. Scaramouche. New York, N.Y.: New American Library (Penguin Putnam), 2001.

Sandoz, Mari. Crazy Horse the Strange Man of the Oglalas. New York, N.Y.: A.A. Knopf, 1942.

Scott, Sir Walter. Ivanhoe. London, England: The Penguin Group. First published 1814.

Slokum, Joshua. Sailing Alone Around the World. New York, N.Y.: The Century Co., 1900.

Stevenson, Robert Lewis. Treasure Island. New York, N.Y.: New American Library (Penguin Group), 1st Signet Classic Printing, 1965.

Nordhoff, Charles. Men Against the Sea. New York: Pocket Book, Inc. 1961.

William the Conqueror

Harold of the Saxons

Verne, Jules. 20,000 Leagues Under the Sea.

Vagi, David L. Coinage and History of the Roman Empire: Volume One: History. Sidney, Ohio: Amos Press, Inc., 1999.

Wyss, Johann David. Swiss Family Robinson. NewYork, N.Y.: Tom Doherty Associates, LLC. 1996.

Printed in the United States
by Baker & Taylor Publisher Services